Minicomputers and Microprocessors

Martin Healey, PhD, MSc, C.Eng, MIEE

Department of Electrical and Electronic Engineering,
University College, Cardiff.

Hodder and Stoughton

London Sydney Auckland Toronto

ISBN 0 340 20113 4

First Printed 1976
Reprinted 1977, 1978 (twice), 1979, 1980

Printed in Great Britain for
Hodder and Stoughton Educational,
a division of Hodder and Stoughton Ltd.,
Mill Road, Dunton Green, Sevenoaks, Kent,
by J. W. Arrowsmith Ltd., Bristol BS3 2NT

Minicomputers and Microprocessors

To JANET

Preface

There are a large number of text books on the market covering the broad field of digital computers. As an author, one must justify any extension of this list. It is not sufficient just to create an alternative, direct competitor to established standards. True, time creates obsolescence in books as it does in hardware, so that there is always room for the occasional 'new techniques' text, but this one is largely fundamental, covering basic technology that is well established. This text aims to be different in two ways, firstly it concentrates on the small and medium sized machines, known collectively as minicomputers and the modern LSI offshoot, the microprocessor, and secondly the accent is entirely one of 'How does it work?' rather than 'How do you design it?'

The book is primarily aimed at Engineers and Systems Analysts who wish to know more about the machine, which is, when all said and done, simply a component in a system to them. It is the author's opinion that all Electrical Engineering undergraduates should take a course on computer fundamentals, such is the impact of these machines on all walks of life. Those students studying computer science or computer design, require far more detail than is included here, but a study of minicomputer architecture and the associated software and peripherals will well serve as an introductory text. This concept, which is not commonly accepted in computer teaching if the standard texts are a guide, is all the more relevant nowadays since the drastic fall in the cost of 'stand-alone' minicomputers means that these machines can be made available for 'hands-on' practice, avoiding the problems of sharing a larger general purpose machine.

The microprocessor is strictly a central processor fabricated on one or two LSI chips. This means that smaller, dedicated, digital computers can be tailored to suit a particular requirement. The fundamental principles of operation of microprocessors are the same as those of minicomputers. These machines will be used in industry to replace the larger systems currently made up of TTL logic chips. This means a drastic about face in the background requirements of the systems engineer. The detailed study of combinatorial and sequential logic will become less important, the need to program a small computer in a low level machine language moving to the fore. It is this problem which leads the author to believe that a broader knowledge of digital computers is required by the next generation of electrical and electronic engineers. It is possible, in the usual conflict for teaching time, that machine code or Assembly Language programming will be considered more important than logic minimisation techniques.

The book is presented in nine chapters. The routine arithmetic, logic, memory and electronic processes are briefly described in appendices, rather than the main text, since, with normal electronic studies, and indeed with the newer maths taught in schools, many readers will be well versed in these topics.

Chapter 1 describes a range of applications of minicomputers and microprocessors, related to larger digital computers. Attention is given to the problem of schematic and conceptual descriptions of the fundamental components used in the make up of a computer.

Chapter 2 explains the basic features of a simple minicomputer, by developing a hypothetical machine. The importance of the relation of the hardware operations that can be implemented to the possible instruction set, constrained by a fixed word length, is stressed.

Chapter 3 contains descriptions of the more refined, but fundamental, features found in modern minicomputers CPUs.

Chapter 4 expands the I/O considerations introduced in Chapter 2, including interrupt structures and block data transfer. The more practical aspects of interfacing are also introduced.

Chapter 5 describes the special features of the microprocessor, concentrating on a typical 8 bit machine. Short descriptions of the peripherals commonly used, including bulk storage devices, are given in Chapter 6.

Chapter 7 is a review of the requirements and availability of software. The scope is extensive but purely descriptive. It is not a programming course.

In attempting to present the facts in a logical progressive fashion, a number of more sophisticated hardware techniques are skipped in the earlier chapters and are grouped together in Chapter 8. In general, the material presented in this chapter covers newer, better methods of doing the more fundamental tasks previously explained.

The final chapter is included rather as a practical warning. In this chapter brief comments are made on the problems of purchasing and installing a computer system. It serves a warning that the purchaser can get carried away with the technical complexity of digital computer CPUs and forget the more important aspects of the *system*.

As a course in minicomputers or fundamentals of any digital computer, this text can be read sequentially from beginning to end. The appendices are only intended for quick reference or revision; indeed separate textbooks are required to do justice to each topic covered.

The text is organised so that the engineer who requires an explanation of microprocessors only, may read Chapter 2 followed by Chapter 5, filling in any further details as required.

A fairly extensive bibliography, constrained largely to textbooks rather than papers, is included. In particular, however, I would like to acknowledge the 'silent men' who prepare the handbooks for the commercial machines. I have referenced the particular handbooks which I have personally used over the years, but I would like to praise the efforts of all such authors, as much as a user as a writer.

I would like to acknowledge the helpful discussions I have had with David Turtle, David Horrocks and Peter Tomlinson. I also would like to thank Bob Churchhouse for the notes which largely form Section 1.7. Finally I must admit that the inspiration to write this book stemmed from my associations with minicomputer seminars and conferences run by Richard Elliott-Green and Bob Parslow (On-line) and Gerry Cain, Yakup Paker and Peter Morse (Minicom). Finally I would like to acknowledge the help of Barbara and Jeanette in the preparation of the manuscript.

MARTIN HEALEY

Contents

Contents

3 Further CPU Features

4 Input/Output

5 Microprocessors

6 Peripheral Devices

7 Software   244

8 Advanced Features   283

9 Selecting a Computer System   298

Appendices

Chapter 1

Digital Computers and Their Applications

1·1 Binary Representation of Information

A digital computer is an electronic programmable calculating machine which works on a binary principle. Electronic circuits are used to represent combinations of binary digits, each of which can be in one of two states, on or off, high or low, open or closed, etc. Logically these two states can be termed true or false but the useful parallel with binary arithmetic makes the terminology 0 or 1 most common; in fact using the 0/1 notation, logical (Boolean) arithmetic can be closely related to normal arithmetic using the binary system. Any reader who is not conversant with binary or logical arithmetic will find the topic well covered in modern elementary text books; Appendix 1 provides a summary of the salient features.

Inside a practical computer the two states are represented by electrical voltages. The actual voltage levels depend upon the technology used in the manufacture of the circuits and vary as new manufacturing techniques are developed. For some time now the TTL (*transistor–transistor logic*) type of circuit has prevailed and logical 0 is represented by a nominal 0 volts and logical 1 by a nominal 3·5 volts. Details of the different types of logic systems are given in Appendix 2.

1

The more recent MOS LSI (*metal-oxide-silicon large-scale-integration*) circuits work with different voltages, but such is the current hold of TTL that the MOS LSI circuits are being 'tailored' to be compatible at their inputs and outputs with TTL systems. Of course the original concept of computers was thought of long before the electronic age, so that mechanical representation of two state systems was envisaged; indeed punched paper tape is just such a system where the punched hole represents, say, 0 and no hole represents 1. For such a system however a tape reader is needed, a device which converts the hole/no-hole system into TTL compatible voltage levels before such information is useable by the computer.

Each *binary digit* is referred to as a *bit*. To represent a meaningful piece of information, bits must be used in combinations, e.g. to represent all possible decimal numbers from 0 to 63_{10}, that is the binary numbers 0 to 111111_2, requires 6 bits. Differing situations may well require differing combinations of bits, but some standardisation has been introduced, the advantages of which should be clear later. The most common combination is the *8 bit* group, called a *byte*. A byte is often too small a combination to be of use inside a computer, so that each computer, according to its design, has an established fixed *word* length. This means that each piece of information is handled inside the machine as a fixed length binary word. Common word lengths are 8, 12, 16, 18, 24 and 32. The more sophisticated machines will allow more than one word length by allowing groups of bytes, but not any number of bits. The pros and cons of a particular word length will be discussed in the following chapters.

The advantage of using a binary system in an electronic machine lies in the elimination of erroneous interpretation while 'transporting' information from one point of the machine to another. Consider a system in which the numbers from 0 to 10 are represented by subdividing a 5 volt supply, as in figure 1.1. In an equivalent binary system four digits are required as shown in figure 1.2. Note that three digits can represent 0 to 7 and four digits 0 to 15; the fourth digit is required to represent 0 to 10, although some combinations are 'wasted'. Thus the number 8 is represented by the voltage level 4·0 volts in the analogue form and by the four voltages 5, 0, 0 and 0 in the binary or digital form.

Now, in manipulating the information in electronic circuitry, it is likely that the voltage levels will be distorted; if the 4·0 volts falls to 3·75 volts then it is midway between the representation of 8 and 7 and an error has been introduced into the system. In the binary system the 0 and 5 volt levels must be distorted to 2·5 volts before ambiguity occurs. In other words errors occur in the analogue system for voltage level

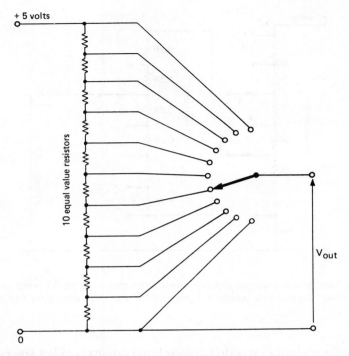

Fig. 1·1 Analogue representation of the integer numbers 0 to 10.

changes equal to about 5% of the 5 volt supply while the digital system is tolerant to changes of around 50%.

The resolution of the analogue system can be improved by subdividing each interval and that of the digital system by extending the number of digits below the LSB (*least significant bit*) as shown in figures 1.3 and 1.4. The digital system shown in figure 1.4, in which each digit

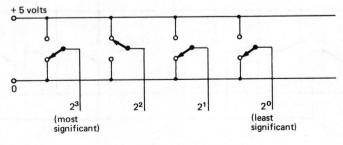

Fig. 1·2 Binary representation of the integer numbers 0 to 10.

3

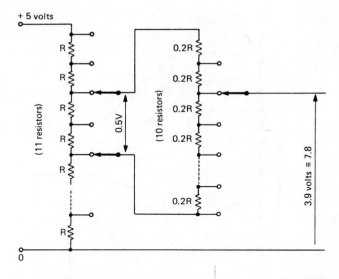

Fig. 1·3 Two decade analogue representation. Note that there are 11 resistors in the primary chain. The two Rs in parallel with the ten 0·2 R resistors is equivalent to one R as in figure 1.1.

of a decimal number is coded as four binary digits is called *binary coded decimal* (BCD). In practice most digital computers use a pure binary number code, which is more efficient than BCD, as in BCD only ten of the sixteen possible combinations of each 4 bits are used. These number systems are discussed in Appendix 1. The resolution of both systems (figures 1.3 and 1.4) can be increased by adding further sections, however, accuracy is a different problem to resolution. It is no use adding further decades to figure 1.3 if the accuracy of the most

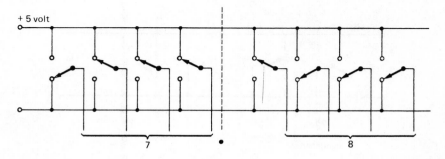

Fig. 1·4 Binary representation of two decade decimal systems using four binary digits for each decade.

significant digit cannot match that of the least significant. On the other hand the accuracy of the binary system is directly related to the resolution, since it is fair to assume that the voltage level changes will never approach the 50% mark at which errors will occur. Thus the accuracy of a digital system is directly related to the number of bits allowed in the word used inside the computer. For those readers conversant with FORTRAN, the Double Precision statement is a direct application of this principle in which the number of bits used to represent the number is doubled over the normal representation, with the attendant increase in accuracy.

In summary a digital computer uses a very simple system to represent information, the binary system, which gives extraordinarily high integrity. The penalty paid for using the binary system is the large numer of digits that are required, e.g. 4 bits to represent one decimal digit. A digital computer then is a proliferation of electronic two-state circuits.

1·2 Schematic Concept of a Digital Computer

All digital computers are capable of executing a limited number of defined operations. Typical operations are to move information from one part of the computer to another, i.e. to and from the memory and the CPU (*central processing unit*), or to take data into the computer from the input and to send data to the output. Other operations involve arithmetical and logical functions, such as add two numbers together. The computer is ordered to execute a particular operation by giving it an *instruction*; each instruction is coded as a combination of binary digits. The computer can only execute one of these instructions at a time; to perform a required task a sequence of these simple instructions must be executed. It is worth while stressing at this point just how simple the instructions actually are; on many machines even the simple operation of multiplying two numbers together is performed by repeated 'shift and add' instructions. However the speed at which these simple instructions can be performed is beyond the comprehension of the human being. For example, a machine was made to move 8000 pieces of data from one memory location to another and to add each number to an accumulator. The program was started by depressing a switch and completion indicated by causing a light bulb to be lit. Despite the 8000 data moves and 8000 additions, all done sequentially, it appears to the human operator that the bulb is lit directly by closing the switch. A high speed idiot is a most appropriate description of a digital computer!

5

When the computer is required to perform another task it must be asked to execute another sequence of its own simple instructions. Thus, since each and every task set by the user of the machine must be converted into a string of simple machine instructions, the same machine can be made to perform any such task without any changes to its electronic components. A sequential list of the instructions to be performed is called a *Machine Code* or *Object Program*; special languages such as FORTRAN or COBOL have been developed to simplify the task of creating the program. Each new problem posed by the user is formulated by writing a new program.

Now each instruction could be fed to the machine via an operator's console, one at a time. Such an approach however, would slow the machine down to the speed of the human operator; use must be made of the incredible speed of the electronic circuitry. Thus the developed program is entered into a store inside the machine, labelled *program memory* in figure 1.5. The first instruction is then transferred from the

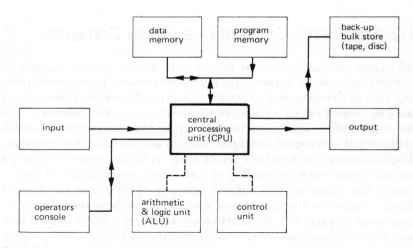

Fig. 1·5 Schematic layout of a digital computer.

memory to the CPU(this only takes around 1 microsecond) where it is 'decoded' by the control unit and executed. When each instruction is finished the next instruction is 'fetched' from the program memory and executed. Note that in executing an instruction, data may be involved and this is made rapidly available by a similar store, labelled *data memory* in figure 1.5. In a clever system the next program is 'loaded' into another part of the memory while the first program is executing, avoiding delays. This 'stored-program' concept is fundamental to the operation of a digital computer; it is the ability to use the same machine for a variety of problems simply by reprogramming that gives the machine its vital versatility.

The physical components of the computer are termed *hardware*, while the programs that control the machine are termed *software*.

Each instruction is simply a binary word; a particular combination of zeros and ones is decoded by the control unit in the CPU. In practice this means that a complex network of logical electronic elements is switched in a pattern determined by the bits in the instruction. A few simple examples are given in Appendix 2, but there are many textbooks available on the design of digital systems. While each instruction does not necessarily require the same number of bits to define the required action, the organisation of the program memory dictates that all instructions are coded into fixed length words, some bits of which may be redundant for a particular instruction. There are many considerations to be taken into account in arriving at a choice of word length (the choice is the machine designers, not the users) as will become clear in later chapters.

Now both the data and the instructions are stored and manipulated inside the computer as fixed length combinations of bits. The memories are 'word orientated' that is the instructions are located in the memory by individually addressing each word – the whole word is fetched down into the CPU, never particular bits of the word* In practice all machines above the programmable calculator level use the same basic word length for both data and instructions so that a common memory can be employed; in this way jobs with small programs and large amounts of data and jobs with large programs and small amounts of data can both be accommodated with a minimum total memory requirement. The program is loaded into one area of memory and data into another. The CPU is initialised by being given the address of the location of the first instruction and proceeds from there by the logical progression of the program, referring to data in other, specified locations. It must be stressed that there is no physical difference between an instruction and a piece of data; both are similar length binary words. If for any erroneous reason (usually an incorrectly written program) a piece of data is fetched into the CPU when an instruction is expected, then the control section will attempt to decode and execute it, with some very puzzling results!

It has already been noted that the memory is addressed as fixed length words and that the contents of any location, either an instruction or data, must be rapidly available on demand by the CPU. Since the

---

* Some machines are byte orientated, where memory is split into individually addressed 8 bit bytes. A 16 bit instruction will automatically be fetched as 2 bytes in one operation.

memory locations may be referenced in any order – a simple program will work through its instructions from consecutive locations, but a GO TO in the program will alter the sequence – it must be possible to access *any* one location in memory as quickly as *any* other. Such a memory is said to be a *random access memory* (RAM); for the most part this is magnetic core store, with LSI semi-conductor memory growing in application. RAM should be contrasted with a sequentially accessible memory such as magnetic tape; used as the main memory on a computer, magnetic tape would be forever spooling back and fore to locate specific words of information. RAM, normally referred to simply as memory or even more loosely as core, is expensive and limited in size by the word length; the reasons for this will be explained in the next chapter. Thus magnetic tape and magnetic disc are used as back-up or bulk stores; a program would be copied from the back-up store to memory as a high-speed block transfer and then executed from memory.

The number of basic instructions that the machine is capable of executing is directly related to the sophistication of the electronic logic circuitry in the CPU. The main feature is the *arithmetic and logic unit* (ALU) which actually performs the desired operations on the data. Associated with the ALU are a number of storage registers, ranging from one to say sixteen, which act as a 'scratch-pad' during arithmetic processing. These registers store data similar to specific memory locations, but are high speed TTL registers, the data from which can be accessed in tens of nanoseconds* rather than the microseconds of core memory. In fact the fixed word length must put an upper limit on the number of types of instruction that can be coded; this often sets the limit on the complexity of the CPU rather than the actual circuit design. It is of no use providing extra functions in the electronics if these extra functions cannot be 'dialled-up' by the instruction!

A word of information, say 16 bits as an example, can be transferred inside the machine, e.g. moved from memory to the ALU, in one of two modes, either *serial* or *parallel*. Serial mode means that the word is transferred one bit at a time along a single path in 16 time intervals, the 16 bits being reformed as one word before being used. Parallel mode means that 16 paths are provided and the whole word is transmitted in one time interval. Clearly serial mode is cheaper but slower than parallel mode. All modern computers; in which hardware costs have become less important, thanks to integrated circuit technology; work exclusively in parallel mode, increased speed being the prime objective. One commonly encountered example of serial transmission of

---

* A nanosecond is a thousandth of a microsecond, that is there are 10^9 nanoseconds per second.

data is the common *teletype*. The character is formed in the teletype and transmitted along a single line one bit at a time, usually a total of 11 bits per character including markers. The string of bits is collated in a 'shift-register' at the computer end and only then communicated to the machine in parallel, as shown in figure 1.6.

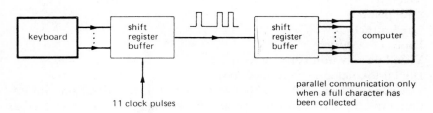

Fig. 1·6 Serial transmission system.

1·3 Communication with the Machine – Input/Output

The computer itself is merely an electronic data manipulator. To be of any practical use it must communicate with the outside world. All the input and output devices supported by the computer are termed peripherals, a category which also includes the back-up storage devices. Both the nature and the number of input and output devices is varied, dependent upon the application. It must be realised that most machines will support both a number of input and a number of output devices. One computer can service a number of I/O devices due to the high speed differences between the essentially electromechanical peripherals and the electronic processor.

Typical input devices are:

Keyboards on teletypes and visual display units (VDUs)

Card reader

Paper tape reader

Analogue-to-digital convertor (ADC)

The basic information transmitted by these devices is converted to digital form before being accepted by the computer. Other signals are fundamentally in binary form, such as the output from another computer, or more generally a communications system, or digital transducers. Single bit digital information such as switch closures, are common in process controls and must be treated as individual pieces of data – it is possible that a whole byte must be allocated to handle one bit of information since this will be the smallest unit handled *inside* the

9

computer. Data from the bulk storage devices, magnetic tapes, discs or drums, is a specialised form of input and such peripherals are not normally classified as input devices, in the I/O sense. Magnetic tape cassettes are normally considered as substitutes for paper tape rather than bulk storage.

Typical output devices are:

Teletype printer

Line printer

Card punch

Paper tape punch

Visual display unit (VDU) screen

Digital-to-analogue convertor (DAC)

Again units which deal with direct binary transmission (communications) or single bit information and magnetic cassettes are classed as output devices while transfers to larger magnetic tape systems, discs or drums are classed as bulk storage.

The simple schematic diagram of figure 1.5 shows only one input device and one output device, each connected with the computer via individual lines. These 'lines', which will transmit a piece of data as a parallel binary word (or byte), are called *data highways, bus bars* or simply *buses*. A bus consists of a number of wires, one for each bit of the data. In practice one bus is used for both input and output, called an I/O bus, to which all the I/O peripherals are connected, only one of which can use the bus at a time – this is no constraint since at the heart of the computer the CPU only executes one instruction at a time. Bus structures and operation of I/O devices are a rather complex problem which is dealt with in the following chapters. For the sake of the current discussion realise that *one* of the input devices can be sending data to the computer *or one* of the output devices can be receiving data from the computer. The electronic circuitry which connects each device to the computer is called an *interface* or a *device controller*. Thus the same peripheral design can be used by different computer manufacturers by appropriate design of the interface.

The bulk memory devices transfer data by blocks of words, rather than individual words and always to or from memory. Whereas a particular input device may store consecutive pieces of data at 'spread out' memory locations, the blocks of data from a disc, say, always go into contiguous (consecutive addresses) memory locations. Thus bulk storage/memory transfers are simple but require high speed. Such devices are connected direct to the memory, rather than to the memory under control of the CPU, by a special connection known as a *direct memory access* channel (DMA).

Yet another common device encountered is a control panel or console. This allows an operator, by means of switches and lights, to override normal operation and to interrogate and display a particular condition. This is the most direct means of communication. Lights are commonly used to display the contents of the memory location currently being accessed (on for a 1, off for a 0); during normal operation the data displayed change as an instruction is executed, giving rise to the flashing lights encountered in Startreck!

The general I/O features introduced in figure 1.5 and discussed above are summarised in figure 1.7. One and only one I/O device can have connection to the I/O bus at a time. Peripherals like a teletype, which have an input and an output device in one physical unit, usually have the two interfaces tailored into one unit also.

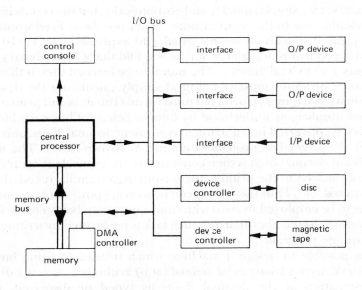

Fig. 1·7 Peripheral connections to the computer.

The physical aspects of communication have now been explained in principle, if not in detail. Thus a character on the teletype keyboard is struck which causes an electronic buffer register to be set to a particular code.* This is then transmitted to the computer via the I/O bus, where it is processed by the CPU under the control of a particular program. It is worth noting that the teletype printer is *not* connected to the keyboard; it is the kind-hearted programmer who decides that the first thing to be

---

* One standard code used in the 8 bit ASCII code. One bit is used for parity which leaves $2^7 = 128$ possible combinations to define specific characters. The 36 alphanumerics plus the +, −, =, etc. and special 'control' characters are the obvious ones.

done with the data received from the keyboard is to 'echo' it, that is to send the same code back to the printer, resulting in the apparent typing of the key pressed.

For more physical problems this concept is probably sufficient; e.g. a temperature is sensed by a transducer which generates a voltage proportional to the temperature; this voltage is converted to a binary number by the ADC, which piece of data is accepted by the computer and processed. The temperature–voltage–binary number relations are of no consequence to the human operator, as long as the programmer has got his scale factor right so that everything behaves correctly. Human interaction however poses extra problems. Consider a simple payroll calculation. The computer, as programmed, calculates Fred's wages, tax, etc., simply, quickly and economically; but the results inside the machine are in the form of pure binary numbers. Fred would be most pleased initially to see his usual £30 expressed as £11110 but would become most irritated when he was told that £11110 binary was still only £30 in 'real' money. The moral to be learned then is that the computer program must not stop at simply calculating the desired value in its own (binary) form, but must format this data and print it as a normal number, as understood by human beings. Thus each binary number is converted into a string of equivalent decimal digits, only two for Fred's wages but probably four for A. Brown-Cow's. The most significant decimal digit is then converted to the equivalent ASCII code and transmitted to the printer; the second digit is similarly coded and transmitted, etc. Thus the high speed processing power of the computer has to be employed to assist with communications between machine and master. Remember that any such task is performed by writing the appropriate program.

It is possible to design a machine which instead of using binary arithmetic, uses a *binary coded decimal* (BCD) arithmetic. BCD is a direct representation of the decimal digits as typed or displayed. BCD arithmetic is however inefficient compared to binary arithmetic; it also requires more bits to represent a given number and is thus more expensive inside a computer. The choice then lies between easier I/O, more difficult processing, and more awkward I/O, easier processing. Only pocket and desk calculators amongst modern machines commonly encountered use the BCD mode.

1·4 The Range of Digital Computers

It should first be stressed that the computer *system* is of more importance than the computer itself. The cost of peripherals and software has become such a dominant feature that one can jokingly ask whether

12

the manufacturer is giving away initialled ball-pens or central processors with his systems! Machines range in cost from a few hundred to hundreds of thousands of pounds. To categorise digital computers rigorously is impractical and pointless and would probably be out of date before this book is published, such is the rate of change in the industry. For the purpose of this book three obvious groups can be defined (i) the larger, general purpose, data processing systems, (ii) the smaller, cheaper general purpose systems and (iii) the dedicated, special purpose systems.

(i) The larger machines, typified by the IBM, Burroughs and ICL, systems, support printers, punches, etc. but not 'on-line' devices like ADC and DACs. They are usually organised to run multiple jobs and require a controlled environment to run in, such as an air conditioned room. These systems fall into two groups, on the one hand data processing, e.g. payroll calculations, stock control, and on the other scientific processing. The former are typified by small programs with a lot of data and the latter by large programs with little data. Most installations will cope with a mixture of both types of work, although many reasonably sized computer bureaus exist with a small central processor, supporting many peripherals which would not be capable of scientific calculations. Similarly some very expensive computers do not support sufficient peripherals to do data processing work with any efficiency.

(ii) The smaller, cheaper systems, which are still capable of general purpose use, are usually required to perform more specific operations. Many classifications of such machines have been attempted such as micro, mini and midi computers, but the term *minicomputer* is now used to cover all such machines. They are more rugged than their larger counterparts, requiring no special environmental conditions. They are used in a wider range of applications, many of which involve 'real-time' or 'on-line' operation such as control of a steel mill or a sophisticated data-logging system. Minicomputers have become increasingly powerful, while retaining their relatively low cost and are now challenging the lower end of the market previously reserved for the larger machines. In fact the more advanced mini's are more powerful and considerably cheaper than many data processing machines. That said it must be pointed out that the supporting software for the mini's is only just adequate to make a serious challenge in that market. Many mini's, because of their real-time applications, have a superior 'interrupt' system, a feature which allows rapid servicing of peripherals, as will be explained later.

(iii) The variety of special purpose uses to which smaller digital computers are put is enormous. Such devices as calculators, digital process controllers, 'intelligent' terminals, controllers for peripherals in large systems and pin ball machines may be included on the list, which is as variable as it is endless. Many of these systems use standard minicomputers, often produced on simplified frames. Others use integrated circuit components, quite the most interesting of which is the *microprocessor*, which, is quite simply a CPU on its own. The microprocessor is built up onto a circuit board along with the necessry memory (nearly always semiconductor), interfaces and power supplies, so as to form a tailor-made *microcomputer* – a digital computer made up on these lines can approach the power of a conventional minicomputer. The tailor-made microcomputer and the cut-down minicomputer are now competing as the new circuit component. After the transistor came integrated circuits and now central processors! Some of these special purpose devices are smaller, but straight forward, minicomputer systems loaded with a particular program in the normal manner; others have their programs developed and then fixed by storing them in *read-only-memory* (ROM). The hand calculator is an obvious example of a microprocessor system with a ROM program store; the program is fixed and cannot be altered by the user although its execution can be controlled by push-buttons. The more sophisticated calculating machines have a small RAM program area in addition to the ROM into which the user can write a sequence of the allowable operations – the allowable operations e.g. sine, exponential, add, etc. are fixed by the manufacturer in the program stored in the ROM. At the smaller end of the scale the advantages of programmability (step-by-step development, updating, etc.) makes the microcomputer a competitor to hard-wired logic systems.

This textbook concentrates on the function of a basic minicomputer system. A chapter is included to discuss the particular details of the microprocessor, but it must be stressed that this is really in principle an isolation of the CPU of the minicomputer. Minicomputers and microprocessors are not isolated topics. The larger machines all operate on the same principles as the minicomputer, but with greater sophistication; the material covered here will serve as an introduction to *any* digital computer.

1·5 Definition of Minicomputers and Microcomputers

Summarising the comments made in the preceding section, the definitions used in this book are:

A *minicomputer* is used in a small to medium sized system. It is a low cost machine without any special environmental requirements. The architecture is reasonably simple, although such a statement is impossible to define, with a good interrupt structure. A number of word lengths are used, 8, 12 and 18 being encountered, but dominated by 16 bit words. Both magnetic core and semiconductor memories are used. A wide variety of peripherals are available, many being 'scaled down', particularly in cost, versions of the heavy duty data processing peripherals; of particular importance are DAC and ADC systems for real-time applications.

A *microcomputer* is a computer made up of an LSI CPU, called a *microprocessor*, with the necessary power supplies, clocks and buffers and the interfaces and memory as required. Such a system could be built up to be a rather poor minicomputer; the advantage in these systems lies in tailoring them to suit the particular application, e.g. minicomputer memory is available in 4K and 8K blocks (K means 1024 words in the computer world); many specialised, smaller applications only require a few hundred words of program. Memory is in practice always semiconductor, although in principle magnetic core could be used; programs, once developed, are stored in ROM while RAM is used for the data areas. Most microprocessors use either 4 or 8 bit words. Units can be used in parallel to create longer words on some systems or programmed so that a 16 bit word can be stored in two memory locations. Currently, because cost and density dictates the use of MOS instead of *Bipolar* semiconductor technology, microcomputers are an order slower than minicomputers.

The situation is becoming more confused since developments in semiconductor technology are being applied as they are developed. Currently Bipolar techniques are faster than MOS, but are more expensive since less components can be packed into the LSI chip. The power consumption of MOS is also lower than Bipolar. The earlier MOS systems were 'p-type' and required a large negative supply voltage; newer systems are 'n-type', using positive supply voltages and are thus easier to interface to TTL. New techniques and modifications of old ones are constantly changing the picture, for example *Silicon-on-sapphire* (SOS) systems which approach Bipolar speed with MOS packing density. The effect of this changing situation is summed up by one manufacturer who claims that if the same computer logical design was re-built each year using the latest technology, it would be twice as fast at half the cost. These comments are expanded in Appendix 3.

To meet the challenge of the microprocessor, or rather to take advantage of the technical developments, the minicomputer manufacturers who specialise in selling large quantities of machines to *other equipment manufacturers* (OEMs), have redeveloped their CPU on LSI technology. The computer is sold with CPU, memory and limited interfaces on a single board, without boxes, panels or power supplies. Indeed one conventional minicomputer has been simply refurbished by constructing the CPU in SOS LSI, and the rest must surely follow. Thus the future will see the difference between a microcomputer and a minicomputer as one of tailoring the former to suit only the specific requirement, with no surplus power as would accrue from a 'standard' mini. This tailored concept will be most economic on very simple systems and those where very large quantities of the same design are used.

1·6 Some Applications of Minicomputers and Microcomputers

Most digital computer systems can be considered to function in one of three modes of operation, which are discussed in more detail in Section 7.8. These modes are:

(a) *Off-Line*. The data to be processed is prepared away from the computer, e.g., punched tape or cards, and is brought to the computer for processing at some later time; also termed *Batch* processing.

(b) *On-Line*. The data to be processed is communicated direct to the computer system or from the computer to a display, i.e. a terminal. Usually such a system will invoke only short delays between entering and requesting processing of data and receiving appropriate answers.

(c) *Real-Time Operation*. This is a form of on-line operation where direct communication between the computer and a physical system is involved. The computer is dedicated to servicing any requests made by external events as rapidly as possible; results of computations may be returned fast enough to control the condition of the physical system.

The larger, *general purpose* or *mainframe* computers are used for both Data Processing and Scientific work. Some machines are capable of processing large amounts of data, running more than one program concurrently. Mini and Microcomputers cover a range of machines from small calculators to medium sized general purpose machines, which, coupled to some unique features related to real-time operation, means that they are used, to some extent, in all possible computer applications. The efficiency of a system is largely related to the software which controls the allocation of peripheral resources and time, termed the *Operating System*. A good operating system makes an installation easier to run but demands an overhead in time and memory space; thus smaller systems will have simpler, less effective operating systems. Most mainframe machines are dedicated to *Batch* processing; the data is prepared on cards or tape away from the machines and presented as a batch to join a queue of similar jobs. Some machines allow data and source programs to be entered via VDU's direct into the machine files and then to be queued for batch processing by the operating system, often termed a *foreground/background* mode of operation. Few mainframe machines offer true on-line operation.

1·6·1 Commercial Data Processing

Commercial or business data processing is, simply speaking, the automation of accounting functions e.g. Payroll, Order processing, Sales and Purchase Ledgers, Personnel details, Stock evaluation, etc. In a large organisation the volume of data and the interrelation of data files makes a large machine essential; indeed large machines have also been used by Bureaux selling 'time' to a number of smaller users. The bigger minis are now in use in these applications.

At the small end of the scale, accounting machines have moved from the mechanical age through electronic aids and into small inbuilt computers. Thus mini and microcomputers are involved at all levels.

Microcomputers are used in data preparation equipment, e.g. key-to-tape, or key-to-disc machines. Data is keyed into the machines, verified, edited, compressed and recorded on magnetic tape (reel or cassette) or discettes. A VDU, formatted by the computer, aids the operator. The tape or cassette is then unloaded and sent to the mainframe machine readers. More sophisticated machines can support multiple key stations, the computer collating the data on the files. The machine may also send data, once collected, via a telephone line direct to the main computer.

With an accounting machine the main problem lies in storing files of information which are both visual and machine readable. The common solution is a device called a Visible Record Computer (VRC). Data is typed on to an A4 sized 'ledger card' which can be filed in a cabinet. A magnetic strip, about 2 mm wide, is bonded onto the card vertically, onto which, like a tape recorder, the data typed on each row is recorded. The card is placed into the VRC card handler, like a typewriter, where it is drawn into the machine, reading the data from the strip into the computer; the computer then ejects the card to the position of the next unused line. In this way information such as customer's name and address, product description, unit price, together with accumulated totals can be made available to the machine without typing. New data is now entered which is both typed and recorded. Such details as total price, VAT, etc. can now be calculated automatically and used with the information copied from the card to cause the VRC to print a detailed document, e.g. an invoice. The earlier VRC's used dedicated, rather crude, electronic devices but the latest

17

machines use mini and microcomputers to which extra peripherals such as card and tape readers can be added.

The flaw with the VRC is that the machine can only retain information from a few cards at a time. Thus with a customer's ledger on one card and stock lines on others, cards will have to be read by the machine more than once to complete the cross referencing needed. Cassette tape recorders are added to act as buffer stores to improve the problem. The problem can be eliminated by storing the data on a magnetic disc which provides random access to all data. Data need only be entered once but the files created can be accessed by many programs; it is possible to sort and merge files, a major problem with ledger cards. Thus small computers with VDU input, a printer and a disc file will replace the VRC. A second VDU will however be necessary so that the data stored on a file can be displayed on request, since a feature of the VRC is the ability to pull a card for visual check. The lower cost systems use 'floppy disc' stores (250 000 characters on-line) and the others, cartridge type discs (over 2 million characters).

It can now be noted that the smaller disc based accounting computer is in fact a similar machine to a key-to-disc system but with more versatile and more powerful software. If data communications facilities are provided with the system, so that selected data can be transmitted to or from a main computer, then the machine acts as an 'intelligent or brilliant' terminal to the main machine. A common variant on this theme is a Remote Job Entry (RJE) terminal, when a minicomputer supports a card reader and other data entry terminals plus a line printer; programs and data are entered into the RJE, checked and collated and then transmitted to a mainframe computer for processing. The processed results are later returned to the RJE store and printed out under local control.

If a medium or high performance mini is used in a disc based system it can provide sufficient power to act as a stand-alone data processing system in many installations. Disc stores from 2 to 200 MByte, line printers and multiple terminals make such a system a direct competitor to the smaller mainframe machines. In addition the minicomputers offer on-line operating systems. Consider as an example, a sales-order entry system. The customer's code number is keyed in and the disc files are searched to display the corresponding name on the screen within the second. This allows confirmation of the correct customer interactively and at the same time displays the current credit limit, etc. The items ordered are next entered, each being checked against available stock. The order can then be accepted, stock levels adjusted and an invoice printed; stock files and Ledger files can be immediately updated from the one set of input data. Statistical reports can also be printed from these files on a weekly or monthly basis.

The mainframe manufacturers have also developed machines to provide smaller computer systems as described above, e.g. IBM System 3, ICL 2903 etc. These 'psuedo minis' are generally much less versatile than the true minicomputer system of similar cost and their future development will be influenced by the small but growing impact of the minicomputer.

Transaction processing is a variant of the on-line system when a large number of terminals are provided for prompt action, e.g. banking terminals, seat reservation systems, etc. These are characterised by the dedicated, similar job of each terminal, compared to the data processing system where the terminal may be running payroll data entry one hour, invoicing routines the next, etc. Special microcomputer controlled shop 'tills' are being used as terminals on a central transaction processing machine; these intelligent 'tills' are called Point-of-Sale (POS) terminals.

1·6·2 Stock and Production Control

The first part of a stock control system is a parts schedule from which a bill-of-materials can be generated, listing all the components required for a specific order. The second part is an inventory list containing data for all items. Typically the following information will be stored for each item: Quantities in stock, on order and allocated against a sale; Reorder quantities and minimum stock level; Bin location; Bought out or made in-house; Lead time for delivery or manufacture; Product description.

The above data files can be used to produce lists of jobs to be marshalled on the shop floor each day. Any new sales or purchase orders must update the quantities on file; deliveries can be checked against outstanding purchase orders. The information can be integrated with the normal accounting system procedures, e.g. ledgers, stock evaluating, costing, etc.

Reorder quantities and levels can be established by past experience; there is always a conflict since the cost per unit is cheaper the larger the order but the cost of holding the stock goes up. Thus the computer can use data relating the utilisation of stock items over the previous months to statistically adjust the reorder data on a monthly basis.

Production control involves the scheduling of machines in a production workshop. In some cases this can be directly related to the stock control system, which given data relating the time to manufacture each component, can request action from the sales order and stock level data. The process becomes much more complex if control is required of an item as it moves through a factory from one machine to another.

19

Such a system requires feeding of data at each step from the shop floor to the computer, involving large numbers of terminals, some of which are specially designed for the job, e.g. punched card readers. With such a detailed breakdown of data, accurate costing by product and by work centre can be undertaken. True scheduling of production is a very complex problem.

1·6·3 Scientific Calculations

Minicomputers can never compete with the extremely powerful computers used for scientific calculations. However many minicomputer systems have been installed which support a number of teletype terminals at which simpler programs can be run. Thus one minicomputer can be used by a number of programmers in a 'time-sharing' system giving 'interactive' facilities to aid program development. These systems are common in both educational establishments and in industry, often relieving the larger computer of tasks which by its standard are trivial. BASIC is the common language used in these systems, which function in an on-line mode.

1·6·4 Calculators

Pocket and desk calculators are specifically programmed microcomputers with particular input (keyboard) and output (display) facilities. The latest trends are to provide extra storage for simple user programs and interfaces for extensions to the I/O, e.g. connection via an ADC to a sensor. These machines are becoming more like simple minicomputers with an accent on decimal input and display and hence BCD internal operation. Like all modern computers these machines operate on a data word in a parallel mode, but only for the 4 bits used for each digit. Thus to add two numbers, each with ten decimal digits, requires ten sequential addition operations, each using 4 bits of information; the processor is so designed to cause a carry when a number exceeds 9, wasting six of the possible combinations. This serial/parallel processing of the decimal numbers means that these machines are slow by minicomputer standards, although fast enough for any limit set by the display and of course the human operator! There is a danger of programmable calculators becoming too sophisticated and finishing up as poor, slow and expensive minicomputers. Note also the development of the most ingenious 'bulk' storage (for programs) on magnetic 'cards'. This is essentially an on-line mode of operation.

1·6·5 Sequence Control

Industry employs a large number of machines operating under sequence control. Common examples are in the food and packaging industries. One operation is initiated, the next operation is started by the completion of the first, and so on. When alternative possibilities occur, such as reject a packet which has been underfilled, the logic of the sequencing can become complex. Hardwired logic controllers are commonly used, that is the logical decisions are implemented by a specially designed controller, manufactured from commercially available integrated circuit gates. This same logical control can be implemented by a minicomputer or microcomputer. The advantage of using a computer is simply that if, for any reason, the logical sequence must be modified, the hardwired system may need complete redesign while the computer system need only be reprogrammed. It is claimed that a system that required around forty TTL chips or more is cheaper when implemented by a microprocessor. The computer also offers many side advantages, such as arithmetic processing, data logging, display and alarm control. This is a real-time mode of operation.

Security systems are an interesting related application. A number is fed to the logical controller by pressing buttons in sequence; if the correct sequence is pressed then the logic circuitry detects this and activates an 'opening' mechanism. Using a microcomputer in such a system the code can be changed by programming, as often as required!

1·6·6 Data Logging

The physical variables in some process are to be monitored and recorded. Transducers are attached to the process, which sense these variables, e.g. temperature, pressure, position and velocity. There are a variety of transducer techniques available, the majority of which produce outputs as (a) voltage levels (b) frequency of an a.c. voltage or (c) digital signals, all roughly proportional to the physical variable. These signals are converted to binary numbers by electronic devices, typically an ADC for (a), a specialised frequency to digital convertor for (b) and binary counters for (c). For the purpose of this brief description consider (a) only, which is by far the most common anyway. The datalogger, with no computer, incorporates a *digital voltmeter* (DVM), which is a sophisticated, accurate ADC with gain changing for scaling and excellent signal to noise characteristics. These DVMs incorporate a decimal display, for which reason the available output is coded in BCD. A simple serialising unit can then be attached to send each of the BCD characters in turn to a printer, following each complete decimal number with appropriate spaces, line feeds and carriage returns. Most applications involve logging of more than one variable, so that an input multiplexor is used to connect one channel at a time to the DVM. The DVM system is now becoming complex and rather limited, so that a computer controlled logger is required. Early systems merely used the computer to control a DVM, but this is unacceptable due to the BCD character, which is not directly compatible with the minicomputer, and due to many redundant features which increase the cost. The maximum speed of a DVM was typically 20 samples per second, whereas a modern ADC with excellent noise rejection can function at speeds of up to 100 samples per second. Other ADCs will sample up to 1 million samples per second but care must be taken with signal-to-noise ratio since noise rejection is low. Multiplexors can be designed to suit, using reed relays for the slower systems and FET (*field effect transistor*) switches for the faster ones. A typical system is shown in figure 1.8, which for completeness indicates how digital inputs can be multiplexed with the output from the ADC.

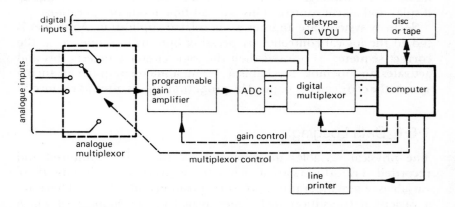

Fig. 1·8 Schematic diagram of a computer controlled data logging system.

Thus the computer can be programmed to select any input, in any order and at any rate within the range of the system. The amplifier gain can be programmed to match a specific input channel to give amplitude scaling. The processing power of the computer enables the data read-in to be scaled, linearised, converted to engineering units, etc. Checks can be made for out-of-limit variables, detected errors causing alarms to be set. All the data can be stored but, under program control, the printed output can be more selective.

This is a real-time mode of operation; indeed the system incorporates a digital clock in the computer in order to control the timing of sampling. More details of the ADC, multiplexor etc., are given in Section 6.7.

With the computer in the system, processing of the data collected can proceed in real-time; such techniques as digital filtering, spectral analysis and correlation are commonly encountered. Factory data collection and patient monitoring systems are typical of the many related systems, when other than the analogue inputs dominate.

1·6·7 Automatic Control

The use of feedback or closed loop techniques in process control and electro-mechanical systems (servomechanisms) is well established. Briefly, the variable to be controlled (temperature, position, etc.) is monitored and the output from the sensor monitoring this variable subtracted from a reference signal. The difference signal resulting from the comparison is a measure of error, called the actuating signal, which is used as an input to the process. This will cause the controlled variable to change in such a direction as to tend to force the actuating signal to zero. A typical system is shown schematically in figure 1.9.

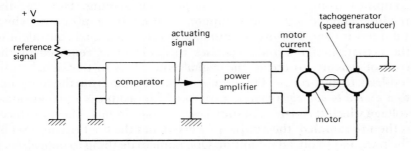

Fig. 1·9 A velocity control system using negative feedback.

The motor speed is the variable to be controlled, while the potentiometer setting generates the reference signal. The tachometer acts as a speed transducer, generating a voltage proportional to speed. The comparator is an electronic device which feeds a voltage to the amplifier proportional to the difference between the reference voltage and the tacho-voltage. If the speed is low for any reason, the actuating signal is positive, causing the amplifier to feed more current to the motor which increases the torque and therefore the speed. If the speed is too high the actuating signal is negative and the motor reduces torque and slows down. Clearly a stable operating speed will be reached when the tacho-voltage is roughly equal to the reference voltage and hence the speed is proportional to the potentiometer position. Externally applied loads try to slow the motor down, but this causes the actuating signal to increase, the motor developing more torque to counteract the external load. The speed of the output shaft, which may be delivering thousands of watts can be controlled simply by turning the reference potentiometer.

The advantages to be gained from the use of negative feedback are (i) regulation against unwanted disturbances, (ii) indirect control of what may be a high power or inaccessible variable by the low power reference signal and (iii) a reduction in the undesirable effects of nonlinearities.

There is a wide variety in the performance of such systems and in many cases the comparator is much more complex; it is normally called a controller. Thus a minicomputer can be used as the controller; this is referred to as *direct digital control* (DDC), although far more complex digital control schemes are being configured.

The output from the transducer is sampled at regular intervals of time, close enough together so that the output cannot change appreciably between samples. This information is converted to binary form by an ADC and stored by the computer; in this sense the input to the computer from the process is simply data logging. However the reading entered into the computer is used by a program which subtracts it from a reference number to create a digital equivalent to the actuating signal and processes this further as required by the control scheme, to create the digital equivalent to the signal to be fed-back to the process. This number is thus output from the computer to a *digital to analogue convertor* (DAC) which produces a proportional voltage which stays constant until reset (a hold circuit). The transducer is then re-sampled, the sample processed and the hold circuit reset by the DAC, and so on, ad infinitum. One immediate thing to note about a computer control system is that the computer becomes part of the process and must operate for as long a period as the process itself. Unlike a data processing installation, the computer is not available for routine maintenance at regular periods of the week.

The reference signal used by the control program may be a fixed number (a set point), but it may be varied by resetting from a teletype say. Alternatively it may be a digital reference signal transmitted from another computer; hierarchy in large scale systems is becoming common, where a number of small computers control local functions, supervised by a central computer. The reference signal may itself be continually varying and the ease with which this can be handled in the computer is one advantage of digital control.

While it may prove practical by using specially tailored microcomputers, with the program stored in ROM, to control a single system as just explained, the economic use is for one computer to control say fifty closed loops. One transducer output is sampled, processed and used to set the hold circuit feeding the appropriate process input. This, since the computer is so fast, may only take, say, one hundredth of the time before another sample is required. Thus a number of process outputs are multiplexed into the computer with an appropriately 'ganged' demultiplexor feeding the hold circuits. In this way, the computer is 'time-multiplexed' to control fifty or so individual loops, before repeating the first loop etc. This is shown schematically in figure 1.10.

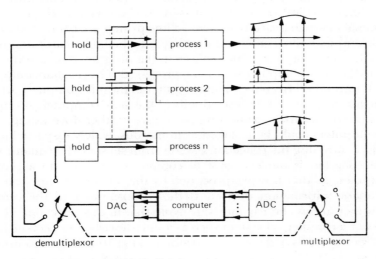

Fig. 1·10 A multiplexed closed loop digital control system.

Clearly additional sequence control, data logging, alarm checking, etc. can be incorporated into the closed loop control scheme as required.

Common examples of computer control exist in the process industries; e.g. chemical plants, oil refineries, and steel works; sophisticated mechanical systems; e.g. radar systems, tracking telescopes, aircraft control systems and machine tools; and electrical control mainly in power systems.

1·6·8 Data Communications

Minicomputers are used in a number of applications involving transmission and routing of digital data; in most cases the minicomputer acts in a subservient manner as part of a system such as a data communications network. Often the minicomputer is used as a sophisticated peripheral to a larger computer system. The usual fields of application are given below.

(a) *Data concentration.* A number of subsystems are connected to the minicomputer which collects the data, at the slower rates of the subsystems and groups it into files. A certain amount of processing can be carried out at this stage, such as code conversion, removal of redundant data, error checking and any possible 'book-keeping' chores. The collated data is then transmitted between the minicomputer and the main computer at the maximum rate of the data transmission lines. Typical of this sort of system is the *remote job entry* (RJE) terminal in which a card reader and a line printer are connected to the minicomputer. Programs and data are punched onto cards and read into the minicomputer. Once collected, the program data is transmitted to the main computer where it is processed. The resultant output is then transmitted from the main computer to the minicomputer, which controls the print out, independently of the main computer. A similar application occurs in collecting data for weather forecasting. Microcomputers could be installed at numerous, widely dispersed locations, controlling the collection of data from sensors. The quantity of data collected is too excessive to communicate direct to a central computer, so that it is pre-processed by the microcomputer and the pertinent information derived is then transmittted to the central computer at, say, hourly intervals. Note that in this sense one of the tasks of a commercial system such as a VRC described in Section 1.6.2 may be to act as a data concentrator linking to a larger computer system.

(b) *Message switching.* The minicomputer is used to check and route messages passed between one out-station and any other, as in a telephone exchange. Firm wired connection between each station and every other one is very expensive and unnecessary, since data flow usually occurs in bursts. Thus all stations are connected to a central minicomputer so that the appropriate connections can be made as requested, using the computer on a time multiplexed basis. Systems can be large and rather complex, with several levels or areas of substations, so that a message may traverse one of a number of alternative routes. The minicomputer may then possibly be used to identify the most efficient path at any given time. One further feature that is made possible by using a minicomputer is message retrieval, provided that a bulk storage system is supported by the computer.

(c) *Front-ending.* A minicomputer can be linked to a large computer, dedicated to handling the computationally unsophisticated, routine tasks. Thus a front-end computer can buffer and interrogate messages, monitor terminals, etc. Simple processing, such as collection of characters and conversion to binary words and formatting of data can also be devoted to the minicomputer. A common application is as a front-end processor to a large computer in a time-sharing installation, as in figure 1.11. The multiple terminals are connected via modems and Post

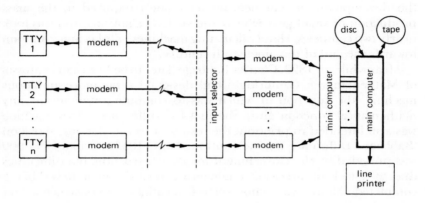

Fig. 1·11 A minicomputer as a front-end processor in a time-sharing system.

Office telephone lines to the central installation; all the input lines are serviced by the minicomputer, controlling the connections to the machine (there may be more terminals than input ports) collecting the input data as typed, book-keeping (time, cost, etc.) and passing the programs and data to the main machine for processing. In this way the main machine is relieved of the routine input/output chores and can concentrate on the more computationally demanding problems, such as compiling, arithmetic processing, etc. The implication should be noted that the minicomputer is as efficient as a main frame computer at data handling, due to excellent on-line i/o features, while being much cheaper; the main frame machine really shows its paces on more sophisticated processing. However there are minicomputers and there are minicomputers, so that a realistic time-sharing system could use one simpler mini, front-ending a more sophisticated mini!

1·7 A History of Computer Development

1·7·1 The Pre-electronic Age

The earliest known example of a calculating machine is due to Pascal who, in 1642, designed a machine which could be used for addition and subtraction. Many such machines were constructed and a few still exist.

It was applied, apparently with great success, to tax collection in France. In 1694 Leibnitz built a superior version of the Pascal machine which was capable of multiplication and division as well as addition and subtraction.

The production of such machines on a commercial basis had to await the development of engineering techniques required in the mass production of small gear wheels and such mechanisms, and this took nearly two centuries. Hand calculating machines only became common towards the end of the nineteenth century.

Meanwhile, in 1822, Charles Babbage (later to be Lucasian Professor of Mathematics at Cambridge) had designed a far more ambitious machine, the function of which was to compute automatically any mathematical function given the first five differences. This machine was also intended to print out the results of its calculations. Work on 'Babbage's Difference Engine' continued until 1833 and about £17 000 was provided by the Government for its construction, but difficulties due to a lack of precision engineering resulted in it never being completed. Many years later such a machine was constructed and worked well.

By 1833 Babbage had come to the conclusion that it should be possible to construct a machine which would be capable of performing any calculation specified to it by an operator and not merely calculations based on differences. This machine 'Babbage's Analytical Engine' is the true fore-runner of the modern computer and it is extraordinary how many features of modern machines were foreseen by Babbage.

The Analytical Engine was to consist of two main parts 'the mill' and 'the store' – which in modern machines correspond to the CPU (central processing unit)' and 'the store'. The store was to consist of 1000 columns of 50 counting wheels (comparable today to 165 000 bits of storage). For input Babbage proposed to use a modification of the punched cards which were then being used in the weaving of complex designs in the Jacquard looms. Output of the results was to be achieved by causing the engine to set up a block of type for printing. Finally Babbage also proposed that the machine should be capable of choosing one of several alternative courses of action in a way not previously known to the human operator: the 'conditional transfer instruction' of the modern computer.

Thus, in the Analytical Engine Babbage introduced the following ideas:

(a) CPU
(b) Storage,
(c) Card input,
(d) Printed output,
(e) Conditional transfers of control,

and

(f) The concept of computer programming.

The machine could not be built in Babbage's day. He was born one hundred years too soon. In 1937 Howard Aitken at Harvard began to build a machine called 'ASCC' (Automatic Sequence Controlled Calculator), or the Harvard Mark 1 Machine, which was a small version of the Analytical Engine. In collaboration with IBM it was completed in 1944. Ironically, by that time new developments had occurred which rapidly made the Harvard Mark 1 obsolete.

1·7·2 The Electronic Age

It is now possible to say that an *electronic* computer, that is one whose CPU and store contain no mechanical parts, could have been built at any time after 1919. In that year W. H. Eccles and F. W. Jordan showed how a pair of triode valves could be connected to form a circuit having two stable states. Today the 'Eccles–Jordan trigger' is commonly known as a 'flip-flop'. It is clearly capable of representing binary digits (zero and one) and hence is fundamental to computers.

In fact no proposal for an electronic computer was put forward until 1943 when J. P. Eckert and J. W. Mauchley of the Moore School of Electrical Engineering at the University of Pennsylvania proposed the building of an all-electronic machine based on the Eccles–Jordan trigger to be used by the U.S. War Department for the calculation of ballistic tables. This machine, called the ENIAC (Electronic Numerical Integrator and Calculator) was completed in about two years and began work on February 15th, 1946. Nothing comparable had ever been seen before for it contained 18 000 valves, it used 100 Kilowatts of power and occupied a room 30 metres in length. It was predicted that a machine with so many valves could not possibly run for more than a few seconds and there is a legend that when the current was switched on the starting transient always blew at least three valves. Nevertheless the machine was very successful and ran for over nine years, being finally switched off on October 2nd, 1955.

ENIAC was an enormous advance on all its predecessors but it was not a general purpose computer since it was not programmable in the modern sense. It was intended to perform specific calculations and a change in the problem to be solved required the replugging of various parts of the machine. ENIAC worked in decimal scale throughout with only twenty accumulators for storage, each of which could hold a ten digit decimal number and its sign. Addition and subtraction took 200 micro seconds and multiplication took 2300 microseconds. Special units were provided for division and square root operations. Input and output were by means of punched cards. In addition to its ballistics calculations ENIAC was used in the solution of partial differential equations and, as an extra, it computed π and e to 2000 decimal places.

Whilst ENIAC was under construction Dr. John von Neumann put forward a proposal for a *stored program* computer (June 30th, 1945). Von Neumann and his colleagues had given a great deal of thought to the optimum form of a computer and they concluded, as Babbage had done, that a 'large' storage capacity was essential. They decided that a computer should have a storage capacity of the order of 4096 words and that, given this, *both instructions and data could be stored in the same unit.* The ideal word length, they decided was between 6 and 12 decimal digits (20 to 40 bits). Desirable characteristics of the store indicated that the best type of storage available at that time was the mercury acoustic delay line. The machine thus designed was the EDVAC (Electronic Discrete Variable Automatic Computer); it used only 3500 valves. Because of delays brought about mainly because Eckert and Mauchley had left to form their own computer company, it was not completed until the early 1950s. In the meantime however Maurice Wilkes, who had spent the summer of 1946 with the computer design group at the University of Pennsylvania, returned to Cambridge in 1947 and began building EDSAC (Electronic Delayed Storage Automatic Computer) and this ran its first program, the first stored program to run anywhere in the world, in May 1949.

In 1949–50 another computer was designed and built at Manchester University. This machine formed the basis of the first computer sold commercially in Britain (the Manchester Mark 1 machine, by Ferranti Limited). Even more important, the machine contained a number of registers, known originally as 'B-lines'.

The first commercially available machine in the world was the Univac 1. This machine was built in the USA by Remington Rand and the first Univac was delivered to the US Bureau of the Census in April 1951. The machine was based on EDVAC.

In 1953, IBM, who had at first shown no great interest in stored program computers, produced the 701 followed in 1955 by the 704, the first really successful scientific computer. From this time on IBM has remained the dominant computer company in the world with nearly 70% of the total world market. It was on the 704 that IBM introduced FORTRAN (February 1957).

The first generation of electronic digital computers were constructed of thermionic devices, particularly triodes. The next generation (1960) used semiconductor technology, replacing the triodes with transistors which gave a marked increase in speed and reliability and a reduction in power consumption, with its related heating problems. The third generation (1966) arrived with the introduction of integrated circuits whereby a number of transistors plus the required resistors and capacitors are fabricated on one semiconductor 'chip'; this further increased speed and reliability, but equally important, greatly reduced size and cost. The definition of a fourth generation is vague indeed, so suffice it to say that currently the scale of the circuit integration has increased and the cost decreased. The terms MSI and LSI have been coined to describe the medium and large scale integrated circuits.

1·7·3 Mini and Micro Computers

The earlier minicomputers were developed for aerospace applications and appeared around 1960–62, e.g. the Burroughs D210, Hughes HCH-201 and Univac Add-1000. Commercial minis appeared around 1966 from such manufacturers as Honeywell, Xerox Data Systems and Hewlett–Packard. The first machine to be sold in large quantities, particularly as a stand alone machine, rather than part of a system, was the Digital Equipment (DEC) PDP-8.

Around 1962 the process control, 'midi' computers, were introduced which were probably the first practical machines for on-line control. Typical machines were the G.E.312/412, IBM 1130 and Ferranti Argus 200. This size of machine is nowadays being superseded by the more powerful of the 16 bit minis.

The first commercial microprocessor, the Intel 4004, appeared in 1972, although it is likely that aerospace machines had been produced by companies such as Rockwell before that. The Intel 8008 and 8080 and the National Semiconductor 'multiple chip set' processor soon followed. In fact all the big semiconductor manufacturers are involved in producing calculator and microprocessor chips of one sort or another.

In 1973/74 Computer Automation and General Automation announced LSI versions of machines which had already been successfully marketed as standard minis. The G.A. machine was probably the first to use silicon-on-sapphire technology.

1·8 Diagrammatic Representation of the Components of a Digital Computer

The advent of integrated circuitry means that electronic units are available which perform some basic function. No longer need logic circuits be configured in terms of resistors and transistors, but in terms of functional units such as gates, registers, amplifiers, etc. These devices are packaged as small ceramic or plastic encapsulated chips, nicknamed 'bugs', with standard pin configurations to ease mounting problems. The simpler units, such as inventors or gates are usually packaged two or more in the one bug; more complex units, such as a memory or microprocessor are presenting more problems in packaging and particularly in pin allocation. The simpler units are referred to as ICs, with the terms MSI and LSI (medium and large scale integration) applied to successively larger units.

The details of how a unit works are of relatively little importance. They are selected simply by what function they perform, how fast they operate and whether or not they are compatible with other ICs, so that they can be simply wired into a circuit. Thus in a text such as this, the operation of a computer can be explained by defining only a few simple functional devices, with no consideration given to the electronics necessary to implement them. Three basic types of unit are defined, gates, registers and busbars.

1·8·1 Gates

There are in practice a number of types of gate, NOT, AND, OR, NAND, NOR, etc., described in Appendix 2. For purely descriptive purposes the NOT, AND and OR gates only are needed, although the others are more common in actual system implementation. These three gates are shown in figure 1.12. In theory there can be any number of inputs to gates (a) and (b) although there are practical limits. For the AND gate the output, X, is logical 0 for all combinations of A, B and C except when all three are logical 1; this sets X to logical 1. Remember that in practice logical 0 is typically 0 volts and logical 1 is +3·5 volts approximately.

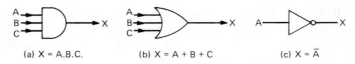

(a) X = A.B.C.   (b) X = A + B + C   (c) X = $\overline{A}$

Fig. 1·12 (a) 3-input AND gate. (b) 3-input OR gate. (c) Invertor or NOT gate.

The two-input AND gate has exceptional importance as it is used as a switch to control the 'flow' of information around the computer. Thus for the AND gate of figure 1.13, the input marked X_{in} is incoming data and the input C is a control signal. Now if X_{in} is 0, X_{out} is 0 for C either 1 or 0; however if X_{in} is 1 then X_{out} is 0 if C is 0 but 1 when C is 1. By studying the summary of this data, given in the truth-table of figure 1.13 it can be seen that X_{out} is 0 if C is 0, but $X_{out} = X_{in}$ if C is 1.

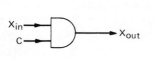

C	X_{in}	X_{out}
0	0	0
0	1	0
1	0	0
1	1	1

Fig. 1·13 A 2-input AND gate and its truth table.

Thus if X_{in} is a bit of data it can be transmitted, via X_{out}, to another part of the system, under control of the signal, C. Used in this sense, the gate is said to be *inhibited* when C is 0 and *enabled* when C is 1.

For the OR gate, figure 1.12(b), the output, X, is 1 if any one, or any combination, of the inputs is 1 and 0 only when A, B and C are all 0.

The NOT gate, or invertor, figure 1.12(c), outputs 1 for a 0 input and vice versa; it is said to *complement* the input data.

A situation regularly arises in which the desired output is one of a number of inputs. Figure 1.14(a) shows how gates can be arranged such that X is either A or B dependent upon whether C_1 or C_2 is 1; if both C_1 and C_2 are 1 then X is the logical OR of A and B. The system of figure 1.14(b) is similar except that a special type of gate is used, the output of which *floats* when not enabled. Thus the OR function can be implemented simply by wiring the gate outputs together, so that if gate 1 is inhibited, the output from gate 2 may be 1 or 0 without affecting the first gate and vice versa. Gates with this type of floating output when inhibited are called 'Tri-state'. If both C_1 and C_2 with the tri-state gates are enabled at the same time damage can be caused, so that this *must* be avoided.

In summary when a conventional TTL gate is inhibited, the output is held at logical 0; when a tri-state gate is inhibited the output is *disconnected* and floats to any level.

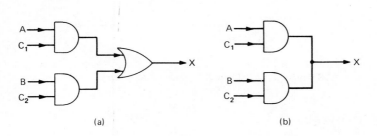

(a) (b)

Fig. 1·14 Logic network for X = A if C_1 = 1 *or* X = B if C_2 = 1 (a) using AND and OR gates (b) using tri-state AND gates (C_1 and $C_2 \neq$ 1).

33

There is an alternative type of gate which can be connected as in figure 1.14(b) termed an 'Open-collector' gate which is a true equivalent to figure 1.14(a), i.e. with C_1 and $C_2 = 1$, X is the logical OR or A and B. These gates are also used for connection to bus bars. Tri-state output devices are becoming more common in integrated circuits.

1·8·2 Registers

While a gate can control the flow of information, it cannot save any data, e.g. in figure 1.13, if C is set to 1, X_{in} is transferred to X_{out}, but when C is cleared to 0, X_{out} becomes 0, irrespective of X_{in}. The basic storage element in logic circuitry is the electronic *flip-flop* or *bi-stable*. This device has two stable states, 1 or 0 and can be *set* to 1 and *cleared* or *reset* to 0 by an input signal, retaining the desired state until it is either set or cleared again as appropriate. A number of variations on the basic set/reset (R-S) flip-flop are discussed in Appendix 2. The flip-flop circuit of importance here is usually called a register, although this term usually implies a group of flip-flops, one for each bit of a computer word, with associated input and output gating.

The use of a gate to control the storage element is shown in figure 1.15; when C is set to 1, the value of X_{in} is transferred to the input of the flip-flop which causes the output, Y, to take the same value, i.e. $Y = X_{in}$. However, when C is returned to 0, inhibiting the gate and causing X to be 0, Y remains unchanged. X_{in} can now be modified without affecting Y; Y will only be affected while the gate is enabled. In summary the register can be made to store the value X_{in} by enabling the gate via C for a short time interval, sufficient only for Y to reach its new state; as long as C is 0, X_{in} can be modified without affecting Y. It must be stressed that this is a schematic representation only. These devices are used for saving information, commonly referred to as *buffers* or *latches*, particularly when the input data is transient.

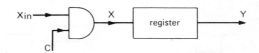

Fig. 1·15 A 1 bit register with data input X_{in} and control input C.

1·8·3 Bus Bars

Data is transferred from one part of the computer to another by a connecting wire called a *bus bar* or more simply a *bus*. Usually, in the modern *parallel* computer each bus bar has a number of wires, one for each bit of the word. In practice a voltage relative to earth is established on each wire to represent zero (0 volts) or one (+3·5 volts). If the output from one gate or register is connected to the bus and the input to another gate or register is also connected to the same bus, then data will be transmitted from the first to the second device. Data is said to 'flow' along the bus, although this is only a descriptive term. Note that the output from only one device should be connected to the bus at any one time, which establishes the voltage level, i.e. 'sends' or 'transmits' the data in the descriptive sense. Any number of devices can have their inputs connected to the bus to 'receive' the data. The sending device is often said to be the bus 'master' while all receiving devices are 'slaves'. In a practical computer there will be a number of bus bars, used for specific purposes, e.g. I/O bus or memory to CPU bus.

Figure 1.16 summarises a situation common inside the computer CPU, although more than the two registers shown will probably have access to the bus. Effectively the outputs from gates 2 and 4 are connected together, via the bus. One or other of these two gates will be enabled so that their outputs should be connected via an OR gate. With the *bus* concept this is impractical, so that tri-state or open-collector gates must be used.

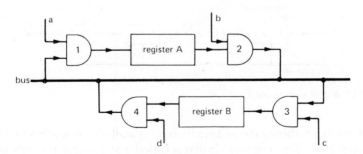

Fig. 1·16 A bi-directional bus.

It can now be shown that data 'flows' in one or another direction along the bus, determined by which gates are enabled; this bus is said to be *bi-directional*. If gates 2 and 3 only are enabled (a = d = 0 and b = c = 1) then the output of register A is connected to the input of register B so that the data stored in A is copied into B; note that the data stored in A is unaffected. Thus when all gates are again inhibited, the data from A has been stored in B (remember that c going back to zero sets the outputs of gate 3 back to zero, but does not alter the data just stored by the register; c must be set to one again to allow a change in the stored data). Similarly enabling gates 1 and 4 for a short interval of time will copy the data stored in B into A. Note that for the first example, data 'flows' along the right hand section of the bus from left to right, and in the second example from right to left along the left hand section of the bus. In both cases, neglecting the very short transmission times, the voltage levels at all points on the bus are the same, stressing the purely descriptive nature of the phrase 'data flow'.

Gates 1 and 3 could both be enabled at the same time, in which case both registers A and B would store data from the bus, which would have been established by some other device not shown in figure 1.16. However gates 2 and 4 cannot both be enabled or else two conflicting pieces of data will attempt to establish control of the bus at the same time.

1·8·4 Word Orientated Data

The preceding comments apply to single bits of information. However since information inside the computer is handled in groups, called words, the grouping of registers, buses, etc. must be considered. The device shown in figure 1.17 is a general purpose 4 bit register; only 4

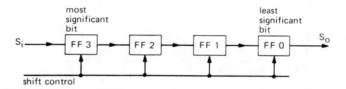

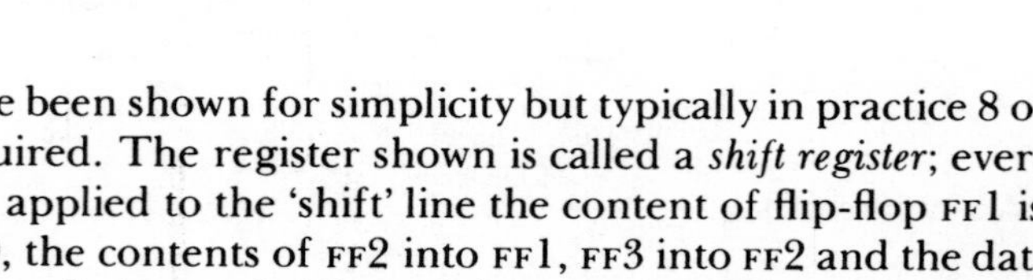

Fig. 1·17 A 4 bit shift register.

bits have been shown for simplicity but typically in practice 8 or 16 bits are required. The register shown is called a *shift register*; every time a pulse is applied to the 'shift' line the content of flip-flop FF1 is copied into FF0, the contents of FF2 into FF1, FF3 into FF2 and the data on the input line, S_i, into FF3. The original contents of FF0 is available on S_o while the shift pulse is at 1 but is lost when it falls to 0. Note the standard numbering system starting at 0, not 1. In this way data can be transferred from one register to another in 4 time intervals by applying 4 consecutive pulses to the shift line when the S_o line of the sending register has been 'gated' through to the S_i line of the receiving register. Thus in figure 1.18 if gate a is enabled, the 4 shift pulses will transfer the contents of the 4 bit register A to the 4 bit register B. The original contents of B are lost and, since gate b is inhibited, S_i of register A is at 0

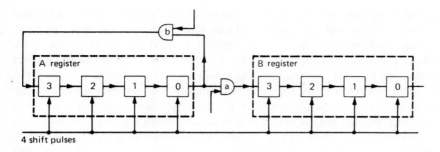

Fig. 1·18 Serial transfer of a data word by shifting.

and the final contents of A will be four 0's, i.e. it is cleared. If however gate b *and* gate a are both enabled, the contents of A will be transferred to B *and* the contents of A will be *rotated*, so that the original contents of A are restored at the end of the 4 pulses in addition to the copy in B. Note that only one bus is used, with data transmitted in *serial* mode.

The alternative to the shift register of figures 1.17 is to use independent flip-flops for each bit of the word, with gating as shown in figure 1.19.

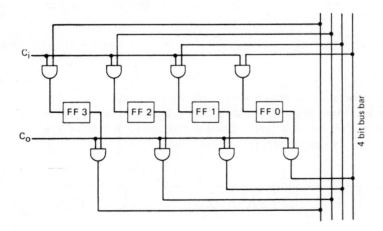

Fig. 1·19 A 4 bit register with parallel input and output connected to a common bus bar.

Assume that normally both C_i and C_o are at level 0. If C_i is changed to 1 the data on the bus bar are copied into the 4 flip-flops of the register and are stored after C_i is returned to 0. Similarly by raising C_o to level 1 the contents of the register are presented to the bus bars; returning C_o

to 0 zeros the bus bar which of course has no memory. This is a *parallel* mode, using multiple gates and bus lines but only one time interval. Note that only the two control signals, C_o and C_i, are required, each being common to each bit of the register – it is not possible to connect say only bit 2 to the bus bar; the whole word or nothing.

Integrated circuits are readily available with 16 bits, in either the shift register or the parallel input/output type including the associated gating. In fact registers are available with both figures 1.17 and 1.19 combined, e.g. data can be shifted in serially and output in parallel. Shifting operations are also used in arithmetic units for other reasons than data transfer as will be explained in the next chapter.

In earlier systems using discrete components, the serial mode had the advantage of lower cost; in all modern systems the parallel mode is used so as to take advantage of the higher speed, integrated circuits having reduced the cost differential. Since as explained above, individual control cannot be exercised over individual bits, the diagrammatic representation of figure 1.20 is used, the double line indicating that there are in reality a number of individual lines, one for each bit of the word.

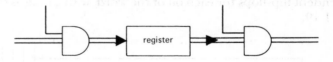

Fig. 1·20 Diagrammatic representation of a multiple bit register with parallel input and output.

There is a standard notation for numbering the bits of a word, with the least-significant-bit (LSB) labelled 0 at the right-hand end and the most-significant-bit (MSB) labelled n-1 at the left-hand end. A 16 bit example is shown in figure 1.21.

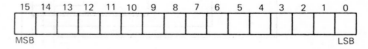

Fig. 1·21 Standard labelling of a 16 bit register.

A simple notation for describing data transfers is also used, thus: Symbols such as A, B, FRED, refer to memory addresses, the contents of which are signified by parenthesis, e.g.

$(XYZ) \rightarrow R2$ means copy the contents of memory location XYZ into register 2.

38

(R2) → TOM   means copy the contents of register 2 into location TOM.

Note that XYZ and TOM are mnemonics for memory locations and are directly replaceable by memory addresses; a specific program relates specific addresses to given *labels*.

Thus

TOM → R2   moves the number equivalent to TOM into R2, *not* the contents of the memory location.

When referring to a CPU register, the parenthesis are superfluous, e.g. (R1) → R2 and R1 → R2 are similar since there is no address and therefore no number related to R1.

The importance of understanding the concepts discussed in this section cannot be over-stated. More detailed discussions are given in Appendix 2 where some further 'basic' devices such as *Adders* and *Decoders* are shown to be simply combinations of basic gates.

In the following chapters the operation of a digital computer is explained in terms of this concept of digital data storage and flow under the control of signals fed to one of the inputs of the gates.

Chapter 2

A Rudimentary Digital Computer

2·1 Introduction

The digital computer to be described in this chapter, the DUMB 1, could be constructed and would work. The objective behind explaining the operation of this simple, hypothetical machine is merely to give the reader an understanding of the fundamental principles. The common refinements of this simple machine which are to be found on the commercial minicomputers are described in the next two chapters, while the more sophisticated techniques are explained in Chapter 8. This chapter is also used as a basis for the discussion of microprocessors conducted in Chapter 5.

In this and the next chapter, the concentration will be on the *central processor unit* (CPU) and its communication with the main, random access memory. Discussion of the *input/output*, (I/O) will be simple here, being constrained to a switch console and input and output devices, each directly compatible with the word length of the computer. Realistic I/O systems are explained separately in Chapter 4.

The word length of this simple machine, the DUMB 1, is chosen as 16 bits since this is the most common in practice. The effect of different word lengths will be expounded as the description progresses.

2·2 The DUMB 1

The DUMB 1 is a 16 bit, parallel, two's complement* minicomputer, the sales of which are expected to reach 1000 a month if only the price can be kept below £20 or $50, whichever is the lower.

A schematic layout of a computer system was shown earlier in figure 1.5; referring to that figure, the back-up store will for the moment be

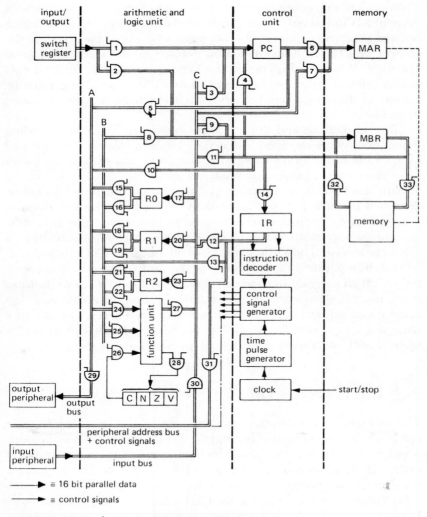

Fig. 2·1 Schematic layout of a simple digital computer

* See Appendix 1

completely ignored and it should be remembered that the data and program memories are in practice different locations of the same memory. Thus figure 2.1 is the same system as figure 1.5, but shown in much greater detail using the diagrammatic techniques explained in Section 1.7. The functions of the individual gates are summarised at the end of this chapter.

The list of instructions, i.e. the program, is already stored in the memory, by methods that will be explained later. The program is so written that the computer works through the list of instructions sequentially unless deliberately instructed to 'branch'. An instruction is fetched from the memory into the *control unit* where it is decoded; the control unit then causes the action defined by the instruction to be executed. When the instruction has been executed, the next instruction is fetched from memory, and so on. The control unit must be capable of deciding where the next instruction to be executed is stored in memory.

All arithmetical and logical operations are performed, when demanded by the decoded instruction, by the *arithmetic and logic unit* (ALU). Communication between the computer and the outside world takes place via the *input/output* system.

With this basic overall picture in mind, each of these blocks will be discussed in turn. It is perhaps worth noting first however, that the computer must be presented in a useful physical form. The electronic components are mounted onto *printed circuit boards* (PCB), sometimes a few large ones and other times more, smaller boards. These boards can be bought separately for mounting by the user in his own equipment, the so called *original* or *other equipment manufacturer* (OEM), but are more normally mounted in a standard size box, complete with fan cooling and power supplies. The front panel is usually arranged as a basic operators console, providing switches and lights to manually operate and interrogate the machine, as explained in Section 2.7.

2·3 The Memory Unit

The memory unit is the main storage area of the computer. In most machines the main memory is a magnetic core store (often the memory is simply called the *core*), with an increasing use of LSI semiconductor stores. Both systems are explained in Appendix 4. The important features of such memories however are as follows:

(a) Information (instruction or data) is stored by the word or byte. For the sake of this chapter, the DUMB 1 stores, and of course accesses, information as 16 bit words; byte orientated stores will be explained in the next chapter. In any case individual bits of a word cannot be accessed; any operations on individual bits must be performed by passing the whole word to the ALU, which can perform logical arithmetic operations to extract an individual bit.

(b) Entering information into the memory is termed *writing*; extracting information is termed *reading*.

(c) Each location in the memory can be accessed in the same time as any other; each location is said to have a unique address. Thus if data is read from location 100 in one instruction, the next read will be completed in the same time whether it is from location 101 or location 1001. This gives rise to the term *random-access-memory* (RAM).

(d) The time taken to complete a memory access, either read or write, is termed the *memory cycle time*. The actual cycle time depends upon the type of memory and the quality; typical memory cycle times in 1974 are:

   (i) magnetic core 0·5 to 2 μ secs.
   (ii) LSI MOS semiconductor 0·4 to 0·7 μ secs.
   (iii) Bipolar semiconductor 0·1 to 0·4 μ secs.

The memory cycle time is one of the fundamental restrictions on the speed of operation of the computer, but by no means the only factor involved!

(e) Reading data from magnetic core memory is a destructive process, so that the word just read out must be copied back into the same memory location to avoid corruption of the data. Thus each instruction, either read or write, requires two time intervals; the memory cycle time is the total time. Three possible modes of operation can be defined:

   (i) clear/write – the write instruction
   (ii) read/restore – the read instruction
   (iii) read/modify/write. This mode is used for such instructions as increment the contents of a memory location; the contents are read, passed to the processor to be incremented (modify) and the modified data written back into memory. Since the modify phase is conducted by the electronic circuitry of the CPU, the time taken for all three modes is often identical, although mode (iii) may take a little longer on some machines.

Reading from semiconductor memory is a non-destructive process so that there are only two modes, read or write. This single phase operation accounts for much of the speed advantage of semiconductor memory over magnetic core. The increment-a-memory-location-contents instruction quoted above requires special memory control hardware if the two types of memory are to be compatible, i.e. the read/modify/write mode must be simulated.

(f) The size of the memory is restricted by the range of addresses as determined by the machine instruction set, which will soon be

43

explained. Commercial minicomputer core is available in 4, 8 or 16 K blocks* of 16 bit words, which can be built up, as and when required, to the maximum limit. Semiconductor memory is available in smaller units, typically 256 words; bigger units of memory become available almost monthly.

(g) Different types of memory can be mixed together in some machines, but this is uncommon. Most microcomputers use semiconductor memory exclusively in practice; programs in *read only memory* (ROM) and data in RAM. The term ROM may be a little misleading, since it is strictly a *random access memory* which can be read from but not written into. Minicomputers tend to be supplied with either magnetic core or semiconductor memory. Only in the larger machines are mixed memories common, where semiconductor stores are used for high speed foreground work, magnetic core for background work with the usual disc for back-up store. Mixed memories are thus uncommon but are technically feasible. To take advantage of possible differing memory speeds, asynchronous operation is essential, otherwise the memory cycle time would be fixed to that of the slowest device. Asynchronous and synchronous operation are discussed in the next chapter.

(h) Some memories require a power supply to maintain their data, i.e. if the power is switched off and then switched on again the original stored information will be lost, being replaced by 'rubbish'. Such a memory is said to be *volatile*. Normal semiconductor RAM is volatile while magnetic core is non-volatile. ROM is clearly non-volatile by definition. Obviously the semiconductor registers in the CPU are volatile and precautions are often taken to safeguard against power failure, as discussed in Chapter 8. Semiconductor memory can be made essentially non-volatile by providing stand-by battery power supplies. One VRC dumps the whole of its semiconductor memory contents to an internal magnetic cassette when power fail is detected.

The rate of development of memory technology is so great as to make the cycle time quoted laughable, even before this book is published, if past history is any guideline. For the record, in 1974 one microsecond was the norm for memory cycle time with costs for both magnetic core and semiconductor memory averaging about one penny per bit.

Viewed by the CPU, the memory should look like a black box with an input 'port' and an output 'port', each port of course communicating one word, e.g. 16 lines for a 16 bit word machine. Thus two special 16 bit registers are associated with the memory bank. One is called the *memory address register* (MAR) and the other the *memory buffer register*

---

* The symbol K is used in computer terminology to mean $2^{10} = 1024$, the nearest binary number to 1000.

(MBR). These names are almost self explanatory. The specific word of information to be accessed, either read or written, is located by the contents of the MAR. If information is to be written into this location, the CPU must simply transfer the appropriate word into the MBR. It is then automatically copied to the appropriate memory location without further action by the CPU, in one memory cycle time. Reading the contents of a specific memory location also requires loading the MAR; the read operation is initiated, which at the end of the memory cycle will have copied the contents of the addressed memory location into the MBR; this is then available for use by the CPU. Thus the CPU communicates solely with the MBR, locating different words of memory independent of the MBR by means of the MAR, with a logical command to indicate whether a read or write is required. The memory unit of the computer shown in figure 2.1 is shown in isolation in figure 2.2. Note

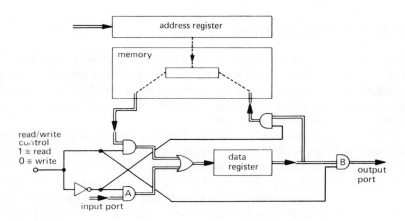

Fig. 2·2 A memory unit

that while separate input and output ports are indicated, these can be wired to a common bus, since the gates A and B cannot both be enabled at the same time. This diagram is often drawn more simply as in figure 2.3.

The maximum size of the memory is fixed by the number of bits in the MAR, thus for a 16 bit machine $2^{16} = 64$K words can be addressed, a limit which is only reached in big installations. From the viewpoint of figure 2.2 there is no reason why the MAR must be the same length as the MBR; this constraint is set simply by compatibility.

In microprocessor systems the 8 bit word is common, which is too short to give an adequate range of addresses. In this case two words are concatenated to give an effective 16 bit address with an 8 bit memory

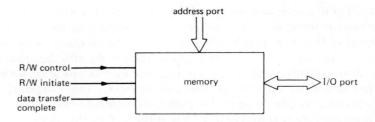

Fig. 2·3 Simplified schematic layout of a memory unit. The extra signal, data transfer complete, is set when the MBR-memory transfer is complete

word; effectively the address port is 16 bits wide while the I/O port is 8 bits. More details are given in Chapter 5.

2·4 The Control Unit

The control unit is the heart of the CPU. It is largely in the detailed development of the control unit that one computer really differs from another. Despite the electronic complexity however, the control unit is conceptually simple, comprising two parts, the *instruction decoder and controller* and the *program counter*.

The *program counter* (PC) is yet another word length register. Its sole purpose is to indicate during the execution of one instruction, the address at which the next instruction to be executed is stored.

Consider a program to be stored in memory with the first instruction to be executed at location 252. To start the program execution, the binary number equivalent to 252 is entered into the PC using the switch registers, say, with the processor halted. A switch is then depressed which starts the computer running. This causes the contents of the PC to be copied into the MAR and to initiate a read memory operation, which, when completed, causes the MBR contents to be copied into the *instruction register* (IR). The IR is part of the instruction decoder and controller. Once the MAR has stored the copy of the PC, the PC itself is no longer involved in this particular instruction. The next instruction to be executed will normally be stored in the memory location following the one from which the current instruction has just been fetched, so that the PC can now be incremented; i.e. one added to the current contents, so that it is pointing to the address of the next instruction in sequence.

The binary number in the IR is an instruction to the computer which is electronically decoded, sending out control signals causing the machine to do what the instruction demands. The specific instruction causes some of the gates in the CPU to be enabled, so that data may be moved, modified or simply tested. Decoding a different instruction generates control signals which cause different gates to be enabled resulting in a different action. In a crude sense the decoding operation can be likened to a telephone network, one number causing a specific connection to be made. However, the computer instruction is much more complex, selecting a number of paths and also requiring interrelated timing of events during execution of one instruction. Note that some instructions will cause data to be transferred to or from memory requiring further use of both the MAR and the MBR; it is for this reason that the next instruction address is kept in the PC, independent of the MAR.

It is vital to realise the importance of timing in the operation described above. The DUMB 1 works in the simplest possible way by synchronising events to an internal processor *clock*, an electronic circuit which generates accurate pulses at regular intervals in time, often crystal controlled for accuracy and stability. A 1 microsecond memory cycle time is typical, but synchronising pulses are required at specified, regular subintervals of this period, requiring basic clock frequency of say 5–10 MHz. The use of asynchronous operation alters this picture somewhat, as shown in Section 3.2.

The following is a step by step summary of the preceding paragraphs:

(a) Copy the PC contents into the MAR and initiate the memory read cycle, thereby loading the MBR.

(b) Restore the memory location just read if magnetic core is being used.

(c) Increment the PC.

(d) Copy the instruction now in the MBR into the IR.

(e) Decode the instruction.

(f) Execute the instruction.

(g) Repeat from (a) etc.

Each of the above steps can be initiated by consecutive clock pulses, except for step (f) which, dependent upon the instruction, may require more than one time interval. For the present assume that step (f) only requires one time interval. If the operations in the list are studied it can be noted that steps (b), (c) and (d) could be arranged in any order without any overall effect. More important, each of these steps is conducted in independent parts of the computer. Thus it is quite practical to cause all of these three steps to occur in the same time interval, thereby speeding up the operation.

Steps (a) and (b) constitute the normal read/restore memory cycle, so that this simple synchronous concept implies that the processor clock is controlling the memory cycle time. This timing sequence is shown in

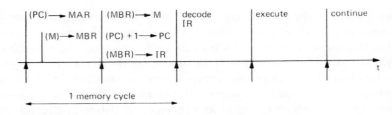

Fig. 2·4 Simple timing sequence

figure 2.4. The notation in this diagram was introduced in Chapter 1 and used here for the first time. To stress the notation for future examples,

(PC) → MAR copy contents of PC into MAR

(M) → MBR copy contents of addressed memory location into MBR

(MBR) → M restore addressed memory location

(PC) + 1 → PC increment PC contents

(MBR) → IR copy contents of MBR into IR

Now the system of figure 2.4 has its maximum clock frequency set by the speed of the memory, say, 1 μ sec. memory cycle time. However the electronic CPU operations of steps (d), (e) and (f), still neglecting more complex execution operations, do not need the 1·5 μ sec. allocated in figure 2.4. In practice 0·5 μ sec. will be adequate. Further, the PC can be incremented at any time after the MAR has been loaded; these two operations in sequence can therefore be performed while the memory read operation is completing, i.e. during the first half of the memory cycle. In effect the CPU operations do not normally conflict with the memory operations so that they can run in parallel. Thus one interval can be subdivided as indicated in figure 2.5. Note that this requires the electronics of the instruction decoder and controller to be sophisticated enough to organise the correct sequence within the one clock period.

It has been stressed that the time allowed in figure 2.5 for execution is only adequate for the simpler instructions, those which only effect the high speed electronics inside the CPU, e.g. clear a register in the

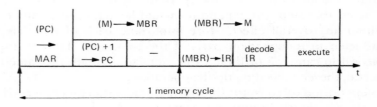

Fig. 2·5 Timing sequence compacted into a one memory cycle

ALU, The other type of instruction to be considered now is one which involves transfer of data between the CPU and memory, e.g. store the contents of an ALU register in a specified memory location. Consider now step (f) for this particular instruction. The specified memory address, as implied in the instruction (see Section 2.8.3), must be loaded into the MAR and the data transferred from the ALU register to the MBR; since this is a memory write instruction the clear cycle is also initiated, followed by the write cycle which transfers the new MBR contents into the addressed memory location. This operation requires a complete memory cycle and so cannot be packed into the 'execute' slot in figure 2.5. Thus this type of instruction, termed a memory reference instruction, requires two complete memory cycles to complete as shown in figure 2.6. The names *fetch* or *instruction cycle* and *execute cycle* are given to these two memory cycles. The word cycle would seem to be in use for too many slightly different actions and the terms fetch, instruction and execute are not truly descriptive of the function, but these are the terms in common use.

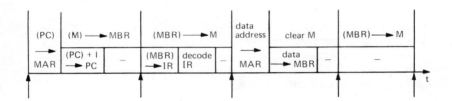

Fig. 2·6 A two memory cycle instruction sequence

The range of instructions available is governed by two factors. The first of these is the hardware configuration, i.e. how many gates have been included to make specific actions electronically feasible, often related to the sophistication of the ALU. The second factor is the word length, which governs the number of combinations that can be uniquely defined and coded into an instruction. The make-up of a typical instruction set will be discussed in Section 2.8 when the cursory explanation of the rest of the machine has been completed.

2·5 The Arithmetic and Logic Unit

The ALU is that part of the computer where all arithmetical and logical operations are performed. It is constructed exclusively of high speed electronic components. The heart of the ALU is a sophisticated piece of circuitry, shown as the function unit on figure 2.1, which will perform some specified operation on the data presented to its inputs. Any operation of which the function unit is capable is executed by a particular set of command signals, which are generated by the instruction decoder at the appropriate time as determined by the specific instruction being executed.

A typical function unit is shown in some greater detail in figure 2.7. On figure 2.1 the input gates were 'summarised' as gates 24, 25 and 26.

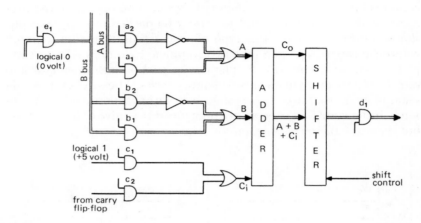

Fig. 2·7 A typical function unit

The *adder*, which is described in more detail in Appendix 2, generates the sum of the three inputs A, B and C_i. A and B are full word length data while C_i is a single bit (least significant). The *shifter* is a network of gates which can route the input data either directly through or shifted, i.e. the bit pattern is displaced one bit right or left. The carry bit, C_o, may well be involved in shifting type operations, which will be discussed further in Section 2.8.4.

Closely associated with the ALU are the four single bit registers (*flip-flops*), often called 'condition flags', labelled C, N, Z and V. Often these flip-flops are grouped together as one status word, usually full word length, with the other bits wasted or used for other functions within the control unit. Seldom are all four flags provided, but they are set to one if, respectively; a carry occurs*; the result is negative, e.g. the MSB (the sign bit) is one; the result is zero; and an arithmetic overflow occurs. These flags can be tested by following instructions to determine conditional jumps in the program sequence.

---

* The carry flag is often termed the *link*; on some machines it is complemented by a carry rather than set to one.

Some of the typical operations are executed as follows, with a summary in figure 2.8.

(i) *Add.* The two words of data are placed on the A and B buses and gates a_1 and b_1 enabled. No shift is used and the sum can be passed on by enabling gate d_1. Some examples in which the condition flags are set are given in Appendix 1.

(ii) *Subtract.* (A–B) is performed by adding the two's complement of B (see Appendix 1) to A. The two's complement is derived by complementing and adding 1. Thus gates a_1, b_2 and c_1 are enabled.

(iii) *Complement and Negate.* The former is achieved, assuming the data to be on bus A, by enabling gate a_2. For the latter, gates a_2 and c_1 must be enabled.

(iv) *Increment.* With the data on bus A, a_1 and c_1 are enabled.

(v) *Decrement.* The two's complement of -1 is all the bits of the word set to one. Thus with the data on bus A, gates a_1, b_2 and e_1 are enabled.

(vi) *Shift.* With the data on bus A, gate a_1 is enabled and the appropriate shift control set. Note that combinations such as add and shift the results are possible with this arrangement.

Operation	Gates Enabled
Add $(A + B)$	a_1, b_1
Subtract $(A - B)$	a_1, b_2, c_1
Complement $(\bar{A})$	a_2
Negate $(-A)$	a_2, c_1
Increment $(A + 1)$	a_1, c_1
Decrement $(A - 1)$	a_1, b_2, e_1

Fig. 2·8

In the DUMB 1, the sources of data which can be fed to the function unit are the three registers labelled simply R0, R1 and R2 and the one bit carry-in. Other computers have far more registers, others only one, in which case the second input to the function unit must come from memory via the MBR. Some machines use temporary 'buffer' registers to communicate between the function unit and other parts of the machine.

The function unit itself is not a store, so that if the result of any operation is required it is saved by writing back into either R0, R1 or R2, overlaying the previous contents of that register. This often leads to the term *accumulator* being applied to this type of register. To appreciate this consider a simple example of a program to add the contents of two memory locations together and save the result in another location. The sequence of events will be as follows.

(i) Fetch and execute the first instruction which reads the first number from memory into R1.

(ii) Fetch and execute the second instruction which reads the second number from memory into R2.

(iii) Fetch and execute the third instruction which causes the instruction decoder to enable the appropriate input gates to effect the addition. The function unit output gate and the input gate to R1 are then enabled, writing the resultant sum into R1; the function unit input gates must be inhibited at the same time to stop cycling the new contents of R1 back into the function unit. All other gates will of course be inhibited automatically at the end of the operation.

(iv) Fetch and execute the fourth instruction which causes the contents of R1 to be written into the appropriate memory location.

Note that the methods of indicating the particular memory locations have not yet been discussed. The first, second and fourth instructions are two-memory-cycle-instructions as in figure 2.6, while the third instruction is a single-memory-cycle-instruction as in figure 2.5. This example should emphasise the relative speed of the circuitry in the function unit compared to memory transfers. It also, by studying (iii) above, should give some indication of the true complexity of the timing problems faced by the computer CPU designer; this type of system involving the enabling and inhibiting of specific gates in specific related time intervals is termed *sequential logic*.

In the above example the final contents of R1 are the original contents plus another number. In this sense R1 is accumulating a sum, hence the common term accumulator. It is not a very good term however since with a subtract operation the final contents of R1 will be the original contents minus another number! If the machine is so designed that the results can be stored in one specific register and no other, then it is more reasonable that this particular register be termed the Accumulator.

The number of possible functions that are built into the electronics of the function unit are restricted by cost and the number of unique codes that can be incorporated into the instruction. The ALU related instructions can be vaguely split into three groups; to be explained in Section 2.8:

(a) Arithmetical instructions e.g. Add, Subtract.

(b) Logical instructions e.g. AND, OR, Exclusive OR.

(c) Manipulating instructions e.g. Shift, Test.

Thus the function unit of figure 2.7 must be more complex in practice so as to incorporate the logical operations.

Instructions in the Test category use the ALU, but seldom use the result, merely setting the condition flags. Thus to determine the relative magnitudes of A and B, the operation $A - B$ is performed, but the output gates from the function unit are not enabled. The operation will affect the N flag so that it will be 0 if $A > B$ and 1 if $A < B$. If $A = B$ then the N flag will be 0 and the Z flag 1. Thus both Z and N must be 0 for $A > B$, while $N = 0$ (Z either 1 or 0) is sufficient for $A \geqslant B$. Another common instruction in this class is *increment and skip if zero*; the data is incremented and if the Z bit is set the PC is incremented by one, causing the next instruction in sequence to be missed.

The ALU is used by the control unit for a number of tasks other than the basic arithmetic and similar instructions. It has already been indicated that the PC must be incremented early in the instruction cycle; by studying figures 2.5 and 2.6 it can be seen that there are no conflicting requirements for the ALU; so that while the memory read cycle is active, the PC contents can be placed on bus A, and gates a_1 and c_1 (figure 2.7) enabled. The output gate d_1 is also enabled and the result transferred back to the PC, overwriting the original value. The ALU is also used by a number of addressing modes, which will be discussed in Section 2.8.3. Note however that these 'control' uses of the ALU must not affect the condition flags, hence gate 28 on figure 2.1.

2·6 Input and Output

The whole concept of I/O will be discussed in detail in Chapter 4. Thus the I/O shown in figure 2.1 is over simplified; only one input and one output peripheral device are shown although there will be many in practice. Peripherals either transmit data to the computer (input) or receive data from the computer (output) along the 16 bit I/O buses. Peripherals that use 8 bit bytes simply connect to 8 of the 16 wires, the other 8 being unused. It is clear that control information must be sent to the peripherals in addition to the data. The most important features are the address of the peripheral (to distinguish one from another) and whether the peripheral is an input or an output device. Far more control signals are required in practice as will be discussed in Chapter 6. Control and data could be time multiplexed onto the I/O buses, but more likely there will be separate data and control lines.

A multiplexor could be used to feed individual peripherals as shown in figure 2.9. However the 'party-line' system of figure 2.10 is the common method used, where the I/O bus and the control lines are passed from one device to the next, in a chain. The input and output buses shown in figure 2.1 are replaced by the one common I/O bus, which means that gates 29 and 30 must not both be enabled at the same

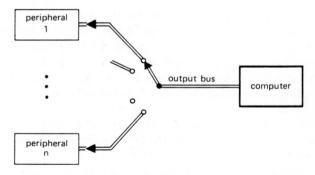

Fig. 2·9 A multiplexed output bus

time. Each peripheral has a unique address code pre-wired into the code comparator. If a match between the code in the comparator and the address line is made, the comparator enables its associated gate and connects that, and only that, peripheral to the I/O data bus. Note that a nonsense situation will occur if the computer tries to send data to an input device, and vice versa. The gates and code comparators of figure 2.10 form the essential parts of the so called *interface*, one per peripheral. Far more is required of the interface in practice to account for the extreme differences in the speed of the CPU and the peripherals, as will be explained in Chapter 4.

Simple I/O data transfers are between the peripherals and the registers R0, R1 or R2. If this were the only I/O operation, then a read from an input device should be followed by an instruction to copy the register contents into memory, if the data is to be saved. On some machines other instructions allow data to be moved between the peripheral and memory locations. Special forms of I/O such as *direct memory access* (DMA) and *block data transfer* will also be discussed in Chapter 4.

Manual I/O will now be discussed separately.

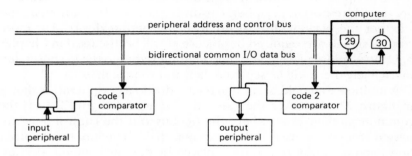

Fig. 2·10 A 'party-line' I/O bus

2·7 The Control Panel

The basic control panel carries switches to enable the operator to work the computer and lights to indicate what is happening. The fundamental feature is a bank of switches, one for each bit of a word, which directly connects to an electronic register. The appropriate bit of this 'switch register' is cleared with the switch down and set with the switch up.

A set of lights, again one per bit, is also aligned with the switches. These lights can be used to display the contents of selected registers inside the computer, not note, the switch register. The light is lit for a one and unlit for a zero. Often more sets of lights are provided, one for addresses, another for memory data and another for CPU registers.

A further set of individual switches control the function of the machine, typically:-

(i) *Halt.* This switch stops the CPU clock and aborts any computation.

(ii) *Start.* This spring loaded switch causes the processor to run when depressed, provided the Halt switch is returned to the run position.

(iii) *Load Address.* This switch causes the number set up on the switch bank to be transferred from the switch register to the PC, indicating that address on the address light bank.

(iv) *Examine.* This switch causes the PC to load the MAR and to read memory. The resulting contents are displayed, via the MBR, on the data light bank. Since the PC will have incremented as soon as it loaded the MAR, depressing the examine switch again will display the contents of the next memory location on the light bank, and so on. The internal CPU registers R0, R1 and R2, will possibly be displayed on a separate light bank.

(v) *Deposit.* This switch causes the contents of the switch register to be written into the location addressed by the previous Load Address. The switch register is used first for the address and then for the data. Great care must be taken with the Deposit switch since it is modifying memory. It is often arranged that the Deposit switch does not increment the PC, so that if Examine is depressed after a Deposit, the newly entered data will be read and displayed.

(vi) *Single Instruction.* After a Halt, if the machine is put in the run mode, by raising the Halt switch, it can be caused to execute one instruction only by depressing the Single Instruction switch rather than the Start switch. By repeatedly depressing the Single Instruction switch the operator can manually run through a program and examine the result of each instruction. Additional lights are usually provided to indicate which part of the instruction cycle is operative. A further switch is often used to subdivide each instruction into *single cycles.*

2·8 Instruction Sets and Addressing

2·8·1 Instruction Word Format

All the instructions that are possible on a given computer are termed the *Instruction Set*. The instruction set can be divided into a number of types of functions, for example:

(a) move data between memory locations and the CPU registers;

(b) perform arithmetical, logical and shift type operations;

(c) alter the program sequence by 'jumping' or 'branching' to a new address, including Subroutine Call and Return;

(d) modify and test the result to determine whether or not to alter the program sequence – a conditional jump;

(e) transfer data to and from the peripherals, e.g. I/O;

(f) various control operations, e.g. halt, set or clear a register, etc.

These instructions are usually put into one of three classes:

(i) *Memory Reference* instructions which involve operations on data stored in memory.

(ii) *Non-Memory Reference* instructions which either operate on data stored inside the CPU or require no data.

(iii) *Input/Output* instructions.

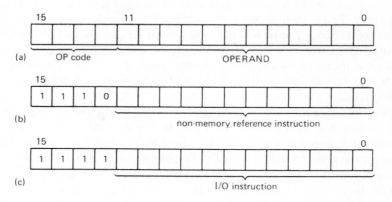

Fig. 2·11 Instruction word formats. (a) is a memory reference

Each instruction is a binary word. The basic format for these instructions for the DUMB 1 is shown in figure 2.11. The type of instruction is determined by the left hand four bits; all four bits set to 1 designates an I/O instruction, three 1's and a 0 designate non-memory reference instructions while the remaining fourteen combinations, 0000 to 1100, are all memory reference instructions.

It is most convenient to express the 16 bit instruction as an equivalent octal number e.g.

$$1 \quad 011 \quad 101 \quad 001 \quad 110 \quad 001_2 = 1 \quad 3 \quad 5 \quad 1 \quad 6 \quad 1_8.$$

With this notation the first two octal digits, 13 in the example, define the type of instruction. Thus instructions $00XXXX_8$ to $15XXXX_8$ are all memory reference instructions, while $16XXXX_8$ are all non-memory reference instructions and $17XXXX_8$ are all I/O instructions.

The use of octal numbers simplifies the identification of an instruction, mnemonics make the problem easier still. Thus mnemonics such as ADD, MOV (move), INC (increment), etc. are introduced in the following text. While these mnemonics are in the first place aids to explanation they have a much greater impact, since programs can be written in terms of them and an automatic aid used to convert this code into the binary instructions required by the machine. This mnemonic coding is termed the *assembly language* and the program which converts the assembly code into binary machine code is called an *assembler*. These points are discussed in detail in Chapter 7.

2·8·2 Memory Reference Instructions

The memory reference instruction is split into two parts, the Operation Code (Op-Code or Order Code) and the Operand. The fourteen possible op-codes define the possible types of memory reference instruction, while the operand defines the location of the data, in memory.

The operand will be discussed after describing the op-codes; the symbol n is used to denote the *effective address* in memory calculated from the operand.

The memory reference instructions for the DUMB 1 are:

(i) LDr n   Load register r (R0, R1 or R2) with the contents of location n.

(ii) STr n   Store the contents of register r into location n.

(iii) JMP n   Unconditional jump. The next instruction to be executed is stored in location n.

(iv) JMS n   Jump to subroutine. The first location of the subroutine is n.

(v) ISZ n   Increment and skip if zero. The contents of location n are incremented by 1; if the result is zero, the PC is incremented by 1.

(vi) DSZ n   Decrement and skip if zero. The contents of location n are decremented by 1; if the result is zero, the PC is incremented by 1.

With three instructions for both (i) and (ii) ten of the possible fourteen instructions have been implemented. The four unallocated op-codes will be discussed in Section 2.9.

The op-codes allocated to date are tabled in figure 2.12.

Mnemonic	Operation-code		Number of	Condition Codes
	Binary	Octal	Memory Cycles	Affected
LD0 n	0000	00	2	N, Z
LD1 n	0001	01	2	N, Z
LD2 n	0010	02	2	N, Z
ST0 n	1000	10	2	none
ST1 n	1001	11	2	none
ST2 n	1010	12	2	none
JMP n	0100	04	1	none
JMS n	0101	05	2	none
ISZ n	0110	06	2	C, N, Z, V
DSZ n	0111	07	2	C, N, Z, V

Fig. 2·12 Operation codes for memory reference instructions

The purpose of most of the above instructions is clear from previous discussions. The load and store instructions are obvious. The jump instruction causes the effective address, n, to be written into the PC; thus the next instruction will not be found in the next sequential location, but in location n. This is the equivalent of the FORTRAN GO TO statement. Note that among the memory reference instructions the JMP only requires one memory cycle to execute, figure 2.5, all the others requiring two cycles, figure 2.6.

The remaining three instructions are used to create control statements in the logical execution of a program. In terms of FORTRAN these are equivalent to CALL to subroutine and DO loops.

2·8·2·1 Subroutines

In writing programs it becomes clear that a number of groups of instructions are used repeatedly, e.g. a routine to convert a binary number to a string of ASCII coded decimal characters. Instead of including the code each time the routine is required, as in figure 2.13(a), it is written as a subroutine. By using a subroutine the code is included only once, an individual instruction branching to the subroutine each time it is needed as in 2.13(b); each time the subroutine is 'called' there must be some means of transferring back to the 'calling' program so that processing can continue. It is the necessity to provide a return that makes the jump-to-subroutine instruction different to the jump instruction. The method used here is to save the current PC contents in the first location of the subroutine before branching. Thus

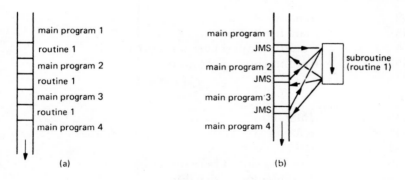

Fig. 2·13 (a) In-line code (b) Use of a subroutine

the instruction JMS n writes the current PC contents (which will have been incremented during the instruction read cycle) into location n, and then transfers n + 1 into the PC. Thus the address of the location following the JMS instruction is saved in the first location of the subroutine and the next instruction to be executed is in the second location of the routine. The last instruction of the subroutine causes the contents of the first location to be loaded into the PC, returning the program to the instruction in the main program following the JMS instruction. The execution timing is shown in figure 2.14.

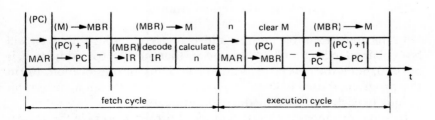

Fig. 2·14 Timing sequence for JMS n instruction

As an example consider a subroutine which computes some number X as a function of two other numbers A and B.

Memory Location	Contents
50	. . . . .
51	JMS 400

52	data for A = a_1
53	data for B = b_1
54	result x_1 stored here on return
55	continuation of program
$\vdots$	$\vdots$
132	JMS 400
133	data for A = a_2
134	data for B = b_2
135	result x_2 stored here on return
136	continuation of program
$\vdots$	$\vdots$
400	return address stored here by JMS;
	= 52 for first call,
	= 133 for second call.
401	LD0 * 400, place a_1 or a_2 in register R0
402	ISZ 400, increment contents of location 400
403	LD1 * 400, place b_1 or b_2 in register R1
404	ISZ 400, location 400 now contains 54 or 135
$\vdots$	$\left\{\begin{array}{l}\text{Calculate } x_1 \text{ or } x_2 \text{ from data in R0 and R1, leaving} \\ \text{the result in R2.}\end{array}\right.$
420	ST2 * 400, put x_1 in location 54 or x_2 in 135
421	ISZ 400
422	JMP * 400, the return from subroutine

In the above example indirect addressing, e.g. * 400, is used. As will be explained in Section 2.8.3 this means that the effective address, n, is not 400, but is the *contents* of location 400. Thus the one location, 400 in this program, is used to keep a tag on locations in the calling program, unique to each call, used by the subroutine itself.

In some machines a special register is provided to save the return address, rather than using the first memory location. This is faster, but if 'nested' subroutine calls are to be allowed, i.e. a JMS is one of the instructions in the subroutine, then the contents of this register must be saved by the first instruction of the first subroutine and restored after the second subroutine is finished. Otherwise the return address for the second call will destroy the return address for the first call. By saving the return address in a memory location, a unique store is provided for each subroutine.

Further comments are made on using stacks with subroutines in Section 3.6. Problems arising from interrupts are discussed in Section 4.3.3.

2·8·2 Loops

It is often required to execute a similar sequence of instructions a given number of times. A location is allocated as a loop counter which is tested by the DSZ (or ISZ) instruction each time around the loop. A jump to the beginning of the loop follows the DSZ instruction which is skipped when, and only when, the count has reduced to zero. Thus the following program moves the five numbers from locations 100 through 104 to locations 200 through 204.

400	LD0 * 500; R0 is used as a
401	ST0 * 501; temporary 'buffer'
402	ISZ 500; increment contents of locations
403	ISZ 501; 500 and 501, no skip will occur
404	DSZ 502
405	JMP 400; skipped when contents of location 502 are zero
406	continue with program
⋮	⋮
500	100; starting address of 'source' data
501	200; starting address of 'destination' data
502	5; loop count

The two's complement number, -5, must be initially stored in location 502 if ISZ 502 is used in location 404.

The two instructions LSZ and DSZ make use of the read/modify/write mode of memory cycle, discussed in Section 2.3. During the execution cycle, the contents of location n are read into the MBR during the first half memory cycle; the data is then transferred from the MBR to the ALU where it is incremented or decremented by one, being returned to the MBR before the memory write phase is completed. The time taken to increment or decrement the data is negligible compared to the read and write times so that the read/modify/write cycle is no longer than the normal cycle. The condition codes are set when the data is passed through the ALU so that the skip is implemented simply by adding the z flag to the PC contents, since this flag will be one only if the result of the arithmetic operation, increment or decrement in this case, is zero; this can take place during the write cycle.

Further skip instructions are described in Section 2.8.4. The previous example shows a good comparison between a skip and a jump operation, both of which cause nonsequential program execution; the skip is simpler to implement since no new address need be specified, merely incrementing the PC, while the jump is more general, branching to any new location.

2·8·3 Memory Addressing

Referring to figure 2.11(a), the 12 bit operand must define the effective address at which the data is located.

The simplest approach is to use all 12 bits as a memory address; this will set the maximum size of memory to $2^{12} = 4K$ words. The memory could be increased above 4K physically, but the extension could never be used because it could never be addressed! There is a second objection to using all 12 bits as the memory address, in that there is then only one mode of addressing, which leads to lack of versatility.

Thus let bits 10 and 11 of the instruction be assigned to specify the mode of addressing, allowing four possible modes. The four modes used here are probably the most common while various alternatives or extensions are introduced in the next chapter. Bit 9 of the instruction is used to indicate an indirect address as used in the example programs in the previous section; more of this after the modes have been introduced.

Thus the 9 bits, 0 to 8 of the instruction, remain for numeric address information. The symbol D is used for this part of the operand, from which the effective address n is found. D is sometimes called the *address field*.

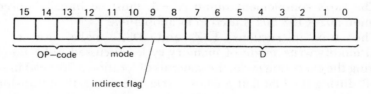

Fig. 2·15 Memory reference instruction format

The mnemonic notation used for this type of instruction is

$$XYZ\,m,\,i\,D$$

where XYZ is the op-code, e.g. ISZ, LD2, etc.
m is the mode, 1, 2 or 3. If m and the comma are omitted mode 0 is implied.
i is omitted for direct addresses and is * for indirect.

2·8·3·1 Indirect or Deferred Addressing

If an indirect address is specified, then the value of n calculated does not point to the memory location required for the data, but to a location which contains the address of the required location. Since each memory location is 16 bits long, $2^{16} = 64K$ locations can be reached from any instruction by an indirect address. One memory location can contain an 'address pointer' to a table of data; the same pointer is used as an indirect address which is incremented at each step. An example of this technique is given in the programs used in the previous section. Thus:

```
100   LD0 200      loads the number 300 into R0
101   LD1 * 200    loads the number 400 into R1
  .
  .
200   300
  .
  .
300   400
```

An extra memory cycle is required for the indirect address. The data read into the MBR is copied back into the MAR and the memory cycle repeated. The extra cycle inserted is called a *defer* cycle as shown in figure 2.16.

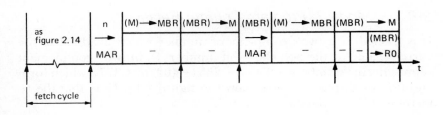

Fig. 2·16 Timing sequence for LD0*n

The four modes are defined in figure 2.17.

Bit 11	Bit 10	Mode
0	0	0 = Page 0 address
0	1	1 = Register 1 relative
1	0	2 = Register 2 relative
1	1	3 = Program Counter relative

Fig. 2·17 Addressing modes

2·8·3·2 Mode 0 = Page 0 address

D is the absolute address in memory. With 9 bits to specify D the maximum number is 512. Thus memory is considered to be made up of *pages*, each 512 words long. It must be stressed that there are no physical page boundaries; paging is entirely created by the limit on the range of addresses imposed by the word length of the computer, e.g. an 18 bit word length computer with the same 7 bits allocated to op-code, mode and indirect flag, leaves a page size of $2^{11} = 2K$ words.

Note that a full 16 bit word can address $2^{16} = 64K$ memory locations. The 16 bit word could be considered thus:

$$0000000XXXXXXXXX = 000\ D_8$$
$$0000001XXXXXXXXX = 001\ D_8$$
$$0000010XXXXXXXXX = 002\ D_8 \quad \text{etc.}$$

The first 7 bits form an address to a page, each page being 512 (1000_8) words long. The particular memory location is then given by the page number and D. With the addressing structure formulated here there is no means of addressing the pages so that, by default, only page 0 can be reached, e.g. mode 0 specifies that D addresses locations 0 to 511 (0 to 777_8) absolutely.

2·8·3·3 Mode 3: Program Counter Relative

D is treated as a two's complement number which is added to the current value of the PC. The 9 bit number, D, in two's complement represents the numbers -256 to $+255$ (-400_8 to $+377_8$) which form an offset or displacement as shown in figure 2.18. Note that the PC increments *before* the offset is added.

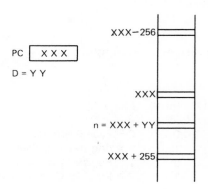

Fig. 2·18 PC relative addressing

The effect of this mode of addressing is to make a band of addresses, of the same length as a page, accessible. Note that since the PC is continually being incremented the absolute addresses that can be reached change, i.e. this is a dynamic addressing mode. Statistically it is obvious that most instructions require branches to and data from locations not too far away, so that this can be a very powerful mode of addressing.

This mode of addressing uses the ALU in calculating the effective address. Referring back to figure 2.14 the event labelled 'calculate n' means that D, extracted from the full instruction during the previous 'decode IR', and the PC contents are fed to the ALU and the resultant sum stored in the MAR. Note that the effective address, n, is a full 16 bit word and that the condition flip-flops must not be affected.

An earlier technique employed was to use the left hand 7 bits of the PC contents to define the current page. The effective address was then the 7 left hand bits of the PC with the 9 bit D completing the 16 bit word. This method is simpler in that the ALU is not involved in calculating n, but is far more restrictive to the programmer. For example, consider page 3, that is addresses 3000_8 to 3777_8; if the PC is at location 3770_8, then all addresses more than seven locations ahead are on the next page, and cannot be reached by this mode. Paging of this nature is looked on as a great constraint on the programmer; the term paging has however been revived to describe a sophisticated virtual memory operating system function as mentioned in Section 7.8.5, the term being handed down from large data processing machines. Another alternative method was to provide a separate *page register* which could be set by a previous instruction; in this example the page register would be 7 bits long, being concatenated with the 9 bits of D to create a 16 bit n.

2·8·3·4 Modes 1 and 2: Register Relative

These modes are similar to mode 3 except that either register R1 or R2 is used instead of the PC. These modes are also called *base register relative* or *indexed*. Strictly speaking there can be differences between register relative and indexed addressing when indirect addresses are used, but this will not be discussed until Section 3.4.1.

These modes are used in working with tables of data (arrays). Thus the program used as an example in Section 2.8.2.2 can be re-programmed as:

```
400   CLR 1        clear R1
401   LD0 1, 100    move contents of location (100 + contents of R1)
                    into R0
```

402	STO 1, 200	move contents of R0 into location (200 + contents of R1)
403	INC 1	increment R1
404	DSZ 3, 2	PC contains 405 ∴ n = 405 + 2 = 407
405	JMP 3, − 5	alternative to JMP 401
406	JMP 3, 1	equivalent to an unconditional skip
407	5	contains the number 5 initially
408	continue with program.	

Note that this program stresses the simple differentiation between instructions and data. By commencing the program at location 400 the JMP at location 406 will stop location 407 ever being accessed as an instruction. This program is superior to the previous version since indirect addressing is avoided, reducing the execution time.

An important feature of this program is that by avoiding mode 0 the same instructions could be loaded into, say, locations 500 through 508, and it would still function as required. The data locations however are still 100 to 104 and 200 to 204. To use data locations outside page 0, R1 must be pre-loaded with the appropriate base address.

It is not inadmissible to use, say, mode 2 with an LD2 instruction. n would be calculated as the initial contents of R2 + D; the contents of location n would then be written into R2.

Only two of the three registers in the machine can be used as base registers. R0 cannot be used as a base register simply since a fifth mode would have to be defined, which would require a third bit to be allocated to mode specification. This could be incorporated at the expense of a bit less in D, giving an 8 bit number and leaving a 256 word page. This is the sort of dilemma that faces the machine designer. This example has deliberately been introduced to stress the point that the machine performance cannot go on being increased by additional hardware, unless the instruction set can incorporate commands to use the extra electronic capability!

With this arrangement the registers R1 and R2 are called *index registers* in some machines, although in most respects they do not differ from R0.

2·8·4 Non-Memory Reference Instructions

Instructions with the op-code 16_8 i.e. 1110 in the four left hand bits, are all non-memory reference instructions, sometimes termed operate instructions. The remaining 12 bits, which supply the operand for memory reference instructions, can be used to define other instructions which do not use memory locations. It is possible to define $2^{12} = 4K$ non-memory reference instructions but it is usual to define the function of specific bits more directly. This class of instruction is here split into three groups:

Group 1: Register to register arithmetical and logical instructions
Group 2: Register modify instructions
Group 3: CPU Control and Skip instructions.

Figure 2.19 indicates the format of these instructions, each of which execute in one memory cycle.

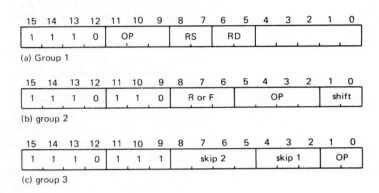

(a) Group 1

(b) group 2

(c) group 3

Fig. 2·19 Non-memory reference instruction formats

2·8·4·1 Group 1 Non-memory reference Instructions

Bits 9–11 (OP) is a three bit code which will define 6 group 1 operations (0 to 5). 6 and 7 bits 9 to 11 define group 2 and group 3 instructions respectively.

Bits 7–8 (RS) define the *source register*, R0 to R2.

Bits 5–6 (RD) define the *destination register*, R0 to R2.

Bits 0–4 must be zero unless used in combined instructions, Section 2.8.4.4.

Instructions in this group are *double operand* instructions, e.g. two pieces of data are used.

RS or RD	Register
00	R0
01	R1
10	R2
11	unused

Fig. 2·20 Source (RS) and destination (RD) designations

The 6 operations defined, with mnemonic notation, are listed in figure 2.21.

Mnemonic	Bits 11–91 Binary	Octal	Function
ADD RS, RD	000	0	Two's complement add contents of RS to contents of RD and place sum in RD. Establish all condition flags.
SUB RS, RD	001	1	Two's complement subtract contents of RS from contents of RD and place difference in RD. Establish all condition flags.
CPR RS, RD	010	2	Subtract contents of RS from contents of RD. Result is not saved, but all condition flags are established so that comparisons can be tested.
MOV RS, RD	011	3	Copy contents of RS into RD. RS is unaffected. N and Z are established, C is unaffected. V is cleared.
AND RS, RD	100	4	Place logical AND of the contents of RS and RD in RD. N and Z are established, C is unaffected, V is cleared.
OR RS, RD	101	5	Place logical OR of the contents of RS and RD in RD. N and Z are established, C is unaffected, V is cleared.

Fig. 2·21 Group 1 non-memory reference instructions

Some attention must be paid to the way in which the condition flags are affected. Fundamentally N and Z are determined by the 16 bit result; Z is set to 1 if all 16 bits are zero and N is set if the MSB is 1, i.e. N is a copy of bit 15. V is determined by the result of an arithmetic operation, details of which are given in Appendix 1, and this flag is deliberately cleared by the non-arithmetic operations. Similarly C is affected only by arithmetic operations, but its previous value may be of some use, so that unlike V, it is unaffected. This difference in philosophy stems from the fact that C performs useful functions, while V is only an error indicator.

Bits 0 to 4 are unused, so that Skip and Shift operations can be combined, as will be explained later.

The following program calculates $X = A + B - C$.

150	LD0 3, 6	load A into r0, using mode 3
151	LD1 3, 6	load B into r1
152	ADD 1, 0	$A + B$ in r0
153	LD1 3, 5	load C into r1
154	SUB 1, 0	$A + B - C$ in r0
155	ST0 3, 4	store $A + B - C$
156	HLT	halt, or alternatively JMP 161 to continue
157	data for A	
158	data for B	
159	data for C	
160	store for result, X	

The arithmetic operations need no explanation. The compare instruction (CPR) is used in conjunction with skip instructions to effect conditional jumps. The logical operations are used for bit manipulation 'inside' a word:

(a) AND. Each bit of the result will be 1 only if the corresponding bit in the contents of RS and RD are both 1, e.g.

	RS	1	0	1	1	0	1	0	1	1	0	0	0	1	1	1	0
Original	RD	1	1	0	1	1	0	0	1	1	1	1	0	1	0	0	1
Final	RD	1	0	0	1	0	0	0	1	1	0	0	0	1	0	0	0

The contents of RS are considered to be a *mask*; the effect of the AND instruction is thus to clear each bit of RD which corresponds to a 0 in the mask. Bits of RD corresponding to 1's in the mask are unaffected, *not* set to 1. A variant on this instruction is the 'Bit Clear' instruction, which does a logical AND between the complement of RS and RD. The only difference is that bits in the mask stored in RS which are set to 1 (as opposed to 0 in the AND operation), clear corresponding bits in RD.

(b) OR. Each bit of the result will be 1 unless the corresponding bit in the contents of RS and RD are both 0, e.g.

	RS	1	0	1	1	0	1	0	1	1	0	0	0	1	1	1	0
Original	RD	1	1	0	1	1	0	0	1	1	1	1	0	1	0	0	1
Final	RD	1	1	1	1	1	1	0	1	1	1	1	0	1	1	1	1

If the contents of RS are again considered as a mask, then all bits in RD which correspond to a 1 in the mask are set while bits corresponding to a 0 in the mask are unaffected. This instruction is also called 'Bit Set'.

Minicomputers and Microprocessors

As an example of the use of logical instructions, to detect if bit 4 of the contents of R1 is a 1 or 0, establish the mask.

0 0 0 0 0 0 0 0 0 0 0 1 0 0 0 0

in R2. Assuming that the contents of R1 must not be destroyed the following instructions will set the z flag to 1 if bit 4 is 0 and clear it otherwise.

MOV 1, 0   copy contents of R1 into R0
AND 2, 0   clear all except bit 4 of R0. The mask in R2 is unaltered, c = ?, v = 0, z = complement of bit 4, N = 0.

2·8·4·2 Group 2 non-memory Reference Instructions

This group of instructions all have the 16_8 for the op-code and 110 in bits 9–11. These instructions are all single-operand, i.e. data is contained in one of the registers or one of the condition flags. Although the condition flags may be physically grouped in one status register, they are treated as individual '1 bit words' in this sense.

Bits 6–8 (R or F) define the register or condition flag, as shown in figure 2.22.

Mnemonic	R or F Binary	Octal	Operand
0	000	0	Register R0
1	001	1	Register R1
2	010	2	Register R2
	011	3	unused
C	100	4	Carry flip-flop
N	101	5	Negative or sign flip-flop
Z	110	6	Zero flip-flop
V	111	7	Overflow flip-flop

Fig. 2·22 Register/condition flag designation

Bits 2–5 (OP) define the 16 possible operations, as shown in figure 2.23. Note that NEG is equivalent to CPL followed by INC.

The condition flags are attached thus:
OP 1, 2 and 3 applied to registers determine N and z; c is unaffected and v is cleared.
OP 4 is similar except for the exceptions noted in the footnote.
OP 5 to 10 are arithmetic operations and affect all flags.

70

Mnemonic	Bits 5–2 Binary	Octal	Function
	0000	0	Shift only; see following description of bits 0 and 1
CLR R (CLR F)	0001	1	Clear register or condition flag
SET R (SET F)	0010	2	Set register or condition flag
CPL R (CPL F)	0011	3	Complement register or condition flags, i.e. change all zeros to ones and all ones to zeros
NEG R	0100	4	Negate register, i.e. replace contents with two's complement†
INC R	0101	5	Add one to content of register
DEC R	0110	6	Subtract one from content of register
ADC R	0111	7	Add carry to register contents
SBB R	1000	10	Subtract c (borrow) from register contents
		11	unused
		17	unused

† An error occurs with the largest negative number. As an example consider the 4 bit numbers with the range $+7$ to -8 (0111 to 1000). The two's complement of 1000 is 1000. Note also that negating 0000 leaves the correct answer, but sets the carry flag.

Fig. 2·23 Group 2 non-memory reference instructions

The two instructions ADC and SBB are used in double precision arithmetic, i.e., using 5 bit words in this example, simply to avoid writing 16 bits,

A_1 A_0

A | 0 0 1 0 0 | 1 0 1 1 1 |

B_1 B_0

B | 1 1 0 0 0 | 1 0 1 0 1 |

C_1 C_0

$C = A + B$ | 1 1 1 0 1 | 0 1 1 0 0 |

Carry | 0 | | 1 |

Both A and B will use two consecutive memory locations. The second word in each case is an extension (less significant) of the first so that its most significant bit is *not* the sign bit; there is only one sign bit, that of the most significant of the pair of words. In this example A is a positive number while B is negative, even though both have a 1 in the left hand bit of the second word. The sum is calculated by adding the two lower significant words to give the lower significant word of the answer and then adding the two most significant words *and* any carry from the first sum to give the most significant word of the answer. The following program adds two double precision words.

50	LD0 101	load A_0 into R0, using mode 0
51	LD1 103	load B_0 into R1
52	ADD 1, 0	$R0 = A_0 + B_0$, affecting carry
53	ST0 105	store C_0, carry not affected
54	LD0 100	load A_1 into R0, carry not affected
55	LD1 102	load B_1 into R1, carry not affected
56	ADC 0	add carry to A_1
57	ADD 1, 0	$R0 = A_1 + B_1 + C$
58	ST0 104	store C_1
100	data A_1	
101	data A_0	
102	data B_1	
103	data B_0	
104	store for C_1	
105	store for C_0	

Note that the order of instructions 56 and 57 cannot be reversed; the ADD would affect the carry, destroying the information from instruction 52.

Bits 0 and 1 (SHIFT) define shift operations. The code 0000 in bits 2–5 of these groups 2 instructions defines a shift instruction. Shift instructions move the bit pattern in the word either right or left. The shift instructions used here only displace by one bit, although some machines have multiple bit shifts.

There are two fundamental types of shift, termed *rotate* and *arithmetic shift* which differ in the treatment of the LSB, MSB and the carry.
(a) **Rotate.** Rotate left (ROL), for instance, causes all bits to be shifted left with the MSB 'rotated' into the LSB, e.g.

		0	1	1	0	1	0	1	1	0	0	1	0	0	0	1	1
becomes		1	1	0	1	0	1	1	0	0	1	0	0	0	1	1	0

It is more usual in practice to involve the carry bit in the shifts; thus for a ROL the MSB is shifted into the carry flip-flop, the previous contents of which are shifted into the LSB. This is shown schematically in figure 2.24(a).

The rotate instructions can be used to access a specific bit of a word, e.g. after one ROR, bit 0 of the original register contents is in C, and can thus be treated separately. Rotating n times places bit n-1 into C. Note that the register contents are displaced, but not destroyed.

(b) **Arithmetic Shifts.** Arithmetic shift left (ASL) performs a signed multiplication by 2. All bits are displaced left and the MSB moved into carry; unlike ROL however, the LSB is cleared. Arithmetic shift right (ASR) figure 2.24(b) performs a signed division by 2. All bits are displaced right and the LSB shifted into C; unlike ROR however, the MSB retains its original value.

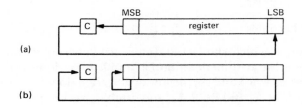

Fig. 2·24 (a) Rotate left through carry (b) Arithmetic shift right (÷2)

Using a 5 bit word for simplicity in this example, the results of the shift operations are shown in figure 2.25.

Operation	Carry	Register (5 bit)
Original	X	1 1 0 1 0
after ASL	1	1 0 1 0 0
after ASR	0	1 1 1 0 1
after ROL	1	1 0 1 0 X
after ROR	0	X 1 1 0 1

Fig. 2·25 Effect of shift operations on a 5 bit word

With the 5 bit word used above, the range of numbers in two's complement is $+15$ to -16. Thus for instance 8×2 should overflow, i.e.

$$0 \quad 1 \quad 0 \quad 0 \quad 0 \equiv +8$$

after ASL becomes
$$1 \quad 0 \quad 0 \quad 0 \quad 0 \equiv -16$$

73

Similarly with ASR, the MSB must be replicated, otherwise the sign could change, thus -14 divided by 2 is

	1	0	0	1	0	$\equiv -14$
after ASR becomes	1	1	0	0	1	$\equiv -7$

If however C had been 0 the -14 becomes,

	0	1	0	0	1	$\equiv +9$
after ROR						

One other point to note is that division by 2 using ASR truncates the answer, i.e. there are no halves!
Thus

	0	1	0	0	1	$\equiv +9$
after ASR becomes	0	0	1	0	0	$\equiv +4$
and	1	1	0	0	1	$\equiv -7$
after ASR becomes	1	1	1	0	0	$\equiv -4$

An example which shows the difference between arithmetic shifts and rotates is the arithmetic shift of a double precision word. Let A_1 be the high order word and A_0 the low order, then double precision ASR is given by ASR A_1 and ROR A_0, and double precision ASL is given by ASL A_0 and ROL A_1.

In the instruction code the specific shift is determined by bits 0 and 1. Bit 0 determines Right (0) or Left (1) and bit 1 determines Rotate (0) or Arithmetic shift (1). In summary, bits 0 and 1 of figure 2.19(b) are shown in figure 2.26.

Mnemonic	Bits 1 and 0	Function
ROR	00	Rotate through carry 1 bit right (no-shift when combined with other operations)
ROL	01	Rotate through carry one bit left
ASR	10	Arithmetic shift right 1 bit ($\div 2$)
ASL	11	Arithmetic shift left 1 bit ($\times 2$)

Fig. 2·26 Shift operation codes

Recalling that 0000 in bits 2–5 define the operation 'shift only', then the instruction 'arithmetic shift right the contents of R1' is given the mnemonic ASR 1 and codes up as shown in figure 2.27.

This example can be used to stress the importance of using mnemonics for the instructions, since the simple octal code loses its direct significance, e.g. the above instruction is equivalent to 166102_8; by direct comparison with figure 2.27 and the appropriate tables in this

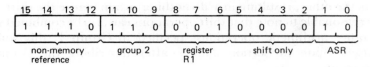

Fig. 2·27 Instruction format for ASR 1

section. The first two digits, 16, uniquely define the non-memory reference instruction; the third digit, 6, uniquely defines a group 2 instruction; the fourth digit, 1, uniquely defines register 1; but the last two digits are a combined effect of the operation and shift functions (Note: if the operation where 0001, then the last 2 digits would be 06). Octal code is still simpler than binary, but individual digits cannot be relied on to refer directly to individual parts of the instruction.

Γy considering figure 2.27, note that some combinations are illegal, e.g. the operand can only be R0, R1 or R2; the other codes specified by bits 6–8 refer to the condition flip-flops, which cannot be shifted.

The ALU of figure 2.7 allows combination of any operation which uses one of the registers with a shift operation. However with operations such as DEC, CLR, etc., bits 0 and 1 must both be zero to specify no-shift, so that only three of the four shift operations may be combined; the instructions are the constraint, not the hardware.

As an example the instruction mnemonic

INC 2, ASR

causes the contents of register 2 to be incremented by 1, and then the result divided by 2.

CLR 0, ASL

causes register 0 to be cleared first, the ASL by shifting the MSB into C also clears the carry. Often a special mnemonic, say, CLRC 0, can be defined to be equivalent to common 'trick' combinations like this.

Thus

DEC 2   ≡ 1 1 1 0   1 1 0   0 1 0   0 1 1 0   0 0

while

DEC 2, ROL ≡ 1 1 1 0   1 1 0   0 1 0   0 1 1 0   0 1

This final instruction is equivalent to

DEC 2

ROL 2

There are obvious advantages of combining the two instructions into one in both storage space and execution time.

The decoded instruction independently sets up the adder input gates and the shift control. The correct sequence is automatic since the shifter can only operate on the result of the arithmetic operation. A shift only instruction applies the data to one of the adder inputs and clears the other, resulting in a 'do nothing' action before the shift. It is now reasonable to note that shift operations can also be combined with the other arithmetic operations specified in Group 1; this will be enlarged upon in Section 2.8.4.4, after describing the Group 3 instructions.

2·8·4·3 Group 3 Non-memory Reference Instructions

The format of Group 3 non-memory reference instructions is shown in figure 2.19(c).

Bits 0 and 1 specify a CPU control operation. These, with mnemonic notation, are shown in figure 2.28.

Mnemonic	Bits 1 and 0	Function
HTL	00	Halt. The CPU clock is halted. The machine must be restarted from the console
WAIT	01	The CPU clock is halted, but it can be started again by an interrupt (see Chapter 4)
	10	Skip. When the skip condition specified by bits 2–8 is 'no skip' then this becomes a 'do nothing' operation, which wastes a machine cycle of time. It is used to help synchronising or timing of events. The mnemonic NOP is used for this instruction
	11	not used

Fig. 2·28 Group 3 non-memory reference instruction operations

When Halt or Wait are specified, bits 2–8 are ignored.

Bits 2–8 specify Skip actions. Skip actions test for a specific condition. If that condition is not met then no action takes place; if however the condition is met, then the PC is incremented by one (in addition to the normal increment) so that the next sequential instruction is missed out. The instruction following the skip instruction is usually a JMP instruction so that the program sequence will branch if the condition is not met, but will continue if it is. An example was given in Section 2.8.2. when explaining the ISZ and DSZ instructions. The skip instructions considered here do not reference memory as do the ISZ and DSZ instructions, but determine specific conditions by the current state of the condition flip-flops, inside the CPU. The condition codes themselves will have been set or cleared by some previous action of the CPU, so that the skip instructions follow instructions such as ADD and in particular, CPR (compare).

Seven bits are allocated to specifying conditional skip actions, so that up to 128 actions could be defined. However, for reasons of combination with Group 1 instructions, to be explained in Section 2.8.4.4, they are split into two groups. *Bits 2–4* specify the basic 8 conditions and *Bits 5–8* a possible 16 additional conditions. This is a good example of how dedicated use of specific bits reduces the total possible combinations, (from 128 to 24, in this case).

The immediately obvious skip instructions are directly related to the condition flags, e.g. skip if carry is clear. However various combinations have more significance in arithmetic operations and these are therefore grouped as skip 1 in figure 2.19(c). The arithmetic conditions are determined by combinations of the z and N flags as shown in figure 2.29. (Note: 'greater than' means that the result of the previous arithmetic operation was greater than zero, i.e. positive. Each phrase means relative to zero.)

Condition	N	Z	Boolean Expression
Greater than (GT)	0	0	$\bar{N} . \bar{Z}$
Greater than or equal to (GE)	0	0 }	$\bar{N} . \bar{Z} + \bar{N} . Z = \bar{N}$
	0	1 }	
Less than (LT)	1	0	$N . \bar{Z}$
Less than or equal to (LE)	1	0 }	$N . \bar{Z} + \bar{N} . Z = N + Z$
	0	1 }	
Equal to (EQ)	0	1	Z
Not equal to (NE)	?	0	$\bar{Z}$

Fig. 2·29 Arithmetic conditions, relative to zero

Thus the eight skip 1 conditions are as listed in figure 2.30.

Mnemonic	Bits 4–2	Function
	000	No skip
SGT	001	Skip if greater than zero
SGE	010	Skip if greater than or equal to zero
SLT	011	Skip if less than zero
SLE	100	Skip if less than or equal to zero
SEQ	101	Skip if equal to zero
SNE	110	Skip if not equal to zero
SVC	111	Skip if no overflow occurs $(v = 0)$

Fig. 2·30 First group of Skip conditions

Skip if v is clear was included as the eighth possible condition, since it also relates to arithmetic operations.

The sixteen Skip 2 conditions are listed in figure 2.31.

Mnemonic	Bits 8–5	Function
	0000	No skip
SKP	0001	Skip unconditionally
SCC	0010	Skip if c = 0
SCS	0011	Skip if c = 1
SNC	0100	Skip if n = 0
SNS	0101	Skip if n = 1
SZC	0110	Skip if z = 0 (≡SNE)
SZS	0111	Skip if z = 1; On single register machines this is equivalent to skip if accumulator is clear. (≡SEQ)
SVS	1000	Skip if v = 1

Other combinations are not yet defined. Some may be related to I/O considerations, i.e. skip if interrupt-on is set, etc.

Fig. 2·31 Second group of Skip conditions

Conditions from both groups cannot be combined, thus for a Skip 1 condition, bits 5–8 are all zero, while for a Skip 2 condition, bits 2–4 are all zero.

Some examples are:

SGT ≡ 1 1 1 0   1 1 1   0 0 0 0   0 0 1   1 0

      Non-   Group 3   NSK   SGT   Skip
      memory
      reference

SCS ≡ 1 1 1 0   1 1 1   0 0 1 1   0 0 0   1 0

The skip code in bits 0 and 1, but with 'no-skip' in both groups is a 'do nothing' operation, for which the mnemonic NOP is used, thus

NOP ≡ 1 1 1 0   1 1 1   0 0 0 0   0 0 0   1 0

The skip instructions do not themselves affect the condition flags. Thus two or more skip instructions can occur which test the result of the same operation e.g.

ADD 1, 2   add contents of r1 to r2
SVC   test for overflow

JMP n_1	jump to routine if overflow occurs
SGT	test for positive, non-zero result
JMP n_2	jump to routine for negative or zero result
XXXX	routine for positive result
$\vdots$	
JMP n_4	avoid other routines
n_2 SNE	
JMP n_3	jump to routine for zero result
YYYY	routine for negative result
$\vdots$	
JMP n_4	avoid other routines
n_3 ZZZZ	routine for zero result
$\vdots$	
JMP n_4	avoid other routines
n_1 VVVV	routine for overflow
$\vdots$	
n_4	continue with program

2·8·4·4 Combined Instructions

To allow the combination of functions such as add and skip in the one instruction, control must be exercised over the timing of events. Referring back to figure 2.5, it can be noted that one time slot is allocated to execute the instruction. Now the CPU is fast compared to the memory restore cycle, so that the execute time slot may possibly be further divided into two units, each of which is long enough on its own to execute a specific function such as increment the PC, etc. This is not strictly practical with modern memory systems since they are becoming so fast, e.g. one machine manages during slot 2 to test for a skip, but if the condition is met it is forced to a second memory cycle just to increment the PC. Asynchronous operation is the real approach as described in Section 3.2.

On some machines it is possible that the 'execute slot' be divided into more than two sections, but this is not necessary on this machine, since only the skip operation could clash with the others. Thus the arithmetic (or logic) operation and any shift are always correctly timed by virtue of the hardware arrangement, which passes data through the adder to the Shifter. The skip however must be determined by the result of the operation and thus must be timed to occur *only* when the

79

arithmetic/shift operation has completed. In this simple machine the arithmetic/shift operations are all executed in slot 1 and skips in slot 2. If non-combined instructions are specified then the alternative execute slot is simply not used, e.g. *all* arithmetic/shift operations use slot 1 and *all* skip operations slot 2.

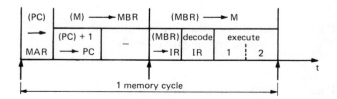

Fig. 2·32 Timing sequence for a non-memory reference instruction

With the hardware implied by the timing diagram of figure 2.32 all combinations of arithmetic/shift and skip instructions are possible. However there is always the additional constraint of specifying the combined instruction; the practical constraint is of course set by the limit to the combinations which can be created with, in this case, 16 bits. It will now become clear that certain arrangements used in specifying the functions of non-memory reference instructions were specifically deployed to assist in making combined instructions.

Group 2 instructions, figure 2.19(b), simply allow combination of the specified operations and three of the four shift functions. Since some of these operations are arithmetical, e.g. ADC, it is reasonable to ask if shifting and the more complex Group 1 arithmetic operations can be combined; more so since the hardware (adder/shifter) used is the same in both cases. From the instruction format of figure 2.19(a) it is clear that bits 0 and 1, which specify the shift, are not used in the Group 1 instruction, so that combinations are possible. However, as with combined Group 2 operations, one of the four shift codes possible *must* be used to specify no-shift, so that in comparison with figure 2.26, zeros in bits 0 and 1 means no-shift when used with combined instructions. Rotate right (ROR) cannot be combined with a Group 1 instruction, not because of a problem with the hardware, but because it cannot be incorporated in this particular instruction set.

With further reference to figure 2.19(a), bits 2–4 are not used for Group 1 instructions, so that one of the seven 'skip 1' operations can be combined with a Group 1 instruction. It can now be appreciated why the skip instructions in Group 3 were split into two groups; again the 'skip 2' operations could be combined in the hardware, but not in the available instruction code. Note that, unlike the shift codes, no-skip is already defined as zeros in bits 2–4, so that all 'skip 1' operations can be combined. Finally, note that a Group 1 operation can be combined with one of the three allowable shifts *and* one of the seven allowable skips; the skips will be determined by the *result* of the arithmetic/shift operation.

Thus the instruction

ADD 0, 1, ASL, SVC
$\equiv$ 1 1 1 0   0 0 0   0 0 0 1   1 1 1   1 1

Non-memory reference   ADD   R0   R1   SVC   ASL

causes the contents of register R0 to be added to the contents of register R 1; result is multiplied by 2 (ASL) and saved in register R1, destroying the original contents of that register and establishing the appropriate condition codes. The V flag is then checked and if it is clear the PC is incremented by 1.

Note that the above instruction is equivalent to

ADD 0, 1
ASL 1
SVC

Thus the advantage of the combined instruction is twofold; (a) it requires only one, as opposed to three memory locations and (b) it requires only one, as opposed to three, instruction cycle times to execute.

The combination of simple instructions into one more extensive instruction is often referred to as microprogramming, e.g. the one machine instruction is a *program* of two, or possibly more, low-level instructions. The term microprogramming is now commonly used for a more sophisticated extension of this technique, whereby even the machine instructions such as ADD are made up of a sequence of lower level instructions, e.g. enable or inhibit specific gates, so that *all* machine code instructions execute by running through a 'micro-program' of the 'micro-instructions'. This interesting topic is discussed at length in Chapter 8.

2·8·5 Input/Output Instructions

From figure 2.11(c), all I/O instructions are characterised by the op-code 1111. The 12 remaining bits are used to define the actual I/O operation.

By definition the term *input* implies data transmission from a peripheral to the CPU while *output* implies the reverse. Little has yet been said about I/O, which is discussed in detail in Chapter 4. It is sufficient here to note that there are four basic types of instruction,

(a) *Input* data from a peripheral device

(b) *Output* data to a peripheral device

(c) Establish (set or clear) flags in or associated with a peripheral device, to *control* that device

(d) *Test* (skip or jump) flags in or associated with a peripheral device, to determine the current state of that device.

Note that a peripheral device number will never be the same for an input and an output instruction, e.g. a teletype will have one buffer for the keyboard and one for the printer; each buffer is given a unique device number for identification in an I/O instruction.

There will be a number of single bit flip-flops or flags associated with each peripheral, typically to determine whether the device is, or is not, ready to send or receive more data. There are further flags, some inside the CPU, which deal with the *interrupt* system, which is also explained in Chapter 4.

Each I/O instruction must specify the following:

(a) whether the operation is input, output, control or test.

(b) the device address

(c) any specific function within the selected peripheral

(d) the location of data inside the CPU.

The format for the I/O instruction in the DUMB 1 is shown in figure 2.33.

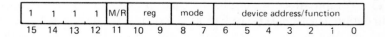

Fig. 2·33 I/O instruction format

Bits 7–8 define the mode as indicated in figure 2.34.

Bits 8 and 7	Mode
00	Input
01	Output
10	Control
11	Test

Fig. 2·34 I/O modes

Bits 9–11 are used with modes 0 and 1 to define the data source/destination inside the CPU. Bits 9 and 10 specify one of the registers in the usual sense of figure 2.20. Bit 11 specifies whether a register or a memory location is to be used. If bit 11 is zero, the register specified by bits 9 and 10 is used directly. If bit 11 is one, then the specified register contains the address of the memory location to be used.

In the latter case the memory address must be loaded into the specified register by a previous instruction; typically the contents of this register will be incremented after each I/O instruction so that consecutive input/output data are written/read into/from contiguous locations in memory. This can be done either by a separate INC r instruction or automatically as part of the I/O memory reference instruction. Note that an extra memory cycle is required for the memory access compared to the direct to register mode. This technique of using an independent register for the memory address is introduced since there are insufficient bits available in the I/O instruction itself.

Bits 0–6 specify the peripheral device to be used. Some peripherals, e.g. the teletype printer, have one clearly defined function. Others, e.g. a VDU, have many functions, such as generate vectors, bright up the screen, generate characters, etc. One viewpoint is to consider each individual function to appear to the computer as though they were independent peripherals, allocating one of the possible 128 unique device addresses to each. An alternative approach is to use say, bits 0–4 to specify 32 possible peripherals and bits 5 and 6 to define 4 possible functions in each. If no data is involved, i.e. modes 2 and 3, then bits 9–11 could possibly be used to define further peripheral functions. The former, with 128 possible codes, is more versatile, but possibly requires more complex logic in the peripheral interface.

The simplest control and test functions relate to enabling a device and determining its current state; additional functions are introduced in Chapter 4. Thus, associated with each peripheral, there are one or more flags or flip-flops built into the interface which can be established or tested by an instruction. The simplest possible example is a teleprinter which requires only one flag, commonly called a 'busy' flag. When the printer is waiting for data the busy flag is at zero. An output instruction can then be used to set the printer in action. The interface is so designed that acceptance of the data, i.e. copying the data on the I/O bus into the buffer register, activates the print and also sets the busy flag to one, that is an output and a control function are combined. If another output instruction follows, the data will not be accepted and a programming error ensues. It should again be stressed that while the action of a printer may appear fast to the human eye, the computer is capable of executing hundreds and even thousands of instructions while the printer deals with one character. Thus the computer must test the busy flag and send new data only when it is clear. This is done by repeating the test, using a skip-if-busy-flag-clear instruction, until it is satisfied.

Let the mnemonic for the output instruction be

OUT r, d   or   OUT * r, d

where r is the register, * means the memory location addressed by the contents of r and d is the device number.

The input instruction mnemonic is similarly

IN r, d   or   IN * r, d

The mnemonic

SKBYS d

means skip if device d is busy (set), while

SKBYC d

means skip if device d is ready (busy flag clear).

Special mnemonic may be defined for individual peripherals, since their control and test functions will not necessarily be similar.

The following program prints a ten character string which is stored in consecutive memory locations. The printer is device 7.

1000	LD1 3, 7	load start address of data into R1
1001	SKBYC 7	test printer for busy
1002	JMP 3, −2	jump, PC relative mode, back to 1001. This loop repeats until printer is ready.
1003	OUT * 1, 7	move data from memory to printer
1004	INC 1	R1 points to next word of data*
1005	DSZ 3, 3	count number of characters printed
1006	JMP 3, −6	repeat
1007	JMP 3, 12	jump beyond array to continue program
1008	1010	start address of character string
1009	10	number of characters in string
1010	XXXX	character 1, etc.
⋮	⋮	
1019	XXXX	last character
1020	continuation of program	

---

* If the I/O memory reference instructions were to automatically increment the 'pointer' register, this instruction must be deleted.

Any attempt to use IN r, 7 would be abortive.

Note that this example is wasteful in that full 16 bit words are used to store characters when 8 would suffice. (See Section 3.5.1 for further discussion on byte addressing.)

Consider now the keyboard; the major difference between this and the printer is that the printer action is initiated by the computer OUT instruction while the keyboard action is initiated by depressing the key, the data being available to the computer on completion of the peripheral action. Thus in the keyboard case, not only is a busy flag required, but also a 'done' flag. Both are normally clear. The busy flag is set by striking a key; when the appropriate data is available in the buffer register, the busy flag is cleared and the done flag set. The device will now remain inactive until the data is read from the buffer by an IN instruction; the done flag is also cleared by this instruction. Programs similar to the previous one can be used to loop, testing the done flag, until true data is available.

Neither of the previous examples require isolated control operations since the control functions are combined with the IN and OUT instructions. Now many teletypes have a paper tape reader/punch attachment. Provided the reader/punch is mechanically activated, data presented to the printer will also be punched; no additional computer actions are needed. However, while the reader is also 'in parallel' with the keyboard, using the same buffer register, etc., its operation is controlled by the computer. A further flip-flop in the interface, often termed a reader-enable flag, causes one frame of the tape to be advanced and read, when set to 1. This flag is cleared by the interface electronics as soon as the busy flag is set and cannot be set again until both busy and done flags are clear.

Thus if the keyboard/tape reader is device 6 and the mnemonic for the control type I/O instruction which sets the enable flag is ENB d, (note that a general mnemonic with a device number may be inappropriate due to the differing control functions in differing devices; an appropriate set of instructions with mnemonics could be defined for each peripheral) the following program causes a tape to be read until a blank frame is detected. The ASCII character for the blank frame corresponds to the arithmetic number 0; striking the zero key on the keyboard generates an ASCII character 060_8.

The mnemonics SKDNS d and SKDNC d are used for the test type I/O instructions 'skip if done flag in device d is set or clear', respectively.

```
200   1200            pointer to storage array address
   :
   :
400   ENB 6           cause one frame of tape to be read
```

401	SKDNS 6	test for completion of read
402	JMP 3, −2	loop test
403	IN 1, 6	more data to R1
404	SEQ	skip if last operation, load R1, is zero, i.e. blank frame detected
405	SKP	new data available
406	JMP 3, +3	blank frame, finish reading
407	ST1 * 200	store data indirect, i.e. first data at 1200
408	ISZ 200	increment contents of 200 (cannot be zero)
409	JMP 3, −10	read next frame
410	continue	
⋮		
1200		data to be stored here
1201		
⋮		

On many machines I/O instructions take longer to execute than, say, memory reference instructions, since the control signals required on the I/O bus are more complex than those of the memory access bus. This is incorporated by allowing an extended execution cycle, often called a *pause*. Asynchronous operation, as discussed in Section 3.2, eases this problem.

2·9 Modifications of the Basic Machine

A basic digital computer and its associated instruction set have now been introduced and explained.

Look now from a computer designer's viewpoint. The instruction codes have been specified and the desired execution explained schematically by simplified timing diagrams such as figures 2.5, 2.6 or 2.32 and by block diagrams such as figure 2.7. On every timing diagram there appears a slot marked 'Decode IR', which is quite adequate for the purpose envisaged here. The computer designer however has only just begun at this stage. He must design and construct a network of logic that causes the CPU to behave as demanded by the instruction. Imagine the sequence of events. The first four bits must be interrogated to determine which type of instruction; as a result of this the remaining twelve bits will be interpolated in differing manners, e.g. for non-memory reference instructions the group will next be determined, etc. The point to be made here is that it is only reasonable for the designer to draw the line at just how much of the specified conception of a computer he can hope to achieve in a given time. Thus, when a machine is marketed, it is common for a user to criticise the performance by the lack of what might appear to be some reasonably obvious feature.

With reasonable sales, the manufacturer can now ask the designer to consider modifications to the machine to increase its power. With MSI, using TTL chips, it is relatively easy to add hardware; with LSI new chips must be designed with a high development cost, but virtually no increase in production cost.

The designer has two paths open to him. Either he modifies the current design or he produces a completely new design, which based on the experience of the previous (and other manufactures!) machine should be superior. This point may be demonstrated by highlighting a few features of the machine just described which can be modified. In the next chapter a whole variety of alternative techniques will be discussed.

Some of the points which could be improved on in the DUMB 1 are:
(a) more registers
(b) more addressing modes
(c) arithmetic or logical operations on data in memory.

The cost of extra hardware is negligible, so that the limit to any improvement is set by the instruction set, to which no major change of format can be considered since that is consistent with a major redesign.

From figure 2.12, it appears that there are four unallocated op-codes for memory reference instructions. Thus two more registers could be included (R3 and R4) with the instructions LD3, LD4, ST3 and ST4. However, referring to figures 2.19(a) and 2.20 only one further register can be used. Modifying the Group 1 non-memory reference instructions would require 3 bits each for RS and RD which eliminate possible combined arithmetic/shift/skip instructions. Thus only one extra register, R3, can be considered. This, fortunately, is also usable by Group 2 non-memory reference instructions as can be seen in figure 2.22.

If the extra register is included, instructions LD3 and ST3 are needed, but two further memory reference instructions could be specified. An arithmetic operation such as ADD A, B which means add the contents of memory location, A, to the contents of memory location B and leave the result in location B is not possible, because two operands with memory addresses are required. ADD A, r where r is a register is more feasible. However with only two unallocated instructions, only two of the four registers could be specified. A better compromise is to define two operations, e.g. ADD A and SUB A, which add (subtract) the contents of memory location A to (from) the contents of R0, leaving the answer in R0. Only R0 is used, since there are simply not enough op-codes to specify the others. ADD A would execute in a manner similar to the non-memory reference instruction ADD 1,0, except that the data is read (in one extra cycle) into the MBR and the outputs of the MBR and R0 used as the inputs to the adder. The compromise made by the designer could be further compounded by sticking to three registers and, referring to figure 2.21, introducing ADD A, SUB A, CPR A and AND A. Note that if R0 is used 'by default' as the destination operand, as discussed here, then it is fairly termed the Accumulator. In this way, specific registers acquire special names, even if they are fundamentally general purpose registers.

With reference to figure 2.15, it can be seen that further addressing modes could be introduced by increasing the number of bits used to three. This would give four further modes. The cost in terms of ease of programming would be high since the page size would be halved to 256 locations, which would be tolerable, at a pinch. Further addressing modes are explained in the next chapter when the wisdom of incorporating them in this design can be considered.

2.10 Resumé

To summarise this chapter, the following table describes the use of the gates shown schematically on figure 2.1. Each of these gates will be enabled at the appropriate time, that is in the correct sequence, by the control signals generated by the decoded instruction.

Gate	Function
1	Used by 'Load Address' switch on console
2	Used by 'Deposit' switch to load data into memory
3	Place result of an arithmetic operation into the PC. Used to increment the PC or Jump using indexed addressing
4	Transfer contents of the MBR into the PC for jump
5	Transfer contents of the PC into the function unit, via 24. Used to increment the PC or PC relative addressing
6	Load the MAR from the PC for the next instruction
7	Load the MAR from the C bus; via 12 for page 0 address; via 27 for relative address; via 11 for indirect address
8	Load contents of register into MBR via 16(R0), 19(R1) or 22(R2)
9	Load the MBR from the function unit. Used with 10, 24

	and 27 to modify MBR contents (ISZ etc.) and for input to memory, via 30
10	Transfer contents of the MBR into the function unit for ISZ etc. May also be used for ADD from memory and, via 29, for output
11	Load registers from the MBR via 17(R0), 20(R1) or 23(R2)
12	Transfer the displacement of a memory reference instruction to the C bus and via 7 to the MAR
13	As 12, but to the B bus. Used as displacement in relative addressing; added to register or PC contents before loading the MAR
14	Load instructions from the MBR into the IR
15	Output of R0 to the A bus. Used with 25 for arithmetic/logic/shift operations and with 29 for output
16	Output of R0 to the B bus. Used with 25 for arithmetic/logic/shift operations and with 8 for store
17	Load R0 with data from the C bus. Used with 27 for destination of arithmetic/logic/shift operation and with 11 for load
18, 19, 20	As 15, 16 and 17 but for R1
21, 22, 23	As 15, 16 and 17 but for R2
24	First input to function unit
25	Second input to function unit
26	Carry input to function unit

These are actually sets of gates as shown in figure 2.7, the appropriate combination being enabled by a particular operation

27	Output from the function unit
28	A set of gates which allow the condition flip-flops to be established during an execute cycle, but not by increment PC or address calculations
29	Output from bus A to the output bus, via 15(R0), 18(R1), 21(R2) or 10(MBR)
30	Input from input bus to bus C; to R0 via 17, R1 via 20, R2 via 23 or MBR via 9
31	Address of peripheral for an I/O instruction
32, 33	Connect the MBR to the memory. A detailed version of these gates is shown in figure 2.2. Further comment is given in Section 3.3.3.

Computer organisation as depicted in figure 2.1, is discussed in more detail in Section 3.3. Some comment however can be made on the problem of redundancy in logic systems. Two specific examples have been deliberately introduced into figure 2.1.

(a) Gate 4 is redundant since its function can be implemented by enabling gates 3 and 11. It can simply be omitted.

(b) The second example of redundancy concerns gates 1 and 2, which however requires some rearrangement. If the output of gate 1 were connected to bus C instead of to the PC and gate 2 removed, then the function of the original gate 1 is achieved with the new gate 1 and gate 3 while the function of the original gate 2 is achieved with the new gate 1 and gate 9.

Chapter 3

Further CPU Features

3·1 Introduction

In the previous chapter the basic function of a digital computer was explained by reference to a particular, hypothetical machine. All modifications or extensions to the basic computer were related to that particular machine. In this chapter and the next a number of features which are commonly encountered in commercial minicomputers will be described, while the more sophisticated techniques are introduced in Chapter 8. Unlike the previous chapter there is no common thread to this one. It would be impossible to incorporate all the features described here in the one machine. Many of the newer features introduced by one manufacturer are incorporated in new versions of another manufacturer's machine, but it has already been stressed that there is a limit to the extent of the modifications that can be implemented.

Assuming that integrated circuit construction makes the hardware costs of secondary importance, the major problem lies in the instruction set. Quite the simplest way to allow a greater range of instructions is to increase the word length; indeed this is done in the larger machines. However there are a lot of attractive features in keeping to the 16 bit word length for minicomputers; (a) cost, each memory location as well as the CPU registers must be extended, (b) compatibility with other machines and (c) exactly two bytes can be stored per word. Clearly the larger machines can justify the use of longer word lengths, but they will also expect yet more sophistication in the instruction set. Thus, in all machines, the efficient utilisation of the available word is of paramount importance.

The only way, given a fixed basic word length, in which the effective instruction can be extended is to use multiple words per instruction. Some machines will have some single word, some double word and even some treble word instructions; these will become apparent in the following sections. Since multiple word instructions require multiple memory cycles to read into the CPU, they must show distinct advantages over groups of simpler instructions; double word instructions must not be introduced when single word equivalents can be devised.

The second feature which can improve the efficiency of the computer is speed. Memory cycle times are continually being improved, but this is not the only feature which affects the speed of 'through-put', the instruction set itself is totally relevant. Thus in one machine the transfer of data from a peripheral to memory may require one instruction to read the I/O bus into a register and a second instruction to store the register contents in memory; on another machine a single input-to-memory instruction saves at least one memory cycle since only one instruction need be fetched and decoded. Some of the speed improving features commonly encountered are discussed in the following sections.

3·2 Synchronous and Asynchronous Operation

Synchronous operations are timed by a clock. Asynchronous operations initiate a new operation immediately on completion of the current one. The machine discussed in the last chapter was essentially synchronous in operation. Each instruction took one or two complete memory cycles to execute.

With a synchronous system, using for example a 1 MHz clock, then if event A takes $0·2 \mu$sec, event B $0·9 \mu$sec and event C $1·5 \mu$sec, the first two each require 1 cycle and the third 2 cycles. With an asynchronous system the completion of event A starts event B, the completion of which initiates event C. Allowing say $0·1 \mu$sec for the logic which detects the end of one operation and initiates the next, the three events above take $0·2 + 0·1 + 0·9 + 0·1 + 1·5 + 0·1 = 2·9 \mu$sec compared to $1 + 1 + 2 = 4 \mu$sec with the synchronous system. This is shown in figure 3.1.

It is clear that the advantage of asynchronous operation is an increase in speed. There is however a disadvantage in that extra logic circuitry is required to detect the end of an event; this can be far more costly than the simple clock required by synchronous operation. Thus asynchronous operation is faster but more complex than synchronous operation.

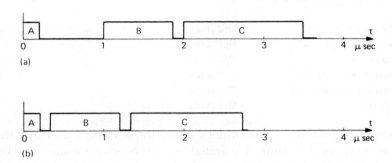

Fig. 3·1 Example of (a) synchronous and (b) asynchronous operation

There are numerous points in the computer system where these principles can be applied. One of the commonest is in the I/O system. Thus for an output instruction, data is placed on the I/O bus and the processor made to 'pause' until the receiving peripheral sends back a pulse to acknowledge receipt of the data. A similar mode of operation is possible with some memory systems, a common example being used in the microprocessor explained in Chapter 5. Asynchronous memory system operation is essential if mixed types of memory are used.

Inside the CPU, where the increase in circuit complexity is not so important, (increase in I/O complexity affects *every* peripheral) asynchronous operation has great scope. Consider the timing diagram of figure 2.32. Execution of the instruction begins by copying the PC contents into the MAR. A pulse generated by completion of the MAR load can initiate both the memory read cycle and the incrementing of the PC. In practice the read will take longer than the increment PC; this is irrelevant if the next event is initiated by the completion of which ever finishes last, e.g. both the MBR loaded *and* the PC incremented pulses have occurred. The restore memory cycle can now commence completely independently of any CPU action. The CPU operation commences at the same time as the restore cycle by copying the MBR contents into the IR. Completion of the copy causes the control signals from the decoder to be established, which in turn initiate the execution. If more than one event is required in sequence by the one instruction, then completion of the first again initiates the second, and so on. Now, in direct comparison to figure 2.32, the next instruction fetch cycle will not commence until both the memory restore and the execution(s) are complete.

Consider as an example that the actual times for the specific electronic operations involved are:

Increment PC	$0.2 \mu sec$
MBR to IR	$0.1 \mu sec$
Decode IR	$0.2 \mu sec$
Execute operation 1	$0.3 \mu sec$
Execute operation 2	$0.2 \mu sec$
PC to MAR	$0.1 \mu sec$

Figure 3.2 shows the asynchronous operation with (a) $2 \mu sec$ and (b) $1 \mu sec$ memory cycle time. The initial load of the MAR is assumed to be included in the quoted memory cycle time. The actual time taken by the read cycle only is called the *access* time, 800 and 400 nsec for (a) and (b) respectively. In practice quoted figures usually include an allowance for a possible modify state.

In case (b) the net instruction time is $1.3 \mu sec$. The next instruction cycle can commence immediately. Thus execution times for different instructions will not necessarily be multiples of the memory cycle time. In fact the actual time may depend upon the operation, as was the case when the execute 2 operation, originally expressed in figure 2.32, was a skip function; if the condition is satisfied then the PC must be incremented, but not otherwise. Thus if the execute operation takes, say $0.1 \mu sec$ to check the condition codes and $0.2 \mu sec$ to increment the PC, then the execute 2 time slot may be either 0.1 or $0.3 \mu secs$ and the instruction of figure 3.2(b) could take either 1.2 or $1.4 \mu sec$.

Asynchronous operation is also helpful when non-destructive-read-out memory is used, e.g. semi-conductor LSI. Figure 3.2 is still applicable except that the restore memory section is eliminated. Again if a read/modify/write memory mode is used, the modify phase is asynchronously entered, the write cycle commencing upon completion of the modify. The increment and skip if zero (ISZ) instruction is one which uses the modify cycle as shown in figure 3.3.

A lot of confusion is introduced by simply calling a computer synchronous or asynchronous. In fact an asynchronous processor could be used with either a synchronous or asynchronous I/O system. When used without qualification one can probably assume both CPU and I/O are as specified, but some caution is wise.

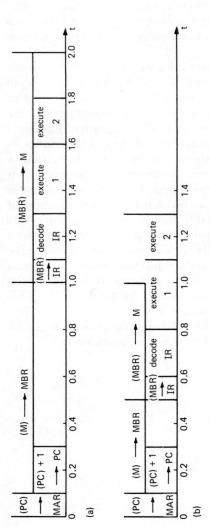

(a)

(b)

Fig. 3·2 Timing sequence for asynchronous operation of a non-memory-reference instruction with memory cycle times of (a) 2 μsec and (b) 1 μsec.

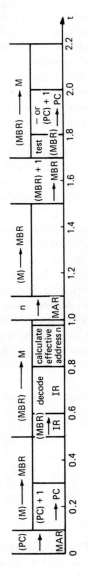

Fig. 3·3 Timing sequence for ISZ instruction which uses a read/modify/write memory cycle

3·3 Processor Organisation

3·3·1 Internal Bus Structures

One of the main differences between computers is the basic architecture; in particular the variety in the arrangement of the data bus systems which allow communication between one part of the machine and another.

The basic computer shown in figures 2.1 and 3.4 is clearly a multiple bus machine, with the data buses A, B, C and the input and output buses. The arrangement of the diagram of figure 2.1 was dictated by the desire to accentuate the break down of the functional parts of the machine e.g. I/O, ALU, control and memory. The diagram of figure 3.4 is re-arranged to accentuate the organisation of the bus structures.

The system of figure 3.4 can be simplified from the logic circuitry viewpoint by realising that if only one input to the function unit is enabled, then it will pass the data unmodified. Thus, by enabling gates 24 and 27, data can be transferred from bus A to bus C. The machine of figure 3.4 can therefore be simplified to that of figure 3.5. Since only one instruction at a time can be executed, both gates 29 and 30 cannot be simultaneously enabled. Similarly, device controllers either take data off the output bus or place it onto the input bus, thus both bus bars cannot be simultaneously in use. It is common therefore to use only the one *bidirectional I/O data bus* as was shown in figure 2.10. This modification is also incorporated in figure 3.5.

Comparing figure 3.4 and 3.5, the following equivalences can be deduced; note that gates 14 and 31 have been repositioned.

Figure 3.4	Figure 3.5
6	5, 24, 27 and 7
12	13, 25 and 27
14	10, 24, 27 and 14
11	10, 24 and 27
8	25, 27 and 9
31	13 and 31

For the simpler type of machine where one register is dedicated as an accumulator and another as an index register, the system can be further simplified, as shown in figure 3.6. R0 is designated as the accumulator and R1 as the index register. R2 is omitted.

For this machine the only arithmetic operations allowed are of the type 'Add data from memory to the data in the accumulator and leave

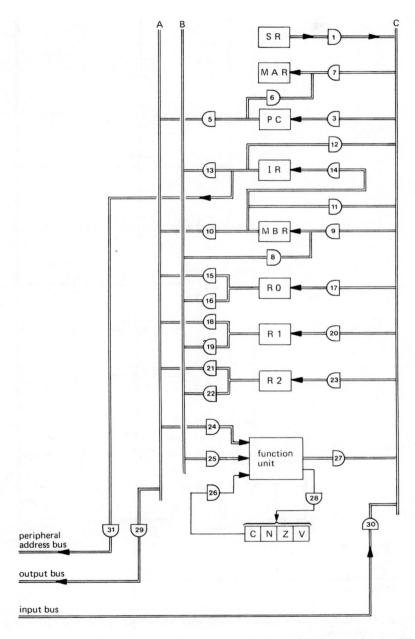

Fig. 3·4 The basic machine of figure 2·1 with the modifications suggested in Section 2·10

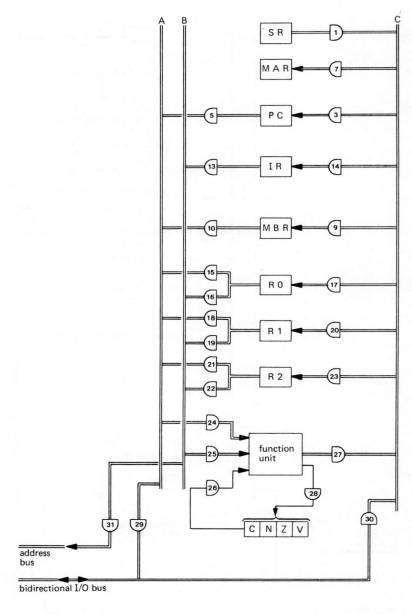

Fig. 3·5 Modified version of figure 3·4 which uses the function unit to transfer data from one bus to another

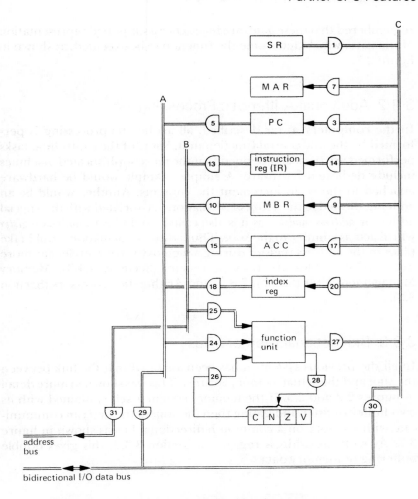

Fig. 3·6 A dedicated Accumulator, Index Register variant on figure 3·5

the result in the accumulator'. For this reason gate 10 has been reconnected to the B bus. Thus for example a register relative address is determined by adding the offset from IR to either the PC or the index register contents, placing the result in the MAR. Loading the accumulator (or index register) requires gates 10, 25, 27 and 17 (or 20) to be enabled.

In these simplified structures of figures 3.5 and 3.6 it would appear that gates 24 and 25 are superfluous, since both buses A and B will be clear unless a register is deliberately connected to them with the specific intention of communicating with the function unit. However it must be remembered that these gates are in practice a simplified representation of the gates which determine the function to be executed, as shown in figure 2.7.

3·3·2 Additional Arithmetic Processing

In the computers so far described, all arithmetic processing is performed by the one central function unit. Some of the controlling tasks performed are so clearly defined that the more sophisticated machines include dedicated hardware. A simple example would be hardware attached to the PC to increment the contents. Another would be an adder dedicated to the address calculations. Associated with this special adder, or *address modifier* as it is also called, could be an *address register* which acts as a buffer to the MAR. Thus address calculations could take place in the address register during a memory refresh cycle. Far more extensive examples are DMA processors (Sections 4.4.3), Memory Management Unit (Section 7.8.5) and Arithmetic Processors (Section 8.3).

3·3·3 Bidirectional Memory Bus

In all the previous systems it has been assumed that the link between the MBR and the actual memory is direct. This was shown in more detail in figures 2.2 and 2.3. If the memory system is self contained with its own buffer register and gating then the MBR in the CPU can communicate with memory on a common bidirectional bus as shown in figure 3.7. As with the address register in Section 3.3.2, this gives double buffering of memory data.

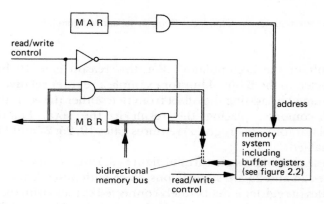

Fig. 3·7 Bi-directional memory bus connecting the MBR to memory

The buffering is used by a memory access technique called *direct memory access*, which will be explained in Section 4.4.3. The more sophisticated systems incorporate a simple arithmetic processor with the buffer inside the memory unit, another example of the extensions mentioned in Section 3.3.2, which is also discussed in Section 4.4.3.

3·3·4 External Bus Structures

There are two basic lines of communication with the CPU (i) the I/O bus and (ii) the memory bus. It could also be argued that there are four lines since both of these buses are bidirectional or six lines since there are additional address and control buses. There is however an alternative whereby a *single bus* is shared for both I/O and memory transfers. Both structures are shown in figure 3.8, where it is obvious that the phrases 'single or double' refer to groups of data, address and control buses, external to the CPU.

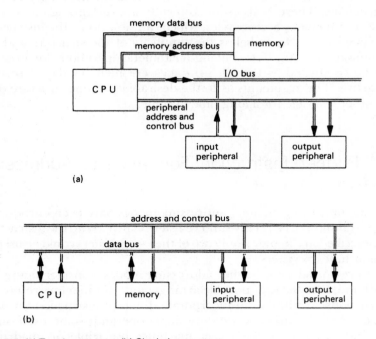

Fig. 3·8 (a) Two bus system (b) Single bus system

With the two bus system, I/O and memory transfer are completely independent. Separate instructions are required for memory transfer and I/O. To transfer a piece of data from peripheral 1 to peripheral 2,

101

one I/O instruction is required to transfer data from peripheral 1 to a CPU register and a second I/O instruction to transfer from the CPU register to peripheral 2. It should be noted that the logic requirements for control of the two buses will be different.

With the single bus system the data buffers in each peripheral device are effectively other memory locations. Each interface will contain a buffer register which is addressed as though it were a memory location. Thus no special I/O instructions are required. One device at any instant will become 'master' of the bus and can communicate with any other device, which is then a 'slave'. Memory can only be a slave device, but the peripherals can be masters. Thus one peripheral can become master and transfer data to the CPU, memory or another peripheral device. The big disadvantage of this system is that the control logic is the same for memory and peripherals, and because of the lowest common denominator factor is necessarily over complex when compared to the two bus system. There is a time penalty to be paid in acquiring control of the bus, even for normal memory store or load instructions. There is also some difficulty in overlapping CPU operations and memory access cycles, which can slow down the instruction execution time. Nevertheless the simplicity of the structure and the minimisation of I/O data moving (arithmetic operations for instance can be conducted as though I/O data were memory data) are very attractive. The arguments as to the desirability of one structure over the other will rage for a long time to come.

3·4 Further Instruction Formats and Addressing Modes

To date only three memory addressing modes have been introduced, page 0 (absolute), PC relative and register relative. With the instruction set described in Chapter 2 only two of the CPU registers could be used as base or index registers.

Before considering further addressing modes, consider figure 3.9 which indicates the four possible arrangements for memory reference instructions. Machines can incorporate different instruction formats, but most minicomputers use only single operand; some use double operand, while only the larger machines use triple or quadruple operand instructions. For the DUMB 1 the instructions employing double operands could only use one operand in memory at the most; the second operand (or both operands) would be CPU registers. Memory addresses are therefore implied by the expressions 'double operand', etc.

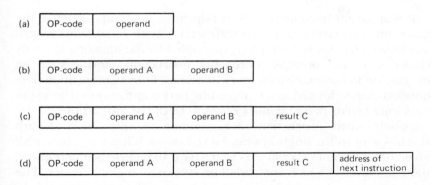

Fig. 3·9 Memory reference instruction formats

The combination of skip operations with arithmetic operations, as explained in Section 2.8.4.4, constitutes to some extent a method of controlling the address of the next instruction.

Thus to add the contents of locations A and B and place in result in C would require the typical code:

(i) Single operand instructions

```
LD1        A
LD2        B
ADD 2, 1
ST1        C
```

(ii) Double operand instructions:

```
ADD        A, B   place result A + B in B
MOV        B, C   copy contents of B into C.
```

Alternatively, avoiding corruption of B,

```
MOV        B, C
ADD        A, C
```

(iii) Triple operand instructions

```
ADD        A, B, C
```

(i) requires four instructions with three memory data accesses.
(ii) requires two instructions with four memory data accesses, B to temp; temp to C; A to adder; C to adder (result loaded back in C on the write cycle).
(iii) requires one instruction with three memory accesses.

Approximately, ignoring the effects of asynchronous operations and that the multiple operand instructions will take longer to decode; (i) requires seven memory cycles, (ii) six and (iii) four.

It is apparent from figure 3.9 that the more operands included, the more bits are required in the instruction. With fixed word length machines, and this is dominantly controlled by the memory, the only choice is to use multiple words per instruction, storing such an instruction in consecutive memory locations. Thus the execution time improvements claimed in the preceding paragraph may well be lost in requiring two or more memory cycles to fetch the instruction.

Double word instructions are common in short word length machines, even for single operand instructions. Thus a machine with an eight bit memory system may well have a 16 bit instruction register, the two halves of which are loaded on successive memory cycles. The microprocessor described in Chapter 5 is just such an arrangement. 16 bit machines could use the same technique, having a 32 bit instruction register. This is not desirable however since 16 bits are adequate for many instructions, which would result in some 16 bit and some 32 bit instructions. In more sophisticated machines there may well be some 8, 16, 24 and 32 bit instructions. In such cases part of the op-code in the first word must indicate the number of following words (or bytes) required for that specific instruction. Thus minicomputers use the one 16 bit basic instruction register and can effectively extend the instruction by special utilisation of the other CPU registers. Some of these points will be incorporated in the following list of addressing modes, which are additional to the three so far mentioned. It is worth bearing in mind that a major objective is to arrive at a 16 bit effective address, with the constraint of the relatively few bits (9 in the DUMB 1) available in the operand part of the instruction.

3·4·1 Additional Addressing Modes

It must be realised that if further addressing modes are introduced, then more bits of the word must be allocated to define them. The extra modes defined here can not be incorporated into the instruction set of the machine used in Chapter 2 without major modification. The following is a description of various modes that are commonly encountered.

3·4·1·1 Literal

The operand is the data, rather than an address pointer. This is very convenient for handling simple constants, e.g. add 10 to the contents of a register. If the constant, 10, is part of the instruction then separate memory locations need not be allocated just to store constants, as in the example program in Section 2.8.5.

3·4·1·2 Immediate

The data is stored in the location immediately following the instruction. The PC contents are copied into the MAR to fetch the instruction and then incremented, as usual. The PC contents now point to the location following the instruction location, which stores the data; thus the PC contents are copied into the MAR on the next memory cycle and the PC incremented again. The double incrementing of the PC leaves it pointing to the next instruction, as required. This is an example of how two words are used to form the one extended instruction. Note that the usual operand part of the instruction is only required to define the mode. This addressing mode could therefore be introduced into the instruction of Section 2.8.3.3 as a special PC relative mode by noting that zero displacement is never normally needed, e.g.

LD0 3, 0; load R0, mode 3, displacement 0

would load the contents of the next memory location into R0.

If now, with, and only with, zero displacement, the PC is incremented twice, instead of once then the immediate mode of addressing results. On some machines the largest negative, −256 (100000000), rather than zero displacement is singled out to create the immediate mode.

A special set of mnemonics are commonly created for immediate mode addressing, e.g. LDIr n which loads the number n in register r. LDr # n is an alternative notation, the symbol # implying the number n, rather than location n. In terms of the instruction set of Chapter 2

LD0 20 ≡ 0 0 0 0   1 1   0   0 0 0 0 1 0 1 0 0

Op-code   Mode   +20

                3   Direct

while

LDI0 20 ≡ 0 0 0 0   1 1   0   0 0 0 0 0 0 0 0 0

0 0 0 0   0 0   0   0 0 0 0 1 0 1 0 0

Note that numbers in the range +32 767 to −32 768 can be specified

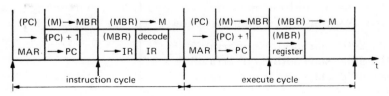

Fig. 3·10 Timing sequence for a memory reference instruction, Load Register, using Immediate mode.

with immediate mode, while $+255$ to -256 is the range with the single word literal address, even if some method of specifying this latter mode could be found. The timing sequence is shown in figure 3.10 for a load register, immediate instruction.

3·4·1·3 Base Relative and Indexed

No differential was made between base relative and index addressing in the previous chapter. Indeed they are very similar.

With direct addressing there is no difference in the function; the effective address is calculated by adding the displacement, D, to the contents of a specified CPU register. Conceptually a difference could be classified thus: (a) base relative, the register contents are fixed and the displacement is modified after each instruction and (b) indexed, the register contents are modified while the displacement is kept constant.

A more powerful arrangement is to allow both base relative *and* indexed addressing in the one effective address. One CPU register is used as a base register and another as an index register; the effective address is then the sum of both these registers and the displacement. Referring to figure 3.4 the output from the MAR would have to be gated back to the A bus so that the function unit can be assessed twice, using the MAR as an accumulator. Note also the comments in Section 3.3.2 about buffering the MAR.

With indirect addressing further differences appear, determined by whether the address additions are made before or after the indirect memory fetch. Thus (a) *Pre-indexing*, the index register contents and the displacement are added to give an address, the contents of which location give the effective address. (b) *Post-indexing*, the displacement is used as an indirect address pointer to a memory location, the contents of which are added to the index register contents to give the effective address. These techniques become more powerful still when combined; thus base relative, indirect, indexed causes the sum of the base register contents and the displacement to give an indirect address pointer to a memory location, the contents of which are added to the contents of the index register to give the effective address.

This class of addressing mode is commonly used in handling data in arrays. A sophisticated example follows:

100	200	start address of array A
101	300	start address of array B
102	400	start address of array C
$\vdots$		
200	a_0	first data word in array A

201   a_1 second data word in array A

$\vdots$

300   b_0
301   b_1

$\vdots$

400   c_0
401   c_1

$\vdots$

Define register R1 as the base register and R2 as the index register, then the nth data word in the Nth array is accessed by a base relative, indirect, indexed address if; R1 contains 100, the starting address of the table of array start addresses; D, the displacement, is N−1; and R2 contains n−1.

This is an example of the dedicated use of CPU registers to increase the flexibility of the instruction set, without increasing the word length, i.e. with dedicated base and index registers they need not be specified in the instruction.

3·4·1·4 Increment and Decrement (Auto indexing)

One of the common requirements is to work through tables of data (arrays) sequentially. This involves a pointer being used to locate the current word in the array. The pointer is then incremented (or decremented, dependent on whether it is required to work up or down the array) after each memory access, to which end the INC and DEC instructions were defined. An improved method is to use a specific addressing mode whereby the pointer is automatically incremented or decremented whenever it is used. A standard convention, which is important in using stacks, explained in Section 3.5, is that with autoincrement the pointer is used and then incremented, while with autodecrement the pointer is decremented and then used.

Reconsider the example used in Section 3.4.1.3 above. If the index register, R2, is autoincremented, then repeating the same instruction will locate the n + 1th element in the Nth array. It is rather too much to expect a machine to incorporate in one mode base relative, indexed and autoincrement though! More simply R2 would be loaded with the address of the first word of the array by a previous instruction and used with an autoincrement mode.

To avoid the problem of specifying the extra modes in the instruction set, some minicomputers dedicate hardware to the memory system which automatically increments or decrements the contents of certain memory locations whenever they are used as indirect addressed locations. The contents are read into the MBR, incremented or decremented before the restore cycle, and the result transferred to the MAR as the effective address. Usually about eight locations are allocated to autoincrement and probably another eight to autodecrement. Note however that the autodecrement decrements before using the pointer, so that it cannot be used in stack processing. This dedicated memory technique could be incorporated in the DUMB 1 without affecting the instruction set in any way.

3·4·2 Double Operands Instructions in 16 Bit Word Machines

With the 16 bit word length of the conventional minicomputer, referring to figure 3.9, it is clear that double operand addressing cannot be incorporated by the conventional methods so far described. Some means must be developed by which double or triple words can be combined to form one instruction, as with immediate mode addressing. Two such methods are given below.

(i) The first word is relatively conventional, except that one bit must be used to denote whether this word is a single or double operand instruction, effectively increasing the op-code. If it is a single operand then the instruction is similar to those already described. If however it is a double operand instruction, then the displacement in the first word forms the first operand while the second operand is contained in the following word. Now no op-code is required in the second word so that the second operand is effectively 5 bits longer than the first. Probably all the usual modes will apply to the second operand but with a larger displacement. The necessity to use the extra bit in the first word to denote the number of operands often means that some of the addressing modes must be restricted or the displacement reduced for the first operand.

An alternative approach would be, on detecting a two operand instruction, to use internal registers to store the 11 bits (assuming a 4 bit op-code + 1 bit single/double operand flag) from the first word and concatenate them with the full second word. Using internal CPU logic the 27 bits can be split into two similar operands (quite how to split 27 in two creates a small problem). This however would slow the machine down, since it would have to wait for the second memory access to get the full information for the first operand.

Assuming the first operand to be in the first word and the second in the second word, then immediate mode addressing could be possible on the first word, since it would sandwich the immediate data word between the two words of the instruction.

(ii) The displacement in the operand is completely dispensed with. An effective displacement, if required, is stored in one of the CPU registers. The operand now only requires to specify the addressing mode and the reference register. A simple structure used by one common commercial minicomputer, the DEC PDP-11, is to allocate 3 bits to specify one of eight modes and another 3 bits to specify one of eight registers. The eight possible registers must cover those used in all addressing modes, e.g. the PC, index, base, and all general purpose registers or accumulators. The PC, must be included as one of the group of registers to give program counter relative addressing. Thus there would be a maximum of seven general registers compared to the three in figure 3.4. No special names need to be given to specific registers other than the PC since they can all be used as general, base or index registers, etc. One however has a dedicated use in stack processing, automatically used by the JMS and interrupt system.

Thus each operand is defined by 6 bits and a double operand instruction can be coded into one 16 bit word, as shown in figure 3.11.

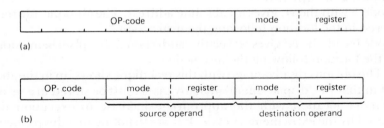

Fig. 3·11 Instruction word format for PDP-11. (a) Single operand and (b) Double operand

Eight possible addressing modes at first sight seems too good to be true, but this is tempered since direct or indirect must be also included. One further innovation is to allocate one mode to mean register direct, i.e. non-memory reference. Thus the instructions to increment a memory location and to increment a register are the same, apart from the mode, greatly increasing the simplicity of the instruction set.

All through this text stress has been laid on the designers problem of compromise between the range of possible functions and the range allowed by the instruction format, which is inevitably limited. The reader may like to ponder on the choice made by the designers of the PDP-11 and perhaps to contemplate some alternatives from the modes discussed previously. The PDP–11 modes are:

0   Register direct, i.e. a non-memory reference
1   Register deferred. As 0 but indirect, using the register as a pointer. This can be likened to a 16 bit page 0 address, with the contents of the specified register acting as a displacement, or alternatively as an index register with zero displacement.
2   Autoincrement. As 1, but the register contents are post-incremented.
3   As 2 but an indirect address.
4   Auto decrement. As 1, but the register contents are pre-decremented.
5   As 4 but an indirect address.
6   Indexed. Specified register acts as the index register, but the displacement, which cannot be included in the word, is saved in the location following the instruction.
7   As 6 but an indirect address.

Combination of the above modes specifically with the PC, results in other modes previously defined, e.g.

Mode 2 with the PC gives the normal immediate mode, with the data following the instruction.

Mode 3 with the PC gives an absolute address. The absolute address is stored in the location following the instruction.

Mode 6 with the PC gives PC relative addressing, the offset being stored in the location following the instruction.

The obvious disadvantage with this technique shows up in the above list in that the 'displacement' in many cases must be stored in a second memory location with the appropriate increase in execution time caused by the extra memory cycle. It is worth noting that this particular computer is a single bus machine, so that the operand may refer to either a register, a memory location or a peripheral, all with the same basic instruction!

3·5 Further Instructions

In this section a number of instructions which are commonly encountered are described. Needless to say they cannot all be included in any machine.

3·5·1 Byte Operations

Many computer applications use principally 8 bit data words, in particular character handling devices, e.g. data processing or data communications. Indeed a number of machines on the market are fundamentally 8 bit computers, concatenating 8 bit words to make longer instructions. It was largely to avoid the multiple fetches of 8 bit data words per one instruction that the 16 bit machines were developed. Character handling in 16 bit word machines is simply achieved by using half of the word only, but this wastes the other half. Thus certain instructions have been developed to enable two bytes of data to be stored and accessed in one 16 bit word.

The best technique is to address the memory by bytes. Thus a 16 bit word can address 64K bytes or 32K words. All words are then addressed by even numbered addresses as shown in figure 3.12.

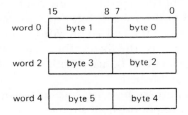

Fig. 3·12 A byte addressed 16 bit memory system

The obvious disadvantage of this system is that all word addresses go up in twos, so that to increment the PC after an instruction fetch, *two* must be added, etc. A simple way round this is to retain the more normal memory address systems but to load the MAR arithmetically shifted one place right. Thus if the effective word address is 4172_8, then

Effective address

$$0 \quad 0 \quad 0 \quad 0 \quad 1 \quad 0 \quad 0 \quad 0 \quad 0 \quad 1 \quad 1 \quad 1 \quad 1 \quad 0 \quad 1 \quad 1 \quad \rightarrow$$

MAR contents

$$0 \quad 0 \quad 0 \quad 1 \quad 0 \quad 0 \quad 0 \quad 0 \quad 1 \quad 1 \quad 1 \quad 1 \quad 0 \quad 1 \quad 1 \quad 0$$

Byte addresses would be loaded directly. The disadvantage of the even numbered word addresses is the problem of thinking in twos. The advantage is that words or bytes are similarly addressed, e.g. byte 260 is the right byte of word 260. With the alternative system the addresses are normally numbered in increments of one, either word or byte, so that byte 260 is the right byte of word 130.

In either case special byte orientated instructions are required to supplement the usual instructions. Some machines use a word/byte mode flip-flop inside the CPU which can be controlled by a special instruction. If the flip-flop is in the word mode then instructions use full 16 bit data words; if the flip-flop is in the byte mode, most instructions use 8 bit bytes of data, the exceptions being addresses referring to instruction storage, e.g. Jump.

It is better still to define special byte instructions, since then byte and word data instructions can be more easily intermixed in a program. Most important are Load byte and Store byte instructions. Store byte instructions copy the right half of a register's contents (bits 0–7) into a half word of memory. Load byte instructions copy a byte from memory to the right half (bits 0–7) of a specified register. Some variants of the Load instruction are however encountered: (a) the left half of the register is unaffected, (b) the left half of the register is automatically cleared, (c) the left half of the register is 'sign extended' i.e. if bit 7 is 0, bits 8–15 are cleared but if bit 7 is 1, bits 8–15 are set. Case (c) would appear to be superior since the full 16 bit word is the same number in two's complement form as the byte; thus the normal arithmetic operations on the registers can be used with byte data, the condition codes being correctly established.

Instructions such as Zero-right-byte, Zero-left-byte and Swap-bytes, all on data in registers but not normally in memory, are common. The Swap-bytes operation is shown in figure 3.13, along with a Rotate-byte-right (RORB) instruction, the latter being typical of byte mode variants of normal instructions.

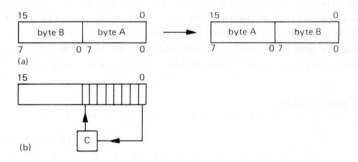

Fig. 3·13 (a) Swap-byte and (b) Rotate-byte-right operations

Many machines cannot address bytes in memory directly, making them inefficient for character handling. The full word must be taken into the CPU and the left half zeroed to access the right byte, while a swap operation is required in addition to access the left byte. Zeroing of half the word often has to be done with a logical AND between the word and a mask specially stored in another register.

3·5·2 Bit Operations

Quite one of the weakest features of the digital computer, created by the 'word orientation' of the memory, is the processing of single bit data. Single bit data is commonly associated with binary external events such as the closing of a switch, the activating of a solenoid, the lighting of a lamp, the sounding of an alarm, etc. Individual pieces of binary information can be treated as the numbers 0 or 1 and saved in a full word (or byte), but this is most wasteful. One word can be allocated to store 16 binary pieces of information, one per bit of the word, provided the individual bits can be isolated to test them and to alter them. This is particularly true of an I/O instruction when one peripheral device can in fact be a 16 channel digital controller.

On most machines the data word concerned must be transferred to a CPU register. The Rotate instructions can then be used to isolate the desired bit in the carry or sign flip-flop. This can then be tested, set or cleared as required. If a modification to the data is to be made, e.g. set or cleared, then the rotate operation must be reversed before the full operation is complete. Note that up to eight rotate operations may be required to reach a bit in the middle of a word; multiple shift instructions, to be described in Section 3.5.4, are most helpful. Nevertheless it is clear that, say, to set a specific bit in an output device, a number of instructions are required. Masking operations (Bit set or Bit clear) may also be used.

Some machines incorporate special bit operate instructions, which give very superior performance in this respect. Typical instructions would be:

BITS n, A; set bit n in word A; the normal address modes apply so that A may refer to a register or a memory location contents.
BITC n, A; clear bit n in word A
BITT n, A; test bit n in word A. This merely requires bit n to be copied into, say, the z flip-flop, when the usual skip instructions can be used.

3·5·3 Conditional Branches

Conditional branches or jumps have, using the instructions defined to date, been executed by combining conditional skip instructions, with an unconditional jump instruction (see the examples in Section 2.8.4.3). Conditional branch instructions are similar to skip instructions except that if the condition is met, the location to which the program sequence is transferred is specified in the instruction. Usually the branch is defined as a program counter relative address, the displacement being stored in the instruction. For this reason the conditional branch can only cause jumps to memory locations local to the location where the instruction is stored, i.e. with, say, an 8 bit displacement, $+127$ to -128 locations about the instruction location. For branches to locations further away the conditional branch must be indirect. Programming with branch instructions is very similar to the IF($-$) GO TO – types of statement in high level languages. As an example the instruction 'Branch if equal (to zero)' is

BEQ + 30 ≡ $\begin{cases} \text{SNE; skip if not equal} \\ \text{JMP 3, +29; jump, mode 3.} \end{cases}$

Branch instructions are somewhat easier to use than skip and jump combinations.

3·5·4 Multiple Shifts

In Section 2.8.4.2 four shift type operations were specified, i.e. rotate and arithmetic shift right or left. Other instructions of this type can be defined by differentiating between rotates which either do or do not include the carry bit, and by 'long shifts'. Long shifts involve two words which effectively form a 'double precision' 32 bit word. Thus a long arithmetic shift left causes the second (least significant) word to be shifted with the right bit cleared. The first word is also shifted left, with the MSB shifted into the carry flip-flop, but the LSB is filled with the MSB from the second word. Examples of long shifts are shown in figure 3.14.

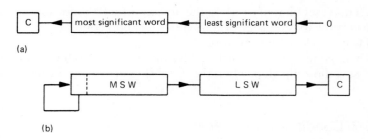

(a)

(b)

Fig. 3·14 (a) Long arithmetic shift left (double precision multiply by 2) (b) Long arithmetic shift right (double precision divide by 2)

A further possible variant is an unsigned arithmetic shift right, which differs from the more usual ASR by filling the left hand bit with zero rather than replicating the previous MSB. A most useful extension to the shift instructions is to include multiple places of shift. Eight places need specifying for rotates provided both right and left shifting is available, but more may be needed for arithmetic shifts. At least 3 bits of the instruction would be required to dictate how many places of shift are called for. A separate register is usually allocated as a 'shift counter'; this is employed to count the number of times the data is looped through the shifter, being shifted one place each time. Each place shifted takes about quarter to half a memory cycle. With modern LSI technology, a more sophisticated shifter can be implemented which will cause multiple shifts internally, rather than re-cycle the single place shifter.

3·5·5 Multiply and Divide

Extensive consideration must be given to the problem of multiplying and dividing numbers. The basic multiplication technique is related to the multiple shift operations just mentioned. For multiplication the data is looped back through the adder-shifter, not just the shifter; 'long-shifts' are also necessary.

Consider the problem of multiplying two *unsigned* positive integers together.* As usual using 5 bit words for numerical descriptions, find $X = Y \times Z$ when $Y = 5$ and $Z = 20$.

Y =					0	0	1	0	1		multiplicand
Z =					1	0	1	0	0		multiplier
				0	0	0	0	0			partial product 1
			0	0	0	0	0				partial product 2
		0	0	1	0	1					partial product 3
	0	0	0	0	0						partial product 4
	0	0	1	0	1						partial product 5
X =	0	0	1	1	0	0	1	0	0		

Note that X may be a 10 bit number. (Two 16 bit numbers give a product of length 32 bits, leading zeros, as in the above example, included.) There is no need to save all the partial products and then sum, they can be accumulated as they are found. In practice the first partial product is found and then shifted right one place to which the second partial product is added; this sum is again shifted one place

---

* Multiplication of two's complement numbers is more difficult, see Appendix 1. The simpler unsigned multiplication is included here as an introduction to the problem, which is expanded upon in Section 8.3.

right and the next partial product added, etc. Note that there are n partial products for n bit multiplicand and multiplier.

Now with binary numbers the ith partial product is simply the multiplicand when bit (i–1) of the multiplier (remember bit 0 is defined as the LSB) is 1 and zero when it is 0.

The multiplicand is stored in a CPU register, B, and the multiplier in a register MQ (this stands for multiplier/quotient, as it is also used in division). The result must be stored in two registers, the most significant half in A and the least significant half in A_0.

The basic algorithm for multiplication is thus:

(a) clear carry and A
(b) if bit (i–1) of MQ is 1, add B to A
(c) long rotate right A and A_0
(d) repeat (b) and (c) n times, i = 1, 2, . . . , n.

In practice the convenient way to test the bit of the multiplier is to arithmetically shift it right so that the LSB, bit 0, is in carry; a second shift puts bit 1 into the carry, etc. Accepting that this destroys the original contents of MQ, the multiplier register MQ can serve as A_0, since the accumulated sum of the partial products 'grows' into A_0 at the same rate as the multiplier is shifted into the carry. An initial shift on MQ is required to load carry with bit 0. The algorithm, related to figure 3.15, then becomes

(a) clear A
(b) ASR MQ; bit 0 to carry
(c) if carry is 1, add B to A, re-establishing carry
(d) long rotate right A and MQ through C
(e) repeat (c) and (d) n times; the shift-count register can be used as a counter.

The double precision product is left in A and MQ.

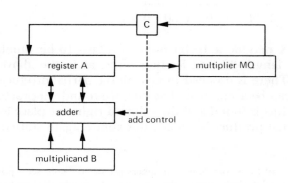

Fig. 3·15 Multiplication register arrangement

On single accumulator machines, A is the accumulator, B is the MBR but a special additional hardware register is required for MQ. On a machine as shown in figure 2.1, the three general registers could be used.

Many problems remain to be discussed such as division, handling of signed (two's complement) numbers and alternative hardware arrangements. Further details are given in Appendix 1 and Section 8.3.

3·5·6 Multiple Operations in One Instruction

There are a number of examples of commonly used sequences of operations which are performed by a sequence of instructions. There are alternative practical examples of machines with special single instructions which perform the combined sequence of operations. Thus while the actual execution time is unaffected, only one instruction need be fetched and decoded, so that the total time to complete the sequence of operations is reduced, as is the memory storage for the instructions.

The simplest examples of combined operations per instruction are the grouping of various non-memory reference instructions. Some examples were given in Section 2.8.4.4, e.g. 'Clear a register' and 'Clear carry' which can be combined to the one instruction 'Clear a register and carry'. Arithmetic operations such as combining Add and Add Carry are other examples. There are however some more sophisticated examples as follows:

(a) *The multiply and divide routines*, introduced in Section 3.5.5.

(b) *Load and store all the CPU registers*, e.g.

ST0, 100
ST1, 101 $\equiv$ STALL, 100
ST2, 102

These instructions are used in interrupt service routines, as will be explained later. They can also be used in power-fail servicing. Note that the one operand, 100 in the example, implies an array of locations *starting* at 100.

(c) *Double precision operations.* Such operations as 'double precision add' require four words of data; the two lower significant words are added and the carry is then added along with the two higher significant words. The add, add carry and the second add can be specified as one instruction, thus, if R0 is implied in the single ADD instruction:

DADD, n

adds the double precision word stored in memory locations n and n + 1 to the double precision word stored in R0 and R1, leaving the result in R0 and R1.

Some machines have a separate flag register which specifies single or double precision operation, the same instruction mnemonics being used, effectively giving an extra bit to the instruction; the programmer must be careful to allocate one or two words for the data as appropriate. The flag is set by a separate instruction. This is a very powerful technique since most of the instruction set can be usefully employed. Thus, rather similar to (b) above, transferring data between two registers and two consecutive memory locations, becomes one instruction.

Note that, whether a double/single precision flip-flop is used or an extra set of instructions somehow incorporated, only one operand is used to specify the data, two consecutive numbered memory locations or registers being implied in double precision. Long shifts are further examples.

(d) *An Exchange instruction*; this moves the contents of one location to a temporary register, the contents of a second location to the first location and the contents of the temporary register to the second location. Particularly useful between a CPU register and a memory location.

(e) *A memory scan instruction*. Registers are used to specify the start of an array in memory and either the last address or the number of words in the array. The array is then 'scanned', each word in turn being brought into the CPU as the start address is incremented, and compared with the contents of a specific register. The scan is stopped either when the end of the array or a match is reached. Thus the existence and location of a specific word in memory can be detected.

Looking through the minicomputer manufacturers' literature a number of specially configured instructions will appear. Some are very powerful in specific applications areas, but they may well be 'window dressing'.

3·6 Stack Operations

The principle of stacking data in an array is related to the 'last-in, first-out' principle (LIFO). An array located in memory used for this purpose is called a *Push-down Stack* or simply a *Stack*. A register inside the CPU is allocated to track the location of the 'top' of the stack; this register, which may be a general register allocated the task by the programmer, is called the *stack pointer* (S.P.).

The stack pointer is loaded initially with the address of the first memory location of the array allocated as the stack; the length of the stack, i.e. the number of contiguous memory locations used, is determined by the programmer. Any area of memory can be allocated as the stack.

The first piece of data to be placed on the stack is transferred to the memory location addressed by the current contents of the stack pointer; this can be done using an index mode with zero displacement. The stack pointer contents are then incremented (or decremented) by one; incrementing uses memory locations starting at the initial value and increasing in address, decrementing decreases the address, e.g. to use locations 300 to 500 inclusive as a stack, the initial address is 300 if the stack pointer is incremented, 500 if decremented. Data can be added to the stack by repeating the process, the stack pointer pointing to the next available location. To take data off the stack, the stack pointer must first be decremented (or incremented) before being used to address the data. Data is said to be *pushed* onto the stack and *popped* off of it.

Using the mnemonic code for the DUMB 1 instructions, the following program could be used, with R2 acting as the stack pointer:

100	300	the start address of the stack
101	LD2 100	load start address in s.p. (R2)*
102	ST0 2, 0	store contents of R0 into location
		(0 + contents of R2) = 300.
103	INC 2	move s.p. on
104	LD0 1000	move some data from locations 1000
105	LD1 1001	and 1001 into the CPU
106	ST0 2, 0	store contents of R0 on stack
107	INC 2	move SP on
108	ST1 2, 0	store contents of R1 on stack
109	INC 2	move SP on
⋮		
300		Area to be used as the stack starting here
301		
⋮		

Assume now that R2 is dedicated as the stack pointer, then instructions 102, 106 and 108, each followed by INC 2 are similar except that one of the other two registers, R0 or R1, must be specified as the location of the data to be stacked. Thus a new instruction can be

---

* The instruction LD2 300 could be used; LD2 3,0 would be in location 100 and 300 in location 101. See Section 3.4.1.2.

defined to replace the block of code, i.e.

PUSH 1 is equivalent to ST1 2,0
INC 2

In addition

PUSH X is equivalent to LD? X
ST? 2, 0
INC 2

where X is an operand defined by the usual addressing modes. The ? has been used in the equivalent code since there is no need to transfer the data from the MBR to a register and then from a register to the MBR to execute the store. The PUSH instruction therefore transfers data from a memory location onto the stack, without using other registers.

Similarly

POP X is equivalent to DEC 2
LD? 2, 0
ST? X

which takes the piece of data from the top of the stack and stores it at X.

The autoincrement and autodecrement addressing modes, when available, allow stacking to be readily incorporated. The PDP-11, briefly discussed in Section 3.4.2, has autoincrement and autodecrement modes, coupled with double operand addressing. Thus the instruction

MOV X, (SP) +

which means move data from X to the location whose address is indicated by the contents of the register SP and then increment that register's contents, is directly equivalent to PUSH X, while

MOV −(SP), X

is directly equivalent to POP X. Any of the 8 PDP-11 registers, except the PC, could be used as the stack pointer, but certain hardware features automatically assume one specific register. Note that the autoincrement mode increments *after* using the address, the autodecrement decrements *before*, as required by a LIFO stack.

As a point of convention, which must be adhered to because of the hardware utilisation, the PDP-11 'grows' the stack with decreasing addresses to that

PUSH X ≡ MOV X, −(SP)
and POP X   ≡ MOV (SP)+, X

Note that the initial address to be set in the stack pointer should be one word higher than the first stack location because of the decrement before use.

There are two fundamental areas in which stack processing can be applied, (a) to save information relating to a program when its normal operation has to be temporarily suspended; data such as the CPU register contents are pushed onto the stack, so that the interrupting routine can use them, and then popped off stack to their original locations so that processing can continue as though never interrupted. (b) in a form of arithmetic calculations known as *Polish mode*.

3·6·1 Stacks Used with Subroutines

The use of a stack in interrupt servicing will not be discussed until the need for such interventions in the simple program sequence have been established, namely in the next chapter. The stack can however be used to advantage in subroutine calls and returns, these being a program dictated break in the sequential execution of instructions, which, unlike a jump, must retain contact with the particular 'jump-to-subroutine' instruction, as previously explained in Section 2.8.2.1. In that section the technique was expounded of using the first memory location of the subroutine to automatically store the address following the JSR instruction, which can then be used to locate data (the argument list, remembering that there may be many calls, each with specific data, to the same subroutine) and to enable the return from the subroutine.

A faster subroutine technique is to allocate a special CPU register to store the current PC contents, rather than a memory location. By using the stack, any one of the general CPU registers available can be indiscriminately used. Thus the JSR r, FRED instruction causes the contents of register r to be pushed onto the stack and the current contents of the PC, which now points to the address following the JSR instruction, to be copied into register r. The address corresponding to FRED is then copied into the PC, effecting entry to the subroutine. Inside the subroutine, register r can then be used as a pointer to data related to the call, which would be stored in the locations following the JSR instruction. Each time a data word is accessed using register r as a pointer, the contents of that register must be incremented. If there are n pieces of data associated with the subroutine, there must be exactly n data locations following the JSR instruction. The subroutine terminates with a Return instruction (RTS) which causes the contents of register r to be copied into the PC and also re-establishes the original contents of register r by popping the stack.

The real power of the technique just explained lies in the fact that subroutine calls can be 'nested' and made 're-entrant' as will be explained in Section 7.4.3. Nested subroutines, i.e. one subroutine calls another, which calls another, etc., are possible since the contents of register r will be pushed onto the stack by successive calls and then popped off in the last on–first off order required. Note however that each subroutine must terminate correctly, e.g. a jump or branch instruction must not miss out an RTS instruction or else the stack pointer will get out of step, with disastrous results!

3·6·2 Polish Mode Arithmetic

Polish notation is an arithmetical or logical notational system using only operands and operators arranged in a sequence (or string) in such a way as to eliminate the use of factor boundaries, e.g. parenthesis.

Consider the simple example, using the 'normal' notation,

$$A = B + C$$

The essential feature of expressing this equation as a 'polish string' is to place the operator e.g. $+, -, \times, \div$, etc. *after* a pair of operands, rather than *between* them. The expression is evaluated from left to right, using the result of a previous operation where appropriate; the string is terminated by the left side of the normal equation, thus the above expression in Polish notation is:

$$BC + A =$$

Similarly the expression

$$A = (B + C) . (D + E)$$

is equivalent to the Polish string.

$$BC + DE + \times A =$$

This is evaluated as B and C added together; D and E added together; multiply the two immediately previous current operands which are now the results of the two sums; equate A to the immediately previous operator, which is the desired result.

The main rules for converting the right-hand side of a 'normal' arithmetic expression into a Polish string are shown in figure 3.16. Note the temporary use of the Delimiter List while building the string.

The importance of Polish mode expressions can be directly related to the use of stacks. This is of specific importance in certain larger computers, the architectures of which are built around stacks and

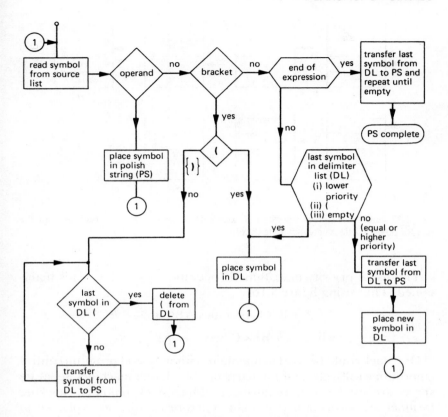

Fig. 3·16 Flow chart for converting a 'normal' arithmetic expression into a Polish string

which use the Polish strings as integral parts of the compilers, and multi-programming executives.

Thus to evaluate the above Polish string:

(i) push B onto stack

(ii) push C onto stack

(iii) pop stack into adder; pop stack into adder; push result onto stack.

(iv) push D onto stack

(v) push E onto stack

(vi) pop stack into adder; pop stack into adder; push result onto stack.

(vii) pop stack into multiplier; pop stack into multiplier; push result onto stack.

(viii) pop stack and store at A.

This is shown in figure 3.17.

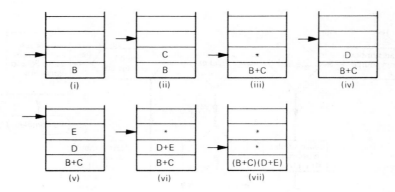

Fig. 3·17 Successive stack operations. Locations marked * are not modified, but the pointer position effectively eliminates them.

The usual priority in arithmetic operations ($\times$, $\div$, $+$, $-$) is maintained. Thus using figure 3.16

$$A + B \times C \text{ becomes } ABC \times +$$

$$\text{while } (A + B) \times C \text{ becomes } AB + C\times$$

One stack could be used to maintain arithmetic and program control (subroutine calls, etc.). Often, particularly in larger machines, separate stacks are established, requiring multiple stack pointers. Stacking facilities are incorporated in many microprocessors, as explained in Section 5.4.7.

3·7 Resumé

In Chapter 2 a relatively simple digital computer was developed, in which all the suggested instructions could be incorporated in the order code, within the constraint of the 16 bit word. In this chapter a number of further instructions and related details, e.g. addressing modes, have been introduced. No attempt has been made to include these extensions into the previously developed instruction set; it will of course be impossible to incorporate all possible instructions and modes in any one machine.

A number of techniques have been suggested to extend the instruction set. In particular the dedicated use of specific registers has been outlined, a technique which avoids the necessity of defining which register is to be used in the instruction, but which reduces the versatility. The alternative, or indeed additional, technique of using multiple word instructions, again often making specific uses of internal registers, has also been outlined.

The techniques introduced in this chapter are by no means an exhaustive list. A bare minimum has been said to date about I/O, since the next chapter is devoted to this topic, and Chapter 8 is used to discuss further techniques which are commonly encountered, but which are considered rather more than fundamental.

Chapter 4

Input/Output

4·1 Basic I/O Considerations

The modern digital computer, of all sizes, is essentially a general purpose machine. The dedicated fields of application are related more to the peripheral devices used, than to the computer itself, provided the computer has adequate processing power. Thus the CPU has evolved around an efficient internal structure, to some extent with disregard to the outside world. In particular two's complement binary arithmetic is an efficient internal system, but one not directly related to human assimilation. Binary coded decimal (BCD) arithmetic is far easier from the input and display viewpoint, but less efficient in terms of electronic storage and manipulation. Thus only those devices which are dominated by simple keyboard input and decimal displays, with relatively low speed arithmetic requirements, such business machines and calculators, would use BCD.

In the conventional digital computer, programs must be written to take data from particular input devices and to convert received data strings into pure binary form before being manipulated. Similarly data to be communicated with the outside world must be processed into a suitable form before transmission, e.g. an internal 16 bit number is

126

converted into a string of five decimal digits, each converted to the equivalent ASCII character. Thus, as shown in figure 4.1, two interfaces are required to attach a peripheral to the computer, (i) a 'Software Interface' to process the data to or from binary form as required by the peripheral design and (ii) a 'Hardware Interface', an electronic controller which allows communications to proceed.

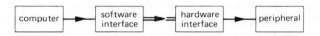

Fig. 4·1 CPU/peripheral communication

The actual design of the peripheral will determine the program required to effect the software interface. Such programs are usually termed *device drivers* and are discussed in Section 7.7.1. The peripherals are discussed separately in Chapter 6, although many features will be introduced during this chapter.

The three fundamental types of I/O operation will be unfolded in this chapter, (i) Programmed I/O, (ii) Data break and (iii) Direct memory access.

The first two use the I/O bus mentioned during the two previous chapters. The third requires more extensive hardware modification to allow access to the memory without CPU intervention. (ii) and (iii) are used for high speed transmission of blocks of data.

Most peripheral devices are electro-mechanical and as such are fundamentally slower than the CPU. Thus if the computer needs to send two consecutive pieces of data to the same peripheral, it must wait until the first piece of data has been accepted and used before further data can be transmitted. The alternative is for the computer to send the first piece of data and then continue with some other task. When the peripheral is ready to accept the next piece of data, a signal is sent to the computer which causes a pause in the current program; the computer sends the next piece of data and then returns to the program it was executing when the pause was requested by the peripheral. This is known as an *interrupt* and is used only with programmed I/O. Block data I/O can be considered as a special sort of interrupt operation.

4·2 Programmed I/O Data Transfer

An introduction to programmed I/O was given in Sections 2.6 and 2.8.5. To recap there are four types of instruction:

(i) input data (peripheral to CPU)
(ii) output data (CPU to peripheral)
(iii) control some function in the peripheral
(iv) test or sense the state of the peripheral

4·2·1 Input and Output Data Operations

The peripheral device must be capable of communicating its current state to the computer, otherwise there will be nothing to stop new data being transmitted before the previous data is finished with. The commonly encountered *busy* and *done* flags, which are set to 1 when the device is completing and has completed, respectively, were introduced in Section 2.8.5. Other 'state-of-the-peripheral' flags will be built into the interface if required by a specific peripheral, with appropriate skip-type test instructions defined.

The data transfer operations cause data to be placed on the I/O bus, connecting one of the CPU registers and the buffer register in the selected peripheral. The instruction must include information, defining which particular peripheral is being serviced; this information is decoded by the interfaces, enabling one and only one device, as shown in Section 2.6.

Most input instructions simply transfer data from the peripheral via the I/O bus to one of the CPU registers. One useful modification is to save the logical AND of the incoming data and the initial contents of the receiving register; in this way certain unwanted bits of the data accepted can be masked out.

Byte orientated I/O instructions are common. They are in fact similar to the normal word instruction except that the unused half word is either left unaltered or definitely cleared to zero, dependent upon byte memory storage details as discussed in Section 3.5.1.

I/O data operations and test functions may be combined into one instruction. Thus an output type instruction may repeatedly test the busy flag and send the data as soon as it is clear, i.e. from the programs in Section 2.8.5.

PRINT r, d

is equivalent to

SKBYC d
JMP 3, −2
OUT r, d

Similarly

READ r, d

is equivalent to

ENB d
SKDNS d
JMP 3, −2
IN r, d

Note the execution timing for both these instructions is indeterminate, since the peripheral, not the CPU, will determine how many loops are needed before an operation is completed. These operations are something more than simple microprograms of multiple instructions into one instruction, see Section 2.8.4.4, since the individual instruction executions cannot be slotted together in time. The print and read instructions would require quite specific hardware.

4·2·2 Control Functions

In addition to transferring data to and from peripherals, many features of these devices can be controlled by instructions from the CPU. The most obvious example is to turn a device on or off; another example was introduced in Section 2.8.5 where an *enable* flag in the paper tape reader interface could be set, which caused a frame of the tape to be read. The advantage to be gained by using the control function I/O instructions, is that the peripherals can be automatically computer controlled.

Many control functions are essentially two state operations, i.e. set or clear a flag, the interface being designed to appropriately respond to the state of that flip-flop. Note the indirect nature of the operation, the computer controls only the flag, the interface is specifically designed to react to the flip-flop. Interface hardware will be discussed in Section 4.5.

In addition to the done, busy and device enable flags, an *interrupt enable* flag is also commonly encountered, the use of which is explained in Section 4.3.

Other peripherals require rather more complex control functions so that instead of one or two independent flag flip-flops, the interface contains a multiple bit register. This register acts as a buffer for control information and can be loaded from or read into the computer as though it were a data buffer. Loading of this buffer is treated not as a simple control operation, but as a normal data I/O operation. The control register is allocated an address of its own, so that there will probably be more than one device address allocated to one peripheral. The register can be established by manipulating data inside the CPU, probably using logical and masking instructions, and then transferring it with an OUT instruction. Some combinations of this register can also be used to give the peripheral status information, so that it can be read into the CPU by an IN instruction and interrogated by a program. This would not be as simple as specialised test operations, i.e. SKBYC, but may provide more versatility for more sophisticated peripherals.

As an example of this technique consider a multiple channel *analogue-to-digital-convertor* (ADC) system. The input multiplexor may scan consecutive channels or it may be possible to select any specific channel. The control register allocates one bit to select scan or single channel mode and other bits to address the desired channel. Loading the address will probably cause the channel to be selected and the conversion to commence; busy and done bits as well as an interrupt signal will also be needed. A more sophisticated ADC may have program controlled gain setting of the amplifiers and a number of selectable scan rates. Thus more than one word length control register, or two consecutive entries into the one register, may well be needed. Further details of ADC systems are given in Section 6.7.

In summary when a peripheral has few control requirements, special I/O control function instructions can be specified, dealing with single bit flags. For more complex control requirements full buffer registers of control flip-flops are used, serviced by the normal data I/O instructions.

4·2·3 Virtual Memory I/O

This technique was first mentioned in Section 3.3.4, figure 3.8(b). Both the memory and all the buffer registers in the peripheral interface are connected, via controlled gates of course, to a single data bus. Each peripheral buffer register is allocated an address as though it were an extension of memory. Typically on a machine with an addressing range of 32K words, the last* 4K i.e. addresses 28672 to 32767, are allocated to peripherals, leaving 28K of memory possible, all of which may not be physically supplied.

The advantages of this system are:

(a) Special I/O instructions are simply not required. To output data to a peripheral a STr d type instruction will suffice, where d is the address of the buffer register. Similarly a LDr d acts as an input instruction. As no I/O instructions are defined, the use of a register for test and control purposes, as described in the previous sub-section, is commonly employed.

(b) All the memory reference instructions, not just store and load, can be used.

---

* 1K would be ample, but memory is usually available in 4K blocks. The restriction to 32K 16 bit words indicates the existence of byte addressing to 64K bytes.

(c) Data can be transferred from one peripheral buffer register to another, without intermediate use of a CPU register. This however requires a special 'double operand' form of instruction set, discussed in Section 3.4.2, in order to take advantage of this practical possibility.

The disadvantages are:

(a) A reduction in the maximum memory size.

(b) One device must take control of the bus (master) which can then transfer data to any other device (slave); thus even for memory reference instructions, time is wasted in acquiring control of the bus, over and above the normal memory cycle time.

The virtual memory concept is extended in some machines to include bulk store, i.e. disk, as an addressable extension of memory. This is associated with a rather complex operating system, Section 7.8.5.

4·3 Interrupt Systems

4·3·1 The Need for an Interrupt System

The I/O program examples given in Section 2.8.5 highlight the problem created by the relatively slow speed of the peripheral when compared to the computer. The straight forward programmed I/O used in Section 2.8.5 and discussed further in Section 4.2 uses a test and loop instruction to cause the computer to 'idle' until the peripheral is ready. This means that the apparent speed of the computer is tied to that of the peripheral. Clearly if a number of peripherals need servicing by the computer, they would have to queue for attention, whereas a high speed computer should be capable of servicing a number of slow speed peripherals apparently simultaneously. Actually, since the computer executes instructions one at a time, multiple peripherals can only be serviced *apparently* simultaneously. In fact the computer should service one peripheral then move to another, and then another, etc. and be capable of returning to give new data to the original peripheral by the time it is ready to receive it, *ad infinitum.*

It is apparent therefore that in most cases the computer cannot be allowed to idle on one peripheral. Thus an entirely different mode of operation is used. Instead of the peripheral being purely submissive, the CPU being required to execute an instruction to determine the current state, it can have the power to 'give the computer a nudge' and ask for some attention when, and only when, it is ready to be serviced. It requests an *interrupt.*

Thus the peripheral is set in motion, either by a computer command, e.g. a control type I/O operation, or by an external event, e.g. striking a key on a keyboard; it then proceeds to completion, entirely independent of the computer. Meanwhile the computer continues with some other task, until the peripheral completes, when it makes a request to the CPU for service. The program the computer is currently executing completes the current instruction and is then suspended. The computer now proceeds to execute the program which services the peripheral. When the service program is completed the machine returns to continue the previous program at the instruction following the one that was interrupted.

Major problems arise in the above example:

(a) *Priority*. When the interrupt is requested the computer may be executing a particularly important program, e.g. a teletype interrupt request must not be allowed to halt a program that is servicing a high speed ADC; thus each peripheral must have an allocated interrupt priority; when an interrupt is requested its priority is compared with that of the program being executed. A higher priority interrupt will be allowed, but a lower or equal one must wait until the current program finishes. With a bad design, the data from a low priority device could be destroyed before it has been accepted by the computer.

(b) *Identification of the source of the interrupt*. Each peripheral has a flag which can be set by the computer to *enable interrupt*. Thus any of the peripherals in which the interrupt system is enabled may have generated the interrupt. A number of systems will be discussed for solving the problem of determining which peripheral is requesting an interrupt. Once the interrupting peripheral has been detected, and the interrupt allowed, then information is available to cause a jump in the program to a subroutine written to service that particular device. This is similar to a jump to subroutine instruction except that it is inserted in the program at a random point, determined by the timing of the interrupt.

(c) *Continuation of the interrupted program*. Each interrupt service routine should finish with an instruction similar to a return from subroutine. A system must be devised for saving the current PC contents when the interrupt is allowed, which can then be copied back into the PC to continue the program. It is quite likely that the peripheral service routine will use the CPU registers and condition flags; if this is so each service routine should store the original contents of the registers and flags in memory as its first move and restore them immediately before the return.

It must be noted that each peripheral service routine is usually in itself a normal I/O program except that the idling loop has been eliminated. An interrupt system is then another way of utilising programmed I/O data transfers. DMA on the other hand is an alternative data transfer system.

4·3·2 A Simple Interrupt System

A simple interrupt system will be explained here and possible refinements discussed in the following sections.

Each peripheral controller has an interrupt enable flag which can be set or cleared by a computer I/O control instruction. A second flag, the done flag, indicates that the device is ready to be serviced. If the interrupt enable is clear, then as previously described, the computer must test the done flag under program control, there is no way in which the peripheral can communicate with the computer. If the interrupt enable and done flags are set then this condition is recognised by the computer and will set the interrupt procedure in motion. This condition is flagged to the computer by an *interrupt Request* flag, which is set when both interrupt enable and done are set.

The interrupt procedure must first complete the current instruction; since the interrupt may occur near the end of an instruction execution, sufficient time may not be available to implement the interrupt procedure so that the interrupt request is 'synchronised' immediately, but may only be admitted at the end of the next full instruction. At this time the PC points to the source of the next instruction, which is the point at which the interrupted program must resume when the interrupt has been serviced. Note that this can be at any point in the original program. Thus the current PC contents must automatically be saved; memory location 0 is often reserved for this purpose. Similarly memory location 1 is reserved to indicate the starting address of the interrupt service routine, so that the contents of this location are copied into the PC, to complete the transfer to the interrupt routine.

When the interrupt has been serviced, control can be passed back to the original program simply by copying the contents of location 0 into the PC; this is achieved by terminating the interrupt routine with an indirect jump on location 0, often given a mnemonic such as RTI (return from interrupt).

If there were only one peripheral device the system just described would be completely adequate. More than the one peripheral is however the norm, so that further considerations must be taken.

When one peripheral has interrupted, further interrupts must be stopped until the current one has been serviced. Thus there is an *interrupt-on* flag in the CPU, in addition to the interrupt enable flags in the device interfaces, which must also be set before an interrupt request is accepted. The CPU interrupt-on flag is automatically cleared when the save PC, etc. routine is entered and must be set immediately before the return from interrupt.

The first task of the interrupt service routine is to determine which device requested the interrupt. This part of the routine could be termed the 'interrupt handler' which will pass control to an appropriate subroutine, of which there will be one per peripheral device. The address of the handler is pre-stored in location 1, common to all interrupts.

The simplest handler is a *software-polling* system which, using I/O test instructions, checks each peripheral in turn to determine whether or not it is requesting an interrupt. This can be done by testing the interrupt request flag. Such a program is shown below, assuming five devices.

0		save PC contents
1	1020	start address of interrupt handler
2	2000	start address of device 1 service routine
3	2050	start address of device 2 service routine
⋮		
6	3000	start address of device 5 service routine
1020	SKIRC 1	skip next instruction if device 1 not requesting interrupt
1021	JMP * 2	device 1 requesting interrupt (indirect jump to location 2000)
1022	SKIRC 2	test device 2 for interrupt request
1023	JMP * 3	device 2 requesting interrupt
⋮		
1028	SKIRC 5	test device 5
1029	JMP * 6	device 5 requesting interrupt
1030	HLT	error!
2000		subroutine to service device 1
⋮		
	INTON	set CPU interrupt-on
	JMP * 0	return
2050		subroutine to service device 2

etc.

Note the use of indirect jumps to the service routines via page 0 to overcome the range of addresses possible.

As previously mentioned, if, as is possible, any of the service routines use any of the CPU registers in addition to the PC, they will corrupt the data being used by the interrupted program. Thus the first instructions in each service subroutine must save the contents of each of the registers to be subsequently used, in allocated memory locations; the instructions immediately prior to the INTON instruction must restore the original register contents.

Equally as important as any registers used, the program should also save and restore the condition flags, carry, overflow, zero and negative, since they will certainly be affected. In the previous chapters no instructions have been provided to achieve this. Rotating a register and saving the new contents (after saving the original) will effectively save C but new instructions must be defined for the others. Quite the best method is to treat each of the flags as one bit of a full 16 bit status register, and define instructions to store and restore it. If, as in the instruction set of Chapter 2, another memory reference instruction cannot be specified a non-memory reference instruction can be used to copy the status word into a register and then store that registers' contents.

4·3·3 Identification of the Interrupting Device

In the previous section software polling was used to identify the particular peripheral requesting an interrupt. This is a slow method since the handler program must be executed (until the device is located) at every interrupt, before the actual service routine commences. For the example program, in the worst case of device 5, after the interrupt occurs there will be one instruction (one or two cycles in the DUMB 1, but perhaps more in other machines) to allow synchronisation, one cycle to store PC in location 0, one cycle to load PC from location 1, five skip operations (one cycle each, although since they are I/O instructions they will be extended cycles on some machines) and one cycle for the JMP, a total of nine or ten cycles at least. There are further reasons associated with priority that make this technique suitable only for simple systems.

On some machines a special I/O instruction is defined which can be executed as the interrupt handler. This instruction, called *interrupt acknowledge*, causes the address of the interrupt requesting peripheral to be copied into one of the CPU registers. This register can be used to cause a branch to the appropriate service routine.

A simple modification is to use a special register to save the PC contents rather than memory location 0. The interrupt procedure is now similar to a conventional jump to subroutine instruction, using an indirect address, as previously described in Section 2.8.2.1. The same register can be used for interrupt and normal subroutine calls, provided that some protection is introduced. This is done by causing either an interrupt or a JSR to clear the CPU interrupt-on flag; the program can then save the contents of the register and set interrupt-on, restoring the register at the end of the routine, without an interrupt corrupting the return address.

A more extensive improvement is to provide extra hardware so that there are multiple interrupt lines, each using specific memory locations. The actual memory addresses are fixed by the hardware design. Thus an interrupt on line 1 stores the PC contents in say location 100 and copies the contents in location 101 into the PC; line 2 stores the PC contents in location 102 and copies the contents of location 103 into the PC, etc. A specific area of memory is reserved for this purpose just as locations 0 and 1 were used in the simple case. If one device only is attached to each line, then that device is automatically identified. If more than one device is attached to the one interrupt line, then, as before, the routine must poll to identify the interrupt source; however only the devices on that line need be polled. There could well be one line per peripheral device, but some priority considerations often place a constraint on their number in practice.

The automatic transfer of program control in response to an interrupt request is often called *vectored interrupt*, since the unique memory locations cause a specific directed change in the program sequence.

One method of achieving vectored interrupts without the proliferation of interrupt lines required by the above technique, is to cause a specific memory address to be placed on the I/O bus when acceptance of the interrupt is signalled by the processor. The actual memory address is hardwired into the peripheral controller and care must be taken not to allocate the same address to two peripherals; the vector address to memory is not the same as the peripheral address. The interrupt procedure then uses the address on the I/O bus as a pointer to the dedicated memory locations for storing the PC and the subroutine start address. In summary a device requests an interrupt; the processor accepts the interrupt and completes the current instruction (and possibly a complete one as well); a signal is then sent from the CPU to indicate that it is prepared to service the interrupt. This signal goes to all peripherals, but only the one with the interrupt request flag set acts on it. The interface so selected then enables gates which connect a pre-wired memory address to the data bus. The CPU hardware then takes this address and commences the save PC, etc. Note that this versatile system requires rather more specialised hardware, including an increase in the device controller complexity.

The obvious advantage of vectored interrupts is the low time that exists between an interrupt being accepted and the specific service routine commencing; this time interval is termed *interrupt latency*.

4·3·4 Priority Systems

In the foregoing it has been implicitly assumed that only one interrupt at a time will occur and that it can be serviced before another one arrives. With a multi-peripheral system this is untrue. However, by not setting the interrupt-on flag in the CPU, which is automatically cleared when the interrupt is accepted, until the return instruction, any further interrupts will be ignored. For this reason the CPU is designed so that it executes at least one further instruction following an INTON instruction so that the return can be completed.

If an interrupt request is still set it will immediately cause another interrupt, not allowing one instruction of the original program to continue until this new interrupt is serviced. The flaw with this system is that the second interrupt may require very fast attention but the service routine for the first interrupt may be long, so long in fact that the second interrupt data may be lost before it gains CPU attention. In short the second interrupt may be of a higher priority than the first. Each interrupt must be granted a level of priority and the system must be modified so that a higher priority interrupt request can cause the service routine of a lower priority to be itself interrupted, e.g. nesting of interrupts. Examples are shown in figure 4.2. The system should be so designed that interrupts can be nested to any level. The notation that priority level 1 is the highest will be adopted here

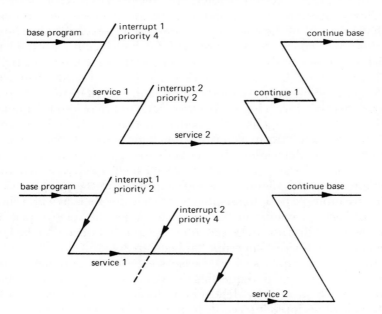

Fig. 4·2 Effect of interrupted interrupts and priority

The problems of determining which of a number of devices, each with their interrupt request flags set, has the highest priority, and that of allowing a higher priority interrupt to nest in are rather different.

Consider the former first. The simple software-polling technique has an inbuilt priority structure arranged by the order in which devices are tested. A second method is to arrange the interrupt acknowledge signal, sent from the CPU when an interrupt request is detected, to be 'daisy chained'. This means that the signal is passed to the first device on the bus, which is accepted as the interrupting device if its interrupt request flag is set. If the flag is clear, the device controller sends the interrupt acknowledge signal on to the next device, etc. The priority structure is determined by the order in which devices are connected in the chain. Thus the device physically closest to the CPU has the highest priority.

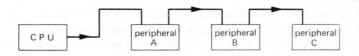

Fig. 4·3 Daisy chaining of interrupt acknowledge

In order to allow nesting of interrupts, the priority level of the device which is requesting an interrupt must be determined and compared with the priority of the interrupt currently being serviced. This should be done by dedicated hardware, without interfering with the CPU, which continues to execute instructions. If the new interrupt is of a higher level it will be accepted; if it is of a lower level it will be ignored. As long as the interrupt request continues to exist, it must be continually re-checked since a higher priority interrupt may join the queue.

If multiple interrupt lines are used, then a given priority level can be allocated to each. Priority determination logic in the CPU hardware can then be used to determine whether an interrupt can be allowed. Thus the priority of the peripherals is established when the system is configured, by the allocation of interrupt lines to the peripherals. If there are multiple peripherals attached to one line then, as with a single line, physical proximity to the CPU determines the relative priority. Note however that no device can interrupt another device on the same line once that devices' interrupt has been accepted.

Multiple interrupt lines were earlier suggested as a unique method of identifying interrupt requesting devices. They are however of more importance as a priority determining structure combined with the technique of vectored interrupts from hardware memory addresses in the controller; in this way devices on the same 'priority' line are still uniquely identified. This is shown schematically in figure 4.4. The address logic will only be required if the vector addresses are tied to the lines. Otherwise, as suggested above, unique addresses will be passed via the I/O bus. The internal interrupts indicated on figure 4.4 are generated by devices such as power fail detection, memory parity error, real time clock, etc.; these features will not be discussed until Chapter 8. Suffice it here to note that they usually are allocated high priorities, with power fail detection highest of all.

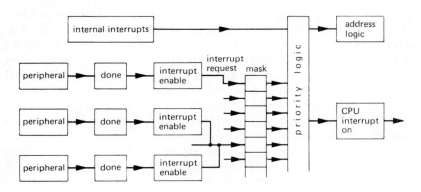

Fig. 4·4 Priority interrupt system

It must now be realised that the priority is fundamentally fixed by hardware when the system is configured. There are many examples however where the priority level could be advantageously controlled by a program. For example, a high priority is associated with a high speed ADC, which scans multiple channels rapidly. Once the data is read it is processed by the service program, but this is a relatively low priority task. There are a number of ways around this. One method is to give all interrupt lines equal priority but to enable, by program control, only devices which are considered to be of higher priority than the current service program. This must be changed at the beginning of each service routine, but it can, if appropriate, be changed during the routine. Each individual peripheral can have its interrupt enabled by specific I/O control instructions. This has obvious uses, but setting the current priority structure for each interrupt is too expensive in computer time, since each service routine would have to set or clear the interrupt in each peripheral, one instruction for each. Thus a mask register is provided which can, as any other register, be loaded as one word in one instruction. In effect there is one bit of the mask in each interrupt line; if that bit is zero, then interrupt requests from that line are ignored; if the mask bit is one, interrupt requests are passed

139

through. (The priority logic is not used in this system, or rather the mask is the priority logic!) Thus the mask will be set to a specific bit pattern at the beginning of each service routine, and of course may be changed during the routine. Thus use of a normal length register for the mask limits the number of interrupt lines to 16 in this system. With more than 16 peripherals, limited it should be recalled by the number of device addresses allocated in the I/O instructions, lines must be shared.

For systems where priority levels are allocated to the interrupt lines by hardware, there is a sophisticated method of program controlled priority. Assume for example that there are 16 priority levels. The single CPU interrupt-on register is replaced by a 16 level system, i.e. a 4 bit CPU register establishes a CPU priority level. The level of any requesting interrupt is compared with this register and allowed only if it is higher. The hardware level at which the peripheral requests interrupt and the level of the priority at which the service routine operates are completely independent. Obviously the programmer will normally set the CPU priority register to a level similar to that of the hardware, but not necessarily. This system creates one extra problem in that the CPU priority level is associated with the current program; if that program is interrupted a new priority level will be established by the new program. Thus the CPU priority level must be saved along with the PC contents when the interrupt is allowed and restored on return. One method used is to share the CPU 'status register' along with the C, Z, N and V flags.

4·3·5 Other Interrupt Features

In the simplest systems with only one set of dedicated memory locations; i.e. locations 0 for saving the PC and 1 for the handler routine start address; each routine must make a copy of the contents of location 0 before enabling the CPU interrupt-on flag if nesting of interrupts is to be allowed. Otherwise the nesting interrupt, which must use the same location, will corrupt the return information. This is less of a problem with multiple interrupt lines and is completely eliminated with vectored interrupts since specific locations are dedicated to each device.

Stacks can be used for interrupt handling, just as they can be used for subroutine handling, Section 3.6.1. When an interrupt is recognised the current PC contents are automatically pushed onto the stack, rather than a dedicated memory location; the return from interrupt merely requires the top of the stack to be 'popped' into the PC. A dedicated memory location is still required for the service routine start address.

Nested interrupts are handled with no further consideration since the last in–first out characteristic of the stack assures correct nesting. Indeed the same stack can be used for subroutine calls as for the interrupts, with one word of warning to check that return instructions cannot be missed out by inadvertent JMP instructions!

It has already been mentioned that any registers, particularly the status register, used by an interrupt service routine should be saved and restored after use. Some machines automatically save all registers as well as the PC and status flags (possibly on the stack). This is quicker than using a set of instructions to save the register contents, but may be time wasteful since all the registers are not used by every subroutine. Other machines define two separate instructions to save and restore all registers starting at a specified memory location.

In all the systems so far explained the interrupt servicing begins by automatically copying a subroutine address from a memory location into the PC, after saving the original PC contents; in other words a JMS operation is simulated. A variant on the theme is to save an *instruction* in the dedicated interrupt location, the interrupt service then merely copies this instruction into the IR and proceeds from there. The obvious instruction is a JMS instruction so that the net effect of this and the previous methods is the same, except that the calculation of the effective address of the JMS instruction may require an extra cycle, dependent upon the addressing mode used, i.e. an indirect address from page 0 is common. If however the interrupt can be serviced by one instruction only, then this instruction can be stored in the interrupt location; copying it from memory under command of the interrupt system logic, rather than normal program control, means that the PC is unaffected, so that the normal program continues without noticing the single inserted instruction, provided that it does not corrupt any register information. Counting of external events is a simple example, the interrupt instruction simply incrementing a memory location's contents. More sophisticated single instructions may transfer 'blocks' of data, as shown in Section 4.4.1.

In summary when an interrupt is requested, its priority must be compared with that of the current level associated with the program executing; this may be set by the hardware level at which the current program was started or by a CPU priority level register. Alternatively interrupts considered of lower priority may have been 'masked' out. If the interrupt is allowed, the requesting device must be identified and the appropriate service routine initiated. Memory locations are dedicated as routine pointers for each interrupt line or by hardwired addresses in the peripheral controllers. The current PC contents must be saved, either in dedicated memory locations, a special CPU register or on a stack, which can then be used to return after servicing the interrupt. It is desirable that the processor status, i.e. status flags and interrupt level, should be automatically saved and restored along with the PC contents. The CPU register contents which will be altered by the service routine should also be saved and restored; sometimes this is automatically achieved along with the PC and status data.

4·4 Block Data transfer

The I/O techniques described to date are ideally suited to handling data that is available as single pieces of information. Even a simple service routine to read and save data will require around ten instructions added to the time taken to acknowledge an interrupt and begin the routine. With a $1\,\mu$ second cycle time, of the order of $20\,\mu$ seconds should be allowed for each data transfer. Many peripheral devices require to transfer 'blocks' of data to or from the computer at much faster rates than the 50K words/second implied above.

The common devices which require high speed block data transfer are bulk storage devices such as magnetic disc, drum or tape. These block data transfers are characterised by the simplicity of the processing, normally requiring just transfer to or from memory, using contiguous locations in memory at that.

Certain high speed peripherals can be considered as block data devices too. A common example occurs in transient data analysis, where a short duration dynamic signal is sampled and passed to the computer via an ADC. Ideally each data point should be processed as it arrives, but if the rate is too high, the sequence of samples is stored as a block of data and then processed after the event.

There are a number of ways in which block data can be handled, ranging from special I/O instructions using the normal I/O bus, to dedicated hardware direct memory access (DMA) channels. These are often grouped as non-program controlled I/O, but this can be misleading since normal I/O operations are usually involved in setting up the block data device, if not in the actual data transfer.

All block data transfers must in one way or another specify the following:
(a) the device address*
(b) the starting address of the array in memory
(c) the number of words of data in the block (word count).
(d) the direction of transfer (in or out).

---

* For a file structured device, e.g. a disc, the particular file identifier must also be specified.

4·4·1 Block Data via the I/O Bus

The simplest aid to block data transfer is to specify a single instruction to implement the input or output operation and the book keeping. Let these be called *augmented* I/O *instructions* with the mnemonics:

AIN d, WC, SA and AOUT d, WC, SA.

Since both a word count and a start address must be associated with these instructions, either two registers or two specific memory locations must be used. The latter is implied above, no register identifiers being used. The easy way is to use the two memory locations immediately following the AIN or AOUT code for the counter and pointer, so that these instructions are 3 words long, as indicated in figure 4.5. When the instruction is assembled the address of the location immediately before the first word of the array in memory is loaded into the third word of the instruction i.e. SA-1. The total number of words in the block is also loaded into the second word, i.e. WC.

n	AIN or AOUT
n+1	word count
n+2	memory location pointer

Fig 4·5 Automatic I/O instruction. The memory location pointer contains the address of the next word −1

When the instruction is executed the following sequence ensues:
(i) Fetch and decode the AIN or AOUT code. The PC is incremented as usual.
(ii) Increment the MAR and read the word count. Decrement the MBR before the restore cycle. If the result is zero increment the PC.
(iii) Increment the MAR and read the address pointer. This initially carries the required address −1; increment the MBR before the restore cycle. Increment the PC and copy the contents of the MBR into the MAR.*
(iv) Test the ready flag on device d and repeat until set. Then execute an input or output between device d and memory via the MBR. Increment the PC.

This instruction takes four memory cycles to execute if the data is immediately ready, but is the equivalent of a DSZ, an increment

* If the memory has an internal address buffer register, then the MAR can be changed during the restore cycle, see figure 3.7.

143

memory and an I/O instruction. Thus the following program inputs one hundred words of data into locations 1610 to 1709 from device 23. Note that no internal registers are used and the peripheral is responsible for presenting the correct data.

```
223   AIN 23 ⎫
224   100    ⎬  equivalent to AIN 23, 100, 1610
225   1609   ⎭
226   JMP 3, −4
227   data transfer completed
```

A clever modification of these instructions can be used with interrupt. In step (iv) there is no need to test the ready flag. In step (ii) if the count is zero a control signal is generated on the I/O control lines to inform the peripheral that data transfer is complete rather than increment the PC. The peripheral can then generate an independent interrupt to make the computer take appropriate action but not until the current instruction has completed steps (iii) and (iv). The significance is that the single (three word) instruction is the complete service routine, apart from the return instruction, and the block is transferred to memory with no interference with other programs other than enforcing periodic hold-ups of 5–10 cycles. Note also the significance with single instruction interrupts mentioned in Section 4.3.5. The result is a virtually CPU independent, or autonomous, peripheral-to-memory data channel. One feature of this system is that the interface required is no more complex than a conventional interface, but it is still relatively slow with maximum speeds of around 100 K words per second.

A limiting factor in the speed of data transmission by the above technique is the necessity to access memory twice, in addition to the data transfer for each word, in order to read the address pointer and the word count and to comply to an interrupt request. If the computer can be dedicated to the block data transfer task, inhibiting all other interrupts, then CPU registers can be utilised. Define another pair of single instructions similar to the three word AIN and AOUT but which transfer whole blocks of data rather than single words. These are termed *block data transfer instructions*, with mnemonics:

$$\text{BIN d, WC, SA and BOUT d, WC, SA.}$$

These assemble as three words, with the I/O code followed by word count and starting address as before. Let register R2 be dedicated as the counter or an additional special register may be provided. The instruction operates as follows:

(i) Fetch and decode the BIN or BOUT code, incrementing the PC.
(ii) Read next word, WC, into R2, incrementing the PC.

(iii) Read next word, SA, into MBR, restore and copy the contents of MBR into MAR. Increment the PC.

(iv) Repeatedly test device ready flag until set then transfer data, via MBR, between device d and memory. Decrement R2 and increment MAR.

(v) If contents of R2 are zero (z flag set) continue next instruction since transfer is complete. Otherwise repeat (iv).

It is because the MAR is effectively used as a location pointer that interrupts cannot be allowed during these instructions. Three memory cycles are required to 'prime' the transfer, and then, provided the data is available, only one cycle is required per data word. Note that this is in fact an I/O cycle which in some machines is longer than the usual memory cycle, but assuming a 1μ second cycle time, data can be transferred at 1 million words per second.

To enable the transfer to take place as an interrupt procedure, thus interleaving data transfer and normal program instructions, as with the AIN, AOUT modification previously mentioned, a compromise can be introduced. Dedicated word count and address pointer registers are built into the device controller. These registers can be set by conventional programmed I/O instructions to prime the transfer. The peripheral generates an interrupt when a data transfer is required; the service routine uses a three cycle variant of the AIN/AOUT instructions which takes one cycle to decode and then reads the pointer address register, via the I/O bus, into the MAR and then reads or writes the data, via the I/O bus, from or into memory; the I/O bus is effectively time-multiplexed by this instruction. Note that it must be one instruction; two normal I/O instructions cannot be used since the MAR will be corrupted by fetching the second instruction. Once the data transfer is sensed by the interface, the word count register is decremented; if this is zero an independent interrupt is generated to inform the computer that the transfer is complete. The data transfer interrupt is cleared, the address pointer register incremented and the process repeats to completion. Compared to the AIN/AOUT system, one memory cycle per word transferred is saved at the expense of increased interface complexity.

4·4·2 Autonomous I/O – Data Break

The system just described can be made more efficient by realising that the PC and CPU registers are unaffected. Therefore a conventional interrupt is not required, saving the PC, etc. A specialised interrupt, called a *data break*, can be requested which merely causes the normal operation to pause as soon as the end of an instruction is reached. Two special machine cycles can then be initiated which load first the MAR from the address pointer register and then transfer data. The program then continues unaffected until the next data break is requested by the next data transfer being ready. Since no interrupt must be accepted and no instruction fetched and decoded, only the two memory cycles are required, giving transfer rates of up to 500 K words/second. Note that special CPU hardware is required now as well as the increased sophistication of the interface.

A further improvement is realised if a separate I/O bus is provided to transmit the address information direct to the MAR. In this way address and data transfer can be implemented in the one memory cycle, giving maximum data transfer rates equivalent to the memory cycle time. To slightly simplify the interface design, a separate data bus, virtually in parallel to the normal I/O bus, is often used.

Since the address and word count are stored and updated in the device interface and not the CPU, any number of devices can share the data break facility, interleaving transfers at random. An independent priority structure is often built into the data break interfaces.

4·4·3 Direct Memory Access

The data break technique is essentially an I/O bus orientated method of data transfer. It was suggested that improvements could be made by providing independent address and data buses, dedicated to the data break, the former linking direct to the MAR and the latter the MBR. This has advantages in that control and identification of normal I/O and data break devices is independent. Nevertheless these additional buses are fundamentally paralleling up the normal I/O bus, so that the data break is in effect interleaving special I/O instructions with normal instructions; the CPU can give attention to either the normal instructions or the data break, but not both simultaneously. This leads to the concept of *direct memory access* (DMA) where the dedicated address and data buses are taken direct into the memory system, by-passing the MAR and MBR. The net result is that the CPU can continue processing operations while the DMA channel is transferring data quite independently. In effect the CPU and the DMA system are independent processors sharing the same memory; the latter being a singularly simple-minded processor! Only when both systems require simultaneous use of the memory does a clash occur. In this case the DMA channel is given priority over the CPU, and the processor is made to *hesitate*. Another phrase used to describe this action is *cycle stealing*.

A major comparison between DMA and data break is that the former can transfer data immediately a CPU instruction has completed a memory cycle, whereas the latter must wait for the full instruction to complete. Also some of the DMA transfers will take place while the CPU is executing non-memory functions. Note that on the machine described in Chapter 2, most execution operation coincides with memory restore cycles, so that only the I/O instructions leave cycles in which no use of memory is being made. Asynchronous operation, Section 3.2, with more sophisticated instructions, generates longer periods during which DMA can interleave without causing overmuch *hesitation*. It must be stressed however that if the DMA channels transfer data at full memory cycle speed, then it will *steal all* the memory cycles, effectively holding up the normal program completely.

To facilitate the direct access to memory, the address and data registers must be 'double buffered' as shown in figure 4.6; the actual

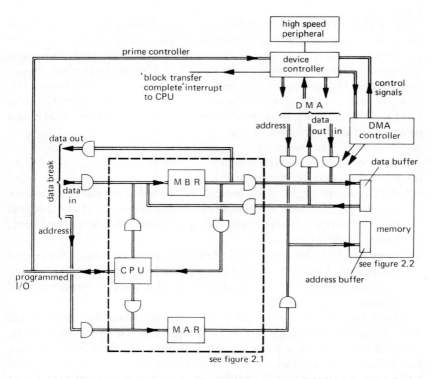

Fig. 4·6 A memory system with program controlled, data break and direct-memory access

memory buffer registers, see figure 2.2, can be linked to either the MBR and MAR in the CPU or to the DMA lines. Nevertheless the DMA channel requires a reasonable amount of additional hardware to implement the cycle stealing logic. The device controller is rather similar for both data break and DMA in that program controlled I/O transfers are required to set the word count and start address registers, etc.

Referring to figure 4.6 it can be appreciated that far more complex memory systems are possible, some comments on this are given in Chapter 8. In particular multiple access ports to the memory unit allow CPU and DMA to access different areas of memory simultaneously.

With a single bus structure; previously discussed in Section 3.3.4, see figure 3.8(b); the CPU execution is independent of the data transfers along the bus, which of course include memory transfers. The DMA controller gains mastery of the bus and transfers an address and data to memory, which is the slave, without any CPU controlled operations. This is a clear example of the device controller acting as a simple processor, with complete autonomy at the expense of interface hardware.

Since the DMA channel controller is a simple processor in itself, it is possible to increase the DMA capability by including simple arithmetic processing. This is most practically incorporated in the logic controller attached to the CPU/memory system, rather than the individual device controllers. The arithmetic processor is used to modify data before the restore cycle; with semiconductor memory it must simulate the read/modify/write cycle, if needed. Some of the capabilities that could be incorporated are listed below:

(a) Write data into memory
(b) Read data and restore memory
(c) Read data and clear memory
(d) Add to memory. Memory is read and added to the data on the DMA input line; the sum is then written into memory. If the address pointer is not incremented, the same location will be accessed, acting as an accumulator.
(e) Logical AND, OR or exclusive OR with memory. As (d) except that the result of the logical operation is returned to memory.
(f) Increment memory. No data is transmitted. Used to count external events.

The DMA processor is not program controlled like the CPU, but will have (some of) the above options implemented, one of which can be selected by a code, say 3 bits, which will be fed to the DMA controller from the requesting device interface. The particular action required will be programmed into the device controlled by normal programmed I/O, along with the word count and start address, when priming the device. Since the action code is transmitted in the one cycle along with the address and any data, devices can still be multiplexed to the DMA port, one of which, say, is simply inputting data, while the other is adding to memory.

On large computer systems the Data Channel, as it is more commonly called, has much greater processing power, so that routine book-keeping tasks such as decoding and sending standard messages to terminals, code checking and converting, data packing and unpacking, queuing and multiplexing of slower peripherals, etc. can be completed without wasting the relatively expensive CPU power. Such is the extent of these systems that minicomputers, complete with memory and fixed programs, are used as Data Channels on large processors. It is quite conceivable then, that dedicated microprocessors will be used as sophisticated DMA controllers on the more extensive minicomputer systems.

4·5 Interfaces and Device Controllers

Communication between the computer and the outside world must be the most important single feature of a computer system. With no input medium the computer is an idle giant, with no output devices an ideal information sink!

The electronic circuit which connects the peripheral device to the computer I/O systems is termed an interface. Some devices require extensive control, increasing the complexity of the interface. In many such cases the full interface components are split, part local to the computer (interface) and the rest to the peripheral (controller). Thus one peripheral may support a dedicated controller, linking to the computer via an interface; the same peripheral can then be linked to any other computer by the appropriate interface, utilising the same controller. The terms interface and controller are not rigorously defined and are regularly used synonymously.

Previously I/O systems have been discussed largely from the CPU viewpoint. The general principles of I/O bus systems so far introduced will be reviewed now and expanded from the viewpoint of the peripheral devices. In particular many of the requirements of an interface and device controller will be introduced, indicating the practical problems of connecting a peripheral device to the I/O bus.

It is not possible to explain in detail how to construct an interface to any computer, since the details will differ from one design of machine to another. The importance of studying the manufacturers detailed literature cannot be overstressed. One point that can be made however, is that buying interfaces from the computer manufacturer can be expensive. If one has the facilities, interface design is not too complex and implementation using the readily available MSI chips is quite practical and much cheaper. A number of MSI chips are now available which are specifically designed for use in this type of application, as will be mentioned during this chapter.

4·5·1 A Review of I/O Bus Systems

All communication between the peripherals and the CPU takes place along the I/O bus. Most machines have an I/O bus independent of CPU/memory transfers; those that do share the same bus for memory and peripheral data transfers are termed single bus systems.

Minicomputer bus structures are discussed in Section 3.3 and microprocessor bus organisation in Section 5.3.

The so called I/O bus in itself can be considered to contain a number of dedicated sub-buses, each of a differing number of wires. The following table indicates the possible sub-groups that may be encountered. As usual the direction of transfer, unless otherwise specified, is relative to the CPU.

Number of lines	Direction of 'flow'	Use
6–9	OUT	Peripheral address (or device number)
3–6	OUT	Function, either control or test
1–3	IN	Response to test function
16	OUT	Out data (to peripheral)
16	IN	Input data (from peripheral)
3–10	Both	Timing, synchronising, asynchronous response, etc.
3–30	Both	Interrupt request, acknowledge, priority, vectored memory location, etc.
3–20	Both	Data Break Control
1–4	Both	Parity checks

Fig.4·7 Table of possible I/O bus lines

With a single bus system the address must cover the full range of memory addresses, which include the peripheral addresses, necessitating sixteen address lines.

On some systems the control and test flags in the peripheral are grouped into one status register which is tested or modified by normal input or output instructions. This technique involves at least two registers per peripheral, data and status, so that while the function lines are not required, more address lines must be used. On other systems, say, six lines are used to address a peripheral and two other lines to select one of four registers in that device. It should be noted that these physical properties are directly related to the way in which the I/O instructions are formulated. To a large extent the address and function lines are loaded by a direct copy of an I/O instruction, except for the op-code itself.

It is quite possible to employ independent, uni-directional input and output lines. However it is common, determined by the gating at the CPU internal bus bars (Section 3.3.1), to use only the one, sixteen line, bi-directional I/O data bus. This imposes few restrictions, since due to the sequential execution of instructions, the CPU can never both send and receive data at the same time.

It is also commonly encountered that the same sixteen way bus is used to transmit the address and function information in one time interval and the data in a subsequent interval, time-multiplexing the one bus. This technique will be explained in detail in relation to the simpler microprocessor system in Section 5.3. Another variant is to use two unidirectional sixteen line buses, one in and one out, and time-multiplex them; thus address and output data use one set of lines and input data and vectored interrupt address the other set.

There are no simple rules to cover the allocation of timing and interrupt lines since machines vary drastically in complexity in this respect. Two obvious categories of timing exist however in synchronous or asynchronous operation, examples of which will be given in the following sections.

If vectored memory locations are transmitted to the CPU in response to an acceptance of an interrupt, in order to cause automatic program jumping, then a specific hardwired address in the interface must be placed onto the bus. A full 16 bit address could be transmitted either via the input data lines or by special purpose lines. In practice the vector interrupt memory addresses are constrained to be in, say, the first 512 locations so that a 9 bit vector address will suffice. Just what these requirements are will depend upon the CPU hardware employed to handle interrupts.

Many block data transfer systems (Section 4.4) use the I/O data bus. The normal data lines are commonly used, although independent lines effectively paralleled inside the computer may be provided. Memory addresses for block data transfers may be provided by the device controller; these may be time-multiplexed on the data-in lines or may use an additional, special purpose sixteen line bus. True DMA interfaces use totally independent bus systems, with their own interrupt system, etc.

The parity lines are used to give parity checks on data transmission. There may well be one parity bit per byte of data.

4·6 Synchronous I/O Bus

With a synchronous I/O system the CPU is responsible for generating timing signals which are used to activate external events. It is implicit in the interface design that the peripheral must be ready for the appropriate timing signal, e.g. when the signal to place data onto the bus is received the correct data must be waiting.

4·6·1 Programmed I/O Operations

The CPU places pulses on individual lines at specific times which the peripheral can use for any suitable purpose. The spacing between each pulse need not be equal to the memory cycle time, since the electronic devices used in modern interfaces are so fast; it is however common to generate all timing pulses in one memory cycle. In this way, with the synchronous approach, the timing of an I/O instruction is similar to that of other instructions. However the fact that the I/O system is synchronous does not directly effect the CPU mode of operation. Thus if, say, three pulses are generated, half a memory cycle apart, then the CPU must enter a pause state while executing an I/O instruction before commencing the next instruction fetch. For this reason many synchronous computers exhibit this anomaly whereby the I/O instruction execution time is not an integer multiple of the memory cycle time.

There are as many variants on the actual functions of the I/O lines as there are computers. This is directly related to the instruction set. Recall that there are four possible types of I/O functions:

 (i) Test (skip)
 (ii) Control (activate)
 (iii) Data transfer to CPU (IN)
 (iv) Data transfer from CPU (OUT)

On some machines these functions may be combined in the one instruction, e.g. transfer data *and* clear a flag, so that the relative times at which the operations start must be controlled. The timing of these signals will also be governed by any necessity to time multiplex I/O lines.

Consider now the simplest case where independent sub-buses are provided for address and function, data in and data out. When an I/O instruction is decoded, the CPU causes the address and function bits to be placed on the lines. At the same time the type of function is decoded; assuming that there is one line for each of the four possible types of function*, the appropriate one will be set. Assume for the moment

---

* The function-type is signalled by one of four lines; the actual function is determined by a combination of these lines and the function lines, e.g. set flip-flop number 3 will set the control type-of-function line *and* function line 3. Whèther the flag is set or cleared will be determined by the wiring in the interface.

that only one type of function will be requested by the one instruction.

The device address lines are presented to every peripheral and each interface has a unique, pre-wired device address, which is compared with the number on the address lines. For the one device that matches, a flag is set in the interface to activate that controller. The logic circuit required to determine the match is relatively straightforward, e.g. for each bit the result should be 1 if both are 1 or both 0, and 0 otherwise. If the address lines data is $A_n A_{n-1} \ldots A_1 A_0$ and the wired address is $D_n \ldots D_1 D_0$, then $X_i = A_i D_i + \bar{A}_i . \bar{D}_i = \overline{A_i \oplus D_i}$

$$\therefore \quad X = \overline{A_n \oplus D_n} . \overline{A_{n-1} \oplus D_{n-1}} \ldots . . \overline{A_0 \oplus D_0}$$

The device is selected if X is 1. In effect the two numbers are subtracted and the result tested for zero. Note that this logic circuit is required in every interface. All other lines are also fed to every interface, but only the selected device will accept them.

For a *test* function, the status of a flip-flop inside the interface of a selected device must be transmitted to the CPU, usually to determine *skip* operations. As described in Chapter 2, the most important flip-flops are the *done* and *busy* flags, although more complex peripherals contain others. The function bits, which are appended to the device address and transmitted at the same time, are coded so that one particular flag can be specified by the I/O instruction. This function may be in coded or decoded form, e.g. three lines can be coded to specify one of eight flags or three separate flags. If the function is in coded form it must be decoded by the interface. The status of the tested flag can then be copied onto a further I/O line and transmitted back to the CPU. Figure 4.8 shows a diagram of the interface requirements for device selection and testing one of these flags.

For a *control* function, specific flags in the interface must be set or cleared, typically to start the peripheral actions. The same function lines can be used for control as those introduced for test functions, since the type of function is clearly differentiated by the type-of-function lines.

For a *data-in* function, the selected interface enables gates that connect the data buffer in that interface to the data input lines.

For a *data-out* function, the CPU must place data on the output bus at the same time as the address lines are activated. The selected interface then gates the data on the data output lines into the peripheral, usually a buffer register.

The main variant on the data transfer functions centres around the fact that a device can either send or receive data, but not both, and that only one instruction at a time can be executed. Thus the direction of transfer required is determined exclusively by the device address so

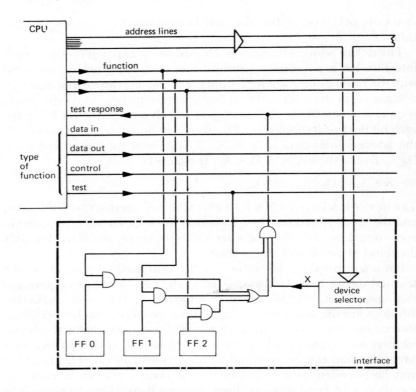

Fig. 4·8 Interface to test the status of one of three flip-flops

that the two lines to specify data-in or data-out types of function can be combined into one data transfer function line. If now a common, bidirectional, data I/O sub-bus is used, the CPU, when decoding the instruction must be prepared to send or accept data, relying on the interface design to respond appropriately. Figure 4.9 shows the components of the interface required for data transfer. The full interface will contain the components of both figures 4.8 and 4.9.

There are few timing problems with an interface as simple as the one described above. The signals placed by the CPU onto the type-of-function lines are timed so that the device selection network is allowed time to operate; they are cleared about 200–500 nanoseconds later, allowing the interface and CPU logic time to take appropriate action. There are a number of variants encountered, however, which allow time-multiplexing of some of the bus lines and also combination of control and data transfer instructions. The latter example is simply accomplished by activating, say, the control type-of-function line almost immediately but delaying the pulse on the data transfer

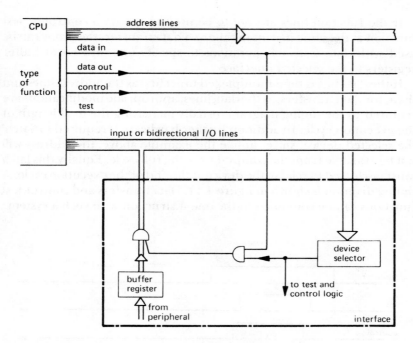

Fig. 4·9 Interface to transfer data from a peripheral to the computer

function lines for around 1 microsecond. In some cases the test and control type-of-function signals are also time displaced. Note that it is not possible that all four lines will be activated by one instruction, even one combinating functions. A typical timing diagram is shown in figure 4.10.

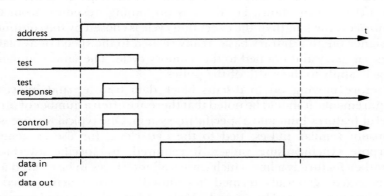

Fig. 4·10 Timing diagram which allows a data transfer and a test/control operation in one instruction

155

If the function lines are not to be used to specify a control or test function at the same instant in time as a data transfer, then they can be used with data transfer operations to specify one of a set of buffer registers in the selected interface.

If the data bus is time-multiplexed to act first as the address lines and then, for data transfers, as the data lines, appropriate modifications are required to the timing diagram, usually increasing the total length of the execution cycle. In addition further hardware is required to 'latch' the selected device, since, unlike the example above, the address will not be available from the computer for the full cycle. Equally this latch must be cleared to release the device at the end of the execution cycle. A timing diagram is shown in figure 4.11. Data transfers and control/test functions can be combined in the one instruction with such a system.

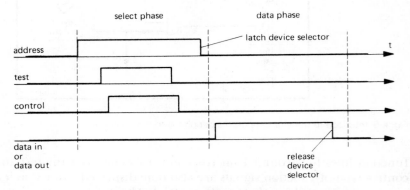

Fig. 4·11 Timing diagram for a system with common data and address lines

The two diagrams of figures 4.10 and 4.11 perhaps stress that while the I/O is synchronous, i.e. there is no 'timing' response from the controller, the length of the execution cycle is chosen by the computer designer on an arbitrary basis, really related to the speed of available logic circuitry and not tied to the memory cycle. The same comments largely apply to the width of the pulses.

Before moving on to discuss block data transfer and interrupt requirements, it should be noted that there are often a number of other useful features built into a specific I/O system. One typical feature is to transmit regular pulses, tied to the CPU clock, for use as general purpose synchronising pulses, if required, by specific interfaces. Another feature is a line which causes all interfaces to be cleared and disengaged, generally termed 'initiallised'. An instruction used at start-up or generated by a panel switch, activates this line and prepares all peripherals to start work. This is most useful after power failure.

4·6·2 Interrupt Systems

An interrupt system is simply a means by which the peripheral can call for attention from the CPU. The simple requirement then is a flip-flop which will be set by the peripheral itself, e.g. an event external to and independent of the CPU, which, provided the interrupt system is enabled, is connected to the CPU to physically request the interrupt. The interrupt request may occur at any instant in time, but it will be synchronised by the CPU so that no other instructions can be left uncompleted. When the interrupt is eventually accepted by the computer a pulse is returned to the interface, termed an interrupt-grant, which clears the interrupt-request flip-flop. The following operations will be normal I/O operations, specific to the interrupt request, which are governed by the device service routines, i.e. software, and so do not require anything further from the interface hardware. However in between the interrupt-request and the interrupt-grant two things must be determined; (i) the priority of the request relative to other devices requesting interrupt and to the current program being executed, and (ii) the CPU must determine which device made the request.

With a simple system employing only one interrupt line and software polling to test the individual interrupt-request flags (which may well be directly related to the done flag) no further interface hardware is required.

The CPU probably supports a number of interrupt-request lines, of differing priority, established either by virtue of the related CPU logic or by a program controlled mask. Thus any one interface is wired to one particular interrupt-request line at a priority level determined by the system configuration. Any number of devices may however be linked to the same line. Thus an interrupt-acknowledge signal is 'daisy-chained' from device to device. This means that the signal is passed to the device nearest to the computer; if the interrupt-request flag in that interface is set, then that device is selected and the interrupt-acknowledge signal is not passed on. However, if the intterupt-request flag is clear, the interrupt-acknowledge signal is passed on to the next interface, and so on. When the interrupt-acknowledge signal is generated, a further line may also be set to hold off any new interrupts.

While the selection procedure is being enacted, the CPU can continue with its normal operation. Once the interrupt-acknowledge signal has been accepted by an interface, the interface generates a device-selected signal to tell the CPU that the interrupt can now proceed; when the CPU has completed the current instruction (plus one extra in some machines) an interrupt-grant is transmitted back to the interface.

   The action taken by the selected interface is dependent upon the system. One system places its own device address on the data input lines, (in that machine the interrupt-acknowledge pulse is not automatically generated, but is generated by an I/O instruction in the interrupt handling routine). A better technique is to cause a number to be placed on the data input lines, determined, rather like the device address, by hard wiring in the interface. The CPU then treats this number as a

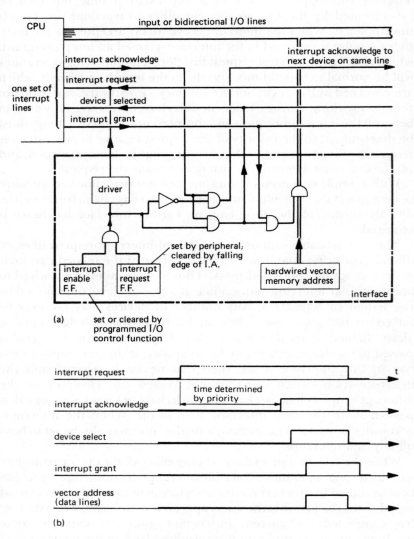

Fig. 4·12 Interface for vectored interrupt control

memory address pointing to a service routine specific to the interrupting peripheral (vectoring). A typical system is shown in figure 4.12.

It must be noted that the interface generates the request for an interrupt, but has no influence (apart from the hardwired choice of interrupt line and position on the daisy chain) on when the request is to be acknowledged. Thus if a request is made by one peripheral, other requests of higher priority may join the queue before the CPU will release its current task, which will be serviced first. Thus the logic in the interface related more to controlling the peripheral device itself, should inhibit further peripheral action until the interrupt has been serviced. Typical requirements are to clear the done flag automatically when the CPU eventually reads data from the buffer into the CPU.

4·7 Asynchronous I/O Bus

An asynchronous interface is a little more complex than a synchronous one, requiring a few more logic components in each controller and a few more lines on the I/O bus. The asynchronous operation is often termed 'hand-shaking', e.g. 'Are you ready?', 'Yes I am', 'Here it is', 'Thank you'.

The CPU places the device number onto the address lines as before, which activates one specific device selector. The device selector in the referenced interface sets a latch, which will effectively channel all the I/O lines into that one device until it is cleared. Once the latch is set, the number on the address lines is no longer required. A pulse is then sent from the interface to the CPU to inform the computer that the peripheral is selected and is awaiting further attention. Data will then be transmitted along the data lines. For an input instruction the CPU will send a pulse to the interface once it has accepted the data, which will disable the interface, and commence the next instruction fetch. Similarly for an output instruction the interface will send a pulse back to the CPU when the data has been accepted.

The significance of asynchronous operation is that devices of differing speeds of action can be serviced by similar instructions. The time taken to complete the instruction execution is determined by the actual speed of response of the logic, whereas synchronous operation requires pulses to be timed so as to give a margin of allowance for the slower interface logic. The possible increase in speed of execution offsets the increase in interface complexity.

4·8 Other Interfaces

Many other types of device controller are required with special considerations. The single, common, I/O and memory bus computer organisation allows one device to transfer data directly to another. To take advantage of this possibility however requires one device to become master of the bus, so that each I/O or memory access is preceded by a sequence to establish mastery of the bus, rather like an interrupt priority system. This imposes a time penalty of around 200 nanoseconds for each use of the bus and in an increase in controller complexity. Since Peripherals and memory use the same bus, asynchronous operation is clearly desirable. The flexibility of such a system is considered well worth the overhead.

Block data transfer controllers are another example. As described in Section 4·4 these devices connect to the computer via special systems. The data-break systems can use the standard I/O bus, requiring in addition a data-break request line to cause the CPU to pause at the end of an instruction. The CPU must acknowledge that the pause state has been entered, so that the controller can transmit the memory address and the data. A DMA controller is similar from the interface viewpoint. Block data controllers must also contain conventional I/O interfaces so that the word count and start address buffers, etc., can be set up by program control. A conventional interrupt is also required which requests program attention when the word count buffer is clear, i.e. transfer is complete, in addition to the data break or cycle stealing requests. Priority of block data transfer devices, since they transmit data as the memory address/data pair, and hence can interleave requests, is simply determined by daisy-chaining the data-break or cycle-steal grant signal.

A block diagram of a disc controller is shown in figure 4.13. This communicates data with the CPU via the DMA channel. Normal programmed I/O is used to initialise the word count and memory address registers and to set up the block address on the disc. The latter will be used to control the positioning of the head and to select the appropriate sector on a track of a specific surface. Status information, which can be quite sophisticated, is also made available to the CPU.

Usually multiple disc drives can be allocated to the one controller. Only one disc can be transferring data at any one time, but others can concurrently be head positioning, etc. In this case the block select register must also define which disc drive to use. In effect one controller with four 2·5 M byte drives looks to the computer like one 10 M byte disc, except that transfer and seek may be overlapped.

Each disc must support its own interface to communicate with the common controller. Many hardware features are built into these interfaces viz:

(a) Writing and checking of error-check characters.

(b) Double buffering of data to allow for a transient delay in the DMA channel.

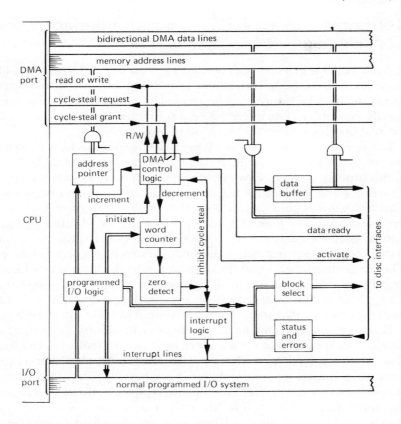

Fig. 4·13 A block diagram of a disc controller

(c) Linking together of sectors to form longer records so that the word count may be larger than the sector size. In this way a whole track can be read/written in one disc revolution.

(d) Set a status indicator to mark a 'bad' sector on a disc, which will be skipped in further use.

(e) Write protection. If the appropriate bit in the status register is set, any attempt to write into that sector will be aborted and an error flagged to the controller and hence to the computer.

(f) Sector verification. The sector address is recorded at the beginning of the sector; this is read and compared with the requested sector before data transfer is allowed.

Further details of magnetic disc drives are given in Section 6.6.

4·9 Some Practical Bus Bar and Interface Logic Considerations

It is not possible in a text such as this to give sufficient details to enable an interface to be built. Indeed this is undesirable since the manufacturers detailed literature *must* be studied, to make an interface for a specific computer. The intention here is to draw attention to many of the real problems that may be encountered.

In the earlier sections of this chapter the use of a party-line I/O bus system was explicitly assumed. This of course is applicable to all minicomputer systems. However the microcomputers shown later in figures 5.4 and 5.5 indicate the use of input and output multiplexors. This technique is quite practical for the simple applications for which the microcomputer is used, effectively creating a dedicated input or output port for each device. It should be noted that the party line system can be used instead of the multiplexors on a microcomputer. The major difference is that the multiplexor is built into the computer, greatly simplifying the interface logic requirements at the peripheral. The disadvantage is the lack of versatility, particularly with the interrupt system, that stems from oversimplifying the interface logic.

However, a major practical point arises with the use of the multiplexor. The multiplexor is itself a TTL (or TTL compatible) device with short leads connecting it to the CPU. The individual multiplexor output lines are required to drive only one peripheral device so that direct connections to TTL interface components is possible; the same is true of the input lines. With a bus bar system a number of devices are competing for use of the same lines, with attendant loading problems, even though, with either system, only one device at a time can be serviced.

A bus bar is quite simply a transmission line and must be treated as such. The time taken for a pulse placed on the line by the CPU to reach the peripherals may be appreciable, compared with the speed of modern interface logic. Equally important, incorrect termination of the lines will result in pulses being reflected back along the line, which may cause erroneous triggering of interface circuits. The data may be placed on the line by one of a number of possible sources, i.e. one device *or* another, but never two. Thus the outputs of conventional TTL logic units cannot be coupled directly to the bus, in case raising one device to a high voltage level burns out another one which is at a low level. In other words the outputs of conventional TTL circuits cannot be 'or-ed' by wiring their outputs to a common connection, such as a bus bar. Thus all outputs to the bus bar, from the CPU or the device interfaces, must come from special driver circuits which display a three state characteristic. When enabled, the output may be logic 1 or 0, but

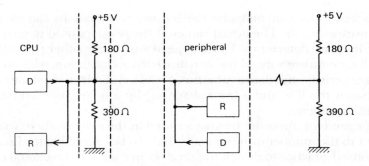

Fig. 4·14 Matching terminations for a bus bar line

when inhibited the output must float. Only one output driver may be enabled at any instant, which will, via the bus bar, force the outputs of the other drivers to the same level, with no effect on those devices since they are not enabled.

Two types of device are used, the open-collector transistor and the tri-state devices. These devices were mentioned in the introduction in Section 1.8, since they are fundamental to the concept of bus bar systems. The open collector units require an external resistor while the newer tri-state devices can be treated as special TTL devices, with no particular output connection problems. As an example of this technology a single MSI/MOS chip is now available which serves as an 8 bit latch, with one input enable line (common to the 8 data bits) and one output enable line, with tri-state output data lines and normal TTL compatible input lines. A typical bus bar line with correct termination is shown in figure 4.14. An open collector driver circuit, suitable for direct connection in figure 4.14 is shown in figure 4.15; note that this circuit

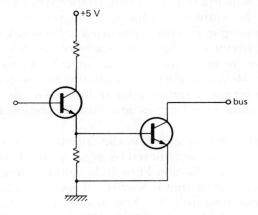

Fig. 4·15 A typical open collector driver circuit

acts as an invertor and that the bus bar terminations complete the transistor circuit. The actual values of the resistors used to terminate the lines are determined by the type of wire used; either twisted pairs or flat multicore wire with alternate earths are common, with nominal characteristic impedances of around 100Ω. A diode is often connected between the line and a low voltage to clip any negative overshoots, limiting ringing.

Dependent upon the transistors used in the drivers, there will be a limit to the number of input loads that can be coupled to the line. It is standard practice to design the receiver in each interface to take only one 'unit-load', with an amplifier to feed parallel connections inside the device.

There is a practical limit to the length of line that can be directly driven from the CPU, determined by the loading and the driver design. A typical figure of around 17m is encountered. To drive longer lengths, or more than around twenty standard TTL loads, a line extender unit is required, which is effectively a receiver linked directly to a driver; loads on the extended line being supplied by the extender driver circuits.

Since many line driver circuits are effectively invertors and also since most MSI TTL logic systems are constructed almost entirely of NAND gates, the voltage levels on the bus lines of all computers are non-standard. It is most common that the data lines use $+3\cdot5$ volts for logic 0 and voltages of $0\cdot7$ and less for logic 1. It is equally likely that, say, the interrupt lines on the same computer use $3\cdot5$ volts for logic 1 and 0 volts for logic 0. It is imperative that these figures are checked in the manufacturers' literature.

Noise immunity is another important feature of interface logic design. Great care must be taken with system earths, preferably returning them all to a common point. In special cases differential line drivers may be employed, (this is analogous to common-mode-rejection in analogue systems as discussed in Section 6.7.2). Differing styles of logic circuit offer different noise rejection characteristics. TTL is rather prone to noise problems, due to its high speed as much as anything else. Most manufacturers, including the computer manufacturers, offer a range of essentially slower, high noise rejection units, but the standard CMOS logic families now available are inherently good in this respect.

Total earth isolation between the interface/computer and the peripheral device can be achieved by using an 'optical coupler'. The sending line drives a Gallium Phosphide light emitting diode, which "shines" directly into a photo-sensitive transistor which feeds the line driver, as shown in figure 4.16. These devices are now becoming faster and longer lived (the lamps fade with age) and are increasingly being

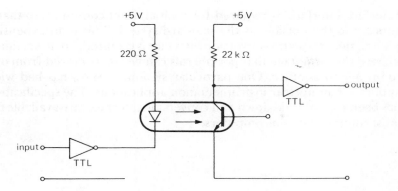

Fig. 4·16 An optical coupler

employed in standard interface designs. They are packaged as single combined units. On some the base of the transistor is brought out as an extra terminal for use in faster switching circuits.

Another similar problem is that of 'skew', when data placed simultaneously on parallel lines may arrive at the destination some tens of nanoseconds out of step. These small time errors could cause errors in high speed logic circuits, so that the CPU response signals are usually delayed by around 50 nanoseconds to allow the skew effect to disappear.

In summary, while stock MSI devices may suffice, it is most desirable to employ specially constructed line drivers and receivers to connect interfaces to the bus bar.

4·10 General Purpose and Standard Interfaces

Most computer manufacturers offer a general purpose interface to ease the problem of connecting special peripherals to the machine, without designing a special purpose interface. The GP interface contains all the line drivers and receivers, device selectors, interrupt system, etc., simply presenting an input and an output port to the actual peripheral device. By its general nature, such an interface is bound to have redundant components for a specific job, but is likely to be cost competitive with a tailor made interface on a one-off basis.

The concept of standard interfaces is far more sophisticated. The idea is that a standard specification for an interface bus system should be formulated. Device controllers are then designed to interface to this common standard, independent of the computer make. Thus a special 'interface-interface' is required for each make of computer, so that it appears to the outside, as the standard system. This is an expensive system, since the extra conversion interface is required, but it is claimed to have the advantage that peripherals can be freely moved from one computer to another. One particular system, CAMAC, has had wide application in nuclear instrumentation applications. The specification has been rigously laid down and conversion interfaces are available for most commercial minicomputers.

Chapter 5

Microprocessors

5·1 Introduction

5·1·1 Large Scale Integration in Computers

A review of integrated circuit technology is presented in Appendix 3. In summary there are two competing techniques for LSI, Bipolar and MOS, with many variants, which may be compared to conventional transistors and field effect transistors, FETs. Bipolar devices are faster while more gates can be packed into one MOS chip. Thus MOS/LSI devices are generally more complex but slower than Bipolar/LSI devices. Needless to say advancing technology may change this picture, but it is really irrelevant to the user who merely purchases a chip, usually encapsulated in either plastic or ceramic with a standardised connecting pin structure, picturesquely termed a 'bug'. All that is important is what functions will the chip perform, how fast, how much will it cost, how much power does it consume and is it compatible with other devices.

Digital computers are largely constructed of many hundred medium scale integrated circuit TTL Bipolar chips, e.g. four two-input NAND gates in one 14 pin bug. This pattern is changing with groups of bugs being replaced by single LSI chips. The initial impact of LSI was in the introduction of semi-conductor memory; see Appendix 4; which by 1974 was in direct competition, both in price and speed, with magnetic core. This was the obvious region to use the new technologies, because of the repetitiveness of the design.

With greatly increased knowledge of production methods, far more sophisticated circuitry is being produced. However, it must be realised that the quite enormous saving in cost that can be achieved by LSI, can only be realised if sufficiently large sales can result to offset the high development cost, which naturally reduces the field of practical application. However, more complex systems were developed for aerospace and military applications, where reliability and weight were more important than cost considerations. Thus the backcloth was set for the introduction of the calculator chips which have proliferated in desk and pocket calculators. These chips are decimal arithmetic processors. They are controlled by programs, stored in ROM, which can be activated by pressing switches. The output from an internal register is connected to a display panel. The more sophisticated machines have an additional RAM memory in which a program of the functions which the ROM can implement, can be stored. Thus the full processing capability is fabricated on one chip.

In the above example of the calculator, the computer consists of the calculator chip, the memories, the keyboard, the display and a power supply. With such a dedicated application, interfacing between these components can be virtually eliminated by including the necessary circuits on the LSI chips.

The calculator chip is effectively a simple CPU. Thus it was a natural step forward to design a more sophisticated, general purpose CPU along the same lines. This has been termed a *microprocessor*, a CPU on a chip. Now just as there is a range of minicomputers, so is there a range of microprocessors. Some are fabricated on one chip, but others utilise a group of three or four chips to implement the full CPU. The simpler microprocessor can be used in the more sophisticated calculators, but since they are GP processors they can be built up with memory chips, power supplies, buffers, interfaces, etc., to form a conventional computer. Such a computer will be called a *microcomputer*, although a *microprocessor system* may be safer and more accurate, since the term microcomputer has been used in the past to describe the 8 and 12 bit minicomputers. It must be stressed that the microprocessor is an LSI CPU only and not a full 'computer on a chip'.

The minicomputer manufacturers are also well aware of the advantages of LSI technology and in 1974 machines were introduced which were in effect older designs with blocks of TTL chips replaced by LSI chips. In retaining the full complexity of the original designs it was necessary to use around ten LSI chips, but this resulted in a great reduction in size since some hundreds of TTL chips were replaced. Note that the new technology has been introduced by the manufacturer who hopes to sell thousands of units, i.e. computer companies who specialise in the OEM market. These machines are called LSI minicomputers.

The problem with LSI systems is speed. The common commercial microprocessors are fabricated in MOS, resulting in speeds which are a decade slower than MSI minicomputer CPU's. Bipolar units are being developed and one of the LSI minicomputers uses a *silicon-on-sapphire* (SOS) variant of MOS which is much faster. One suspects however that the speed differential may well continue to exist for some years, since the MSI systems will also improve. Nevertheless the LSI minicomputers, utilising a number of chips, and probably the microprocessors will rapidly close the gap on MSI machines, with obvious advantages in size and cost.

5·1·2 Microcomputers Versus Minicomputers

A small digital computer can be constructed around a microprocessor by adding a full range of memory, power supplies, a front panel and all the necessary interfaces, including I/O channels. Indeed more than one such machine is commercially available. The result however is an inferior minicomputer, in all respects, including price when compared to the LSI mini's. This is not the way to use a microprocessor.

The microprocessor must be regarded as a sophisticated logic component and used accordingly. It is the modularity of a microcomputer that is its advantage. Thus a system can be designed and built with only the minimum necessary components and no surplus power, e.g. a microcomputer can be used as a dedicated *controller*, as part of a system. The program will be developed off-line and stored in ROM, which will be plugged into the microcomputer. Data can be fed into the machine via ADCs and out via DACs so that the resulting machine, microprocessor, ROM, any RAM for data, power supplies, interfaces, ADC, etc., can be constructed on one tailored circuit board. Such a system, which now has a dedicated logic performance by virtue of the fixed ROM, could be constructed with TTL chips. The net effect is that the design of a hard-wired logic network has been replaced by the development of a microcomputer program. This gives advantages in debugging the system and marked advantages in modifying the system. Thus if a particular microcomputer is controlling a specific process, say an intelligent terminal, then if the system needs modifying for any reason the new program can be developed off-line and implemented simply by plugging in the new ROM in place of the old one. Clearly a minicomputer, particularly an LSI mini on a single board, could be used for the same task, but would be more expensive by virtue of the surplus performance inherent in the general purpose nature of the design.

While the implemented microcomputer will be a special purpose device, reprogrammable rather than programmable, a laboratory development unit will be required. This will in effect be the pseudo-minicomputer mentioned above, with tape readers and teletypes to aid program development. In particular a unit for making ROM will be required, so that the developed program can be transferred to the dedicated machine. This installation may be supplemented, or even replaced, by using larger computers as 'hosts' to create programs for microcomputers, as explained in Section 7.9.

In summary microprocessor systems can be economically used to implement controllers which would require of the order of forty or more TTL bugs, yet do not require the full processing power of a minicomputer. They will be singularly economic in situations where hundreds of the same system will be required, when the program development cost can be averaged out.

There are however many areas of development in which multi-processors are being considered. Thus the performance of one very powerful CPU may be matched by a number, possibly hundreds, of simpler CPUs, since the one CPU must process data one step at a time, while the individual CPUs may be working at the same instant in time. This is generally called *parallel-processing* and is a current research topic. Some simple examples have already been introduced in the use of peripheral processors, e.g. a DMA controller with arithmetic power as explained in Section 4.4.3.

The list of possible application areas is most extensive, some typical examples being:

Industrial sequence controllers
Machine tool controllers
Point-of-sale terminals
Intelligent terminals
Instrument processors
Traffic light controllers
Weather data collection systems
Process controllers

5·1·3 Microprocessor Configurations

One of the main concepts of a microcomputer is its modularity, one module being the microprocessor. However, for various reasons the microprocessor itself may be configured from a selection of chips.

The commercially available microprocessors can be classified* as:
(i) Serial calculator chips
(ii) 4 bit parallel processor chips
(iii) 8 bit parallel general purpose chips
(iv) Microprogrammable multi-chip sets

5·1·3·1 Serial Calculator Chips

These devices were the original LSI *computer* chips. The system was constructed from a number of individual chips such as adder, registers, timing and control, keyboard and display as well as the program ROM. The data is stored and manipulated as 4 bit decimal digits so that a calculator may be configured as a ten digit machine plus two digits for the exponent. The registers where fixed length, e.g. 100 bits, arranged as 25 BCD digits in one system. Since the arithmetic, input and output operations are executed serially, the active register length is controlled by the number of 'time slots' used. The instructions available are simply add and subtract and move data and the programs are stored in 256 word (10 or 12 bit) ROMs up to a maximum of 32.

5·1·3·2 4-Bit Parallel Processor Chips

These devices are the logical extension of the serial calculator chips. They are based on a 4 bit data word, termed a *nibble*. The CPU is fabricated on one chip with which is associated ROM program memory and RAM data memory. Special memory chips are used which include all the interfacing, address decoding, etc., necessary to couple the memory direct to the CPU, and also to function as an I/O port.

The instruction set is rather more extensive than that required simply for calculators, e.g. I/O instructions, and the reduction in the number of chips compared to the serial calculator sets led to these devices being used as microprocessors, in the sense discussed in Section 5.1.2.

Since it has been stressed in the preceding chapters that a 16 bit word length is restrictive, it is important to recognise just how a computer has been developed around a 4 bit word. This is discussed in Section 5.2.1.

---

* This classification is taken from an excellent review of microprocessors by David Wright ('Microprocessors: fundamentals and applications', MINICOM Conference Proceedings, Polytechnic of Central London, 1974).

5·1·3·3 8-Bit General Purpose Chips

The next step after the 4 bit processor is to lose the association with calculator chips and to stress the general programmable nature of the microprocessor. The compromises of cost and circuit complexity have led to an 8 bit word being adopted as standard at present and may well stay so since the LSI minis will dominate the 16 bit systems. Again some detailed consideration must be given to how the short 8 bit word can be usefully employed, as will be explained in Section 5.2.2.

These microprocessors are normally single chips and have a much more powerful instruction set than the 4 bit machines, including logic operations. They have an interrupt system and are designed for use with standard LSI memory. As a result, unlike the 4 bit systems with their specialised memory, a number of MSI circuits are required to interface the memory and I/O to the CPU. The support for this class of microprocessor is growing extensively, particularly in the software area. Although fabricated in MOS, the connections to the microprocessor are, where possible, made TTL compatible to ease the interfacing problem.

This type of system can be considered as the typical microprocessor and will be discussed in some detail in the remainder of this chapter.

5·1·3·4 Microprogrammable Multi-Chip Microprocessors

A system of manufacturing microprocessors which is very similar to the LSI mini is to break the CPU function into a number of modules, each implemented on a separate chip. With the reduction in chip complexity these units can be fabricated in bipolar technology, with an increase in speed.

The CPU is split into three functional units typically (i) an arithmetic and logic units including registers (RALU) (ii) a timing and control unit and (iii) a control ROM (CROM) as shown in figure 5.1.

The actual functions performed on each chip, and the number of chips will vary. One manufacturer puts all decoding and control, both the normal instructions from memory and the microprogram on one chip, with only the arithmetic and registers on the RALU.

Each RALU is a 4 bit device so that simply by paralleling them, word lengths of 4, 8, 12, 16, etc. bits can be used. Note that 4 RALUs give a full 16 bit parallel word as compared to two consecutive instructions with 8 bit data. The timing and control unit combine with the CROM to implement the instruction set. The fundamental micro-instructions are of a low level, but the machine recognises normal instructions, sometimes called macro-instructions, and converts each one to a set of simpler instructions. In effect each machine instruction is converted to

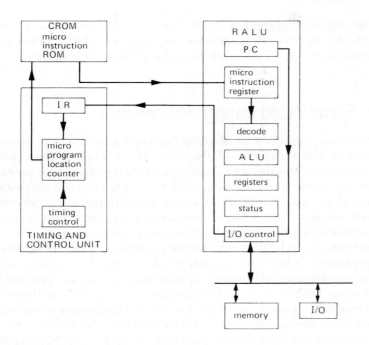

Fig. 5·1 A multi-chip microprocessor

a microprogram which is stored in the CROM and executed by the timing and control unit. This technique is termed microprogramming and is discussed in more detail in Chapter 8. The significance is that a computer can be constructed of these units with a specific instruction set. This instruction set can be altered by changing the CROM. In this way, using the same basic device, an 8 bit system with two RALUS can be developed, with appropriate multiple word, 8 bit instructions, or a full 16 bit minicomputer-like system can be produced with four RALUS.

While in theory a machine can be developed with an instruction set tailored to suit a particular range of applications, the development of the CROM is not trivial. Thus a limited number of standard CROMS are being made available.

The 16 bit system will have to compete with the LSI minis, or possibly the LSI minis will be constructed of the available multi-chip micro-processor units, with differing CROMS. There are a number of other LSI devices, similar in principle to the units considered here which are not strictly microprocessors but are more 'microcontrollers'. Built on Bipolar techniques they are very fast and specifically designed to be microprogrammed to replace groups of TTL chips in existing designs.

The microprogrammed multi-chip microprocessors will not be specifically mentioned again since they can be tailored to behave as anything between a 4 bit machine and a 16 bit minicomputer.

5·2 Short Word Length Processors

In previous chapters a lot of stress has been placed on the problems created by the restriction of the short 16 bit word of the common minicomputer. Because of the application to calculator type problems some microprocessors are restricted to 4 bit words; the majority, by virtue of circuit complexity as much as anything, use 8 bit words. Clearly neither 4 nor 8 bits is adequate for a range of instructions so that multiple words must be used for most instructions.

Attention must be drawn to a small problem in terminology. As will be explained below, due largely to the physical constraint of the maximum number of connecting pins that can be incorporated in a single chip, both memory and I/O data are transmitted from the CPU via the same bus – a single bus structure in minicomputer terminology. Because it is the means of transmitting data in and out of the CPU, this common bus has been misleadingly termed the I/O bus. Such a phrase should really describe communication between the microcomputer and its peripherals, not the microprocessor and its memory. Thus the phrase *data port* is used here to describe the connections for the didirectional bus taking data in and out of the CPU itself. It will also be shown that on the simpler machines the one data port will be time-multiplexed to transmit both addresses and data.

5·2·1 Four Bit Microprocessors

A typical 4 bit microprocessor, figure 5.2, uses 8 bit instructions, stored in consecutive 4 bit locations in ROM with 4 bit data words in an independent RAM. 4K nibbles of ROM are addressable by using a 12 bit address and 256 nibbles of RAM by using an 8 bit address. Inside the CPU the registers are of appropriate length, i.e. an 8 bit IR, 12 bit PC, etc. Since the memory and the data port are in 4 bit units, information must be transmitted in multiple time slots.

The instruction cycle of this machine will comprise a number of time multiplexed events, referred to as *machine states*, thus:
(i) The 12 bit PC contents will be transmitted to the ROM as three consecutive nibbles in the first three machine states. The ROM must contain a 12 bit address register with the necessary logic to collate the 12 bit address from the three nibbles transmitted. Clearly control

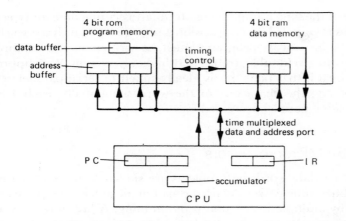

Fig. 5·2 A 4 bit single chip microprocessor with special memories which include time-multiplexing logic control

information must also be sent from the CPU, so that the ROM can determine which of the three states is active. It should be noted that either additional TTL logic or special ROM units are required to implement the external MAR and its control logic.

(ii) In the next two time intervals, the nibbles from the addressed ROM location and the following one are transmitted to the CPU as the 8 bit instruction.

(iii) The instruction is decoded and executed. It may prove however, to be a double word instruction (with some 8 bit instructions, a second byte is required, e.g. ISZ or Jump operations) so that two further machine states are used to fetch two further nibbles from ROM.

(iv) If data is required it may come from one of two sources. (a) Immediate mode, from the next nibble in ROM, which does not require a new address to be transmitted or (b) to or from RAM, which requires an 8 bit address to be transmitted in two further machine states, with a third one for the 4 bit data transfer. Again the RAM, like the ROM, requires additional control signals and control logic.

Thus to fetch, decode and execute an instruction to store a 4 bit data word in RAM from CPU accumulator, an 8 bit instruction, with the RAM address already set up in an 8 bit internal register, requires a total of eight transfers between the CPU and the memories.

Unlike the 16 bit minicomputer, a variety of word lengths are used for differing purposes in this machine, all combinations of the basic 4 bit word, e.g. both 8 and 12 bit addresses, 8 bit instructions and 4 bit data. Time multiplexing is then employed to effect the appropriate combinations. Note that internal CPU registers will also be differing lengths, e.g. a 4 bit adder and accumulator, an 8 bit IR and a 12 bit PC.

Because of the time multiplexing, the total execution time for typical instructions is long. If higher precision is required, and it always will be with only 4 bit words, programs must be written to use multiple instructions to give double, treble, and higher precision. With appropriate decimal instructions this is ideally suited to serial/parallel BCD operations, e.g. the characters of the word sequentially, each 4 bit character being parallel processed.

5·2·2 8 Bit Microprocessors

With an 8 bit data word the problems are similar to those of a 4 bit machine, but a little easier. Again the arithmetic precision can only be increased by multiple instruction programming. A far more conventional approach is used, with standard 8 bit semiconductor memory* being employed in the normal manner, not the individually addressed program and data memories used in the 4 bit machine. Programs are still usually stored in ROM and data in RAM, but these can be intermixed. Thus a program can be developed in RAM and, with the same addresses, implemented in ROM. Since conventional memory units are used, any control logic required must be implemented in additional TTL circuits.

Since an 8 bit word only allows 256 addresses, double words, (16 bits) are used for memory addresses. Thus a jump instruction requires one word for the instruction code and two words for the address, a total of three 8 bit words. Non-memory reference instruction use one word and immediate mode instructions one plus one for the data. Thus there are some one, two and some three word instructions, requiring one memory time interval to fetch each 8 bit word.

The internal registers will also be of mixed length, e.g. a 16 bit PC and 8 bit IR and accumulators.

Again memory addresses may be transmitted as two 8 bit bytes in successive time intervals and collated into a 16 bit address in an external buffer register used by the memory. However the better technique now used is to provide a separate 16 bit address bus and an 8 bit data bus.

Two techniques then are used:
(i) a common 8 bit bi-directional bus, figure 5.3(a), via which the address and data, both memory reference and I/O, are transmitted by time-multiplexing.
(ii) a bus system with a 8 bit data and 16 bit address buses, figure 5.3(b).

---

* Semiconductor memory is common, but there is no technical limitation against using core.

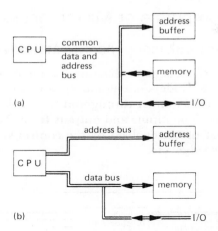

Fig. 5·3 (a) A time-multiplexed address and data bus system. (b) Independent address and data buses

When this is compared with the various bus structures of the minicomputer, discussed in Section 3.3, it can be considered primitive. Case (i) is an order lower than anything previously considered, time sharing the same bus for address and data, while case (ii) is similar to the so called single bus minicomputer structure of figure 3.8(b). Indeed with both of these structures it is most surprising that virtual I/O has not been used, but as will soon be explained, independent control signals are used to indicate an I/O instruction, which can be used by external logic to take appropriate action.

The reason for this constraint on the communication with the CPU is a physical one, quite simply related to the number of external connections that can be engineered in LSI technology. System (i) was used on a microprocessor which was packaged in an eighteen pin bug. Improved technology increased the number of pins to forty, allowing the system (ii) to be implemented. Multi-chip systems are not so restricted. In fact the limitation on the number of pins on the chip is restricting in many ways including the sophistication of the interrupt systems. Thus many of the functions which are explained in the following sections which appear strange may be enforced by this external connection limitation. In any case the bottle neck created by the simple data port to the CPU is a limiting factor as far as speed of execution is concerned.

In an attempt to minimise communication outside the CPU, it is common to use a rather large quantity of internal registers. It is likely in the future that this concept will be extended with fair sized memory 'scratch pads' on the CPU chip.

5·3 Microcomputers or Microprocessor Systems

5·3·1 A System with Independent Data and Address Buses

Figure 5.4 shows the schematic diagram for a microcomputer using a microprocessor with independent address and data buses. Note that tri-state devices are assumed throughout to enable buses to be used without OR gates. The inputs and outputs from the memory, multiplexors, etc. float unless enabled by the control signals read, write, interrupt acknowledge, etc.

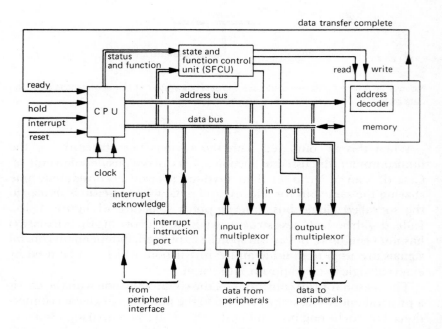

Fig. 5·4 A microcomputer using a microprocessor with independent data and address buses

Since the one data port is used to fetch instructions, which may be multiple words, and to transmit data to or from memory, as well as I/O data, external logic is required to synchronise the external connections with the current internal state of the CPU. The internal CPU state will depend upon which instruction is being executed and what stage of the cycle has been reached.

Usually the information transmitted is grouped as timing signals and external function demands, e.g. read, write, etc.; the 'when' and the 'what' respectively. This information can be transmitted to the external circuits in two ways. The direct method is to use separate connections to the CPU; since pin connections must be used sparingly the information may be in coded form, e.g. three pins can be used to signal eight independent states while another group of pins defines the function. The alternative method of communication is to use the data bus during a time interval that it is not to be used for other purposes, e.g. while an address is being sent out on the address bus. This technique requires that timing information is still transmitted by direct connection, coded or otherwise.

Clearly a combination of the two techniques is the most versatile and since more bits of information are effectively available than would be possible with direct connection only, most information may then be presented in decoded form, e.g. one line for read, one for input, etc.

The status and function information is collected by a logic system shown as the *state and function control unit* (SFCU) in figure 5.4. This will in practice be a conglomerate of TTL chips which converts the status and function information into appropriately timed control signals to activate the other units of the computer. The simplicity of the SFCU is dependent on the degree of coding of the signals from the CPU. As an example a *synch* signal is transmitted to indicate that a cycle has just started inside the CPU, which sends an address on the address bus and places status information on the data bus; the synch signal can be used to enable gates in the SFCU to act on the information on the data bus. The synch signal is followed by another timing signal to indicate that the data line is going to be used for something else, so that the SFCU must inhibit its gating to the data bus, having saved any status information that may be needed later in the cycle. If the signals are not in coded form this is all that the SFCU need do.

Another class of control signals can be *input* to the CPU to govern its mode of operation, overriding the normal clocked sequential program execution. Four such control functions are shown on figure 5.4.

The *ready* line indicates to the CPU that the data on the data bus can be used; if the memory is very slow then the CPU will try to read data at the appropriate time in its own cycle, which will not be available. If the ready line is clear then the CPU will pause in this state until it is set, in this example by the completion of the memory access. In this way asynchronous CPU/memory communication is achieved.

The *hold* line is similar to ready except that it forces the CPU into a wait state, floating the data bus; this is used to allow autonomous external events such as DMA.

The *interrupt* line requests an interrupt, as in a simple minicomputer. The current cycle is completed and the fetch instruction state is entered. The instruction is placed on the data bus from the requesting peripheral itself, allowing different peripherals to be identified. Note that in this system an instruction (probably a jump to service sub-routine), not a vector address or a peripheral address, is transmitted from the interface.

Setting the *reset* line causes the PC and possibly other internal registers to be cleared. When the line is cleared the program now commences at location 0. The reset and hold lines can be used to give a manual override of the program.

The data bus is used to time-multiplex transmission of instructions and data between the CPU and the memory. It is also used for I/O data transfers. On the system of figure 5.4 the SFCU generates appropriate control signals to enable read memory, write memory, input or output functions as and when requested by the status and function information from the CPU. The address of a particular memory location is placed on the 16 bit address bus by the CPU. The same bus is also used to carry the peripheral device address. Usually only one byte of the address is used for peripherals, giving a range of 256 input and 256 output peripheral buffer registers. Input and output multiplexors are shown on figure 5.4 but the more conventional party-line I/O bus could be employed. The system shown concentrates most of the interface logic in the microcomputer by using the multiplexors. Since the data is only available on the data bus for one part of a cycle, it is common to buffer (or latch) the output lines; the same could be said of the input lines except that the peripheral interface normally contains its own buffer. This choice is entirely dependent upon the system design. Note that virtual I/O is quite plausible on this system, allocating memory addresses to the peripherals buffer registers. The use of 8 bit address and the input or output control lines from the SFCU is probably simpler in terms of interface design than the full 16 bit address.

The *clock* is a logic circuit, possibly crystal controlled, which gener-ates accurately timed, phased and shaped pulses, which 'switch' the CPU through its internal states of operation. Normally the clock is required to generate more than one non-overlapping pulse. Thus accurate timing and phasing of internal CPU actions can be adjusted via the (external) clock. It is probable that clock circuitry will eventually be included in the chip, but accuracy and adjustability problems are not trivial.

By using the ready signal on the CPU, memory data transfers are made asynchronous. Thus any mixture of memory types can be used. A typical microcomputer in field service will have only sufficient memory for the purpose, up to 64K bytes with this 16 bit address machine, with the program in ROM and the data in RAM. Magnetic core is seldom used. Details of memory systems are given in Appendix 4.

The CPU itself will be discussed in Section 5.4.

5·3·2 A system with a Common Data and Address Bus

The microcomputer shown in figure 5.5 is typical of a system utilising a common 8-bit bus for both addresses and data. Assuming 16 bit addresses, this bus must be time-multiplexed to control the external components.

Since the data bus carries address information, at no time will it be available to transmit status information. This must be communicated to the SFCU by direct connection, which, with the scarcity of pins, means that coding of information is essential. The SFCU in this system must decode these signals and is thus far more complex than in the system of figure 5.4.

The microcomputer is generally similar to the one just described except for the time-multiplexing, which necessitates the two *latches* (buffer registers with input and output gating). To explain the function of this system some further knowledge of the CPU is required. The machine uses four states, labelled T_1, T_2, T_3 and T_4 (more detailed comments are given in the next section) which are entered sequentially.

To fetch an instruction the action is:

T_1 send out first byte of address and save in latch 1.
T_2 send out second byte of address and save in latch 2.
T_3 enable gates A and B and activate the read line to transfer the instruction from memory to the CPU.
T_4 decode the instruction and execute it if it is a non-memory reference instruction. Note that no external action is required during this state and that in practice it may be twice as long as the other states.

For a memory reference instruction a second cycle is entered, thus:

T_1 and T_2 load address into latches 1 and 2
T_3 read or write data to or from the CPU
T_4 use the data

For a jump type instruction the data is a 16 bit address so that the above cycle must be repeated to fetch the second byte.

For an output instruction the second cycle is:

T_1 send out data for O/P; save in latch 1
T_2 send out peripheral address; save in latch 2
T_3 enable gates D and E and activate the output multiplexor
T_4 not required

For an input instruction the second cycle is:

T_1 nothing
T_2 send out peripheral address; save in latch 2
T_3 enable gate C and activate the input multiplexor (tri-state devices eliminate the need for an output gate from the input multiplexor)
T_4 not required

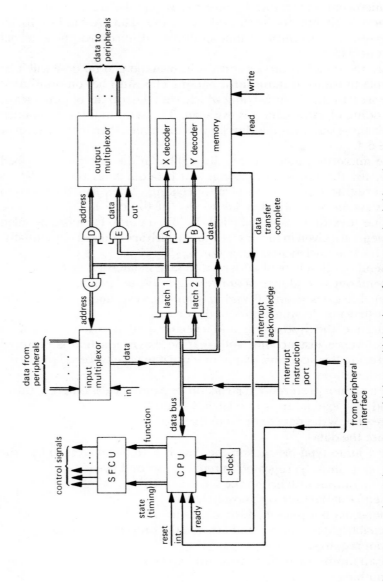

Fig. 5·5 A microcomputer using a microprocessor with time-multiplexed use of a common data/address bus

Since differing use is made of the machine states dependent upon the cycle and type of instruction that is being executed, both timing and function information are needed by the sFCU.

5·4 A Single Chip, 8 Bit Microprocessor

5·4·1 General Architecture

In this section a typical 8 bit microprocessor with a common data and address bus will be examined. A few details of CPUs, with separate data and address buses, and of multi-chip machines will be given, but the differences in principle between the machine described here and the others are reasonably obvious. It is fair to say that any future micro-processors will follow the lines explained here but incorporating more and more of the sophisticated minicomputer CPU techniques previously explained. It is worth repeating that a microprocesor is simply a CPU on a chip. The main reason that sufficient differences between the microprocessor and minicomputer CPU exist to warrant a separate chapter is due to the technological limitations of LSI circuits.

The machine shown schematically in figure 5.6 is an 8 bit machine. All internal registers and buses are 8 bits wide, although some 16 bit registers are effectively created by two 8 bit registers. the machine stores and moves data in a parallel mode, so that two consecutive operations are required for the double length registers.

The microprocessor of figure 5.6 is fundamentally similar to the machines shown in Section 3.3. The main points of difference are:
(a) there is only one 8 bit bus for all memory and I/O operations.
(b) there is a relative abundance of internal CPU registers. In figure 5.6 the registers are allocated to specific tasks; in a multi-chip system the register use will be determined by the microprogram in the CROM. Thus a hardware program counter *stack* is incorporated inside the CPU. Future microprocessors will extend this principle considerably, incorporating sections of the memory inside the main chip.

5·4·2 Machine State, Cycle and Timing

Because of the bottleneck created by the 8 bit data bus, time multiplexing is needed to execute an instruction. Thus in a micropro-cessor timing takes on a greater complexity than in a minicomputer CPU.

The fundamental time unit is determined by an external clock, fed to the *State Timing Generator*. In practice, due to difficulty in accurately sub-dividing intervals inside the LSI chip, the clock feeds in two

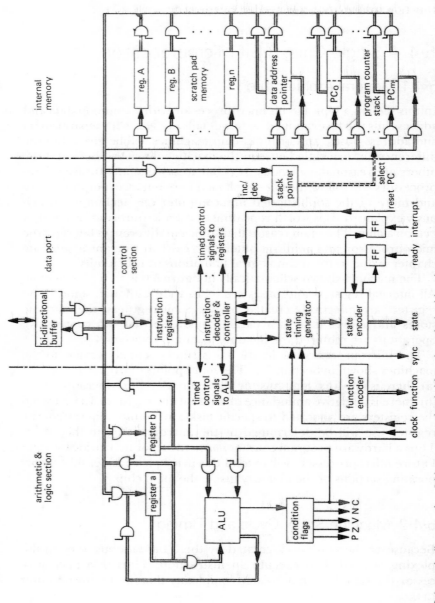

Fig. 5·6 Schematic diagram of an 8 bit, common data/address bus single-chip microprocessor accurately phased pulses for each so called *machine state*; the use of an external clock allows adjustable components to be used which clearly is not possible on the chip! For the sake of ease of explanation let the external clock run at 4 MHz. These clock pulses are used to cycle the CPU through a series of distinct, equal length, machine states. Other states will need defining, but the following four basic states are the minimum requirement:

T_1 send out lower 8 bits of a memory address

T_2 send out higher 8 bits of a memory address

T_3 transfer a word. This may be an instruction moved from memory to the Instruction Register, data from memory to one of the temporary registers (a or b) or data from one of the temporary registers to memory.

T_4 execute an instruction, internal to the CPU, e.g. move data from one register to another. This state may be twice as long as the others, but is assumed to be the same length for simplicity.

During each state a number of distinct actions take place, so that in state T_1 the particular register containing the lower half of the address must be located, its output gate enabled and the input gate to the buffer, enabled. To help the CPU organise this sequence it is common to use up to four clock pulses for each state. Often two clock inputs are used, with an accurate phase displacement between them, but all such details are relevant only to the complexity of the State Timing Generator on a particular CPU. If four clock pulses for each state are assumed at a 4 MHz rate, then each machine state exists for 1 μ second.

The current state of the machine is transmitted from the CPU to the rest of the microcomputer by means of the 'state' lines. One line could be used for each state, i.e. line 1 is at logic 'one' when T_1 is active, etc., but it is more compact to code the state information onto fewer lines. If a 3 bit 'state word' is output, a total of eight states can be 'flagged', the four defined above and others yet to be discussed. The current state cannot be determined by external simulation, by counting the clock pulses, since some instructions do not require every state; the states that are unnecessary are skipped rather than mark-time, to which end a feed-back from the Instruction Decoder and Controller to the State Timing Generator is indicated.

To facilitate co-ordination of the CPU with external equipment, a synch pulse is also sent out. This pulse is locked to the machine state, rather than the clock, i.e. in this example a synch pulse every microsecond.

A *machine, processor* or *memory cycle* comprises the set of necessary machine states. Thus a non-memory reference instruction such as 'add the contents of two internal registers' requires all four states, T_1 through T_4, and takes 4 μ seconds.

As will be explained later some instructions may take up to three memory cycles to execute, possibly totalling up to ten states (not twelve as some states will be skipped), i.e. $10\,\mu$ seconds.

5·4·3 Data Port Buffer

The only data communication link between the CPU and the rest of the microcomputer is the 8 bit *data port*. Most external units coupled to the CPU will be TTL devices, while the CPU is MOS/LSI. Thus an 8 bit buffer is built into the CPU to make the actual data lines from the CPU TTL compatible. The buffer must be bi-directional since data may be moved into or out of the CPU. Whether the CPU is receiving or sending data is a function of the instruction being executed and the current state during that machine cycle; thus the appropriate gates can be enabled, connecting the buffer to the internal data bus, for the specific time interval. When no data is being transmitted, the gates are inhibited and the buffer is 'floating', i.e. *tri-state*.

Due to the physical limitations of the MOS/LSI, the buffer has a low-power-TTL output, and a high power external buffer may be needed.

It was suggested above that all external devices would be TTL, but this is not strictly true. Other devices, in particular MOS/LSI memory, in the same manner as the CPU, have I/O buffers to make them TTL compatible. From the engineers viewpoint this is an excellent technique since there are few problems of interconnection of special purpose devices.

5·4·4 The Control Section

The heart of the CPU is the *Instruction Register* (IR). The machine operates by fetching an instruction from memory, loading it into the IR, executing the instruction and on completion, fetching the next instruction from memory, etc. In this example the basic instruction is an 8 bit word, allowing each combination to specify a unique action to be executed. The instruction, once stored in the IR is decoded to specify a sequence of events, and the enabling of specific gates, required for the particular instruction. In some ways this can be likened to a telephone exchange, but with the major difference that *time* sequencing of events is all important. As previously described, this timing information is supplied by the State Timing Generator. In short the Instruction Decoder decides the 'what' and the State Timing Generator the 'when'.

Control is exercised, using the gates, on both the *arithmetic and logic unit* ALU (and its registers) and the internal memory. In addition some information concerning the particular instruction being executed must be transmitted out of the CPU so as to distinguish between the differing uses of the data port. This, on figure 5.6, is transmitted by the lines marked *function*, again in coded form due to the restriction on the number of external connections. The function effectively tells the external devices what to do with the data coming out of the port or what data to present to the port. Five functions are required:

F_1 transmit an instruction from memory to the CPU
F_2 transmit data from memory to the CPU (memory read)
F_3 transmit data from the CPU to memory (memory write)
F_4 transmit data from an external input (peripheral) to the CPU (input)
F_5 transmit data from the CPU to an external output (output)

The specific memory addresses or peripheral device numbers must be transmitted through the I/O port during one or two of the states of the machine cycle.

Functions F_4 and F_5 can be combined, and an input instruction differentiated from an output instruction by using some of the range of device numbers for inputs and the others for outputs. The resulting four functions could then be coded on to two lines out of the CPU. Note that combining F_4 and F_5 only reduces the information 'flagged' to the external devices from the CPU; internally the CPU fully differentiates its actions between input and output.

There are three other 1 bit inputs to the control section shown in figure 5.6, *ready, interrupt* and *reset.* The first two inputs may be short duration pulses and so they are 'latched' by 1 bit flip-flops. These flip-flops are cleared by the state timing generator after their information has been used.

The *ready* signal is used to indicate to the CPU whether data it is expecting at the data port is or is not available. Normally the ready line will be held at logic '1' and the processor will cycle through its state as required. If however slow-speed memory is being used, an address will be output during states T_1 and T_2 and the data should be available during T_3. If it is not available immediately after T_2 an erroneous piece of data, left from some previous action, would be transmitted during T_3. If this is possible, the ready line must be held at logic '0' during T_1 and T_2; the processor will then go into a *wait* state, rather than progressing to T_3. When the memory has completed its read and the data required by the CPU is available, the ready line will be switched to logic '1' and the processor will move from the wait state to T_3, etc. Note that, unlike $T_1, \ldots, T_4$, the wait state is of indefinite length, although, since it is synchronised to the clock, it will be an integer multiple of the state period.

The *interrupt* signal is used to alter the normal sequence of a program, in response to an external request. The interrupt system is discussed in Section 5.4.8. The acceptance of the interrupt is flagged outside the CPU by denoting a modified T_1 state. Alternatively an independent *interrupt acknowledge* signal could be generated.

A processor *stop* or *halt* is the seventh state. The halt state stops any further normal action, as distinct from the wait state, which can be restarted by the ready signal.

In summary the interrupt state is a modification of the normal T_1 state and the wait and halt states are modifications of the normal T_3 state.

The final element in the control section in figure 5.6 is the *stack pointer*. This is an internal register which indicates which of the double length registers in the internal memory is the current Program Counter. If there are eight double-length registers in the stack, a 3 bit stack pointer is required, etc. A double-length register may also be used as the stack pointer to 'point' to a stack in the main memory. This technique is discussed further in Section 5.4.7.

5·4·5 The Arithmetic and Logic Section

The *arithmetic and logic unit* (ALU) performs a number of operations on two 8 bit words of data. The two pieces of data, termed the *operands* are initially stored in temporary registers, denoted register a and register b in figure 5.6. Data can be shifted into or out of these registers, to or from any of the other internal registers or the data port, when the appropriate gates are enabled by the control section.

The range of ALU operations differs from design to design (the limiting factor is the fixed length of the instruction word, rather than the cost of hardware). The following is a representative list:

ADD	arithmetic, two's complement addition
SUB	arithmetic, two's complement subtraction
OR	logical OR
XOR	logical exclusive OR
AND	logical AND
COMPL	complement, replace '0' by '1' and vice versa
SL	shift left
SR	shift right
INC	increment (add 1)
DEC	decrement (subtract 1)

The first five operations in the above list require two operands and therefore use both registers a and b. The last five operate on one piece of data only, which is stored in register a.

The ALU itself does not store data, so that the result of the operation is stored back into register a, overwriting the original data.

The result of an ALU operation is tested and certain features of the results indicated by the condition flags. The five flags shown will be at logic '0' normally but set to logic '1' by the following:

C   if a carry resulted ('0' for all logical operations)
z   if the result is zero
N   if the result is negative (test for sign)
P   if the parity (arithmetic sum of the bits of the word) is even
V   is an arithmetic operation overflowed, i.e. a number out of the machine range of $+127$ to -128 for an 8 bit word.

The conditions under which these flags are set are discussed in Appendix 1. They are similar to the condition flags encountered in minicomputers, with the addition of the parity flag. These flags are used in the execution of conditional instructions.

The range of operations can usually be extended by simple modifications and combinations of the operations listed above. Some important ones are now given.

(i) *Add with carry*, i.e. the contents of registers a and b are added, together with the initial value of C; this is particularly important with the short word length of the microprocessor since 'double-precision' arithmetic may be necessary, i.e. two machine words to store one effective 16 bit piece of data.

(ii) *Compare* two data words, X and Y. By performing the operation X-Y, the condition flags will be set which can then be tested to establish the relation of X to Y. The following logical identities were noted in Section 2.8.4.3:

$$
\begin{aligned}
X > Y & \quad & z + (N \oplus v) = 0 \\
X \geqslant Y & \quad & N \oplus v = 0 \\
X < Y & \quad & N \oplus v = 1 \\
X \leqslant Y & \quad & z + (N \oplus v) = 1
\end{aligned}
$$

On some machines the v flag does not exist, so that overflow is not detected; the N flag can then be used instead of $N \oplus v$, but an error will exist if overflow does occur, which the programmer must avoid.

It must be noted that the SUB operation will set the condition flags in the same manner as *compare*; the difference is that SUB puts the result back into register a, while *compare* does nothing with the result.

(iii) The range of *shift* operations can be extended to include *rotate* (left or right). *Shift left* moves all digits left one place, pushing the most significant bit (MSB) into the carry and filling the least significant bit (LSB) with '0'; *shift right* moves all digits right one place, loosing the LSB and filling the MSB with the same digit as the original MSB, now one place to the right. Rotate operations differ from shift operations in that, with rotate left, the MSB is pushed into the LSB and vice versa for rotate right. A further variant allows the rotation to include the carry bit, i.e. rotate left through carry pushes the MSB into carry and the initial carry digit into the LSB.

(iv) The *increment* (INC) and *decrement* (DEC) operations are used for counters. They can possibly be combined with condition flag tests to give conditional operations such as 'decrement the contents of a register and jump to a new instruction if the result is zero; otherwise continue with the next instruction in sequence'.

Note that the more complex operations *multiply* and *divide* are not possible in an ALU of this simplicity. The major problem is that multiplying two 8 bit numbers together will produce a 16 bit answer, which cannot be effectively handled. The most successful way of handling multiplication, apart from the slower 'software' approach, is to use a specialised '*hardware-extended-arithmetic-unit*' (EAU) attached to the system as one of the peripherals; EAUs are discussed further in Chapter 8. The instruction set is discussed in greater detail in Section 5.5.

Apart from their use with the ALU, the two registers, a and b are often used as temporary work registers by the processor, e.g. data read into the CPU during the T_3 state is placed immediately into register b and transferred from there to its final location during T_4.

5·4·6 Internal Memory

The *internal memory* of the CPU shown in figure 5.6 consists of three sets of registers, the *scratch-pad memory*, the *data address pointer* and the *program-counter stack*.

The scratch-pad memory comprises of a number, about eight, of single word registers, which are used to store active pieces of data, rather than use the main memory; they are the general purpose registers common in any CPU. As usual some of these registers are allocated special tasks, e.g. accumulator, etc. As a specific example, the Add instruction can only explicitly define one operand, either the contents of one of the registers or a location in main memory; the second operand must be implied and is taken always as the contents of the scratch-pad register A. Thus the instruction *add register B* means add the contents of register B to the contents of register A and place the result in register A. Register A is thus called an *accumulator*.

This is a good example of the influence of software on hardware and vice-versa, in that the hardware (word length) has restricted the ability to 'call' a second operand. This is further exemplified by the fact that the number of registers in the scratch-pad is limited by the number of bits in the instruction that can be used to differentiate between them, and not by the cost, particularly in LSI.

The *data address pointer* is a 16 bit register, accessible as two distinct 8 bit words. It is used as a pointer to the location in main memory of a data word in the 'pointer-address' mode, which is explained in Section 5.5. Since both 8 bit halves of the register are independently accessible, they can be used as two extentions to the scratch-pad memory.

The *program counter stack* is a set of independent 16 bit registers, one of which is at any instant the *program counter* (PC). The number of 16 bit registers in the stack is related to the length of the stack pointer in the control section. The principle of stacking is discussed in the next section so consider here only one PC. Again each 8 bit half of the register must be accessible individually, so that the next instruction address can be transmitted to the main memory in two successive machine states (T_1 and T_2). As in any digital computer the PC contains the address of the next instruction (or part instruction in multiple word instructions). The lower byte of the PC contents will be incremented immediately after it has been transmitted (during state T_1); the higher byte is incremented after transmission (during state T_2) if a carry resulted from incrementing the lower byte.

Internal memories on the LSI chip are often of the 'dynamic' type, that is they are set by a pulse and store the logic output level on a charged capacitor. Since the charge on the capacitor will decay, the memories must be 'refreshed', typically every machine cycle. This action is totally independent of the machine operation from the user's viewpoint and can be completely ignored. The advantage of dynamic over 'static' registers is a reduction in power requirements at the expense of some extra circuitry.

5·4·7 Stacking

Stacking is a technique introduced into the more modern digital computers as discussed in Section 3.6, and therefore in microprocessors.

In the microprocessor of figure 5.6 the stack is used exclusively for the Program Counter; more extensive use of stacks will be discussed at the end of this section.

The PC stack is used when a program sequence is changed to execute a new group of instructions, following which the original program should continue from where it left off. Typical of such operations is *jump to subroutine (call)*; the subroutine will be terminated by a *return from subroutine* operation. Since the subroutine can be called from any part of the main program, indeed it may be called several times from different points, the return operation must be able to find the address from which the current call was made in order to establish the address in the main program from which to continue.

Consider the stack pointer to locate the first register in the stack as the PC. Let the address in this program counter, PC_0, fetch a *Call* instruction into the IR during state T_3, by which time the contents of PC_0 have been incremented by 1, so as to address the next memory location. The call is a special kind of *Jump* operation so that the starting address of the subroutine must now be transmitted to the CPU; this 16 bit address is stored in memory in the two locations following the instruction code, just copied into the IR. PC_0 is therefore currently pointing to the first of these words. State T_4 can be skipped and a second machine cycle commenced, the address being sent out at T_1 and T_2, the data read and PC_0 incremented again during T_3. This piece of data is not an instruction but is part of an address and is therefore saved temporarily. Since this is not an intermediate sum in the sense in which the scratch-pad memory is used, it is saved in, say, Register a. Again T_4 is skipped and the third machine cycle commenced, the data acquired at T_3 being the second byte of the starting address of the subroutine, this is stored temporarily in register b. Note that PC_0 will again be incremented so that it contains the address of the next instruction in the main program to be executed *after* completing the subroutine referenced by the call. Thus immediately after state T_3 in the third machine cycle the CPU contains, in registers a and b, the address of the next instruction to be executed and, in PC_0, the address to be returned to. At this stage, in the third machine cycle, the state T_4 is used; first the stack pointer is incremented by one, making PC_1 the active program counter; the contents of register a are then moved to the lower byte of the program counter, PC_1, and the contents of register b to the higher byte of PC_1. The call operation, a 3 word instruction in this example, is then complete, having taken ten machine states to fetch and execute.

The *return* instruction, which terminates the subroutine, is far simpler; it merely decrements the stack pointer making PC_0 the current program counter.

The main advantage of stacking is that calls can be 'nested'. Thus if subroutine 1 calls subroutine 2, the stack pointer is again incremented, PC_2 now becoming the active program counter; the Return from subroutine 2 decrements the stack pointer returning the sequence, via PC_1, to continue with subroutine 1, etc. With a 3 bit stack pointer and eight program counter registers, nesting up to eight levels can be used.

Nesting in a ninth level will increment the stack pointer, setting it to zero and referencing PC_0 again. In the sense that the ninth level nests in properly, this is correct, but the eventual return to the first level using PC_0, will find the contents corrupted by the ninth level operations.

Incrementing the stack pointers is often termed 'pushing' the stack; decrementing it is termed 'popping' the stack.

Memory Map

Memory Location	Instruction Data
⋮	
N − 1	...
N	Call SUB 1
N + 1 ⎫	Address of
N + 2 ⎭	SUB 1 (S1)
N + 3	...
⋮	(Continue Main Program)
S1 ⎫	Subroutine
S1 + 1 ⎬	
⋮ ⎭	SUB 1
S1 + x	Call SUB 2
S1 + x + 1 ⎫	Address of
S1 + x + 2 ⎭	SUB 2 (S2)
S1 + x + 3 ⎫	Rest of
⋮ ⎬	SUB 1
⋮ ⎭	
S1 + y	Return
S2 ⎫	Subroutine
⋮ ⎬	SUB 2
⋮ ⎭	
S2 + z	Return

Sequence

Active PC	Contents	Comments
0	N	
0	N + 1	
0	N + 2	
1	S1	$PC_0 \Rightarrow N + 3$
⋮	⋮	
1	S1 + x	
1	S1 + x + 1	
1	S1 + x + 2	
2	S2	$PC_1 \Rightarrow S1 + x + 3$
⋮	⋮	
2	S2 + z	
1	S1 + x + 3	$PC_2 \Rightarrow S2 + z + 1$
⋮	⋮	
1	S1 + y	
0	N + 3	$PC_1 \Rightarrow S1 + y + 1$
⋮	⋮	

Fig. 5·7 Nested subroutine calls using Program Counter Stack

It should be carefully noted that incorrect termination of a subroutine, e.g. a conditional jump causing the return instruction to be missed, will result in the stack pointer getting out of step, with disastrous results!

The normal minicomputer stacking technique, using memory locations for the stack, Section 3.6, is also used. Such a machine must have one, conventional, PC and a 16 bit stack pointer register. Pushing the stack will, as before increment the stack pointer, but a more complex transfer of data then ensues. After storing the new program address in temporary registers such as a and b, the current PC contents must be transferred to memory locations addressed by the stack pointer, before reloading the PC with the address from registers a and b. Note that the stack pointer has incremented by 2 for each 'push'. There is in this case no limit to the length of the stack. The physical location in main memory of the stack is simply established by the initial address loaded into the stack pointer register. While this is a slower technique, it can also be made more versatile since data other than addresses can be saved on the stack. A good example is the contents of the scratch-pad memory; if a subroutine needs to use these CPU registers, they will be corrupted when the return to the main program is made. Thus a subroutine should initially save the current contents of the registers it will use, in main memory, and restore these values after completing its own task, before the return instruction.

5·4·8 Interrupts

When an interrupt signal is detected, the current instruction is allowed to complete. When the next cycle commences, which will be a fetch-instruction, F_1, function, a modified T_1 state is entered which simply stops the incrementing of the PC. Note that an instruction and not just a memory cycle must be completed, so that the T_1 state cannot be modified until the F_1 function is requested.

How then is this incredibly simple interrupt procedure utilised? The fact that the requested interrupt had been accepted is flagged outside the CPU when the state information is decoded by the SFCU, in figure 5.5, detecting the modified T_1 state. The unmodified memory address sent out during T_1 and T_2 is completely ignored. During T_3, instead of enabling the memory read line, the interrupt instruction port is enabled. Thus the next instruction to be copied into the IR comes from the peripheral rather than memory. Any instruction can be 'jammed-in' in this fashion, but the obvious one to use is a jump to subroutine. If the peripheral interfaces are so designed that the device requesting the interrupt also feeds its own instruction to the interrupt port, then unique subroutine calls can be allocated. Most jump instructions, since they include the 16-bit memory address, are 3 bytes long. In this case the device interface would have to present 3 different bytes during successive T_3 cycles, resulting in a very complex interface. Thus special single byte instructions are formulated to give jump to subroutine at one of 8 locations only. Typically a 3 bit address is included in this instruction to specify a number, x, which causes a jump to location $x0_8$; the resulting 8 locations between each of these addresses can be used to transfer to longer routines elsewhere in memory.

Since a jump to subroutine instruction is used, the stacking system is automatically employed. When the return is executed the program will repeat the transmission of the original PC contents during the next T_1 and T_2 cycles, giving the correct nesting since the modified T_1 state did not increment the PC.

Note that the interrupt request from the peripheral must be cleared by the interrupt acknowledge signal or else a further interrupt will occur. With this simple system there is no priority system incorporated. The newer microprocessors however follow the main simple minicomputer interrupt system of using an internal interrupt-on flag. This is cleared when the interrupt is acknowledged and must be set by an interrupt enable instruction before another interrupt can be allowed.

If software polling is used to identify the source of an interrupt request, then only one interrupt instruction is required to jump to the interrupt handler routine, and this can be hard-wired in the interrupt instruction port. To achieve software polling, some I/O instructions must be used to read status registers from the peripherals, since there are no test/control type I/O instructions.

5·5 Instruction Sets

Many of the instructions available in microprocessors have been mentioned already in this chapter. In any case the microprocessor instruction set is similar to that of a minicomputer, and clearly different microprocessors will have different instruction sets. Basically the 8 bit instruction typical to microprocessors is rather constraining and results in a limited number and range of instructions. The multi-chip microprocessors are at an advantage here in that longer word lengths can be built up; the microprogrammed control unit can then be developed to produce an instruction set more like a minicomputer. To retain the simplicity and cost advantages however, the best must be made of an 8 bit instruction, using some multiple-word instructions such as the call instruction discussed in Section 5.4.7.

Fundamentally an instruction comprises an *operation-code* (op-code) and a number of *operands*. The op-code decides 'what' and the operands 'what with'. A few instructions such as return and halt require no operand, others one and others two. Two operands are difficult to specify in an 8 bit instruction so that, when required, the second operand is implicitly taken as the contents of a particular internal register, called the Accumulator. It would be ideally simple, (particularly for the designer of the control section of the microprocessor!), if specific bits of the instruction word were reserved for the op-code and others for operands, but this is far too wasteful for an 8 bit instruction. The machine code of a microprocessor is thus rather illogical in appearance when compared to a minicomputer machine code. The use of Symbolic Assembly Languages renders this of little importance, to the relief of all users!

Figure 5.8 is a list of instructions which may be encountered. No one machine will have all of these instructions.

The *conditional jumps* are executed by testing the condition flags or combinations of them as shown in Section 5.4.5. The conditional tests can easily be extended to the *call, return, increment* and *decrement* instructions, e.g. Call subroutine if v is '1' (true). When a conditional test fails, the program continues with the next instruction in sequence. A most common combination is the instruction *decrement and skip if zero* (DSZ); the contents of a register are decremented and the result tested for zero. If zero does result ($z = $ '1'), the PC is incremented (by 3 in an 8 bit machine) so that the next instruction in sequence is skipped; that instruction must be a (3 word) jump which will therefore be executed whenever the result is non-zero. This instruction is used for simple *do loops*, the location tested by the DSZ instruction storing a counter.

The *decimal adjust* instruction is common on microprocessors due to the association with calculators. It facilitates the use of BCD arithmetic, when two BCD characters are stored in the one 8 bit word. If two, 2 character BCD numbers are added, they will be treated as binary numbers with an erroneous BCD result. The decimal adjust instruction corrects this result, which will be saved in the accumulator after the ADD instruction, by the following algorithm:
if x_0 denotes the least significant decimal digit, stored in bits 0–3 and x_1 the other digit stored in bits 4–7, then

$$x_1 x_0 + y_1 y_0 \text{ give } z_1 z_0 \text{ following ADD.}$$

DEC ADJ modifies $z_1 z_0$
if $z_0 > 9$ or there was a carry from bit 3, then replace z_0 by $z_0 + 6$, add any carry to z_1
if $z_1 > 9$ or there was a carry from bit 7, then replace z_1 by $z_1 + 6$, setting the C flag.
Note that an additional carry flip-flop is required to detect the carry from bit 3.

Many double precision instructions have been introduced to facilitate handling of 16 bit address words, e.g.
DADD R_0 causes the contents of the two registers R_0 and R_1, treated as one 16 bit word, to be added to the data address pointer contents.

Operation Code	Operand 1	Operand 2	Comments
MOVE (LOAD and STORE)	d.a./r	d.a./r	Both operands may be r, but only one or the other d.a.
ADD	d.a./r	Accumulator	
SUB	d.a./r	Accumulator	
ADD + CARRY	d.a./r	Accumulator	} The carry bit is used as a one bit third operand
SUB – BORROW	d.a./r	Accumulator	
AND	d.a./r	Accumulator	
OR	d.a./r	Accumulator	
Exclusive-OR	d.a./r	Accumulator	
COMPARE	d.a./r	Accumulator	
INCREMENT	d.a./r	—	Normally r only
DECREMENT	d.a./r	—	Normally r only
COMPLEMENT	d.a./r	—	Normally r only
SHIFT–LEFT	d.a./r	—	} Normally r only, possibly Accumulator only. Rotate may and may not include carry
SHIFT–RIGHT	d.a./r	—	
ROTATE–LEFT	d.a./r	—	
ROTATE–RIGHT	d.a./r	—	
DECIMAL ADJUST	Accumulator	—	See text
INPUT	I/P device number	Accumulator	
OUTPUT	O/P device number	Accumulator	
JUMP	i.a.	—	The 'GO TO' instruction
CALL	i.a.	—	One machine has a 'Restart' Call to one of eight page 0 locations, which is stored in 1 rather than 3 words, see Section 5.4.8
JUMP CONDITIONALLY	i.a.	—	The 'iF' instructions
RETURN	—	—	
HALT	—	—	

Fig. 5-8 r = register identifier; d.a. = data address; i.a. = instruction address. The true operand is the contents of the identified storage locations

With machines which use a 16 bit *stack pointer* (SP), *push* and *pop* instructions can be defined, e.g.

PUSH r decrements the SP and stores the contents of register r in the location addressed by the SP. A variant on the theme may cause the contents of two or more registers to be stacked in consecutive locations.

The distinction is made between data and instruction addresses in figure 5.8 since some addressing modes cannot be applied to both. Indeed, in some machines, usually 4 bit word length, the instructions and data are stored in different memories.

Associated with each instruction the operand must communicate the location of the data. The location of a data word stored in main memory requires a 16 bit address word and clearly cannot be actually included in the 8 bit instruction. The operand part of the instruction therefore must indicate the addressing mode, whereby other registers are used to hold the location of the actual operand. A variety of possible modes are now discussed.

Register mode. The operand is stored in an internal register. The operand part of the instruction need only 'number' which register and, since there are few such registers, can be coded directly into the instruction.

Immediate mode. The operand is located in the memory location(s) immediately following the location of the associated instruction. Since the PC increments as soon as it has located the instruction, it holds the address of the operand. For an 8 bit machine if the operand is an 8 bit data word, e.g. a move data from memory to an internal register, only one word is required; if however the operand is a 16 bit instruction address, e.g. Jump (to a new 16 bit address) two consecutive memory locations are used as described in some detail in Section 5.4.7.

Pointer mode. The operand is stored at any location in main memory. A specific 16 bit (or pair of 8 bit) internal register, called the *data address pointer* (DAP) in figure 5.6, locates the operand. The DAP must be loaded before the instruction is executed. This is a slow mode of addressing since either two Move instructions or a special double precision load instruction are required to load the DAP, in addition to the actual instruction. This mode is not used for two word operands, since two DAPs would be required.

Indexed mode. The operand part of the instruction is added to the DAP to locate the true operand. In this mode the DAP need only be loaded once to locate a set of closely grouped locations. The size of the group is determined by the maximum number which could be coded into the operand part of the instruction; the word following the instruction is used to store the offset.

Program Counter Relative mode. This is the same as the *indexed* mode, except that the PC is used as the DAP (the PC contents must not be changed by the indexing addition). In this way the 'local group' of memory locations addressable moves as the program executes. Again this mode cannot be used with short word lengths.

The concepts of *Direct* and *Indirect* addressing can be considered. Direct addressing is as described above. Indirect addressing uses the contents of the memory word located, not as the operand, but as an address to the true operand location. Indirect addressing is not commonly used on 8 bit machines due to the double word address problem. In a 16 bit machine it could be used with the associated Auto Incrementing and Decrementing modes.

The normal 8 bit instruction word of the microprocessor means that Register, Immediate and Pointer Modes are the only ones usually encountered, with no Indirect addressing. Longer word lengths and microprogramming means that most minicomputer instructions and addressing modes can be incorporated.

5·6 Programmable Logic Arrays

A programmable digital computer, either mini or micro, is essentially a word oriented device, making it most suitable for arithmetic processing. Processing of logical data, which involves single bits of information can be accomplished by masking operations on internal words. One computer word will be used to store a number of single bits of data. Single bit data processing is thus not very efficient.

A particular logical system can be implemented by a specially constructed collection of random logic elements. The total specification can be formulated in terms of truth and state tables so that the type of logic elements, their position and possible interconnections can be determined. The use of a programmable computer to implement the system can be considered as the system complexity increases. An example of this is the technique of microprogramming to implement the logic of a CPU instruction decoder and controller, Section 8.2. However a general purpose computer must implement the logical (Boolean) equations by treating them as a sequential program.

An alternative approach to the implementation of logical networks is to use a general purpose programmable device, specially oriented to logical, but not arithmetic, processing. Any logical system has a number of input bits, $x_1, x_2, \ldots x_n$ and a number of output bits, $z_1, z_2, \ldots, z_p$. For a combinational logic problem the outputs will be defined by some combination of the inputs. For a sequential logic problem however, the output will be a function of the input and the current condition or state of any internal storage elements. In turn the states, $y_1, y_2, \ldots, y_m$ will be changed as a function of the inputs and the previous states of these memory elements. This can be written as the Boolean state equations

$$y_i(k) = f(x_1(k), \dots, x_n(k), \ y_1(k-1), \dots, y_m(k-1)); \qquad i = 1, \dots m$$

and

$$z_j(k) = g(x_1(k), \dots, x_n(k), \ y_1(k-1), \dots, y_m(k-1)); \qquad j = 1, \dots, p$$

where f and g mean 'functions of', each specific problem being defined by a unique function. The system for implementing these equations is shown in figure 5.9.

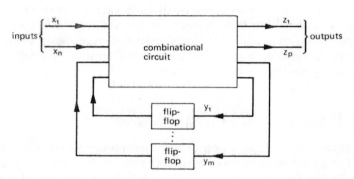

Fig. 5·9 A sequential logic system

If the combinational circuit in figure 5.9 can be programmed then a general purpose device results. In practice all available devices must be programmed with special apparatus, and, unlike the general purpose digital computer, cannot be easily reprogrammed. The simplest device conceptually is a ROM*. The ROM must have $n + m$ input lines and therefore requires $2^{(n+m)}$ words to uniquely specify all possible combinations. Each combination must result in a specific output and new state, i.e. $p + m$ bits, so that each ROM word must be $p + m$ bits long. The particular functions required define the bit patterns programmed into the ROM. Unfortunately a 5 input, 5 output, 10 memory element system requires 491520 bits of ROM.

The system can be simplified by realising that all possible combinations will never be required. In fact the Boolean equations can be shown to be definable by a set of q 'prime implicants'. The prime implicants will be greater in number than the states, but will be logical AND functions of the inputs and the state. The new state and hence the output are created by a logical OR function of the prime implicants as shown in figure 5.10.

* Programmable ROM (PROM) will allow the logic function to be changed.

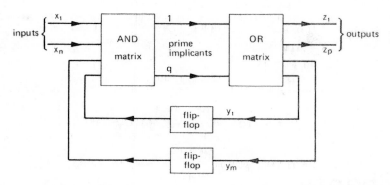

Fig. 5·10 A programmable logic array

Particular combinations of the AND and OR functions can be programmed into the matrices, as with the ROM. These devices are called *programmable logic arrays* (PLA) or *functional memory*; they cannot be reprogrammed, being constructed by masking during manufacture to a user supplied combination. With a PLA the 5 input, 5 output, 10 memory element system with 60 prime implicants requires 1800 bits in the AND matrix and 900 bits in the OR matrix, a total of 2700 compared to nearly half a million for the pure ROM.

PLAS may prove a cheaper, faster way of implementing logical, but non-arithmetic, systems compared to say a microprocessor. However the cost of masking the matrices will be high, so that the cheapness will only be realised for large quantities of the same system.

Chapter 6

Peripheral Devices

6·1 An Introduction to Peripheral Devices

In this chapter, brief descriptions of the peripheral devices normally encountered are given. When choosing a peripheral device it is reasonable to assume that the interfacing requirements will be similar from one supplier to another. A word of warning that must be given however, is not to forget the software situation. Manufacturer A is hardly likely to give you his Disc Operating System (DOS) software with his computer if you buy B's disc system and even if A will sell the DOS, he probably will not support it. If B supplies the disc to use with A's computer, then B must supply and maintain the DOS.

There is no need to differentiate between minicomputer and larger computer peripherals in this general description. The difference lies in the ruggedness of the devices, the capacity, the speed and the cost. The best way of viewing the current situation is to consider the minicomputer peripherals to be scaled-down versions of the data processing peripherals. This situation is very flexible since minicomputers are now being used in data processing applications which, for reliability's sake, must support a full scale line printer, rather than the simpler, cheaper printer suitable for, say, a data logging system. There are also a number of peripherals specifically for use in real-time systems, which are of course the domain of minicomputers, e.g. analogue and digital signal processing equipment.

The peripheral devices can be split into groups:

(i) *Alphanumeric devices* which transmit or display human acceptable data, e.g. teletypes, line printers, etc.

(ii) *Card and paper tape punches and readers, etc.* These are storage media which can be interpreted by a human operator.

(iii) *Bulk data storage systems*, e.g. magnetic tape and disc. These devices simply store data as it is presented, irrespective of any form of coding, e.g. a source program will be saved as coded characters, which are presented to the compiler for decoding; the object program generated may be returned to the disc in pure binary (memory image) form. Any responsibility for the coding of the stored data is that of the service program, not the disc, e.g. the FORMAT statements in a FORTRAN program. Paper tape can also be used for this type of storage; thus if a binary tape, say an object program, is read through a tape reader/printer, then only when the binary data coincidentally has the same hole/space format as that of a legitimate character, will that character be printed, resulting in pure gibberish.

(iv) *Signal processing equipment*, e.g. ADC, DAC, etc. These devices are essentially numeric and therefore preferably use pure binary code, although BCD is often encountered. As with alphanumeric codes, BCD requires some code conversion by software.

(v) *Data communication systems.* These devices, multiplexors, code convertors, etc., are not strictly speaking peripherals themselves, but are units to enable other data transmitting/receiving systems to communicate with the computer, including computer to computer connection. The necessary interface logic is provided to make them program controllable.

(vi) Devices which are used to enhance the performance of the CPU, rather than to communicate with the outside world, e.g. real-time clock, extended-arithmetic-unit, etc. These devices are discussed in Chapter 8, although they will still require an interface as described previously in Section 4.5.

6·2 Parity Checking

In communicating data between two devices, there is a small but finite possibility of an error occurring. This is most common in simpler peripheral devices, particularly magnetic tape systems due to tape 'drop-out', and long distance transmission over telephone or telegraph lines. Thus a number of error detecting techniques have been developed. Any such technique requires that redundant bits of data be appended to the coded information. Parity checking is the most common method of modifying code to create an 'error-checking-code'. More sophisticated techniques can create 'error-correcting-codes' which are encountered in communications systems, but only infrequently in computer systems.

There are two types of parity, odd and even. The data is coded into, say, a 7 bit character (actual data codes, e.g. ASCII, are explained in Section 6.3.1) to which one extra, parity, bit is added. For even parity there must be an even number of ones in the 8 bits, and for odd parity an odd number. The parity bit is generated at source and the number of ones in the received character checked. An odd number of bits in error will then be detected; an even number of errors, including an error in transmission of the parity bit, will go undetected. The parity bit may be appended to a block of data, rather than each character, with reduced effectiveness.

The parity check can be extended to blocks of data by adding a full character at the end of the block, each bit of which forms the parity bit for the corresponding bit in each character in the block. If each character has its own parity bit, as well, then a two dimensional check is made, greatly reducing the likelihood of multiple errors combining to beat the check. A similar effect to the 'longitudinal' parity character can be achieved by performing a running sum on the data and, ignoring overflow, storing the result at the end of the block. The same sum can be performed as the transmitted data is received and checked for error. This is called a 'check sum'. A 'cyclic-redundancy-character' may also be recorded which can be used to correct errors, provided they occur in one track. True cyclic redundancy can be achieved by transmitting the block twice, or even three times, and comparing the received signals. Parity and checksum techniques are much more economical.

6·3 Alphanumeric Devices

6·3·1 Alphanumeric Codes

The 10 numeric digits, 0 to 9, the 26 upper case and 26 lower case alphabetic characters, together with about 20–30 punctuation marks, parenthesis, +, −, =, etc., define around 90–100 unique characters. To this list must be appended about another 20–30 control characters, e.g. start device, line feed and carriage return. The full list of around 120 characters requires at least 7 bits ($2^7 = 128$) to uniquely specify each character. In practice the lower case alphabetic characters are seldom used.

One or two standard codes have been formulated, although small differences in interpretation still exist. Some common ones are:

(i) ASCII (American Standard Code for Information Interchange). This a 7 bit code, usually increased to 8 bits by the inclusion of a parity bit. This is probably the most common code in current use and is listed in figure 6.1. The ANSCII code is similar.

(ii) BCD. This is a 6 bit plus parity bit code which is an extension of the normal BCD number representation. Thus 000101 is 5_{10} with the combinations above 001010 ($= 10_{10}$) attributed to alphabetic characters, punctuation marks, etc. One exception however is that 000000 represents a blank, not zero, which is represented by 001010. Some computers were designed to handle 6 bit characters rather than the standard byte.

(iii) ISO 7. This is another 7 bit code similar to ASCII.

(iv) EBCDIC (Extended Binary-Coded Decimal Interchange Code). This is a full 8-bit code dominantly intended for use with punched card systems. The punched card itself is a 12 bit system, so that directly equivalent 8 bit codes are generated for each 12 bit code punched. The 12 bit card punch code is wasteful and is a hangover from earlier data processing systems. The 12 bit code read from the card must be electronically converted to the 8 bit 'transmission' code.

(v) *Hollerith*. This is the most common 12 bit card code, shown in figure 6.2. Apart from a few characters the 12 bit EBCDIC and *Hollerith* codes are similar. However, an 8 bit equivalent to the Hollerith code has not been standardised, although Hollerith to ASCII dominates.

(vi) *Paper tape codes*. Paper tape is available in 5, 7 or 8 hole widths. 8 hole, utilising the ASCII code dominates nowadays, although minor variants to the code cause irritating incompatibility between systems. The eighth bit is regularly used for a parity unit. Alternative 8 bit and similar 7 bit codes have been used. The 5 channel tape presents problems due to insufficient bits in one frame to create a wide enough range of characters. Two consecutive frames could be used, but the common 5 channel code is the BAUDOT code. One character is used to denote that all following characters are numbers, and another to denote that all following characters are alphabetic; the state exists until a new letter/figure character is inserted. In this way the 5 bits are used to define alphabetic characters *or* numerics. A 2 bit version of this code is used with some two track cassette tape recorders.

Most significant 2 octal digit	Least significant octal digit							
	000	001	010	011	100	101	110	111
0 000	NUL	SOH	STX	ETX	EOT	WRU	RU	BEL
0 001	BS	HT	LF	VT	FF	CR	SO	SI
0 010	DLE	DC1	DC2	DC3	DC4	NAK	SYN	ETC
0 011	CAN	EM	SUB	ESC	FS	GS	RS	US
0 100	SP	!	"	#	$	%	&	'
0 101	(	)	*	+	,	—	.	/
0 110	0	1	2	3	4	5	6	7
0 111	8	9	:	;	<	=	>	?
1 000	@	A	B	C	D	E	F	G
1 001	H	I	J	K	L	M	N	O
1 010	P	Q	R	S	T	U	V	W
1 011	X	Y	Z	[	\	]	↑	←
1 100	—	a	b	c	d	e	f	g
1 101	h	i	j	k	l	m	n	o
1 110	p	q	r	s	t	u	v	w
1 111	x	y	z	{	|	}	~	DEL

Bit 7 is the parity bit. Thus with *even* parity
1 0101 010 = * and 0 0110 110 = 6

The symbols, with particular reference to a teletype, Section 6.3.2, mean

NUL	Null or tape feed (control-shift P)
SOH	Start of heading; also SOM, start of message (control A)
STX	Start of text; also EOA, end of address (control B)
ETX	End of text; also EOM, end of message (control C)
EOT	End of transmission; also END (control D)
WRU	'who are you?'; also ENQ, enquiry (control E)
RU	'are you . . .?'; also ACK, acknowledge (control F); duplicated on some machines by 174_8
BEL	Ring bell (control G)
BS	Backspace; also FEO, format effector (control H)
HT	Horizontal tab (control I)
LF	Line feed (control J)
VT	Vertical tab (control K)
FF	Form feed to next page (control L)
CR	Carriage return (control M)

SO	Shift out; change print colour to red (control N)
SI	Shift in; change print colour to black (control O)
DLE	Data link escape (control P)
DC1	Device control 1; XON, turn reader on (control Q)
DC2	Turn punch on (control R)
DC3	XOFF, turn reader off (control S)
DC4	Turn punch off (control T)
NAK	Negative acknowledge; also ERR, error (control U)
SYN	Synchronous idle (control V)
ETC	End of transmission block; also LEM, logical end of medium (control W)
CAN	Cancel (control X)
EM	End of medium (control Y)
SUB	Substitute (control Z)
ESC	Escape (control-shift K)
FS	File separator (control-shift L)
GS	Group separator (control-shift M)
RS	Record separator (control-shift N)
US	Unit separator (control-shift O)
SP	Space
DEL	Delete, rub out.

Fig. 6·1 ASCII Code

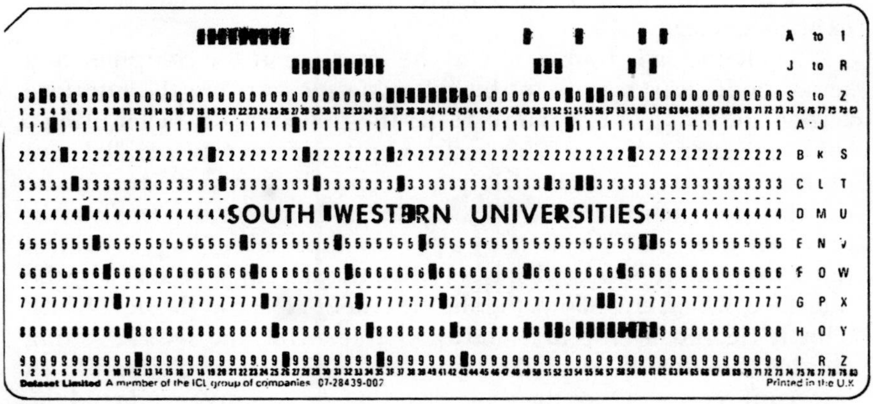

Fig. 6·2 Hollerith Code

6·3·2 Teletype Terminals

The teletype terminal must be the commonest computer peripheral. It comprises a keyboard and a printer, with a possible paper tape reader/punch attachment. Although similar in layout to a conventional typewriter, it must be stressed that the keyboard and printer are independent units. It should also be pointed out that the keyboard layout differs from a typewriter; in particular lower case alphabetic characters are not provided. Nevertheless a conventional shift key is used for some characters such as (, etc. There is also a second shift key, called *control*, which if depressed when one of the other keys is pressed will generate a control character. These were listed in figure 6.1. A few keys provide local action at the terminal, e.g. Run-out generates a leader on paper tape, but most control functions merely generate a specific ASCII character; the device receiving this informationn must decode it and create the appropriate action itself.

When a specific key, or pair of keys, is depressed an ingenious mechanical linkage causes the appropriate logical ones or zeros to be connected to seven positions of a rotatable eleven port mechanical distributer. The first position on the distributer is permanently wired to generate a 'start' pulse and the last two positions 'end of character' spaces. The remaining position on the distributer, equivalent to bit 7 of a resulting 8 bit character is filled by a parity bit. The distributer is motor driven via a clutch, which is activated as soon as the character is presented. The speed of rotation, synchronised to the mains, is such that 110 distributer positions per second are connected in sequence to a twisted pair of lines, resulting in 10 characters per second maximum being transmitted serially at 110 bits per second.* A power source is required in the teletype interface to feed the distributer, as will be explained later.

The character is transmitted to the interface at the computer in a serial mode, least significant bit following the start bit; the interface accepts the string of bits and recreates the 8 bit ASCII character using a shift register as a buffer. This buffer register can now be parallel read by the computer. A 110 cycle per second clock is provided in the interface to synchronise the shift register to the motor driven distributer in the teletype. The interface also contains a pair of flags to control the transmission. A busy flag is set when the start bit is received by the interface, which also allows the shift register to clock in the next 8 bits. This is cleared by the first end of character bit, the second setting another flip-flop, termed the done flag. This may also generate an interrupt request. Once the done flag is set the computer can read the contents of the buffer, and also to clear the done flag. No further character transmitted from the keyboard buffer will be accepted by the interface buffer until the Done flag is clear.

Serial transmission between the keyboard and the interface ensures that the cost of cabling is greatly reduced. The reduction in speed is

---

* The term *Baud* is often used to mean bits per second. Strictly however the Baud is the number of pieces of information per second so that the two units are only the same for a single pair of wires using a binary code.

quite tolerable considering the speed at which an operator can strike the keys.

The printer is similarly serviced. A buffer in the interface can be loaded with an ASCII character, which automatically sets a busy flag and commences the 11 bit serial transmission. The data is collated by activating solenoids to position the printer head, which on receipt of the end bits causes another solenoid to strike the paper. Transmission of the final bit automatically clears the busy flag and sets a done flag, which can generate an interrupt, requesting more data.

The paper tape unit on the teletype (the usual teletype without paper tape unit is a KSR 33, with paper tape unit an ASR 33, automatic send-receive) is not independent of the keyboard/printer. The paper tape reader feeds the same distributer as the keyboard* and transmits in exactly the same fashion and speed, e.g. the computer cannot distinguish between data arriving from the keyboard or paper tape reader. The difference is that the keyboard is activated by the operator, the reader by the computer. Thus there is a further flip-flop in the interface, labelled *reader enable*, which on setting causes a pulse to be transmitted to a solenoid in the reader, incrementing the paper tape one frame and commencing transfer of the data to the interface. Note then that tape may appear to be reading continuously, but this is only the computer making repeated requests for a new character as fast as the reader can supply them. The reader-enable flip-flop is cleared when the data is received by the interface.

The paper tape punch is simply paralleled to the printer. If the punch is mechanically switched off, no tape will be punched, but there is no way to punch tape and not print at the same time.

There are three possible modes of transmission. (i) *Simplex*, which is unidirectional and could only serve either the printer *or* keyboard, (ii) *Duplex*, which provides independent simultaneous bi-directional communication and (iii) *Half-duplex* which is bi-directional but either one direction or the other at any time. Full-duplex requires independent pairs of wires between computer and teletype, half-duplex only one pair. The full-duplex mode is commonly employed, so that with a third pair of wires to activate the paper tape reader solenoid, a six wire cable is required.

A switch is usually provided on the teletype to run the machine in *local* mode. This provides the appropriate current sources and connects the keyboard output direct to the printer. In this way the terminal is disconnected from the computer and can be used to create punched paper tape and to 'print' paper tape previously punched.

---

* The 'parity' bit will be directly read from the tape, while it will be appended to the 7 data bits by the keyboard as either odd or even parity, dependent upon the specification.

With distances of over 300 metres quite likely to be encountered, standard TTL logic is unacceptable for line drivers and receivers. Teletypes are usually designed such that a 20 mA or 60 mA current must be passed along the line to create logic 1 and a negligible current for logic 0; for transmission over telegraph wires ±80 volts are used. Typical current loop driver and receiver circuits are shown in figure 6.3.

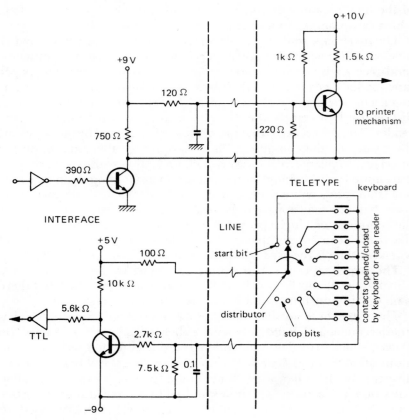

Fig. 6·3 Teletype – interface line circuits

6·3·3 Alternative Keyboard – Printer Terminals

The teletype terminal is essentially an electromechanical device, making little use of modern electronics. Thus a new range of computer terminals is now available. These machines use touch-type keyboards which create the appropriate ASCII character directly in a TTL buffer register. The printers sometimes use the 'golf-ball' principle found in electric typewriters, but the faster machines use a 'dot-matrix' printing head. This device comprises a vertical column of seven pins which can be caused to strike the paper, through the ink ribbon, by electrically operated solenoids. A character is generated by striking the paper five times, incrementing the head position along the paper each time, with controlled selection of the activated pins. In this way a pattern of dots is printed inside a 5 × 7 matrix; 7 × 9 dot matrix characters are also used. A logic circuit inside the printer converts the ASCII character information loaded into the printer buffer register into the desired five patterns of the seven pins. A standard 64 character set is usually programmed in this way. The quality of print achieved is exceptional. Some examples are shown in figure 6.4.

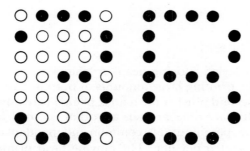

Fig. 6·4 5 × 7 dot matrix characters

These printers will type up to 30 characters per second, three times as fast as a teletype. The same serial transmission system is used, i.e. 1 start bit, 8 character bits, including parity, and 2 stop bits, but for 30 characters per second, at 330 bits per second. With an increase in clock speed the same interface as used with the teletype can be employed, although normal bus line-drivers and receivers can be employed, usually with optical couplers. Normal TTL logic is used at the terminal. Currently these machines are slightly more expensive than a teletype; the real problem however is that the cost of a 30 frame per second paper tape punch is much more than that of the simple 10 frame per second unit on the ASR teletypes. Thus while the teletype is a somewhat inferior printer, keyboard, reader and punch, it is the most economic combination.

6·3·4 UARTS

The *Universal Asynchronous Receiver Transmitter* (UART) is a MOS/LSI chip which performs all the serial to parallel and vice versa operations required by the teletype and similar machines. The send and receive sections are independent. The parallel character (7 or 8 bits) is entered into a register in the UART. This can be shifted out on a series line with the appropriate start and stop bits appended. Similarly a serial input can be loaded into a buffer register, removing the start and stop bits, for parallel reading. The parity bit can be generated or checked by the UART and various word lengths less than 8 bits can be used. All the signals necessary for an interface, e.g. 'data being transmitted', done, etc., are generated by the UART. The UART requires an external clock to set the serial data rate, which can be up to 50 K bits per second for use with VDUS.

For printers with electronic buffer registers, two UARTS are required, one in the interface and one in the terminal; only the interface unit is required for a teletype with its electromechanical distributer system.

6·3·5 Line Printers

The typewriter styled 'moving-head' or 'character-at-a-time' printers are too slow for printing large amounts of output. Fast versions (200 character per second plus) of the matrix printers are now available but higher speed 'line at a time' printers are often essential. Speeds of 200, 300 and 600 lines per minute are common, independent of the number of characters printed per line. The moving head printer must allow time for the head to return to the line beginning (carriage return) or must be programmed to print left-to-right, right-to-left, left-to-right, etc. Average printing rates, varying with the number of characters printed are restricted to around 100 lines per minute. The faster character-at-a-time printers are called serial printers.

Ideally the printer contains a matrix of buffer registers, one per character position across a line, which can be loaded sequentially at high speed by the computer, using parallel transmission for each character (bit parallel, character serial). The printer is then activated to print the whole line of data in one operation.

One method used for line printing is to employ an independent head for each character position, e.g. for the standard 132 column printer, 132 heads. Because of the close proximity, a wheel printing head must be used, rather than the more usual cylinder or ball heads, sandwiched together across the paper width to form a drum. The full character set is embossed on the outer edge of the wheel which is rotated at a continuous, synchronous speed. To print a character requested by the data in the buffer register, a counter is activated by a marker pulse on the head. A synchronised counter then causes a pulse to be generated when the appropriate character is directly opposite the paper, which activates a hammer and types the character. Some medium speed printers use this principle on a character-at-a-time basis, rather than a line at a time, by using a single wheel and incrementing its position across the page. Others print some twenty to twenty-four columns as a block, moving the block as required to complete the line; part lines can be printed by this technique.

Another technique used by bigger line printers is to emboss the character set on a flexible belt, which is rotated so that it moves across the face of the paper, to its full width. Thus at any one instant in time a different character will be opposite each column, with the full character set passing each column in sequence, e.g. when A is opposite column 20, B will be in column 19 position and T will be in column 1. At an instant in time later A will be in column 21 while T is in column 2, etc. Thus with a counter (allowing for the displacement across the paper) and hammer associated with each position, the hammer at any one station can be activated as the appropriate character passes the position. In this way a whole line is printed in the time taken for the 'belt' to move the full width of the paper. Also called a chain printer.

Clearly the dot matrix technique, with a full 5×7 or 7×9 pin head, is a major competitor. Both medium speed moving head and multiple head full line printers will be developed. Alternative methods of printing other than striking the paper through an inked tape are encountered, e.g. 'squirted' ink, electrostatic deposition or thermal, the so called 'non-contacting' methods, often needing special paper.

6·4 Paper Tape and Card Equipment

The peripherals described in this section are used for creating machine readable information. They also form long-term off-line data storage media. The two main types are punched paper tape and punched cards. Unlike the magnetic storage devices explained in the next section, the stored data can be manipulated by hand, although modifications to a paper tape will necessitate splicing. They can also be interpreted visibly.

6·4·1 Paper Tape Readers and Punchers

Punched paper tape equipment was introduced in Section 6.3.2 as an attachment to a teletype terminal. Appropriate punched hole codes were discussed in Section 6.3.1. The paper tape attachment on a teletype is however slow, with a maximum rate of 10 frames per second. It can take the best part of 30 minutes to load a BASIC interpreter from paper tape, using the teletype.

Readers and punches are independent units with separate interfaces, although the two interfaces are often physically mounted on the same card. The interface requirements are similar to those of the teletype reader/punch already described, except that, with higher data rates, parallel transmission is used. It should be stressed that the advantages of serial transmission are related to the possible long distances between the terminal and computer, a problem not relevant to a peripheral such as a reader/punch.

The reader feeds the punched tape over an array of photo diodes, which translate the presence or absence of holes into logical ones or zeros respectively. The punch is a mechanism which cuts holes in tape corresponding to logical ones. Since punches involve far more physical effort, they are much slower than readers. Typical minicomputers peripherals read at 300 characters per second and punch at 50 characters per second.

A variety of techniques are used for the drives, remembering that they are incremental in nature (the computer reads or punches one frame at a time) and therefore must be capable of stopping fully on any one frame. Ratchet wheels driven by a solenoid are frequently used; stepper motors are more commonly being employed, but some means of correctly aligning the frame along the tape is essential. The drive may be positive, via sprocket holes, or by friction rollers. The sprocket holes can be used for alignment.

The tape can either be reeled, in which case tape reel drives will be required for high speed, or it may be 'fan-folded'. Standard tape is 25 mm wide using 8 holes per frame, but other widths and hole configurations have been used. In the data processing field wider tape has been used with the punched data along one side and corresponding printing on the other side, allowing easy visual inspection; this is referred to as 'edge-punched' tape.

Teletypes, in local mode, are often used to prepare original source tapes.

6·4·2 Card Readers and Punches

Punched cards are physically larger, for a given amount of data stored, than paper tape, but a file can be easily edited by replacement of individual cards. They are most useful for storing high-level computer programs, one line of source code per card. The standard Hollerith and EBCDIC codes used for cards were mentioned in Section 6.3.1. The standard card has 80 columns, but a few variants are encountered typically with 96 or 40 columns.

Punched card apparatus is less frequently encountered on minicomputers, although scaled down readers are available, handling some 200–300 cards per minute. On-line card punches would only be used on a special minicomputer system; e.g. a data-preparation, editing system; original cards being prepared on standard off-line data preparation keyboard-card punches.

The interface is more complex than for a paper tape unit. First a card must be set in motion past the reader head; once a card is fed from the hopper it will pass completely over the read/punch head. All 80 columns will be read or punched, each column being handled as a parallel character, one character at a time. The interface must indicate the completion of one card and, under computer control, cause the next card to feed, etc. Due to the use of the highly redundant 12 bit Hollerith code, the interface must contain a code convertor, an electronic LSI device which accepts the 12 bit code and converts it to an equivalent 8 bit ASCII character, which is then accepted by the computer. The punch works in reverse, an ASCII to Hollerith convertor driving the 12 bit punch head. It is also common to flag mechanical card handling errors to the computer; e.g. a photo diode can detect that a card feed request has not resulted in the card arriving at the head.

As shown in figure 6.2 it is common to print the symbol of the punched character at the top of the card, over the column, for easy visual checking. This is done off-line, either by a verifying machine or by the keyboard-punch machines (the verifier is a modification of the keyboard-punch machine, with automatic feed which reads the character and types the code, inhibiting the punch).

6·4·3 Optical and Magnetic Cards

A number of attempts have been made in the commercial field to introduce machine readable media, which are also visually readable by human beings.

Consider a character to be printed by a dot matrix technique, creating either a black spot (1) or leaving the white paper (0) in each of the 35 positions for a 5×7 matrix. An optical reading head, utilising photo transistors, one per position of the matrix, can use the difference in reflectivity to determine the specific combination of data. Since each combination printed corresponds to a unique character, a decoding network (another special purpose LSI device) can convert the 35 bits of binary information into the appropriate 8 bit ASCII character.

A magnetic character reader works on the same principle except that the ink used is doped with a magnetic material, so that the 0 or 1 can be detected electromagnetically rather than optically.

Now the dot matrix technique suggested above is rather wasteful. The 5×7 matrix gives an excellent printed character set, but reasonably legible characters can be created with far less than 35 'zones', simplifying the reader at the expense of quality of the printed character.

Perhaps the most typical example of this technique is the modern bank cheque.

The optical technique can also be used on 'punched' cards, except that the 'hole' is replaced by an ink 'mark'. These card devices are called 'mark-sense' systems. It is the author's opinion that physically smaller mark-sense cards, using an 8 bit ASCII code rather than a 12 bit Hollerith or EBCDIC code, would be a marked improvement over the standard system, particularly in the saving in paper. The disadvantage lies in replacing the enormous amount of existing punch card apparatus.

It is probable that advanced *optical character readers* (OCR) which can detect hand written characters will become available, but these will not become minicomputer peripherals for some while yet!

6·5 Graphic Display Terminals

These are two fundamental methods of drawing pictures under computer control (i) by ink drawings e.g. graph or X–Y plotter and (ii) by a *cathode ray tube* (CRT) display, e.g. a *visual display unit* (VDU). The principle of operation is similar in both cases. A point source acts as a marker, either a pen tip on paper or a spot on a CRT, which is moved to other points on the available display under command of the computer. Two techniques employed are the incremental system and the vector-generator system.

An incremental plotter can move in both the X and Y directions by a fixed distance. Thus the point can be moved to any one of eight positions in its immediate locality in response to +, −, or 0 signals in both X and Y directions, as shown in figure 6.5. Thus a graph is drawn

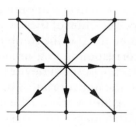

Fig. 6·5 An incremental plotting system

by feeding the plotter with a continuous string of incremental data. There is no guarantee that the line joining two points will be straight, as shown in figure 6.5, but by controlling the length of the increment, any desired accuracy can be attained. A number of algorithms have been devised to minimise the quantity of data required to plot a given graph, but the plotter is strictly under on-line control of the computer. In practice the computer often writes the data to magnetic tape and the tape is read-back into the display.

A vector generator system uses more sophisticated hardware in the display itself. The co-ordinates of a new point on the display are fed to the system and the point is caused to move from its original location to the new point, which may be any distance away, following a specific trajectory. The trajectory is implemented by the display hardware, and is termed a vector. The simplest vector is a linear one, joining the two points together with a straight line. With additional pieces of information more complex vectors can be generated. Thus two points may be joined by an arc of a circle, the radius of which is specified along with the terminal co-ordinates; alternatively two new points may be specified and a vector generated to draw a second order curve which passes from the original point to the end point, through the intermediate point. This system has an advantage over the incremental techniques in that far less input data is required, offsetting the increased hardware costs.

One point that must be stressed with all graphic systems is that special software packages are essential. Without proper software programming aids, the system can never be properly employed.

6·5·1 Graph Plotters

There are a number of mechanical arrangements of graph plotters. The simpler, smaller systems lay the paper flat on a table and mount the pen on a rectilinear carriage above it. The carriage is driven along its Y axis and the whole of this assembly can be moved in the X axis. Either incremental drives, e.g. stepper motors or servo controlled belt-driven drives are used.

The larger systems employ a linear Y axis drive, deployed parallel to the axis of a roll of paper; the X displacement is then achieved by rotating the paper roll from one spindle to another, as shown in figure 6.6. The rotation direction is reversible. With this system the maximum Y displacement is fixed but the X displacement is limited only by the length of the roll of paper.

The simpler commercial analogue X–Y plotters are commonly used with minicomputer systems. These devices create displacements proportional to d.c. voltage levels and can be computer controlled by a two-channel multiplexed digital-to-analogue convertor system.

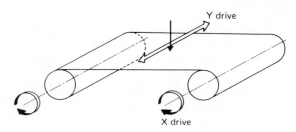

Fig. 6·6 A 'rolled-paper' X-Y plotting system

6·5·2 Visual Display Units

The use of a cathode ray tube, CRT, as a visual graphic display has received a lot of attention of late, largely as a result of the interest in interactive *computer-aided-design* (CAD) and commercial on-line enquiry and data entry systems. Compared to a printer or graph plotter they are faster, the picture can be modified easily and information can be introduced into the system from the display by use of a light pen. They do not however produce hard-copy.

The main problem with a VDU terminal is that to display a continuous picture, the spot must repeatedly retrace the pattern to 'refresh' the image. A rate of around 50 times per second is required to avoid flicker; flicker induced by too low refresh rates can produce quite intolerable effects on human operators. Now a full screen of information represents a large amount of data, so that a computer used to transmit *all* of this data, 50 times a second, is heavily loaded. In fact a computer must be dedicated to 'driving' the display. With modern electronics, particularly with the reduction in data density brought about by vector-generators, storage can be built into the display unit, which can feed the refresh system. The computer is then required only to update the display, by feeding the memories.

An alternative system is to use a *storage* tube in place of the conventional CRT. These displays continue to display the trace created by moving the spot so that they do not require refreshing. In effect the screen acts as a store and display combined. They are more expensive than CRTs (excluding the memory) but the main disadvantage is that local details of the display cannot be changed; to change any part of the picture requires the screen to be cleared and completely re-drawn.

A number of 'operator' devices are used on the more extensive systems such as a 'joy-stick' to position the spot and light-pen to pick-off specific pieces of data from the display, by communicating co-ordinate information to the computer.

Clearly the interface requirements for a graphic display system are fairly extensive.

6·5·3 Alphanumeric VDU terminals

One of the common vector generators in a full graphic display system is a unit to draw alphanumeric characters. The size, co-ordinate of, say, the lower left-hand corner, and ASCII code for the character are input as data. A simple software package can then be devised to 'print' normal typescript on the screen, one line at a time. However a full vector generating VDU is very expensive. A much simpler, cheaper system can be developed, which uses a dot matrix pattern to generate a set of fixed size characters. The screen is effectively divided into, say, 24 lines with 80 characters per line (a variety of sizes are available). The screen is then compatible with a teletype printer. In fact the units are normally supplied with a keyboard so as to be 'Teletype-compatible', except for the paper tape attachment. They are silent and much faster than a teletype using serial 10 or 11 bit transmission systems, via UART's at up to 50 kilo-bits per second, e.g. around 5000 characters per second, filling a complete 24 × 80 character screen in about half a second. Data is entered by character serial, so that the top line is filled, followed by the second, etc. Part lines are created by the equivalents to carriage-return and line-feed commands. When the last line is filled, the next line-feed causes the other lines to be moved up one place, placing the new data on the last line and losing the first line; this simulates the roll-up of a normal typewriter.

A memory matrix is employed, storing one 8 bit character per screen position, deployed as a 24 × 80 stack, to facilitate the memory refresh. Thus when 'roll-up' is required a line pointer register can be incremented, to indicate which of the 24 sets of registers is the top line. Some machines include say 40 sets of registers so that the last 16 lines which have rolled-off the screen can be recalled; nevertheless, roll-down is limited.

The VDU also incorporates a cursor, usually implemented by a flashing underlining bar, one character wide. Additional control keys are used to position this cursor, which can be used as a marker to the next active location. Repositioning of the cursor can be used for selective deletion and editing of the screen display.

A variant on the teletype compatible VDU terminal is used in data processing. The keyboard is used to enter data into the VDU memory in a 'local' mode. The computer may be used to print formats and tabulations, i.e. the computer writes the message CUSTOMERS NAME? and spaces the cursor to a specific column; the operator then types JOE BLOGGS, without the chores of spacing, etc. Once the operator has entered and corrected the data on the display, by using the cursor and overwriting any errors, the full memory is read by the computer; effectively the computer reads the data by the page.

Crude graphs can be drawn on an alphanumeric display by using the character positions as points on the graph, but the much more expensive graph displays must be used for true line drawing.

6·6· Bulk Data Storage Devices

Large quantities of data are stored in specially developed devices. The accent is placed on speed and cost rather than versatility. The most common media employed are magnetic disc and tape, although others will be mentioned.

Data (no differential is made between source programs, object programs or alphanumeric data, as far as the storage system is concerned; the significance of the bit pattern stored is of no concern) is still stored by the byte or word, but in blocks. The storage location is identified by the file, record or block, not by the byte or word. The fundamental unit is a block, typically of 256 or 512 words. The storage handling software then creates a file by allocating the required number of blocks, determined by the amount of data in the file. This is discussed in Section 7.7.2. Data required by the CPU is transferred, by the block, to the main memory and used in a random access mode from there. To facilitate high speed transfer of blocks of data DMA channels are used, as discussed in Section 4.4. Thus with the interfacing requirements explained in Section 4.8 and the software to be discussed in Chapter 7, it remains here to describe the actual peripheral hardware available. It should be noted however that the interface circuitry, or controller as these more complex units are more commonly called, is usually designed to handle more than one device, on a multiplexed basis. Typically one magnetic tape controller will support up to eight tape drives.

6·6·1 Magnetic Surface Recordings

Most bulk storage devices are based on the principle of magnetising a small area of a thin film of a permanent magnetic material, e.g. Iron oxide (ferrite). A simplified recording head is shown in figure 6.7.

For recording, a current is passed through the coil, which establishes a flux path as shown. The ferrite layer is in contact with the head, so

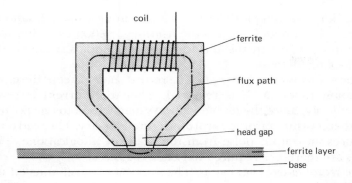

Fig. 6·7 A record/replay head

that the small area under the gap will be magnetised. If the current direction in the coil is reversed, the polarity of the magnetised area of ferrite will also reverse. Thus logical zero or one can be determined by the polarity of the magnetisation . If the coil current is reduced to zero, the ferrite will store the magnetisation. The ferrite layer can now be moved so that a fresh area comes under the head gap and a new bit of data can be recorded. If the ferrite layer is in continuous movement a sequence of positive or negative currents in the head coil will record a sequence of magnetised, individual areas. The speed at which the ferrite can be moved without 'blurring' data areas into each other, is governed by the width of the head gap and the speed at which the coil current and resulting flux can be switched on and off.

While data can be written onto a stationary surface, it cannot be read; however the same basic head can be used for reading by passing the magnetised ferrite across the gap. As each magnetised area coincides with the gap it will cause a flux to pass through the same flux path as shown in figure 6.7; thus the flux will be zero in the interspaces, increasing to a maximum as a magnetised area passes the gap then falling back to zero. The *changing* flux induces an emf in the coil which can be used to set a flip-flop. The alternative polarity magnetisation causes the opposite polarity of the induced emf, thus isolating logical zero and one.

For protection of both the ferrite and the head, the ferrite layer is usually coated with a very thin film of plastic. Alternative magnetic materials to ferrite (gamma ferric oxide) are being considered, notably chromium oxide.

A number of alternative recording modes have been introduced to improve the efficiency both from the signal-to-noise aspect (detecting true ones or zeros from unwanted, random signals) and from packing density.

The simple technique described above, with zero magnetisation gaps between bits of data is termed the *return-to-zero* (RZ) *mode*. Before new data can be recorded the surface must be completely erased. It is a self-clocking method.

Return-to-saturation (RS) *mode*. The record current keeps the tape into saturation unless a '1' is required, when the current is reversed momentarily. Since the ferrite is always magnetised to one polarity or the other, erasure prior to recording is unnecessary. The read out only produces an output pulse from the head for a logical one. Timing pulses are therefore required to isolate the zeros.

Non-return-to-zero (NRZ) *mode*. The inter-bit gap is eliminated so that the ferrite is again always magnetised to one or other polarity. The data to be recorded sets a flip-flop which drives the record head. Thus a train of successive ones causes a constant current to pass through the head coil. On output a pulse is produced when there is a change from zero to one, and the opposite polarity pulse for the change from one to zero. These pulses can be used to drive a flip-flop. However for consecutive ones (or zeros) the output will stay constant for multiple time intervals. Thus a clock pulse is essential to separate these intervals into a chain of ones (or zeros); the same pulse is used to strobe the data into buffer registers.

Non-return-to-zero-invert (NRZI) *mode*. This is an incremental method in that the current polarity is constant until a one occurs, when it is reversed. On play back the reversals of polarity generate pulses, which correspond therefore to the ones. Again a clock pulse is essential since a string of zeros generate no output.

Phase-modulation (PM) *mode*. The data is represented by the direction of the flux transitions, i.e. from positive to negative represents 0 and from negative to positive, 1. When consecutive zeros or ones are recorded, a phase reversal midway through an interval must be induced. This technique has the advantage of high signal-to-noise ratio and is self-clocking.

Simple graphs of magnetic polarity impressed for these modes are shown in figure 6.8. Details of the replay signals and the electronic 'cleaning up' of the data by the use of synchronising pulses are not included in this simple introduction.

The NRZ and NRZI modes simply reverse the current per bit of data, while the other modes must turn the current on and off per bit. Thus the recording density with the NRZ and NRZI modes is higher than with the others and are the most common modes encountered. PM however has the advantage of being self-clocking and is commonly used in simpler systems, particularly magnetic tape cassette and cartridge units.

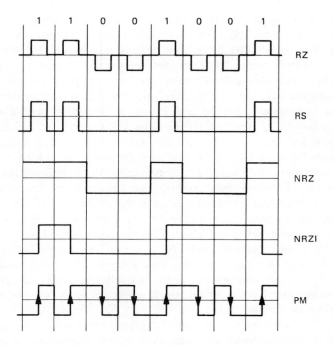

Fig. 6·8 Magnetic polarities for various recording mades

The timing pulses, essential to the RS, NRZ and NRZI modes, may in practice also be used with the other modes to clean up the replay signals. Since these must be accurately synchronised to the data rate, a 'timing-track' is used to record a train of pulses in parallel with the data.

6·6·2 Magnetic Tape Systems

Magnetic tape systems are the cheapest form of data storage, largely since an unlimited number of reels of tape can be used on one drive. These is a wide range of systems available, using Mylar based ferrite tape, about 1·5 thou thick.

The larger machines are loosely termed industry compatible recorders. They use large ($10\frac{1}{2}$ inches diameter) reels of tape from $\frac{1}{2}$ to 1 inch wide. Most $\frac{1}{2}$ inch wide tapes record data in 7 or 9 tracks, 6 or 8 data bits plus a parity bit per frame. For communication with a 16 bit computer with 7 track tape, three frames are read and the resulting 18 bits concatenated into one word (two bits are wasted); with 9 track tape two frames are read to form each word. A timing track is also used in addition to the data tracks, but this is used internally by the read/record

223

system. NRZ or NRZI recording modes are used. Recording densities of 200, 556, 800 and 1600 bits per inch (bpi) are standardised. Tape speeds between 40 and 200 inches per second (ips) give data transfer rates of between 4 and 300 kilobytes per second. It may however take up to three minutes to load a tape and locate a specific block of data, before the transfer can commence. Since the data is recorded in blocks, the tape transport must be given time to decelerate and accelerate between blocks, so that 'interblock gaps' $\frac{1}{2}$ to 1 inch long, of blank tape are employed. A few frames of non-data are appended to the beginning and end of each block of data, usually about six all zero frames (to aid location) and longitudinal parity and/or cyclic redundancy check characters. These are used to detect and possibly to correct reading errors. If these frames are repeated at the end of the block, then the block can be accessed from either direction of tape motion. A further frame must be used to note which tape direction is used for recording, so that the same direction is used for reading. Two heads, or rather one head with two independent magnetic systems, are used, and thus a frame of data can be written and immediately re-read. If the input data and the recorded data do not tally, an error has occurred and the system can be alerted.

With the high speeds of tape handling employed, a number of sophisticated techniques are used in the tape transport to avoid tape breakage. Typically a 'buffer' of tape is created between the reels and the head, so that the tape at the head can be stopped allowing a little longer for the reels to halt; effectively the high inertia of the reels is isolated. Multiple loop tension-arm systems or vacuum columns are the common methods employed, with servo-controlled reel drives. Great attention to detail is paid in the shape of the head, so as to minimise friction and yet to avoid tape/head separation.

Industry compatible magnetic tape systems are normally used on minicomputer systems to facilitate communication with other, larger computers. However a number of tape systems exist which have lower performance at greatly reduced cost.

Specially designed tape transport systems have been designed, which are smaller, slower versions of the larger systems, but usually with differing recording formats. Other systems use incremental tape drives effectively moving the tape one frame per byte of data, in much the same way as a paper tape system, only faster. Others, and these are becoming the standard minicomputer magnetic tape peripheral, use variants of the commercial (domestic) cartridge and cassette systems. The cassette systems are cheap enough to become direct competitors to punched paper tape, with many of the advantages of magnetic tape, particularly the ability to re-use the tape, which is a great advantage when editing and developing programs.

The common, special purpose, minicomputer tape system uses 3·9 inches diameter reels of $\frac{3}{4}$ inch wide tape. Ten tracks are employed, made up of one timing track, one format track and three data tracks, duplicated to repeat the same information across the one frame. A 16 bit word requires six frames (two wasted bits) and data transfer rates of 5000 words per second are achieved. The timing and format tracks are pre-recorded; these are read during a write operation to give exact timing to determine when to write data. A phase-modulated recording technique is used. The combination of the formatted tape and the redundant recording virtually eliminates errors due to tape speed variations and 'skew'. Formatted tape systems are therefore more tolerant of lower quality tape transports.

Phase-modulation recording techniques are standard on cassette and cartridge systems. Cassettes employ only one or two tracks, cartridges one, two or four. Tape speeds of 30 to 150 ips are used with densities up to 1600 bpi; cassettes often use densities as low as 100 bpi. A typical cassette system (two track, 800 bpi) will store about 600 kilobytes and a cartridge (four track, 1600 bpi) about 2 megabytes. Data transfer rates of 10 to 50 K bits per second will result in from 1 K to around 10 K words per second. Time to spool half a tape is around 20 seconds. Typical stop/start speeds result in inter-record gaps of around 1 to $1\frac{1}{2}$ inches.

6·6·3 Magnetic Disc or Drum Systems

A magnetic disc system uses a circular disc, rather like a gramophone record, the surface of which is coated with a layer of ferrite. The disc is continuously rotated at high speed (1000–3000 rpm). The surface is treated as a number of concentric tracks, spaced about 50 to 200 per inch. Data is recorded at densities of 500 to 3000 bpi. A word is recorded bit serially on one track, usually with guard and synch bits appended to the data; typically about 20 bits are recorded for a 16 bit data word. The data word is collected by a buffer register for parallel communication with the computer. One track is usually used to store pre-recorded timing signals. Data transfer rates of 50 K to 500 K words per second are common. Disc systems are predicted with speeds of rotation up to 6000 rpm, with tracks spaced at over 200 per inch and up to 6000 bpi, which will result in a few million words per second transfer rates.

Discs are normally available with between 20 and 256 tracks per surface. Data is usually recorded as blocks or sectors of words, typically 32 to 256 words per sector, resulting in 2 to 4 K words per track. Thus a small system may have a capacity of 64 K words per disc while a big system can store over a million words per surface. Each block of data contains block identifying addresses and the usual parity and cyclic redundancy checking characters. However, since the disc is continuously in motion, inter-block gaps can be very small.

Two types of head arrangement are used, fixed head and moving head. A fixed head disc uses a number of heads, one per track, mounted radially. A moving head disc utilises one head which can be positioned over any one track; this requires an accurate position controlled servo drive to move the head. Positioning 'guide' tracks are often pre-recorded onto the disc between the data tracks; optical techniques are also used.

The head should ideally be in contact with the disc surface, but this would cause excessive wear. Thus the head is designed aerodynamically so that the relative velocity between disc and head creates an air bearing between them. This 'flying head' results in a very accurately maintained, narrow gap. Nevertheless, the surface flatness of the disc is critical. Fixed head discs are more problematic in this way as the effective area of the multiple heads is larger, accentuating the flatness problems.

In most systems the disc is between 1 and 2 feet in diameter, although some up to 4 feet diameter have been used. The disc itself is metallic (aluminium), normally coated with ferric oxide, but chromium oxide is also used.

Larger disc systems use a stack of discs, recording on both surfaces. thus one system uses six discs; the top and bottom surfaces are not used, resulting in ten recording surfaces, with one moving head per surface. Disc pack or cartridge systems are also being used, where the disc or disc stack can be removed and replaced by another, giving some of the endless capacity advantages of magnetic tape. A moving head system is utilised to facilitate disc removal.

A disc system will transfer data at, say, 50 K to 500 K words per sec. However the beginning of a specific block must be located before transfer can commence. This location time is termed the *latency*. With a fixed head disc the average latency is the time taken for half a disc rotation, irrespective of which track is used. With a moving head disc the time to position the head is more restrictive. With a 1500 rpm disc the average latency due to rotation is 20 milliseconds. With a linear hydraulic positioning servo with a typical stroke of 2 inches, the head positioning latency is around 30 to 70 milliseconds. Experiments with electromagnetic positioning systems suggest that this can be reduced to 20 milliseconds.

A magnetic drum works on similar principles to a disc, except that the ferrite is coated onto the surface of a cylinder. One track is then recorded along the circumference, with multiple tracks stacked along the length. Drums have one advantage in that every track is similar (on a disc the inner track is shorter than the outer), but discs have proved cheaper to manufacture and easier to make removable. Drums are currently fading from the market.

All types and sizes of discs can be used with minicomputers; even the high capacity more expensive systems will be utilised by the more sophisticated minis used in commercial applications.

6·6·4 Floppy Discs

Floppy discs or discettes are much cheaper, removable disc systems, competing with magnetic tape rather than conventional disc systems. The disc itself is plastic, about 0·003 inch thick, coated with ferrite, and is approximately 8 inches in diameter. Mechanical stability is achieved by containing the disc inside a rigid plastic envelope. The disc remains inside the envelope at all times, both for storage and transportation and during operation. The plastic is specially prepared to clean and lubricate the disc when it is rotating inside the envelope. A central hole in the envelope allows a spigot on the drive unit to centralise and drive the disc, while a second window allows the record/replay head to be brought into contact with the recording surface. A further hole is used by an optical sensor to identify the beginning of a track.

Note that the floppy-disc is similar to a magnetic tape cartridge system in that the envelope is plugged into the drive unit and the drive connected once in position. Also the head system is brought directly into contact with the recording surface. Unlike a tape the disc rotates continually and avoids the latency problems inherent in spooling a tape. To reduce wear, the head is only brought into contact when the computer requests attention; some units automatically withdraw the head if data has not been transferred for a fixed period of time. This is referred to as 'automatic head unloading'.

The alignment and wear problems do not allow performance compatible with a flying-head disc system. In practice the common rotational speed is 360 rpm, giving an average latency of 83 milliseconds. Moving head positioning is used to differentiate between tracks so that the average time to seek a new data record is of the order of 200 to 500 milliseconds.

Discettes can only be used to store data and must not be used as a 'system' disc in an operating system due to the wear problem. Clearly these devices must be developed to incorporate some form of non-contacting head in the near future, which will greatly enhance the field of application.

There is a standard track format, referred to as IBM compatible, which has 26 sectors per track, 64 words per sector and 77 data tracks per discette. This gives a formatted storage capacity of 121 472 words. Phase-modulated recording is normally used.

Undoubtedly thin, soft, plastic discs, freely suspended and rotating at high speed so as to fly against the head will be developed as replacements for the rigid aluminium disc used in conventional disc systems. These are not to be confused with the simple plug-in discette system.

6·6·5 Other Devices For Large Capacity Storage

There are no real competitors to magnetic tape and disc systems currently available as bulk storage devices. There are however a number of techniques being studied which may well become commercial propositions. Effectively a bulk storage device is a long shift register, i.e. it stores sequential data. Main memory for a computer is characterised by its random addressable feature, and is more expensive per bit than a bulk store, by definition! However the cost of magnetic core and semiconductor memory systems, which are discussed in Appendix 4, have fallen so much recently that far larger main memories are being employed, a trend which will continue for some time. This will affect the main memory/bulk storage concept in a rather unpredictable manner, possibly removing the requirement for speed from bulk stores.

Large banks of semiconductor memory organised in a bit serial form, conceptually rather like tracks on a disc, are already available, with capacities up to forty 264 kilobit banks and data rates of 10 Megabits per second. They are more expensive than disc, but have application where the high speed is needed.

A number of magnetic shift registers are being developed using 'magnetic bubbles' or 'magnetic domains'. These are static devices which record data by the polarity of small zones which are shifted along a path in the material by an applied field. With no moving parts the reliability is very high; high densities can be expected at low cost in the next few years. One magnetic domain shift register is already available, but is not yet engineered into a system.

Charge coupled devices (CCD), or *charge transfer devices* are shift registers, constructed from capacitors in an integrated circuit; 1 or 0 is determined by whether or not the capacitor is charged. Input signals cause the charge to be shifted from one capacitor to the next, creating the shift register. This technique is the semiconductor competitor to magnetic bubble technology and is in about the same state of development.

Holograph techniques, using a laser light source to scan a mask and record binary images on film have been developed, which can store 10^9

bits on a standard 35 mm slide. Using 16 mm moving film at 100 millimetres per second, 10^{13} bits can be stored on a 1000 metre reel, with an access rate of 100 million bits per second. Once exposed however the film cannot be reused; thus this technique is currently limited to large scale archiving activities. *Computer output microfilm* (COM), which is a computer controlled microfiche writable and readable, but not alterable, bulk store is commercially available.

Specifically for minicomputers, large scale semiconductor memory will certainly have uses and there is no reason why, if their development continues satisfactorily , magnetic bubble or domain and CCD units cannot be manufactured into low cost systems. However there are no real challengers to cassette/cartridge magnetic tape, floppy-disc and magnetic disc for the immediate future.

6·7 Signal Processing Equipment

In on-line, particularly real-time, applications, external events must be monitored and communicated to the computer. Similarly the computer may dictate external actions, which must also be communicated to the external equipment.

External signals fall into one of three categories:
 (i) Single bit digital, i.e. opening and closing of switches,
 (ii) Multi-bit digital, i.e. data from a digital voltmeter, and
(iii) Analogue, i.e. voltages from transducers or to actuators.

Apparatus for handling all types of signals, both to and from the computer must be provided, often termed *data acquisition* and *control* equipment.

6·7·1 Digital Signal Processing Equipment

An on-off type of signal requires only one bit of data. Computers however are word or byte orientated and not ideally designed to handle single bits of information. Two alternatives exist.

(i) Allocate the single bit of information to the LSB of a byte with the other 7 bits set to zero. The digital information is then handled by whether the byte represents the number 0 or 1. This is wasteful since 8 bits are used when 1 would have sufficed.

(ii) Up to 16 individual single bit digital signals are allocated to specific bits of a word. In processing the data inside the computer, the specific bit state must be determined by using logical instructions with masks (see Section 3.5.3). This is hardware economic since only one I/O port is required for 16 digital signals, but requires more software than method (i).

Method (ii) is generally employed because, with one I/O port per 16 digital signals, the interface costs are lower. In this case multiple single-bit and single multi-bit data may be handled in the same way.

6·7·1·1 Input Signals

External events can be communicated to the interface as a high or low voltage level or as a contact being open or closed. Voltage levels may come directly from compatible electronic logic systems, e.g. TTL with +3·5 volts for logic 1 and 0 volts for logic 0, but may equally well be non-compatible even to the extent of being a.c. voltages. Thus virtually all incoming signals require some form of 'signal conditioning' so that standard interface logic circuitry can be used.

A range of voltage level convertors will be required, some with rectifiers for a.c. signals. Alternatively the incoming signal may be used to energise a small relay, which can then be treated as a switch closure. With a switch, the state of the contacts can be determined by connecting it in series with an appropriate voltage source.

It is highly likely that the earthing on the computer and that on the external equipment are not carefully controlled. It is thus possible that large voltages can exist between the switch contacts and earth, so that all incoming signals should be isolated from the computer interface. This can be achieved by causing the incoming signal to activate a reed relay, the contacts of which pass the information to the interface. The isolation is created since the relay coil and contacts are separate. Optical couplers, Section 4.9, can be used rather than relays. The effect of the isolator is to make the input differential.

A complete digital input module will comprise a 16 bit buffer register, interfaced to the computer in the usual way, with state, control and interrupt flags, which can be read into the computer by a normal input instruction. The interrupt system often contains another register to note which of the individual interrupt lines created the interrupt; often the act of closing a switch is simply required to generate an interrupt, to initiate a service routine. The input module will be completed by sixteen individual signal conditioners and isolators, which may be of varying types to suit the application.

The simplest buffers will copy the current state of the input signal. However various modifications may be needed. Thus if the signal is transient in nature, i.e. a pulse, then it may need latching, setting a flip-flop in the conditioner which will be cleared when read by the computer. Another technique encountered is to count incoming pulses, transmitting the counter register contents to the computer at specific instants in time.

6·7·1·2 Output Signals

Most of what has just been said about input equipment applies to output equipment. If one of the sixteen output lines is to be changed then one bit of the current word in the output buffer must be modified. The word is read into the CPU, a bit set (clear) instruction executed and the result sent back to the buffer. Care must be taken with the buffer electronics so that it is not cleared and reloaded, since the resulting transient modification of the bits not being processed may cause erroneous external actions.

Again output signals are isolated and may be voltages or relay closures. Standard line drivers may be employed but non-standard voltages can be derived from relays and additional power supplies. The extra power supplies may be part of the signal conditioner or included in the external device. Relay contacts may need relatively high voltage and current rating; alternatively solid state (Triac) power relays may be employed.

Flip-flops, latches and single-shot latches are also employed. The single-shot latch is set by an output instruction and remains set for an interval of time before clearing itself. The time interval is usually adjustable between 1 millisecond and 10 seconds by a potentiometer. Latched relays are often used rather than electronic latches so that they maintain their state in the event of a computer power failure. Solid state output devices are usually protected by a diode to avoid damage when switching inductive loads.

6·7·2 Analogue Signal Processing Equipment

6·7·2·1 Input Signals

Most physical process variables are measured continuously by attaching a transducer or sensor to the plant. Occasionally the transducer will directly generate a voltage proportional to the variable; e.g. a permanent magnet d.c. tachogenerator to measure speed; but most require connection to an electrical circuit, the output of which is the desired voltage; e.g. a strain gauge is connected into a Wheatstone bridge while thermocouples require the reference junction to be held at a constant temperature. Much of this electrical equipment must be included with the signal conditioning unit. The problems of instrumentation are severe and too specialised to be more than briefly mentioned here.

Effectively each transducer unit will have two wires producing a differential voltage signal. Since the computer can only process binary numbers, one word at a time, the analogue voltage must be 'sampled' and each sample converted to an equivalent binary number. The

Analogue to Digital Convertor (ADC) can then communicate its binary output to the computer via a conventional I/O channel. After a fixed interval of time the analogue voltage is sampled again, etc. If the sampling rate is high enough*, so that the change from sample to sample is relatively small, then the discrete information transmitted is a good approximation to the continuous signal. Too high a sampling rate is wasteful of computer resources.

In practice it is likely that a number of transducers must be connected to the computer. Each could be connected to an independent input channel via its own sampler and ADC, but it is hardly likely that transducers require sampling at anything approaching computer I/O speeds. Hence a number of transducers are 'multiplexed' to a common I/O channel, via the same ADC. Since the full scale voltages from differing transducers may vary widely a high class amplifier is also included, the gain of which can be set by an output instruction from the computer, to suit a particular transducer. A typical system is shown in figure 6.9.

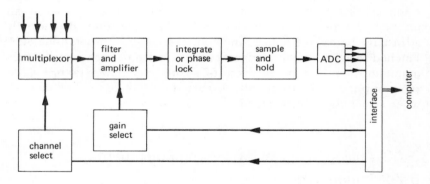

Fig. 6·9 A typical analogue input system

The major problems with analogue input systems are 'noise', i.e. unwanted voltages induced into the connecting wires by stray fields, and the sampling speed. Induced noise voltages will be of two forms, common mode and series mode, as shown in figure 6.10.

Common mode rejection (CMR) is the lesser problem than *series mode rejection* (SMR). By using two pole switching in the multiplexor, the differential inputs can be passed to a differential amplifier, an electronic amplifier the output voltage of which is proportional to the

---

* Shannon's sampling theorem states that to be able to completely recover the information in the continuous signal it must be sampled at least twice as fast as the highest frequency component. Five to ten times as fast is practical. Too low a sampling rate not only loses information, but distorts the rest!

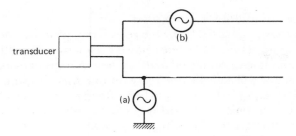

Fig 6·10 (a) Common mode and (b) Series mode noise

difference, voltage between the two input wires, i.e. if due to the common mode line 1 was 10·0 volts above earth and line 2 was 10·1 volts above earth, only the 0·1 volts will be amplified. Screening of the transducer leads will reduce the induced noise and give both CMR and SMR. If the screen is earthed only at the amplifier input, requiring three pole switching in the multiplexor, a further improvement is achieved. To give SMR use is made of the fact that the induced noise is virtually all of normal mains frequency. Two techniques are used:

(i) *Integration.* Each analogue signal is fed to an integrator for exactly one mains cycle, timed by synchronisation to the mains supply. Thus equal amounts of positive and negative charge will have been induced by the series noise, leaving the resulting integrator voltage due only to the signal. This voltage is then clamped and fed to the ADC. The speed of sampling is limited to 50 samples per second by the integrator. To be of any use, the signal itself must not have varied by much during the integration interval, but in any case the integrator produces an 'average' value over the period.

(ii) *Phase-locked sampling.* An internal mains frequency oscillator is phase-locked to the induced noise on the signal. When this oscillator voltage passes through zero a sampler is triggered, which takes an average reading over a very narrow time interval (window) which is then converted. Thus the sample is taken at the instant in time when the induced noise is zero. It is now possible to take two samples per cycle of the mains, i.e. 100 samples per second.

A good quality system will give over 150 db CMR and over 100 db SMR.

For sampling rates over 100 samples per second there can be no SMR so that screening is all the more important. With poor noise rejection, low transducer voltage levels *must* be amplified at source, before connection to the multiplexor. A filter is usually fitted with the amplifier to eliminate 'spikes' of noise. This is most important with a sampling system since the sample window could enclose the spike, giving very erroneous results.

Two types of multiplexor are used.

(i) *Reed relays*, figure 6.11(a). One relay is connected in each line with a common output line. Only one relay is ever activated so that only the selected input line is connected to the system. A register associated with the multiplexor will activate one relay for one specific number, e.g. a 4 bit register is required for 16 input lines. Reed relays will switch at up to 200 times per second, allowing for contact bounce, and have superior electrical characteristics allowing multiplexing of signals in the microvolt regions. The life expectancy of the better mercury wetted contacts is in the region of 10^{10} operations, which is probably sufficient for many continuous day and night operations, e.g. a feed back control of an electromechanical system with a $0 \cdot 1$ second sample rate has a life expectancy of around 30 years.

(ii) *Solid state switches.* A field-effect transistor (FET) is used in place of the relay, figure 6.11(b), connected in series with the signal lines. The FET can be switched to act as a very high resistance, above $1M\Omega$, or a low resistance, about 100Ω ('opening' and 'closing' the circuit respectively) by voltages applied to the third 'gate' terminal. In the 'on' state the FET is not as low a resistance as a relay contact so that it cannot be used to multiplex signals below millivolt levels. They will however switch at megacycle per second rates and having no moving contacts, have a long life expectancy. LSI units are available with multiple 'contacts' and decoded addressing.

A refinement which is sometimes used is the flying capacitor system of figure 6.11(c). The voltage from the transducer charges up the capacitor to an equal voltage. The normally closed contacts are then opened and the normally-open ones closed so that the voltage across the capacitor is actually converted to binary form. In this way the transducers are totally isolated from the amplifier. This technique is usually used with slow speed reed relay systems.

In summary multiplexing applications can be categorised as:

(a) high level, low speed. Any system can be used.
(b) low level, low speed. A reed relay system with SMR techniques must be used.
(c) high level, high speed. FET multiplexors can replace the reed relays, but integration and phase-lock techniques cannot be used, resulting in no SMR. Care must be taken with screening and filtering used to eliminate spikes.
(d) low level, high speed. FET switches must be used and each transducer signal must be individually amplified to a higher voltage at the transducer end. Often single channel 'transient' systems are encountered, without multiplexing.

With any multiplexing system the channel can be selected by activating the appropriate switch, either reed relay or FET. The

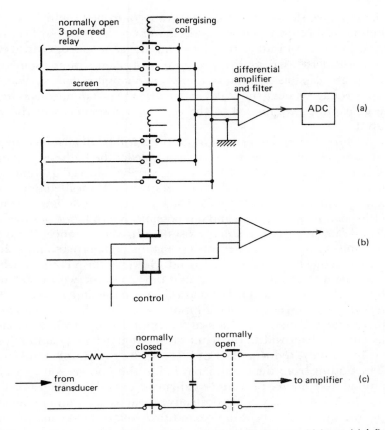

Fig 6·11 (a) A three pole multiplexor with reed relays. (b) A FET multiplexor. (c) A flying capacitor system

simplest systems 'scan' all channels sequentially; variants allow the start and stop channels to be set. The *scan rate* is defined as the rate of switching from one channel to the next whereas the *sample rate* is the rate at which any one channel is activated. Most systems will scan as fast as possible so that each channel is read as near as possible at the same instant as the other channel, i.e. the fast sequential scan approximates to a 'parallel' read. With the more sophisticated multiplexors the mode can be set by computer control with the scan being one mode and random another. With random mode the selected channel is defined by the contents of a 'channel address register'. Thus the address register can be set from the computer so that any transducer can be read, at any time, under program control. A sequence of sequential addresses fed from the computer creates the same effect as the scan mode.

235

To enhance the power of the program controlled multiplexor, the amplifier can be designed so that its gain may also be set by loading a register with an output instruction. Thus the gain appropriate to each channel can be used to give program controlled scaling. Some amplifiers are capable of auto-ranging, i.e. changing gain so that the output voltage is near full scale; in this case the instantaneous value of the gain must be supplied to the computer together with the ADC output.

The cut-off frequency of an input filter will be determined by the characteristics of the signal. As an example let the highest frequency component of a signal be 1 Hz and it is to be sampled 10 times per second. A low pass filter with a cut-off of say 5 Hz will eliminate the higher frequency unwanted noise spikes. The scan rate however may be 100 channels per second and it is possible that full scale positive and full scale negative voltages may exist on adjacent channels. Thus the input voltage to the amplifier must swing through its maximum range in less than one hundredth of a second. However the 5 Hz filter, which is equivalent to about a 30 millisecond time constant, will only change its output by about one third of that voltage, in the time allowed. Thus filters must be included in each input line before the multiplexor. A much neater system uses a filter at the amplifier input which dynamically changes bandwidth; the bandwidth is high while the multiplexor switches rapidly, reducing to 1 or 2 Hz before the sample is taken.

The output from the amplifier is fed to the ADC via some form of sampling system. As previously explained either an integrator or a phase-lock system may be used; in any case at some instant in time the analogue signal must be sampled and that voltage held constant until the conversion has completed. Such a circuit is commonly called a 'sample and hold' amplifier. The width of the sample 'aperture' or 'window', i.e. the time over which the sample is taken, and the duration of the hold will depend upon the particular system.

The ADC is closely involved with the DAC so that both are explained together in Section 6.7.3, with some comments on accuracy and resolution.

6·7·2·2 Output Signals

For control applications and display systems which use conventional analogue signals, e.g. an X–Y plotter or oscilloscope, digital information fed from the computer by output instructions must be converted to analogue voltage levels. The basic Digital to Analogue Convertor (DAC) will produce an analogue voltage output when presented with a binary input number. The output voltage will be maintained as long as the binary input is present.

As with analogue input systems, the rate at which new output data is required is usually low compared to the computer speed, so that one computer output port can be shared by multiple analogue signals. This switching device is usually called a *de-multiplexor*. However once the de-multiplexor switch changes channels the voltage level would fall to zero, so that electronic 'hold' circuits are used with each line. The hold circuit will attempt to maintain its output voltage level until reset by a new input voltage; it must change its output rapidly in response to a new input. In practice the hold output will 'droop' with a time constant probably less than a minute so that it must be reset repetitively, even for a constant desired output. Such a system was shown in figure 1.10.

The alternative to using a de-multiplexor and hold circuits is to employ individual DAC's with one buffer register for each. De-multiplexing is achieved by loading the selected buffer. This method avoids the problem of droop.

6·7·3 Digital-to-Analogue and Analogue-to-Digital Conversion

Two fundamental types of DAC are shown in figure 6.12. In both circuits one switch (a FET in practice) is provided for each bit of the word. In system (a) the switch is open for logical 0 and closed for logical 1. In system (b) a change-over FET switch routes the current back to supply for logical 0 and via the current-to-voltage convertor for logical 1. The current-to-voltage convertor is a 'virtual earth' amplifier which has a very high gain (10^6 or more). If the output voltage is to be of the order of say 10 volts, then the input voltage is only 10 microvolts or less. Thus negligible current flows through the amplifier input circuits so that I_0 is equal but opposite to the current through R_0. Since one end of R_0 is at V_0 and the other at the virtual earth,

$$I_0 = -V_0/R_0$$

$$\therefore \quad V_0 = -I_0R_0$$

The virtual earth means that it appears to the resistance networks that the input to the current-to-voltage convertor is a short circuit. Thus I_0 and V_0 are proportional to the binary number dictating the switch closures. System (a) requires only single pole switches but system (b) employs only resistors of value R and 2R and it is therefore easier to achieve high accuracy. Any variation in the reference voltage, V_{ref}, will cause an error so that again (b) is preferable since the total current drain is constant.

The resolution of the DAC can be increased by introducing further stages. However the accuracy is governed by the individual accuracy of

237

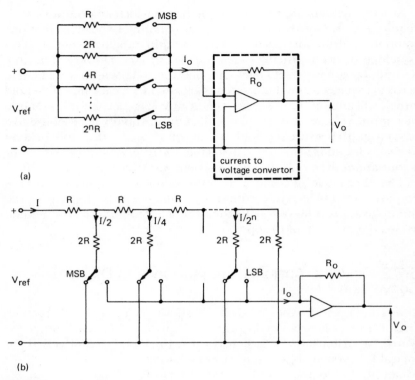

(a)

(b)

Fig. 6·12 DAC circuits

each stage. Thus for an 8 bit DAC the LSB is equivalent to one part in 256, i.e. the resolution is equivalent to about one quarter of one percent. However, to achieve an accuracy of a quarter of a percent, each bit must reach that tolerance; e.g. the MSB corresponds to nearly 50% of full scale, but it must be to a quarter of a percent accuracy. To improve the accuracy to one part in 512 an extra bit is required *and* the accuracy of the other bits must be improved. Thus doubling the accuracy is likely to quadruple the cost.

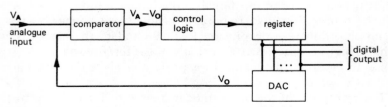

Fig. 6·13 An ADC system

ADC systems work on the principle shown in figure 6.13. The contents of the register, which form the digital output, are fed to a DAC. The resulting analogue equivalent to the binary output, V_0, is subtracted from the analogue input, V_A, and the difference used by a logic circuit to modify the register contents. When V_0 equals V_A the logic 'freezes' the register contents and the conversion is complete.

Two basic logic schemes are commonly encountered:

(a) *servo type* ADCs. The register is connected as a conventional 'up–down' counter. As long as V_A is greater than V_0 the logic causes the counter to count up and vice versa for V_A less than V_0. When $V_A = V_0$, the counting is stopped.

(b) *Successive approximation* ADCs. The register is first cleared and then the MSB is set to 1. If V_0 is less than V_A, then the next most significant bit is set and the test repeated, etc. Whenever V_0 is bigger than V_A, the bit just set is cleared back to zero before setting the next bit.

As an example consider a 12 bit ADC. Type (b) requires twelve operations to convert any number, independent of the previous value of V_A. Type (a) requires sufficient clock pulses to count up the difference between V_A and the previous value.

Thus if an ADC is used to repeatedly sample the same signal, which can therefore be assumed to change little each sample, the servo type ADC is preferred. If however a multiplexed system is used, then successive inputs may come from dissimilar channels and swing from full scale positive to full scale negative so that the successive approximation ADC is preferred.

A slower, cheaper, ADC, often used in digital voltmeters, works on a 'dual-slope' principle. The input voltage is integrated for a fixed period of time, normally 20 milliseconds. The integrator input is then switched to a constant negative reference voltage which causes the integrator output voltage to fall linearly back to zero. A binary up-counter is started when the input is switched which is automatically stopped when the integrator output reaches zero.

Let the input voltage $= V$
the reference voltage $= V_{ref}$
the fixed up-integration time $= T$

and the time to reduce V_{out} to zero $= t$,

then $VT = V_{ref}t$
and $V = V_{ref}t/T$

Since the counter contents are proportional to t, and V_{ref} and T are constant, that register stores a binary number proportional to V.

Finally it is worth stressing that ADC and DAC systems can be over-specified. Thanks to appropriate scaling amplifiers, near full scale levels can be expected, so that only 7 bits are required to give over one percent accuracy. 8 bits is a common compromise, although higher accuracy is readily available.

6·8 Data Communication Equipment

Computers are often interconnected, requiring data transmission between machines, sometimes over long distances. Rented telephone lines are regularly employed. Similarly some peripheral devices may be placed physically remote from the computer, creating similar problems. The advent of 'intelligent' terminals has increased the use of networks in the sense that a larger number of machines of relatively low processing power require to communicate with one, larger, machine.

In a large installation a minicomputer may be employed as a front-end processor to a large machine. The mini accepts the responsibility of sending and receiving data, checking for errors and requesting re-transmission when a fault is detected, organising the data for maximum transmission efficiency, etc. In this way the mini acts as a buffer between the main computer and the communicating devices.

6·8·1 Communications Control Units

A *Communication Control Unit* (CCU) is a peripheral device which interfaces to the I/O bus and/or DMA, with control and status registers to handle the multiplexing of a number of communication lines. With a sophisticated CCU, different types and speeds of line can be mixed at the multiplexor. Since the CCU will be required to perform a variety of processing tasks, e.g. add parity and other error codes on transmission and check and remove the same on receipt, it is in its own right a simple processor. Indeed some minicomputer communication equipment is programmable, so that this, like a sophisticated DMA channel, is an example of a dedicated processor attached to the main CPU.

As previously explained transmission may be one way only (simplex), both ways, but only one way at time (half-duplex) or both ways simultaneously (duplex). The first two only require one set of wires but the duplex requires two.

Transmission can also be serial or parallel. Serial mode is used over long distances, due to the cost of rental of lines. Thus one of the main tasks of the Communications Control Unit is to accept parallel data from the computer, to code it into serial form and to transmit it on one of the (selected) transmission lines. It must also receive serial data and convert it to parallel form before feeding into the computer. It is thus obvious that the CCU must contain registers for each channel, to buffer the data. Double and triple buffers may be provided.

Transmission may also be either synchronous or asynchronous. With synchronous transmission the data is 'clocked' onto the line at a given rate and the receiver at the other end must be synchronised to accept the data. Book-keeping records (synch characters) are often appended at the beginning and end of blocks of data transmitted in this way, which are used by the receiver, but must be extracted from the actual data passed on for processing. Such tasks can be performed by program control in the computer, but are better allocated to the CCU.

With asynchronous transmission, each word of data is transmitted with a proceeding 'start' bit and following 'stop' bit(s). Note that with serial transmission the word may be asynchronously transmitted, but the individual bits will be sent at a fixed clock rate; such a system, as used for teletypes, was explained in Sections 6.3.2 and 6.3.4.

6·8·2 Teleprocessing and Telecommunications Equipment

Historically telecommunications practice was well established before the age of computers. Two systems of telecommunication evolved, the telegraph and the telephone, the former for the transmission of messages and the latter for the human voice.

Lines may be leased, dedicated to a specific task, or they may be routed through the 'Public Switched Network' (PSN). The switched telegraph system is called Telex in the U.K. Switched lines are cheaper for sporadic use, leased lines for near continuous use.

Telegraph lines are the lowest quality, limited to 110 bits per second for leased circuits and 50 bits per second for Telex. D.C. signalling is employed using ±80 volts for logical 1 and 0. Repeaters are used at regular intervals on the line to clean up the distortions introduced by transmission. There are a limited number of lines available, approximately 20 000 in the U.K. Telegraph lines can only be used for teletype communications in the computer system.

Various grades of telephone lines are available, some of which will transmit data at up to 9600 bits per second (2400 on PSN). There are already over eight million connections in the U.K. Specialised data communication systems with speeds up to 240 Kilobits per second are envisaged. D.C. levels cannot be used at speeds above 110 bits per second, due to distortion during transmission. Instead frequency modulation is employed whereby a basic carrier frequency represents logical 0 and a slightly different frequency logical 1. The data to be transmitted is used to modulate the carrier by a device called *a*

241

modulator. At the receiving end a *demodulator* is used to detect the instantaneous frequency and hence to output logical 0 or 1. In a duplex system both a modulator and demodulator are required at each end of the line and these are commonly manufactured on one chassis and termed a *Modem.* Note that modulation techniques are used to transmit multiple channels of data simultaneously along one line by using individual carrier frequencies. Carrier frequencies must be an order higher than the maximum data rate. Modems are commonly configured in minicomputer communications peripherals.

In the U.K. the requirements for connection of apparatus to the public telephone system are most stringent. At present only GPO supplied modems may be used and these must often be connected via a fused isolator. To get around this problem for less permanent installations, *acoustic couplers* are available for connection via a conventional telephone handset, but speeds must be limited to around 200 bits per second.

For systems which transmit data infrequently the Public Switched Network is the cheapest. A conventional dialling and answering hand set can be used to make connection, with a switch to transfer from audio to data. However automatic calling and answering units can be provided with the Communications Control Unit.

6·8·3 The Basic Functions of a Communications Control Unit

To summarise the wide and diverse nature of the available Communications Control Units the basic functions are listed below.

(a) To provide multiplexing of computer input and output lines.

(b) To perform the serial-to-parallel and parallel-to-serial conversion of bits within each character.

(c) To append and delete start and stop bits to each character for asynchronous communication.

(d) To insert and remove synchronising characters at the beginning and end of each block of data for synchronous communication.

(e) To insert and identify control characters, e.g. 'end of message', etc.

(f) To add error checking bits and characters, e.g. parity bits per word and/or block parity characters or cyclic redundancy check characters.

(g) To check error coding on receipt. Most codes only allow error detection so that the CCU can request retransmission. More complex codes allow error detection *and* correction; such codes require more redundant bits than the simple parity bit.

(h) Code conversion, due to the unfortunate lack of complete consistency in code conventions.
(i) Interface with communication lines via modems and line adaptors.
(j) Provide automatic connection (calling and answering) to public networks if necessary.
(k) Some systems use multiple peripherals connected to the one line, called 'multi-drop'. Thus automatic polling may be required to determine which device is the currently active one.

The CCU must of course interface to either the computer I/O bus or DMA. With both data, control and test information passing between the computer and the CCU, more than one peripheral address will be used, possibly using the I/O channel for control and test information and DMA for data.

The simpler CCUs will provide the raw data handling facilities and use the CPU for code conversion, etc. Some CCUs are themselves programmable so that say messages can be stored and printed or transmitted on receipt of a simple reference character. Instead of passing individual characters, the unit could assemble whole messages and form them into queues for transmission. Thus the range extends from the simple minicomputer CCU to a minicomputer controlled communications controller acting as a front-end processor to a larger machine.

Chapter 7

Software

7·1 General Concepts

At the simplest level, computer 'hardware' is the all encompassing term used to describe the electrical, electronic and mechanical components that make up the system and 'software' is the term coined to describe the programs, the suites of instructions, that run the hardware. The advent of ROM however has clouded the issue somewhat. Thus a specially developed program to run a specific microcomputer is written into ROM and wired into the system; this particular piece of hardware differs from conventional memory in that it can only do the one job. Such a compromise has thus fostered the phrase 'firmware'; when ROM is used to execute the primary instruction set, i.e. microprogramming, the term firmware takes on particular significance.

Software can be split into three divisions:

(i) *Applications software.* These programs are the object of the exercise, the software that makes the computer perform the specific job for which it has been bought. Usually Applications programs are written for each development, but there are growing libraries of 'Applications packages' becoming available for many computers. Few are directly applicable but they can be modified to suit relatively easily.

244

Packages will only be available for commonly encountered applications such as data logging, statistical analysis, communication protocol, payroll, etc. Normally detailed features of the computer, in particular the interrupt structure, are built into the package so that they will not be transferable from one machine to another.

Sets of high level language, e.g. FORTRAN, subroutines, e.g. matrix inversion, least squares fit, etc., could be considered as Applications software, but are more aids to scientific computer users. In particular such programs are largely machine independent and do not use real-time facilities.

(ii) *Support software.* In developing Applications programs it is virtually essential to ease the burden on the programmer imposed by coding the binary 'machine code' instructions. Programs developed, supplied and supported by the computer manufacturer for a particular make and type of machine which help in writing and testing applications programs are classed as Support software. The most important examples discussed in this chapter are Loaders, Assemblers, Debuggers, Editors, Compilers and Emulators.

A second type of support software is available as packages of machine code subroutines which can be introduced as blocks of code into the applications programs. Typical examples of this type of software package are mathematical routines; e.g. floating point arithmetic, multiplying, trigonometric functions, etc.; I/O handlers and conversion routines; e.g. conversion from a pure binary number to a string of ASCII coded characters, etc. These packages are also referred to as utility routines.

(iii) *Systems software.* The Application program can be written so that it performs every task required of the computer. However many tasks such as file handling on disc and tape-systems do not differ from one application to another. Thus software dedicated to 'running and organising' the computer system in the wider supervisory sense is classed as System software. In controlling the general operation of the system the System software frees the applications programs from organising standard system tasks. The System software should also be of great help during development stages since the Support software can also be organised. Thus an *Executive* can be defined as a system program that schedules all the other program 'modules' such as the File handling routines, Loaders, Assemblers, etc. The Executive and the support routines are known as the *Operating System.* Operating Systems vary rather widely in versatility, cost and efficiency.

An efficient Operating System will make the best use of the available hardware, so that it may be possible to execute more than one applications program at any one time, i.e. the Operating System contains a *multi-programming Executive.* A *real-time Executive* is one

245

which allows initiation of some of its activities to be related to a digital clock and to efficiently handle interrupt requests.

It must be realised that, to a large extent, Applications software is the responsibility of the user; the System and Support software on the other hand is as much a part of the 'computer' as is the hardware. Some fundamental software will come with the basic machine but the more sophisticated software is very much dependent upon the complete hardware configuration – a *Disc Operating System* (DOS) is of little use without a disc! Usually the cost of the DOS will be included in the cost of the disc, but most manufacturers have now 'unbundled' their software, that is to say software modules can be independently purchased.

Little distinction is made between minicomputers and microprocessors in this chapter. The software currently available for microprocessor systems is but a small subset of the wide range of minicomputer software. However, just as hardware progress , particularly the speeding up of LSI, will make the processor performances more difficult to separate, more and more software will become available from microprocessor manufacturers. The microprocessor software of most importance is the Loader, Assembler and utility packages (often available in ROM). Such programs as the *Emulator,* a software package used for emulating one machine by another one, have far greater use in the microprocessor field than for minicomputers, when in-house data processing and scientific computer installations can be used for developing programs for loading into a microprocessor system.

7·2 Developing an Applications Program

Consider the situation where a computer system has been installed and awaits a program to tell it what to do; the memory is initially totally blank.

The initial means of communication is through the switch register on the control panel; a teletype terminal provides a keyboard and printer and also a paper tape reader and punch.

A simple program is 'keyed' into the machine by setting the appropriate address in the switches followed by the binary code. This program is called a *Bootstrap Loader*. It is written by the manufacturer so that the user knows just what and where to key in code. The object of this small program is to activate the paper tape reader – and no more! To key a program into a machine is a painful exercise, prone to error, so that the simpler the program the better.

The paper tape reader is now active, so that a more sophisticated loader can be read in from a paper tape. Once the Loader is in memory* any other programs stored on pre-prepared paper tape can be loaded. Thus the Assembler can be loaded and the Assembly Language program (*Source Code*) written by the user can be converted to binary machine code (*Object Code*), punched out on paper tape. The machine code can then be loaded back into the machine (overlaying, i.e. over writing, the Assembler) and executed. Various programming aids can then be loaded if necessary to correct any errors in the users program, probably Editing the Assembly language program, re-assembling and re-loading.

A high-speed paper tape reader/punch may well be substituted for the teletype reader/punch, merely changing an identifying address in the Bootstrap. For more sophisticated systems, say a system with a disc, then the DOS Executive must be loaded before it can be used to supervise the system. High-level language compilers may also be used instead of the Assembler.

For the simpler systems the Loader, Assembler, etc. programs are stored on paper tape; these can be more easily saved on magnetic tape or disc, as and when these are available.

The basic modules of software briefly mentioned above, will now be studied in some detail.

Figure 7.1 shows a table of the more usual software units. The Executive in a simple paper tape installation may be the operator sorting out the appropriate tapes and pressing the correct console switches; it may be a sophisticated disc system which responds quickly to simple commands from the keyboard. Enough memory may be available to hold more than one unit at a time, but usually the new

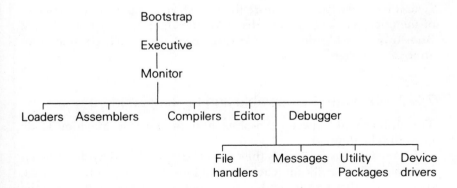

Fig. 7·1 Common software modules

* In software terminology the word 'core' is used loosely to mean the random addressable memory as distinct from disc or tape. We can have the slightly ridiculous situation in some machines of semiconductor 'core'!

"load" overlays the old one and obliterates it, so that it must be reloaded when needed again. The Bootstrap should not be overlayed if possible, and a DOS requires a core-resident Monitor to initiate the disc to memory transfers.

7·3 Loaders

A Loader is a Support program written and supplied by the manufacturer. Its purpose is to activate a peripheral device so that another program can be 'loaded' into memory. There are a variety of Loaders, of varying sophistication.

7·3·1 Bootstrap Loader

The Bootstrap is the simplest loader, which merely activates the input device, i.e. the paper tape reader, magnetic tape unit or disc. The Bootstrap program is very simple although it is reasonable to expect the Bootstrap for a tape or disc system to be a rather longer program than for a paper tape system. The Bootstrap for a paper tape system probably comprises around 10–20 machine code instructions which ask for a character to be read from the paper-tape reader, to store this in a location in memory, increment the memory location counter and then repeatedly test the reader until it has advanced a new character, which is read and stored, etc. The Bootstrap is always used to load a more sophisticated Loader.

ROM is regularly used to store the Bootstrap as a permanent 'corner' of memory, particularly with disc and tape Operating Systems. A ROM Bootstrap is a blessing since keying in at the switch console is an annoying exercise.

7·3·2 Absolute, Relocatable and Linking Loaders

The differential between Absolute and Relocatable Machine Code must first be defined.

(i) *Absolute machine code* is the *Object Code** produced by the *Absolute Assembler*. The significant feature is that some addresses refer to actual, specific, memory locations; thus the program must be loaded into the correct locations in memory, specified to the Assembler prior to

---

* The binary machine code is called the Object Code; the binary equivalent of the Assembly language or high-level language (e.g. FORTRAN) statements is termed the Source Code.

248

generation of the code. If it is required to load the machine code program into a different location, then it must be re-assembled.

(ii) *Relocatable machine code* is the *Object Code* produced by the *Relocatable Assembler.* Any memory addresses generated by the Assembler are relative to a reference level. The Relocatable Loader converts the relative addresses to absolute addresses as the code is loaded, by adding the "displacements" to a base address specified to the Loader prior to commencing the load.* Re-loading the code to new locations in core merely requires a change of base address to the Loader, avoiding re-assembly.

Clearly the Loader and Assembler are related. The Assembler appends certain pieces of information to the generated Object Code which are used by the Loader; thus the Absolute Loader cannot load code generated by a Relocatable Assembler.

Consider the simple piece of absolute code:

500   MOV 550, 560; replace Data B with Data A

   .
   .

540   Data C

   .

550   Data A

   .
   .

560   Data B

The instruction loaded in location 500 means move the contents of location 550 into location 560, thereby overlaying Data B with Data A. Now consider the same code to be incorrectly loaded starting at location 510:

510   MOV 550, 560

   .
   .

550   Data C

   .

560   Data A

   .

570   Data B

The move instruction now overlays Data A with Data C. Before the instruction can be correctly reloaded into location 510, it must be

---

* Do not confuse the base address supplied to the loader with PC or base relative addressing modes.

reassembled as

MOV   560, 570

The same instruction and data can be generated as Relocatable Code, thus:

```
*200
000'   MOV 50, 60
 .
 .
 .
040   Data C
 .
 .
 .
050   Data A
 .
 .
 .
060   Data B
```

The symbol *200 is meant to indicate that the load should start at location 200 and is only supplied to the Loader prior to the load itself. The prime on one of the addresses (which are now relative) i.e. 000', means that the addresses embedded in the code in that line are also relative. Thus the Relocatable Loader will load the code in the absolute locations 200, ..., 240, ..., 250, ... and 260; the code loaded into location 200 will be equivalent to the instruction

MOV 250, 260

Specifying the base load address as 500 loads *exactly* the same code as the first example above, without recourse to re-assembly.

It must be immediately clear from the preceding examples that Relocatable Assemblers and Loaders are more complex than their Absolute counterparts.

The base address can be given to the Loader in two ways; either (i) by writing it into the Assembler Source Code using a pseudo-operation, to be discussed later, when it is included with the Object Code, with a special code to identify it to the Loader, or (ii) as an external reference fed possibly by switch registers or by a Linker.

A linker is another Support program which is used to piece together modules of object code generated as separate entities. The Linker accepts mixtures of Absolute and Relocatable Code and generates a composite Absolute Object Code, which can be loaded by the Absolute Loader. A *Linking Loader* is a Support Program which effectively combines the Linker and Absolute Loader. If each software module being linked is strictly independent, the linking problem is simple. However programs are written as modules so as to share out the development amongst programmers and to reduce the re-assembly load by avoiding assembly of the whole program while working on a sub section; subroutines are the obvious example of modular software writing. It is most likely that some symbols, e.g. the name given to a word of data, are used in a number of modules, so that they must be 'commoned' when loaded. If a symbol used in writing a program module is to be used by other modules, then it is declared to the Assembler as a 'Global'. The Assembler appends a list of Global variables to the generated Relocatable Object Code which is digested by the Linker in order to allocate a unique location in core to that word, calculating the correct calling address in each module as loaded. Note that a Linker usually makes two 'passes' at the Object Code, first extracting all the linking addressing information so that, on the second pass, it can load one module, using information about a module to be loaded later.

In addition to the direct action of transferring code from paper tape, magnetic tape or disc to memory, the Loader can be asked to check for data transmission errors, provided that the Assembler is working in tandem. A common method used is to generate a block of Object Code and then to treat it as a string of bytes of binary data and add them up. The resultant sum is then negated and appended as an extra byte of data, called the *Checksum*, to the block of code. When the block of code is loaded, the Loader carries out a running sum of the code, which, when all the block is read, including the Checksum (which of course is not loaded), should be zero. This can be displayed on the computer display panel, a non zero result indicating an error in the code read in by the Loader. The location of the error in not indicated so that a complete re-load is necessary.

Now consider an example of an Object program, in Absolute Code, which consists of 100 16 bit words of instructions and data, to be loaded from location 500 on, and 200 16 bit words of instructions and data to be loaded from location 3000 on. The loader must not store anything in locations 0–499, 600–2999 and 3199 to the end of core in case other useful programs are already stored there. Thus the code fed from the Assembler to the Loader must contain information specifying the desired locations of the load, in addition to the Object Code. Each group of words of code which fill contiguous locations (consecutive addresses) is termed a 'block'. Three words are then placed before each block of Object Code, (i) a blank or other simple word to mark the beginning of the block, (ii) a word loaded with the total number of words of Object Code in the block and (iii) the address at which the load is to commence. As previously mentioned a Checksum will be appended to the end of each block. In the example above two blocks would be generated, so that the code presented to the Loader would be

0

100

500

$\vdots$ 100 words of Object Code

Checksum 1

0

200

3000

$\vdots$ 200 words of Object Code

Checksum 2

Note that with paper tape systems, one byte of code can be punched in each frame so that two frames are used for each 16 bit word.

The Relocatable Assembler/Loader requires an additional block of data to transmit the relocation addresses which are used by the Loader when loading the blocks of Object Code. Such a block of data is called a *Relocation Directory*.

The Linker or Linking Loader requires a table of Global symbols which are added to the Assembler output as another block called the *Global Symbol Directory*.

7·3·3 Dumpers

A *Dumper* is a Support Program which is used to make copies of the machine code stored in memory. The Dumper usually is selective so that specified parts of the load are dumped. The dump can be made to any external storage device such as magnetic tape, disc or paper tape; the Dumper must format the dump, i.e. words to disc, bytes to paper tape, and must append the usual leading and trailing data such as word count, checksum, etc., so as to be compatible with the Loader. The Dumper may also have a more sophisticated format control, converting each binary word to a string of ASCII characters (6 octal digits for each 16 bit binary word), so that a core load 'map' can be printed.

7·4 Assemblers

7·4·1 Machine Code and Assembly Language

An Assembler is a Support Program which converts Assembly language statements (Source Code) to Binary Machine Code (Object

Code). An instruction is a specific combination of the bits of a word; another instruction is simply a different combination. These combinations are decoded by the Central Processor, establishing a particular pattern and sequence in which gates must be enabled, so as to execute the desired instruction. Let it be said straight away therefore, that the machine code *can* be written directly in binary form, which *could* be a practical disaster!

The use of octal or hexadecimal numbers, as a form of programmers shorthand is helpful and is particularly useful in printing out lists of code.

Consider a 12 bit word instruction, to add data from an address in memory to an accumulator; the first 3 bits are the op. code and the other 9 the operand. Let the op. code for the add instruction be 001 and let the operand be the memory address 115_{10} (= 163_8 = 001110011_2). The machine code for this (over simplified) instruction is thus 001001110011. This is equivalent to the octal number 1163_8. Thus the first octal digit is a mnemonic for the eight possible op. codes and the other three octal digits form the memory address, in octal.

To improve the addressing range in the 9 bit operand, the first (the fourth bit of the instruction) is used to indicate whether the remaining 8 bits form a direct or an indirect address. If '0' indicates a direct and '1' an indirect address, then 1163_8 in the above example represents a direct address. If the operand is 163_8, indirect, then the binary instruction is 001101110011 = 1563_8. Thus the mnemonic interpretation of the octal number fails to highlight the direct/indirect address.

The next stage in the development of an Assembly language is to use simple abbreviations to represent the information in the instruction; such abbreviations, being similar to English, are far easier to remember. Thus, in the above example, the symbol ADD† can be introduced to represent the add to accumulator instruction. Further the symbol * can be used to represent indirect addressing; omission of the * means a direct address. The instructions can now be written as

ADD   163

and

ADD   * 163

Now consider the second instruction in more detail. The seven characters form the Assembly language instruction, the Source Code. These characters plus the embedded blanks are presented as a 'character string' to the Assembler, which it scans to recognise one of the defined Assembly language instructions. When an instruction is

† Many Assembler op. code symbols are three characters, e.g. SUB, MOV, etc. There are however many variants.

identified, the equivalent machine code is created and saved in a file; this will eventually be the Object Code program.

The symbolic nature of the Assembly language can now be extended to include *labels* to represent data variables. The label can be directly assigned at the beginning of the program or attached to a particular word of the Source program, thus

$$A = 163$$

$$\text{ADD} \quad A$$

or
$$\text{ADD} \quad A$$

$$\vdots$$

$$A: \text{data}$$

In the second example the colon following A indicates that the symbol A is a label; if the data is stored in location 163_8, then A is given the value 163_8. The advantage of using labels is immediately obvious in that the Assembler works out the actual value of the Label A, not the programmer; in fact the programmer need never consider specific numerical addresses. The full range of addressing capability of the machine can be introduced into the Assembly language by defining new symbols, thus, say,

$$\text{ADD} \# 123$$

can be interpreted as add immediate mode, i.e. add 123_8 to the accumulator (# can be interpreted as 'the number'). Often this type of instruction requires two words of machine code, the first containing the op. code and a flag to indicate the immediate mode, with the actual number (123_8) in the second.

The Assembler then is largely a one-for-one decoder, although, as in the immediate mode example, the one *unit* of Objective Code may require more than one word of memory.

An increase in the power of the Assembler is achieved by allowing simple arithmetic procedures during assembly, usually only add or subtract. Thus, using the simple running example,

$$\text{ADD} \ 216+111$$

generates the Object Code 1327_8, and

$$\text{ADD} \ A+7$$

where $A = 163_8$ generates the Object Code 1172_8.

Further arithmetic power can be generated by allowing a change of radix in the number system used. The radix can be declared and the Assembler made to convert the written number to the equivalent binary number. Thus the Source Code

> . RADIX 10
>
> .
> .
>
> ADD 115

generates the Object Code 1163_8. The radix will stay at 10 until another . RADIX statement is inserted. Another simple method used is to assume all numbers to be octal unless ended with a point, when they are treated as decimals. Thus ADD 163 and ADD 115. are equivalent.

Most statements in the source program are instructions, but some are Assembler directives. They do not generate Object Code, but assist in the generation of code for proper instructions. Two such Assembler directives have been introduced in the above examples, (i) the direct assignment of labels, i.e. A = 163, which is not to be confused with a 'FORTRAN' type executable statement, and (ii) the .RADIX statement. Statements of type (ii) are called *pseudo operations* and are often identified by the leading dot. The range of Assembler directives is a feature of the sophistication of the Assembler.

The *Assembler Location Counter* is one of the most important directives, usually represented by a period (.) with no extra characters. This symbol represents the address of a current word and generally speaking has a value similar to that which the Program Counter will have when executing the program. Thus the directive

> . =500

means that the address of the next piece of code is to be 500_8. In this way the normal contiguous allocation of core can be controlled, e.g.

> . =500
>
> . WORD 1, 2, 3, 4, 5
>
> . =600
>
> .WORD 6, 7, 10, 11, 12

will load the octal numbers 1, 2, 3, 4 and 5 into locations 500, 501, 502, 503 and 504 and the numbers 6, 7, 10, 11, 12 into locations 600, 601, 602, 603 and 604. The directive .WORD means that the following string of numbers are to be loaded into consecutive words of memory. The Assembly Location Counter can be used in an operand, so that if the instruction

> ADD . +2

is assembled at address 642_8, then the contents of location 644_8 will be added to the accumulator when the instruction is executed.

The Assembly Location Counter can be readily used to allocate blank blocks of core at assembly time, which will be used as data tables during execution, thus

$$. = 3000.$$

$$\text{BUFFER:} . = . +500.$$

$$\vdots$$

will allocate locations 3000 to 3499 as a data area, identified by the label BUFFER allocated to the first word; BUFFER will be equivalent to the number 3000_{10}.

For a Relocatable Assembler further directives are required to indicate whether Absolute or Relocatable Code is to be generated, say . ABS and . REL respectively. Thus the code

```
        . ABS
        . = 100
A:  ADD . +20
        . REL
        . = 10
B:  ADD A
    ADD B + 10
```

will allocate the value 100_8 (absolute) to the label A and 10_8 (relocatable) to label B. Note that the instruction ADD A will be located by the Loader, but the operand, A, is an absolute location. The instruction ADD B + 10, which is located in location 11_8 (relocatable) will reference data at location 20_8 (relocatable). The above example indicates that object code generated by a sophisticated Assembler can contain sections of Absolute and Relocatable Code, mixed together. The Assembler indicates in the Object Code which modules are relocatable, so that the Linking Loader can perform the conversions to absolute addresses when loading, as previously explained.

7·4·2 Macro Assemblers

A *Macro Assembler* is a Relocatable Assembler with an additional facility for handling *Macro* instructions. A Macro instruction is one which corresponds to a group of normal Assembly language instructions. A

Macro, defined by, say,

> . MACRO FRED A, B, C
>
> $\left. \begin{array}{l} - \\ - \\ - \\ - \end{array} \right\}$ group of Assembly language instructions
> using variables A, B and C, e.g. $C = (A + B) \times B$
>
> . ENDM

The argument list is not constrained to three variables as in this example. The Macro name FRED can then be used as an operation in an Assembly language program, e.g.

> ADD B
>
> FRED X, Y, Z
>
> etc.

The resulting object code will contain a copy of the instructions that go to make up FRED. Note that, if FRED is used a number of times the appropriate code will be included each time; compare this with a subroutine where only one block of code is loaded, accessed by Jump to Subroutine instructions inserted at the appropriate points in the program.

Most Macro Assemblers feature a number of useful 'system' Macros to back up the user generated Macros. These are commonly used as directives to an Operating System, particularly file handling statements,

> . FETCH   f,n $\left. \right\}$ copy file from disc to memory
> . READ   f,n
>
> . ENTER   f,n $\left. \right\}$ copy file from memory to disc
> . WRITE   f,n
>
> . DELETE   f
>
> . REWIND   d   rewind magnetic tape
>
> etc.

Note that these directives are included as part of the user program, as distinct from an operator's requests from a terminal.

The more sophisticated systems incorporate an *Optimiser*, making a final pass at the generated code to eliminate redundancy. As an example, consider the two Macros,

```
            . MACRO M1    A, B
            :
            :
            ST1 A;    store contents of R1 in location A
            . ENDM
and
            . MACRO M2    X, Y
            LD1 X;    load R1 from location X
            :
            :
            . ENDM
```

Then the program statements

```
            M1 P, Q
            M2 P, R
```

create the code

```
            :
            :
            ST1 P;    last instruction of M1
            LD1 P;    first instruction of M2
            :
            :
```

The instruction LD1 P is superfluous and will be deleted by the optimiser. Straight forward duplication of instructions may be created by consecutive Macros, which can also be deleted.

It should be quite clear that the Assembler will require to scan the source code to sort out the labels and other symbol values, relocation information, global assignments, etc., before the actual code can be generated. The Assembler usually prints out useful information such as symbol tables at the end of the first 'pass' before making the second pass. At the end of the second pass the Source Code has been assembled into the Object Code which must be filed, either on tape (magnetic or paper) or disc. While each instruction is assembled, the Assembly language instruction, the load address and the machine code (usually in octal form) can be printed out to generate an "Assembly listing". On simple systems with a teletype serving as both printer and punch, generating the listing at the same time as the Object code cannot be done; the Object Code only is punched out on the second pass and a third pass of the Source Code is used to give the listing.

When writing Assembly language programs it is most helpful to include comments. If a semi-colon is inserted at the end of the instruction, then any characters following are ignored by the Assembler, e.g.

FIRST: ADD 100;   LOAD COUNTER

label   Instruction   Comment

Comments are included on listings.

7·4·3 Position Independent and Re-entrant Code

The instruction set on most computers includes a PC relative addressing mode which forms an effective memory address by adding an offset to the Program Counter contents. If a program is written using this addressing mode exclusively, then the only address information actually written into the Object Code is the offsets. This code can therefore be loaded anywhere in core without recourse to re-assembly or relocation and is thus called *Position Independent* or *Program Relative Code* (PIC). PIC may reference Absolute addresses only if the contents of those specific locations are *never* relocated. Due to the machine architecture it is much easier to write PIC for some machines than others.

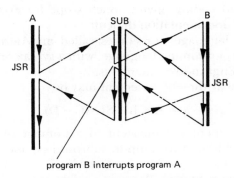

program B interrupts program A

Fig. 7·2 An example of a subroutine which must be written in Pure Code

A routine is said to be *re-entrant* if when part way through its execution it is interrupted and then used anew by the interrupt service routine, it can recommence from the point where the interrupt occurred without error, figure 7.2. For this to be possible the routine must not modify the contents of any of its locations; data must therefore be saved in locations pointed to by the routine, which are not common to each 'call' of the routine. Data areas for the 'input' and 'output' from the routine can be grouped with each calling instruction, in the manner of an argument list in a FORTRAN CALL statement; temporary data and current status values must be located on a stack (see Section 3.6.7) so that the interrupting call locates its own temporary locations further up the stack. The subroutine must begin by modifying the stack pointer to locate the top of the 'temporary area' of the stack and must end by returning the pointer to the bottom of the stack. *Re-entrant Code* is often referred to as *Pure Code*.

Utility packages, such as a set of mathematical routines, are obvious examples of software that should be both position independent and re-entrant. A single copy of the routine can be loaded and shared by more than one program, even when these programs may be competing for Central Processor control.

7·5 High-level Languages

While Assembly language and an associated Assembler make program writing much simpler than using binary machine code, many difficulties remain. First the Assembly language is specific to one type of computer, so that programs developed for one machine will be of no use on another type; programs are not portable. Secondly the instructions are simple so that even uncomplicated programs can require large volumes of coding, giving much scope for error and making debugging and documentation difficult.

A high-level language, sometimes called an *Autocode*, is a more sophisticated programming language, with a syntax oriented towards more 'normal' English-like statements.

Thus a typical arithmetic statement may be

$$X = A + B + SIN(C - D)$$

This single statement is equivalent to a number of machine code instructions, including two jump-to-subroutines, one to multiply and one to find the sine.

A Compiler is a System Program which converts the high-level language source code into machine code. It can be likened to a sophisticated Assembler, as shown in figure 7.3.

The dotted boxes on figure 7.3 are intended to stress that the Assembler, Assembly language and Compiler are specific to one type of machine. In contrast, the high-level language is common to all users, independent of the machine (or nearly so in practice). In practice some compilers generate Assembly code, rather than direct machine code.

Further comparisons between Assemblers and Compilers are:
(a) A Compiler has responsibility for allocating storage for both instructions and data.

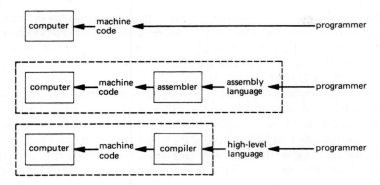

Fig. 7·3 Comparison of methods of generating machine code

(b) There is a one-to-one relation between an Assembly language instruction and the unit of machine code; one high-level source statement can generate large blocks of machine code.

(c) The smaller volume of high-level language code means that programs are easier to write, less prone to error and easier to debug.

(d) A good Compiler may generate code more efficiently in the long run, particularly when use of Assembly language means that the program writing has to be shared among programmers. However many compilers are notoriously inefficient, particularly at generating I/O Code.

High level languages are very much problem orientated. The commonly encountered languages are:

FORTRAN   for scientific (arithmetic) calculations
ALGOL   ditto
BASIC   as above, but with interaction.
COBOL   data processing (commercial, business) applications
RPG   ditto

FORTRAN and ALGOL are strictly for use off-line where data is presented to the program from a pre-prepared file to be processed as quickly as possible and the results placed in a file for printing on completion. BASIC extends this concept to allow the program to request more data as it is required and to print answers as they become available; since this 'interactive' approach effectively slows the program execution down to input/output speeds, it is commonly used in a 'time-sharing' mode, many independent programmers sharing the one machine at the same time.

For data processing applications large files of data must be accessed and updated. New data may be entered as strings of characters,

261

possibly from a variety of sources. Thus COBOL is specifically orientated towards file handling and string processing with poor arithmetic power compared to, say, FORTRAN. RPG is a commercial language which attempts to reduce the user's interaction to that of filling in a form.

Languages such as PL/1 and APL have been generated which attempt to combine data processing and arithmetic power. Other languages such as Extended-FORTRAN and BASIC-PLUS are based on the conventional languages with additional data processing statements defined. The latter, being simple to learn and oriented towards time-sharing, allows easy sharing and allocation of resources among users and is proving very popular in minicomputer based, on-line data processing applications.

None of the conventional languages have proved satisfactory for writing real-time programs, where events may be tied to a clock. In particular I/O procedures required sophisticated handling of interrupt structures and priorities. Again FORTRAN and BASIC have been modified to include real-time statements, e.g. wait for 5 seconds and then read the ADC. Again BASIC has been most successful, but it is very limited in speed. Many real-time programs have been written in Assembly language, but FORTRAN could be used to generate subroutines which could be linked to Assembly language device handlers.

The most hopeful development to date is the introduction of two Algol-based languages, CORAL and RTL/2. These languages are real-time orientated with full arithmetic, logic and data file handling facilities. They generate extremely efficient code, including I/O. Due to their universal appeal these languages could well become dominant in the minicomputer field, but whether the more difficult Algol-like syntax will prove acceptable to programmers versed in the simple minded COBOL syntax remains to be seen.

On mini computer systems BASIC is the best supported language. Generally however it is the most inefficient. FORTRAN is common, ALGOL much less so. RPG is well supported but COBOL has only just been introduced and it is just possible that BASIC-PLUS or CORAL may supersede it before it can become readily available. PL/1 and APL are considered too complex for minicomputer systems to date. CORAL and RTL/2 are available for a limited number of systems.

It is worth noting that some modern Compilers are so efficient at generating machine code, that they can be used to write other Compilers. Thus RTL/2 is being used on one machine for which the Compiler exists to develop RTL/2 compilers for other machines! In this way a highly specialised, problem orientated Compiler can be developed, if the effort can be justified by sufficient applications, e.g. a language tailored to suit process control applications or business applications (RPG is just such an off-shoot). There is a danger however that this would lead to an undesirable proliferation of ill-supported languages.

7·5·1 Compilers

A Compiler is a System Program which accepts the source code statements as input and generates the equivalent machine (object) code. As previously indicated in figure 7.3, it is in this sense similar to an Assembler. The resulting object code can then be loaded and executed. Note that the Compiler is loaded into memory until the compilation is complete, during which time no execution of the program can be considered. After compilation the Compiler is no longer required and it may be overlayed when the Object Code is loaded.

There is a wide range in the quality of Compilers available, particularly measured in terms of the efficiency of the resulting machine code. At the simplest level the Compiler generates a sequence of calls to subroutines. These routines provide the functions to multiply, divide, calculate the sine, etc. and also to handle the I/O instructions, communicating with a disc file via another sub-program which 'formats' the I/O data. Collectively these routines are known as the *run-time library*. The run-time library need only be available in object code form, and it is loaded with the compiled code to complete the executable machine code program. The library should be written in relocatable and re-entrant code. This type of program generation is often termed 'threaded' code.

A better Compiler, while still retaining a run-time library for more complex routines, will insert copies of code direct in the Compiler output, rather than subroutine calls. In this way the executable code will be more efficient. This 'in-line' coding technique however is only effective when hardware arithmetic processing is available, particularly a floating point processor, Section 8.3.4, otherwise calls to multiply, etc. routines *must* be made, which dominate the program and lose the efficiency. This differential is far more relevant to the arithmetic processing languages, e.g. FORTRAN, than to, say, COBOL.

Again the optimising techniques, mentioned in Section 7.4.2, may be incorporated. Attention is usually paid to avoiding unnecessary moving of data to memory, only to be copied back by the next statement, and to elimination of recalculation of invariant expressions inside a loop each time round the loop.

It must be stressed that a more sophisticated Compiler will generate more efficient code but at the expense of longer compilation time. Thus if a job is to be compiled and run once then a simple compiler may be quicker in total compile-plus-run time. For applications where a packaged program is developed to be repeatedly used with new data, then long compilation time is desirable if improved execution timing results.

At the same time as the Compiler converts the Source Code to Object Code it must try to detect and list any errors, usually those related to syntactical mistakes. Other errors may exist which will not manifest themselves until run time, which of course cannot be detected by the Compiler.

The simpler Compilers may be small enough in storage requirement to fit into main memory, taking its Source Code from and placing the resulting Object Code onto paper tape, cassette tape or floppy-disc. The more sophisticated Compilers require storage area and will only function with a disc store. The run-time library must also be loaded with the Object Code generated, which again is simpler using a disc system. Taking FORTRAN as an example a simple Compiler can be as small as 8 K words with a run-time library of around 4 K words. The library may be modular so that only the routines used by a particular compiled program need be loaded. An optimising FORTRAN Compiler may need 24 K words of memory plus disc support with a large, although certainly modular, library.

If a multiprogramming operating system is employed, which may allow more than one source program to be compiled at a time, the Compiler itself must be re-entrant.

7·5·2 Interpreters

BASIC is similar to FORTRAN in the nature of the source program (they are both English-like in character) but is executed quite differently. In BASIC an instruction is decoded and the resulting Object Code executed; the next instruction is then decoded and executed, etc. The immediate difference is that the BASIC Interpreter (so called, rather than Compiler) must reside in memory at all times. BASIC has obvious inefficiencies, (i) the store taken up by the Interpreter cannot be used for instructions, (ii) Looping requires repeated compilation of the statements in the loop. The advantage is equally obvious, simplicity; nothing could be easier to learn than the BASIC language.

Note that the interpretive nature of BASIC means that simple 'desk-calculator' features are incorporated.

This simple structure lends itself to time-sharing operation, each program being loaded into a dedicated area of memory. The Interpreter then takes code from one area, interpreting and executing statements for a fixed length of time. It then leaves that program and reverts to another one, etc., returning to the first program after, say, one second.

In earlier systems the BASIC program was stored as a character string which had to be decoded by the Interpreter during execution. Better systems process the input character string into a simpler form as it is loaded, coded to suit the Interpreter, e.g. Statement numbers, originally stored as three characters, should be converted to the equivalent binary number before storing. Such a system is said to be 'semi-compiled'. The degree of pre-compiling can vary, approaching the concept of a threaded compilation previously discussed. Re-entrant coding of BASIC is also being introduced.

Many of the FORTRAN, COBOL, RPG, etc. packages available on minicomputers are semi-compilers with an Interpreter for run-time execution.

7·6 Editing and Debugging Programs

7·6·1 Modifying User Programs

While a program is being developed the programmer will write the Source Code, which will be assembled (or compiled), loaded and executed. During the development it will be necessary to incorporate modifications to the program, the need for many of which will be found during execution.

The Source program can be changed, reassembled, etc.; however changing Source programs on paper is easier than incorporating the modifications into the Source Code. When the program is punched onto cards, as is common in scientific programming, new cards can be typed and inserted in the deck. Few minicomputer systems support card readers and punched paper tape is the common primary source of transferring the hand written code into a machine readable form. Paper tape can be edited by punching new blocks of code and splicing them into the original tape, but this is not too easy.

A support program is available, called an Editor, or a Text-Editor, which helps in modifying source programs. The Editor reads a copy of the 'text' which is to be edited into memory from the paper tape; the punched paper tape can be read in, then stored and edited from magnetic tape or disc, if available. Once the text is in memory, the Editor can be used by typing commands into a teletype to modify the source text as desired.

The main drawback with modifying programs by editing the source code is that the program must be reassembled, etc. after each modification. Large programs will of course be written in modules so that only one module need be affected at a time. Some modifications may prove simple enough to be incorporated by modifying a few words of the Object Code while it is loaded in memory for execution. This can be achieved with a *Debugging* aid, another support program often called a *Debugger* or an *On-line Debugger*. The Debugging program is in fact much more versatile than a tool for replacing the contents of specific core locations as will be explained in Section 7.6.3.

7·6·2 Text Editors

An Editor is a support program used to modify a users Source program. The Editor must be loaded into memory, together with the Source program, the text, which is to be edited. The facilities of the Editor can be controlled by simple commands typed in on the terminal keyboard.

The most usual facilities of the Editor are:

(a) *Input and output control.* Input commands cause the text to be copied into memory; output commands allow edited text to be punched out or stored on mag tape or disc.

(b) *Listing.* Specified parts of the text can be printed so that they can be examined.

(c) *Text modification.* Specified parts of the text can be deleted or interchanged; blocks of text can be inserted at specified points.

(d) *Searching.* To assist the editing, a character string can be specified and the Editor will locate all places in the text at which that string exists.

To use the Editor, further commands are required to place a 'location pointer' at any desired point in the program, effectively marking the spot for deletion, etc.

The Assembler and Editor are occasionally combined, typically referred to as a *Conversational Assembler*.

7·6·3 Debuggers

Whereas an Editor is an aid to modifying a source program, the Debugging program is an aid to modifying an object program. The Debugging program usually imcorporates features to run parts of the user program to assist in locating errors.

The usual facilities are:

(a) Printing of the contents of any specified location, including the internal registers and buffers. This may be converted to octal or decimal numbers and even Assembler mnemonics.

(b) Entering new data into any specified location.

(c) Locate any specific bit pattern in the object program.

(d) Run the object program. The Debugger can insert breakpoints into the program so that execution can be halted, to examine the contents of specific locations or registers at any stage of the program.

The Debugging program should only be used to make minor changes to the Object Code and it is wise policy to incorporate equivalent modifications in the Source Code for future reassemblies.

Some Debugging programs incorporate simple arithmetic power to help calculate addressing features such as offsets for relative addresses. Since any modifications must be typed in as an octal number, without the aid of Assembler mnemonics, this can be a useful feature.

7·7 Data Handling Programs

7·7·1 Input-Output Control

The user program, at various stages, will require data to be input from peripheral sources and will output data to peripheral devices. Instructions can be coded by the programmer to handle the peripherals. As an example consider a subprogram to handle a teletype terminal.

(a) *Keyboard handler.*

The input data will be typed on the keyboard as a string of decimal characters, with the most significant digit first. When the first character is typed and transmitted to the interface, an interrupt will be requested. When the interrupt is accepted, the machine must start a subroutine which will store the character just typed in the first byte of a 'buffer', established in the routine, and then increment a 'pointer' to the next byte in this buffer before returning. It is common practice to 'echo' the character on the teletype printer by outputting the character just received; to the operator the teletype will then appear to print the character typed, but it is worth remembering that the teletype keyboard and printer are quite independent. Note that if the next character is typed before the interrupt generated by the first character is acknowledged, it will not be accepted since once a character is entered into the local buffer register in the teletype interface, a 'Done flag' is set and the buffer register contents cannot be changed until this flag is cleared. Thus the subroutine, once it has finished with the input character, must clear the Done flag on the teletype. The end of the character string will be marked, say, either by a space or a carriage return character; thus each character is tested by the subroutine as it is received to detect the end of the decimal number. At this point the number has been entered into the computer, but is in the form of a string of ASCII coded characters. A subroutine can now be called which converts the string to a single two's complement binary number for use inside the machine.

(b) *Printer handler*

To print out a number on the keyboard the reverse procedure to the above is required. First a subroutine is called to convert the given two's complement number to an ASCII coded character string. The leading character is then transmitted to the teletype keyboard buffer register, which causes the number to be typed. Once this interface register is loaded a 'Busy flag' is set, which will be cleared when the character has been typed. The computer can repeatedly test the Busy flag in a loop and transmit the next character when it clears; this is simple, but means that the computer is held up until printing is finished. As an alternative the clearing of the Busy flag can be used as an interrupt to the outputting subroutine.

Now each user of the teletype could write his own subroutines to control I/O for the terminal, but this would be most wasteful. Such a standard subroutine is called a *device driver* and can take its place in the library of subroutines available to all users. Device drivers should be written for each peripheral that the computer supports.

I/O Executive programs are often provided which organise the handling of the device drivers, standardising the calling procedures, etc. Macro Assembler features can be used to greatly simplify the calls to the I/O Executive.

Note that the device drivers described above incorporate simple 'formatting procedures', i.e. the conversion from a character string to a binary word. It is worth comparing this with the very sophisticated formatting used in the I/O (READ and PRINT statements) packages in say a FORTRAN Compiler.

7·7·2 File Handling

When bulk storage devices such as a magnetic tape or disc are used in a computer system, they will be required to store a variety of independent *files* of programs or data. It is the ability to transfer files or part-files to and from the bulk store that adds versatility to the system.

A data file may be subdivided into a number of records, e.g. a payroll file will have one record per employee. Each record may be further subdivided into fields, e.g. name, tax rate, etc. Some program files may be similarly subdivided, e.g. subroutines in a source program. Each file and its subdivisions may be identified by a unique name; it will also include information for file protection so that, say, a file created by one person may be read by another user but not amended, etc. Each file must therefore store a *users' identifier*.

Bulk storage devices are organised as a chain of fixed length blocks, typically 512 bytes, each with a unique address. A file will be allocated an integer number of blocks. A specific file can be located directly by the block numbers, but it is possible to isolate the file by name, if a *directory* of all names and equivalent block allocations is created.

There are a variety of ways in which block allocation can be arranged.

(i) An initial area is used for basic information such as device numbers, bootstraps, etc. This is followed by the directories. A *Master File Directory* (MFD) links to a number of *User File Directories* (UFD), one for each user. The UFD contains the name of each file, the block number at which it starts and the number of blocks in the file. A *Spare Block Map* (SBM) contains a directory of unused blocks. The diagram of figure 7.4 shows this layout with four files of differing length recorded.

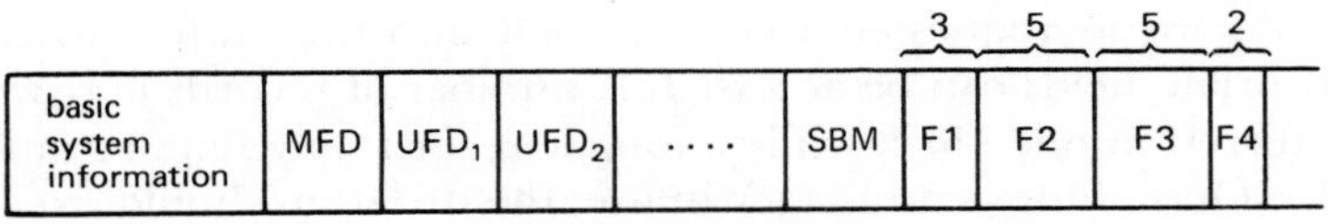

| basic system information | MFD | UFD₁ | UFD₂ | .... | SBM | F1 | F2 | F3 | F4 |

Fig. 7·4 A bulk storage filing system. Each file contains an integer number of blocks

Problems of block allocation occur when files are deleted. Let F1 and F3 be deleted (erasing the names from the directory and updating the SBM is sufficient, as the blocks are erased just before writing) and a new file F5 added. If F5 is three or less blocks long it can be entered where F1 was previously stored; if it is four or five blocks long it will go where F3 was previously stored; if it is six or more blocks long or of indeterminate length it will be stored immediately after F4. Note that if F5 is one block long it will be entered where F1 was stored, leaving two spare blocks. It is clear that repeated entering and deleting of files will result in spare groups of blocks which are too short for most files so that an occasional re-organisation of the store will be required, packing the files 'left' and updating the directories.

(ii) An alternative method of allocating blocks to a file is to terminate each block with a 'link' word, figure 7.5; this word addresses the next

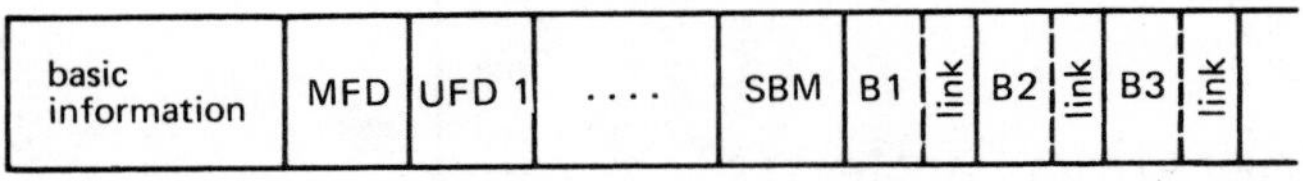

| basic information | MFD | UFD 1 | .... | SBM | B1 | link | B2 | link | B3 | link |

Fig. 7·5 A bulk storage filing system using linking

block to be taken in sequence, to create the file. In this way a new file can be stored in non-contiguous blocks, eliminating any necessity to reorganise.

With method (i) the file length must be pre-determined; with method (ii) it can be extended at any time simply by linking to a new block. In either case file security is related to the file handler which has responsibility for avoiding corruption of the directories, including double allocation of blocks!

The files will be used in differing modes. Commands can be given to the system to transfer whole files, say from disc to memory, simply by typing a request on a keyboard, e.g. to load a compiler. The directory will first be read into the computer which will be processed to identify the specific blocks which can then be transfered as requested. On the other hand many programs, particularly in data processing applications, require access to records during their execution, since the files will be too large to hold in memory. When the program is initiated an OPEN FILE statement will cause the necessary information to be read from the directory and a block-size buffer to be created in memory. Each record as requested will be copied into the buffer, when the appropriate fields can be accessed. A number of records may well be transferred in one block while a longer record may require multiple blocks. Once a file is no longer in use, the program should execute a CLOSE FILE instruction, to free the buffer area.

At the program level, parts of data files can be isolated by index tables, which may also be stored as independent files; there may in fact be multiple levels of indexing. Files which can be accessed by block number only are called *sequential*; those accessed by 'file name: record name' are called *random* and those accessed by index tables, *indexed sequential*. Sophisticated filing structures which allow data files to be accessed by any one of a number of indexes are called *data bases*.

Typical facilities provided by the file handler are:
(a) Create files
(b) Delete files
(c) List files – transfer to memory a block at a time and print
(d) List directories
(e) Transfer files from one storage device to another, including to and from memory. Such a load to memory would be by block via a Direct Memory Access Channel, rather than the Loader.
(f) Storage management such as file renaming, file protection, etc.

7·8 Operating Systems

7·8·1 Executives

An Operating System is a set of programs which control the flow of work through the computer system. All the support programs previously discussed will be incorporated in the Operating System, with a further program which 'manages' the loading, compiling, etc., as demanded by the operator. Such a program is called an Executive, Monitor or Supervisor.

The objectives of an Operating System are twofold:

(i) To relieve the programmer of as much of the simpler, repetitive work as possible, e.g. to find a Source program, load the Compiler, compile the Object program, load it and execute it, all by typing a simple command on the teletype keyboard.

(ii) To optimise, as far as possible, the utilisation of the CPU; in most systems the percentage of time that the CPU is actively engaged is low, even below 10%. This stems from the discrepancy in speed between the CPU and the peripherals; even disc storage which may transfer data at a million words per second, still involves millisecond latencies.

Many features which would have to be written into an application program become standard features of the Operating System, in particular management of the input/output and filing systems. In addition monitoring of programs can detect errors or misuse of resources and take action to prevent collapse of the system. Error diagnostic messages can be generated.

In general the use of an Operating System increases the ease of the use of resources at the expense of increased storage requirements, both memory and bulk store. Some inefficiency may be introduced, compared to say specially written I/O routines for a specific job, but in general the simplicity introduced leads, in practice, to improved efficiency.

There is no doubt that the decrease in hardware costs and increase in programming costs, coupled to increased speed of the hardware will increase the importance of Operating Systems. The development of software modules, the support programs discussed here, greatly assists in the development of Operating Systems.

The variety of Operating Systems is wide, and is related to the hardware configuration available. An 'all singing-all dancing' Operating System would be a very expensive luxury and so, in practice, different types of system are offered, tailored to suit specific applications. They can very roughly be placed in one of two categories (i) *off-line* and (ii) *on-line*, to be explained in the following sections.

For the simplest system, with no bulk storage, i.e. a minicomputer with teletype, paper tape reader/punch or magnetic cassette, the Operating System is little more than a glorified loader-cum-file handler. The Executive would be permanently in memory. With the reduction in memory costs, this is an area that warrants far more attention from the minicomputer manufacturers.

For the larger systems, the Executive itself will be far more complex and quite large. It is common to break the Executive into modules, one of which is permanently in memory while the others are loaded only as and when needed. If the Executive is supplied in modular form, it can be tailored, and updated, to suit the available hardware. The ease of 'generation' of the Operating System from these modules and the associated documentation are important features.

Commands to the Executive are called *Job Control Language* (JCL) statements.

7·8·2 Off-line Operating Systems and Multiprogramming

An off-line Executive schedules the loading and running of programs in response to simple Operator commands. This is the simplest system for data processing, often referred to as a *Disc Operating System* (DOS) in minicomputer systems.

Far more extensive Executives are available on bigger systems to handle *batch* processing. Jobs are submitted to the system on a more or less ad-hoc basis. The Executive queues the jobs, schedules and executes them; new jobs may be added at any time to take their place in the queue. The jobs submitted will vary in nature; some will be regularly required by a certain time of day, some will be required as convenient, some will be required urgently. Each job must be allocated a priority so that on completion of one job the Executive will commence the next job in the queue of the highest priority, not necessarily the one that has been in the queue the longest.

Such a *batch* Operating System as that just described is very inefficient in utilising the hardware if each job is completed before starting the next. *Multiprogramming*, the interleaving of programs using the CPU, greatly increases the efficiency.

As a preliminary to understanding multiprogramming consider the technique of using disc I/O buffers. Consider a job which reads data from punched paper tape and prints results on a line printer. If the program is loaded and the tape read, the CPU will wait for the data; it will also wait for completion of the print. Thus the overall speed of execution is governed by the speed of the tape reader and line printer, not the CPU; the system is 'I/O bound'. If however the tape reader copies directly to a file on the disc while the CPU is executing another job, then the data will be available at disc-to-memory transfer rate rather than tape reader rate. Similarly if the output data is loaded into a disc file, it can be transferred to the line printer from the disc while the CPU is used by another program. By using a number of I/O buffers the CPU utilisation can be greatly enhanced. If any program is held up for any reason while part completed, then a new program can be started, temporarily saving the part executed job if necessary, which can then recommence when possible. In this way the Executive may be controlling execution of more than one program at any time. Note that each job must have its own buffers, otherwise for example, printing an output buffer could have lines of different jobs interleaved; this is called *Spooling*. Allocation and control of the peripherals and their buffers, related to specific program requirements, is under the control of the Executive.

The multiprogramming concept can be further refined in large installations by having enough memory to hold more than one program at a time, thus increasing the efficiency by eliminating delays in 'roll-in' and 'roll-out' of programs between memory and disc, which can take place while another program is executing.

The multiprogramming Executive clearly requires a meticulously accurate logging system so that the location of any data temporarily moved out of memory and the stopping point of any suspended program are recorded. It is equally important to ensure that files are not overwritten and that conflicting demands are not made for the same area of memory. A directory is maintained by the Executive to keep track on each program.

Figure 7.6 shows a simplified 'map' of the main memory for a Disc Operating System. The proportions and locations occupied by the

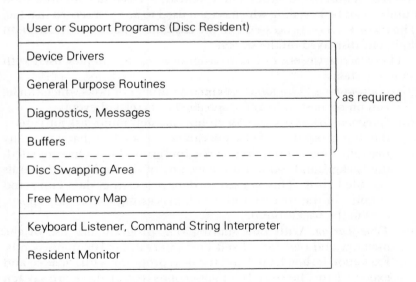

Fig. 7·6 Memory map for disc operating system

various packages are notational only; physical boundaries do not exist. Various methods are however used to make specific areas of memory read-only to applications programs; thus an erroneous application program will not be allowed to corrupt the Executive, say. Memory protection may be extended to prohibit one application program writing into another application program. Since, apart from a few programs such as the Resident Monitor, the load at any time may vary, the areas to be protected must be 'dynamic'. Memory protection can be a hardware feature, an extra bit on each word being set to make that word read-only, the Executive ensuring that the necessary protection bits are set. Registers can also be provided to note the upper and lower addresses of an active applications program, reference to addresses outside that range causing the program to abort. The same techniques can be achieved with software, checking the validity of each address. Hardware is more expensive, e.g. an extra bit on every word of memory, but software increases execution time.

7·8·3 On-line Operating Systems

For a batch program all the input data is first collected in a file; the program then runs to completion, storing any output data in another file; the Executive then schedules the printing program to print the results. An *on-line* system is one which allows data to be processed as it is entered. Thus in an order entry system, a customer identification number can be keyed in, which is then used to access a record in a file. The record is then processed and the customer's name, address, credit limit, etc. displayed on the screen.

There are a variety of multi-programming techniques used with on-line systems:

(i) *Multi-tasking.* The job is split into a number of tasks which can be run on request or by some specified interrelated events.

(ii) *Foreground/Background.* An on-line, possibly multi-task job runs in the 'foreground'. A batch job can be initiated so that it uses any machine time not required by the foreground job. Once initiated, the background job will not have any of the on-line peripherals allocated to it. This is used in data processing, data entry and enquiry in the foreground, batch processing (statistical reports, etc.) in the background.

(iii) *Time-sharing.* With time-sharing one program has use of the memory and CPU for a fixed time interval, say 100 milliseconds. Execution is then halted and the next program in turn loaded and executed for the next 100 milliseconds, etc. If there are say ten programs running, then each program has control of the CPU for 100 milliseconds in each second. Partially executed programs may have to be saved (rolled-out) and then reloaded (rolled-in) to continue from where they left off. It is common in time-sharing systems to allow each program to come under control of individual I/O ports, which may be geographically far apart, communicating to the computer over telephone lines. The slow speed of the terminal means that the user will not normally notice that he is only in contact with the computer for a small percentage of the time, time-multiplexed with other users. The interpretive languages such as BASIC are ideally suited to time-sharing; in fact BASIC was developed for a time-sharing system. The so called *Multi-user* BASIC is a BASIC Interpreter with a simple in-built time-sharing executive and is usually totally memory resident.

(iv) *Multi-language.* If a time-sharing executive also supports a background program then various compilers can be used to develop programs in a number of high-level languages, to be executed in the foreground.

Full multi-programming executives such as (iii) and (iv) allow all programs (legal) access to all files; a program is 'locked-out' only when in conflict for a specific record. With a foreground/background O.S. any file allocated to a background job is locked-out to the foreground job.

Some mainframe computers utilise a foreground mode to enter job control programs and to perform simpler tasks such as Editing, listing, etc.

7·8·4 Real-Time Operating Systems

A *Real-Time Operating System* (RIOS) is a special type of on-line system. The singular feature of a RTOS is that in addition to the normal on-line requests, others may be related to a clock. Such an Executive is required to run the computer for applications in process control, data logging, etc. The major problem with a real-time Executive is the efficient use of the computer interrupt priority system. Certain peripherals require servicing within a given time to avoid loss of information; these are termed *critical devices.* With one critical device an interrupt can suspend the execution of a background program while the service routine for that device is executed; with a number of critical devices there will be conflicting interrupt requests. It is not possible to make a general Executive which will utilise the computer interrupt priority system as efficiently as specifically written applications programs; the general concept of using an Executive to detect interrupt requests, to process them and pass them on to specific applications programs must introduce delays in response. It must be noted that programs which service high priority interrupts *must* be memory resident; they will not tolerate the latency of a disc to memory roll-in.

With a real-time clock in the system, in addition to the normal on-line interrupts, events can be tied to

(a) time of day

(b) after a specific time lapse

(c) repetitively, with a specified frequency of repetition.

While it is not really an Executive it is worth mentioning Real-Time BASIC here. The normal BASIC Interpreter is extended to include special purpose I/O drivers, to support the available peripherals, including a real-time clock. Thus a program essentially similar to a BASIC program can be written incorporating such statements as

$$LET\ X = ADC(4)$$

The function ADC(I) causes the Analogue to Digital Convertor to read the Ith channel and allocate the reading to the variable X. An instruction WAITC causes execution to suspend until a clock interrupt is generated, thus tying operation to real-time. Since with an interpretive language each statement is compiled and executed when encountered, the response time is slow. Such a system, however, should be fast enough to control normal laboratory experiments, it allows the most uninitiated computer user access to the machine in a real-time mode.

Real-time versions of FORTRAN, a compiler with the additional I/O drivers and clock support routines are also available, but are not so common as Real-Time BASIC. A real-time program written in FORTRAN is compiled generating a machine code applications program, which unfortunately is generally inefficient compared to specially written routines, particularly in handling the interrupt structure. It is hoped that the better real-time compiling languages, RTL/2 and CORAL will increase in availability.

7·8·5 Virtual Memory and Paging – Memory Management

The concept of treating memory as though it consists of equal sized block of words, termed *pages*, was introduced in Section 2.8.3. This was brought about by the limited number of bits available in an instruction to create an absolute address. Further it was pointed out that the fixed length page could be located 'dynamically' by adding an address in the page to the contents of another register to create the absolute memory address. From this viewpoint, due to the unavoidably short page length, this addressing system is rather restrictive. Thus methods were stressed which gave a full 64 K range of addresses from the 16 bit word.

This technique can be extended by the operating system, particularly to aid multiprogramming. Refer to addresses written into the program as *program addresses* (PA). When the program is executing, the program address requested by every memory reference is added to a fixed base reference number to give the actual *Physical memory address* (PMA). The base reference number is maintained by the Operating System and is determined when and by where the program is loaded into memory.* The obvious use of this technique is for the Operating System to maintain two (or more) base reference numbers.

As an example consider program A, written to load into absolute locations 0 to 6000 and program B written to use absolute locations 0 to 10000. The first base reference number can be zero and program A loaded into locations 0 to 6000. The second base reference number can be 8000 and program B loaded into locations 8000 to 18000. The second reference number can be any number larger than 6001, provided that the highest address does not exceed the maximum physical memory address available. The Executive can now commence to execute program A. When the program pauses for any reason or when the second program asserts a higher priority, program B can begin. When the second program is activated the current contents of the CPU registers must be saved by the Executive. Special consideration must be given when calculating the PMA, by adding the PA and the base reference number, to allow for dedicated memory locations such as the interrupt vector locations.

Now the simple multiprogramming Executive introduced above carries a high time penalty in that an extra addition must be performed every time memory is referenced. If memory locations used by the Executive Program were employed to store the reference numbers then extra memory cycles would be required for the PMA calculations. Thus the case is easily made for specialised hardware to assist the Executive. This can become fairly extensive and then it is referred to as a 'Memory Management Unit', another example of dedicated processing to ease the burden on the CPU, as was mentioned earlier in Section 3.3.2. This piece of hardware is explained here in a chapter devoted to software since it is inseparable from the Executive.

The simplest aid for the Executive is a set of registers to act as the base reference sources, one per program, which can be called *relocation registers*. Clearly more than the two implied above are desirable. These registers, under control of the Executive program can be loaded from the CPU. A dedicated Adder is also required to compute the physical addresses, without using the CPU ALU. The use of these Executive relocation registers can be likened to base relative addressing in the CPU, but it must be stressed that they are external and additional to the

* This technique must be compared with that of *relocatable loading*. The loader calculates the PMA and modifies the program accordingly as it is *loaded*. In the system above the Executive creates the PMA when the memory reference is *executed*.

CPU registers. In an extreme case a machine with base-relative, indexed addressing, (Section 3.4.1.3) relocated by the Executive will add the offset in the instruction to the base register contents, add the contents of the index register and then add the relocation register contents before arriving at the PMA.

Since the PMA is the sum of the contents of a relocation register and a normal program address, the range of physical addresses is increased. Since the Executive must load the relocation registers it is necessary to keep them to standard length. Thus in a 16 bit machine, the maximum address increases from 64 K to 128 K. Any one program is still constrained to 64 K maximum, but these 64 K locations may be anywhere in the physical range up to 128 K.

The system just described places a lot of responsibility on the Executive to avoid overlapping, and therefore corruption, of programs. Systems *security* or *integrity* is difficult to assure. Further by direct addition of the PA to the contents of the relocation register, the additional 16 bit register only succeeds in doubling the range of addresses. Thus the concept of paging, the curse of the simpler minicomputers, is reintroduced at a much higher Executive level.

The memory system is treated as though made up of a number of pages of maximum size, say, 8 K, giving 8 pages to the standard 16 bit limit of 64 K; a maximum physical memory size of 256 K is equivalent to 32 pages, etc. Thus when the Executive loads a program it keeps a record of the page used. A program longer than a page length can use multiple pages, again tracked by the Executive. To maintain security the Executive must simply ensure that the same page is not used twice. If when executing a program a page outside its own allocation is referenced, an error must have occurred and that particular program is aborted, without affecting the other programs.

The 8 K page is quite a large unit and it is often subdivided into blocks of say 64 bytes, so that part pages can be allocated to different programs. This appreciably increases the complexity of the Memory Management Unit hardware, but noticeably increases the efficiency of memory utilisation. If the allocation of each block is uniquely recorded by hardware registers in the Memory Management Unit, then there is no need for a program to be loaded into contiguous blocks. Thus a program using addresses 0–1000 could finish up loaded into, say, locations 512–1012 and 8192–8692. Any program addresses in the range 0–500 would use one page allocation register, which adds 512 to the program address, while in the range 500–1000, the appropriate page allocation register causes 8192 to be added. In the extreme case, with a minimum unit of the 64 byte block, the 16 bit register could address 2^{16} blocks = 64×64 K bytes, i.e. 4194304 bytes!

One system used is to allocate one register to each 8 K of the program addresses, each register dictating the PMA and the number of blocks allocated, up to the full page. Any one program can then require up to eight registers to cover the normal 64 K range of program addresses. Multiple sets of registers are then used for each program, often dedicated to different modes of operation such as Executive or User. If it is possible to write programs in pure code, with data separately stored in stacks, then different program allocation registers can be used for instructions and for data. In this way a priority structure can be maintained by the Executive.

Since each page is individually 'managed' it is possible to impose specific conditions on any one block such as read only, read/write or prohibited, under dynamic control of the Executive.

A further extension is possible in the concept of *virtual memory*. It was shown above that over 4 million bytes could be addressed by the system, far more than are likely to be available in RAM. Thus the calculated address is termed the *virtual address* (VA) of which. say, the first 256 K are PMA's (RAM) and the remainder are disc or drum locations. When a VA is derived that is out of memory and into the disc, the Operating System automatically causes the appropriate page to be copied into an area in memory, updating the management registers, so that the new VA is a valid PMA. Care must be taken in handling two dimensional arrays, since badly structured data could cause consecutive words to be alternatively in one page and then another, which could cause a disc to memory transfer for every instruction executed!

A dedicated use of the virtual memory concept has been described previously as a method of handling I/O instructions, Section 4.2.3.

Another hardware feature which is related to the operating system is duplication of the CPU general registers. In some machines as many as sixteen sets of registers can be introduced. Thus one set is allocated to one program. When a new program interrupts, instead of saving the register contents in memory, a complete new set of registers is used. If more programs are being run than there are register sets, then and only then, must saving and restoring be used.

In summary the Executive is a system program which manipulates disc to memory and I/O transfers, organises a priority system, detects memory reference errors, etc. using the Memory Management Unit, when available, as a 'book-keeping' aid.

7·9 Developing Programs for other Machines

It is possible to use one machine to develop and test programs for another machine, even a different type of computer. This is of importance when a largish, well supported system is already available but the machine to be used in a particular application will be 'bare', with a few peripherals. This is of singular importance with the advent of microprocessors, since the microcomputer will not have the advantage of a Disc Operating System. Indeed most microcomputer installations will have no terminal, having dedicated connections to the process under control via ADC's and DAC's. A laboratory type microcomputer system, with terminal, should be available for program development, but this will still be restricted.

There are three support programs which are available:

(i) *A Cross-Assembler.* This program when loaded into the host computer, accepts an applications program, written in the Assembly language of the satellite machine and generates machine code for that satellite machine. The machine code thus produced can then be loaded into the satellite machine. The machine code can be punched out on paper tape by the host machine if the satellite machine has got a tape reader, in a format compatible with the Loader of the satellite machine. For microcomputer systems the program will be loaded in ROM so that the host machine must support a ROM programming system – microprocessor manufacturers offer a service to 'convert' programs from punched tape to ROM, but see Appendix 4 for comments on programmable ROM (PROM).

(ii) *A Cross-Compiler.* This program accepts a high-level language source program and generates Assembler code for the satellite machine. Alternatively machine code for the satellite machine may be punched out.

(iii) *A Simulator* or *Emulator.* This program causes the host machine to simulate the actions of the satellite computer and its peripherals. Program development can then be conducted before the applications hardware is available. This is particularly useful during preliminary stages of development.

An off-line simulator uses a printer to indicate the state of the system after each instruction is 'executed', e.g. time elapsed, register contents, flag conditions, etc.

An on-line simulator causes the host machine to execute a program written in the machine code of the satellite computer, in real time. In practice the host machine must be fundamentally faster than the emulated machine to allow for possible non 'one-to-one' instructions, with built in time delays where appropriate to give correct timing. Microprogramming of the host machine may be possible.

It is common, but unfortunately inconsistent, to call the off-line program a Simulator and the on-line program an Emulator. Peripheral actions can be simulated off-line but the actual units can be used with the Emulating machine.

Note that these particular programs, like any other support programs, are in the machine code of the host computer. It is most desirable that the source programs for the Cross-Assembler, Simulator and Emulator should be written in a high-level language, say FORTRAN, so that they can be compiled and used on any host machine with the minimum of machine dependent modifications. Thus FORTRAN source programs could be supplied by each microprocessor manufacturer, so that, with a collection of programs, each user could use the one host machine (virtually irrespective of make) to develop programs for all microcomputers. Because, say, an Emulator is available written in FORTRAN, this does not mean that FORTRAN programs can be written for the microcomputer.

7·10 Summary

In summary the range of software available is already high and growing daily. As the systems software get better, the task of writing applications programs becomes easier. Normally the better the support software, the higher the hardware requirements but this is compatible with the falling cost of hardware and the increasing cost of program writing (manpower).

Often a variety of users require similar programs which are not available from the computer manufacture, which therefore get developed in isolation, with undesirable duplication of effort. The relatively common User Groups, organised by the computer manufacturers, help with co-operation through better communication and can assist with many problems.

With the continual improvement in hardware it is most undesirable that new machines should proliferate, rendering all developed software, particularly support and system programs outdated. One method is to ensure that new models are 'upwards compatible' with the model they replace, that is a program written for the old machine will run on the new machine, the new machine however incorporating new ideas and instructions which make new programs superior. The use of microprogramming helps in this respect, when a new machine can be microprogrammed to execute programs developed on an earlier generation machine.

Historically computer hardware developments came independent of software development. Software was written to take advantage of the hardware improvements. Currently the far more desirable situation exists, and will continue to exist, whereby hardware and software are developed hand-in-hand, the benefit to the user coming from superior support and systems programs, e.g. the memory management unit described in Section 7.8.5.

Finally it must be pointed out that it is most difficult to assess the quality of software provided by a computer manufacturer – there are FORTRAN compilers and there are FORTRAN compilers! It is most regrettable but quality is a feature which can usually only be determined by experience, often bitter. It is most advantageous before buying a computer, to look at the independent 'consumer reports' nowadays available. If possible test programs, called benchmarks, should be run and compared on various machines. Such programs should be as near typical of the users requirements as possible, which makes the task of specifying international standards for benchmark programs exceedingly difficult. Current users opinions whenever available, should always be sought.

Chapter 8

Advanced Features

8·1 Modular Construction and Options

Apart from specially designed and dedicated microcomputers and calculating machines, computers are constructed on a modular basis. Components are built onto a flat fibreglass card, a printed circuit board, with connecting pins along one edge which can be plugged into a socket. The sockets are mounted inside a box which also contains power supplies, cooling fans and a front panel or console. The physical size of the box and the rating of the power supply limit the maximum number of sockets. Extension cases, with power supplies and fans but no front panel, allow further expansion. All interconnections are made by wiring at the back of the sockets, with appropriate interconnectors to expansion boxes.

The size of the cards is a matter of choice in the design. A large number of small cards is more expensive than a few large cards but the former allows greater versatility and easier maintenance. Often cards are split so that two or three plug in across one socket. The cards are usually mounted vertically in the box, but some of the larger card systems are slotted in horizontally.

With this modular concept in mind, it is common practice to build the basic CPU onto one board and to configure the rest of the system by the selection of a number of optional additional cards. The obvious optional cards will include blocks of memory and interfaces to specific peripherals; other options are aimed at increasing the power of the basic CPU. Thus two computer systems constructed around the same basic machine may have widely differing performance and, of course, cost.

Some of the options have already been described, e.g. DMA controllers, interfaces and memory management units. Others will be described in this chapter.

8·2 Microprogramming

Microprogramming is not an option in the sense implied in the last section, but it is a method of implementing the control section of the CPU which offers the possibility of changing the instruction set.

Referring back to figure 2.1, the Instruction decoder and Control signal generator activate the processor by requesting that specific gates be enabled and inhibited in a particular pattern and sequence. A different instruction requests a different gate control action.

There are two fundamental ways in which this control unit can be implemented (i) hard-wiring and (ii) microprogramming. Most computers utilised hard-wired control until recently, since microprogramming was too slow, but the current swing is strongly towards microprogramming with the latest, faster, electronics.

Ideally the Instruction decoder should simultaneously look at all 16 bits of an instruction and establish the appropriate actions accordingly. This however allows 64 K possible combinations and is too expensive to implement. Thus advantage is taken of the structure of the instruction set. Using the instruction set of Chapter 2 as an example, the left-hand 4 bits can be decoded first, thus determining how the remaining 12 bits are to be decoded. If it is a memory reference instruction, the next two bits are decoded to determine which addressing mode is being used, which in turn will determine how the displacement is to be used, e.g. direct to the MAR by enabling gates 12 and 7 for mode 0 or to the adder for mode 3 for addition to the PC contents. In mode 3 gates 13 and 5 are enabled together with the appropriate combination of gates 24 and 25 to activate the addition, followed by enabling gates 27 and 7.

Other instructions are similarly decoded by considering a group of bits and using the result to route the remaining bits to one of a number of possible lower level decoders.

For a hard-wired control unit, the necessary logic required by the decoders is implemented by a complex network of TTL gates and flip-flops. Asynchronous operation also requires further logical information from the CPU to be taken into account; synchronous operation requires timing signals from the clock.

To appreciate the concept of microprogramming reconsider the above description of the instruction decoding process and recognise that it reads rather like a sequential program of events. First look at the *op-code*; for a particular op-code take a specific action determined by the remaining bits of the instruction. With the hard-wired approach a number of events can be simultaneously executed, e.g. enable gates 7 and 12, but alternatively the whole operation can be considered as a sequence of individual, simple events. Thus the control unit can be implemented by a 'microcomputer' within the main CPU. Each machine code instruction is treated by the microcomputer as a call to a subroutine which is executed sequentially. The microcomputer's own instructions are termed microinstructions, so that each machine code instruction is implemented as a program of microinstructions, termed a microprogram.

The microcomputer must have its own PC, IR, memory, I/O, etc. The memory stores the microprogram subroutines, the input accepts the machine code instruction and the output sends signals to the gates. The clock may be used by the microcomputer, but it will make use of asynchronous techniques to operate at maximum speed. Other inputs to the microcomputer are required to create asynchronous links with the main memory, etc.

The microcomputer memory must now be ROM, programmed to implement a specific instruction set, and must be fast. Memory access times as low as 40 nanoseconds are employed so that the full (sequential) microprogram can be executed in speeds comparable with hard-wired logic although never quite as fast. Note therefore that the commercial microcomputer, as discussed in Chapter 5, constructed around a LSI microprocessor, while conceptually similar, is far too slow for this application; it is also far more sophisticated than is necessary. Indeed some microprocessors are fabricated on multiple LSI chips, one of which is a control ROM, microprogramming the microprocessor!

The microinstruction word length need not be the same as that of the 'outer' computer. With a short microinstruction length only simple operations can be carried out per instruction; with a longer word length more overlapping of data transfers and more complex micro-operations can be allowed. From 16 to 64 bits have been used in minicomputers and up to 90 bits in larger machines. The shorter microinstruction word length necessitates more microprogram steps and is thus slower than a longer microinstruction.

When an 'outer' machine instruction is to be executed, a micropro-gram is initiated which causes the new instruction to be fetched into the main IR. The op-code is then transferred to the microcomputer PC so as to act as a jump to the desired microprogram subroutine.

The disadvantage of microprogramming compared to hard-wired processors is that it is generally slower. The advantage is that the machine code instruction set is not irrevocably fixed. A new instruction set can be created by developing new microprogram subroutines and plugging the new control ROM into the CPU. Ideally any user can create his own instruction set. This however is not practical, since it is not a trivial task to create the control programs and since each new instruc-tion set would require new software support packages. Nevertheless the manufacturer may provide two or three alternative control ROMS for specific tasks.

A better philosophy is to fabricate the control ROM on more than one chip. The basic instruction set can then be created on one ROM with an extended instruction set on another. The more specialized instructions could then be constrained to the extended set. A modern innovation is to include a small RAM as part of the control memory so that the instruction set can be modified during operation. This is aimed at a multiprogramming environment so that, say, one extended instruction set can be loaded for use while compiling a FORTRAN program and a different one when executing the the program. This is a good example of hardware and software development moving hand-in-hand.

From a manufacturer's viewpoint microprogramming allows new designs to be made 'upwards–compatible' with existing machines. The new machine can be brought into service with a microprogram emulating the instruction set of the older machine so that all existing software can be used. The instruction set can then be updated as new software becomes available.

Nowadays, the control memory is exclusively semiconductor ROM, although magnetic core ROMs have been used in the past. One of the commonest 'intelligent terminals' uses a dedicated area of disc to store the control program, which is very slow but adequate for the task.

The implementation of the control unit of the CPU by programming raises the question of what is hardware and what is software. In practice this 'programmable-hardware' is called 'firmware' or more pictur-esquely 'soft-hardware' or 'hard-software'.

8·3 Arithmetic Operations

There are four basic arithmetic operations, add, subtract, multiply and divide. Each requires two operands. There are however a number of different formats in which numbers can be stored in a computer, introducing a requirement for more than one form of each operation.

Details of arithmetic operations are given in Appendix 1. In summary there are two basic number types, integer and floating point. Integer numbers are usually treated as two's complement form although occasional use is made of unsigned numbers. They may however be single or double word length (precision) and possibly longer in special cases. Floating point numbers require a mantissa (or fraction) and an exponent; the number of bits in the mantissa determines the number of significant digits, while the exponent determines the range of numbers. Sixteen bits is inadequate to store a floating point number so that two, three or four word formats are commonly used. Two word floating point numbers are considered single precision and four word double. Integer numbers can be interpreted as fixed-point numbers by implying the position of a decimal or binary point. Fixed point arithmetic requires careful software tracking of binary points (scaling) which is avoided by using floating point representation. Fixed point arithmetic is however generally quicker than floating point. Note also that multiplication of two 16 bit integers creates a 32 bit product, which requires careful consideration with regard to the position of an implied binary point, if the multiplier and multiplicand are known not to produce a product greater than $2^{16}-1$, then only the least-significant of the two words of the product need be retained. Again the problem is avoided by using floating point, i.e. any operation on two 32 bit floating point operands produces a 32 bit floating result.

Addition and subtraction of single precision integers are fundamental operations included in the simplest of instruction sets. The treatment of two's complement and unsigned numbers is identical. Multiple precision add and subtract operations are also catered for by the 'add-carry' instruction, Section 2.8.4.2. All other arithmetic processes require rather more complex and detailed treatment. A simple introduction was given in Section 3.5.5 to the multiplication of two unsigned single precision integers, but, unlike addition, multiplication and division of two's complement numbers differ from that of unsigned numbers.

In addition to the four basic operations, the variety of number formats means that operations must be introduced to communicate between routines. Thus instructions to convert from integer (single or double) representation to floating point (2, 3 or 4 word) representation and vice versa are required. Other operations encountered are normalise, negate, complement, clear, set, compare, etc.; in fact any of the functions usually included in the instruction set for single precision integers could be required for other word formats.

There are four methods of handling the arithmetic operations required which are described in the following sections.

8·3·1 Software

A standard library of subroutines can be provided. If a Macro-assembler is available, macro instructions can be defined, with argument lists, to create simple calls to the subroutine. The subroutine must be re-entrant, so that methods are defined for locating the data either in pre-specified registers or in the group of instructions (the Macro) which call the subroutine.

Subroutines, for conversion of a number in each format to a string of ASCII coded characters, are also supplied to aid print out and the dual for reading in numbers by the character.

8·3·2 Extended Instruction Sets

Unspecified combinations of the instruction can be used to create new instructions to aid the arithmetic operations. It must however be clear that there can only be a limited number of instructions unspecified in any machine, so that the full range required may not be provided. Typically single word integer multiply, divide and normalise instructions are added, which are used by a modified software package to provide the double precision, floating point, etc., operations. The modified routines, taking advantage of the additional instructions, will be speeded up. Such *extended instruction sets* (EIS) can be incorporated by hard-wiring, but this is an example of the advantages that can be accrued with microprogramming. The hardware for the EIS can be made modular, e.g. one optional card provides the integer multiply and divide while a second option may extend this to floating point.

8·3·3 Extended Arithmetic Units

These devices are in fact peripherals, connected to the normal I/O bus and accessed with normal I/O instructions. Typically the *Extended Arithmetic Unit* (EAU) will contain two or three buffer registers and control flags to select one of the range of operations available in the hardwired electronic circuitry. Two output instructions are used to transfer the operands to buffer registers in the EAU, followed by a control instruction to initiate the selected operation; the control instruction may well be combined with the second data transfer in practice. When the operation is complete, the result is available in the

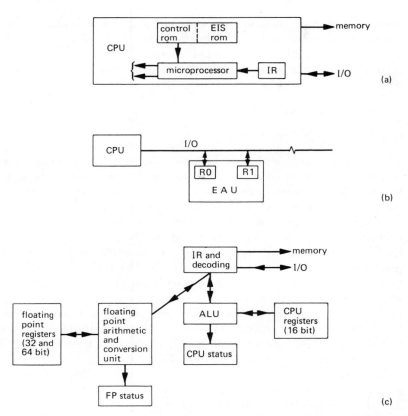

Fig. 8·1 (a) Microprogrammed extended instruction set. (b) An extended arithmetic unit. (c) A floating point processor.

buffer registers and can be transferred back to the CPU by further input instructions.

An EAU probably takes less than 10 microseconds to complete the selected operation. It may be designed to suspend further CPU operation until complete. Alternatively a number of non-conflicting instructions, which use up the 10 microseonds, may follow the EAU initiating instruction: if no further useful operations can be executed before the result is ready for the input instruction, an appropriate number of NOP instructions must be used.

In essence an EAU and an EIS perform similar operations, the former with dedicated external hardware and the latter with modified use of existing CPU hardware. Since EAU's are special purpose electronic devices, they will be faster than extended instructions, but carry the overheads of the I/O instructions. It is quite practical to design EAU's for any number format and arithmetic operation. Normally however they only provide single word integer multiply, divide and normalise operations and, as with the EIS, are used to speed up more varied subroutines.

8·3·4 Floating Point Processors

The most powerful arithmetic processing technique encountered is to create a second processor, with its own registers and arithmetic unit to function in parallel with the conventional CPU. Only one PC and IR are used so that a program is still executed sequentially, but it may use one or other of the processors. The arithmetic processor is a floating point unit (integer multiply/divide will commonly be provided by an EIS) so that its operations will take longer to complete than the normal processor operations. Operations can take place simultaneously in the two processors, since they are physically independent, as shown in figure 8.1(c). A *floating point processor* (FPP) may well incorporate 32 and possibly 64 bit registers and arithmetic processing hardware, even with a 16 bit machine. However, the single 'load–double–precision–floating–point–register' instruction will invoke four transfers of 16 bit data words from consecutive memory locations.

A whole new set of instructions appropriate to the FPP must be defined. Typical instructions are
ADDF   add two floating point numbers
MULF   multiply two floating point numbers
DIVF   divide two floating point numbers
LDF   load two 16 bit words from consecutive memory locations into one 32 bit FPP register
STF   save the contents of a 32 bit register in two consecutive memory locations
ITF   load FPP register with floating point equivalent of an integer number
FTI   store contents of a FPP register as the equivalent integer.
Double precision combinations must also be specified, i.e. DIVD or FTID which converts a floating point number into a two word integer.

Independent status flip-flops are provided with the FPP, established by the floating point arithmetic and conversion operations including such error flags as overflow, underflow and divide-by-zero. The choice of single or double precision floating point arithmetic can be made by establishing a mode control flip-flop, rather than defining two sets of instructions. Thus with single precision mode, LDF loads a 32 bit FPP register from two 16 bit locations, while with double precision mode the same instruction loads a 64 bit FPP register from four 16 bit locations.

It must be realised that this technique gives far the fastest arithmetic processor since it is a high speed dedicated electronic unit, without the overheads of employing I/O instructions. An instruction such as LDF causes two memory accesses for the one instruction–fetch–cycle, whereas a floating point EAU would require two I/O instructions to perform the same task. The existence of the FPP registers also gives a large advantage; the alternative methods must use the processor registers as pointers to stacks in memory for the operands.

Again the problem of specifying unique codes for the new instructions arises. If they cannot be incorporated in the normal set, an alternative method is to provide a mode flag in the main CPU, which can be established by a normal instruction. When the Assembler creates the machine code it will insert appropriate mode flag set or clear instructions. In this way independent 16 bit instruction sets can be used for normal and floating point processors.

Operation	Software	EIS	EAU	FPP
ADD	1			
ADD (32 bit)	3			
MUL	80	4	10	
DIV	150	6	12	
MULF (32 bit)	200	30	20	7
DIVF (32 bit)	350	50	25	8
ADDF (32 bit)	100	20	18	5

Fig. 8·2 Typical timing of arithmetic operations, assuming all data to be in CPU registers, not memory The floating point software routines could be speeded up by normalisation with an EIS or EAU

The following two programs indicate the manner in which the parallel operation of the two processors can be utilized.

LDF 1, 100   load FPP register 1 with the contents of memory locations 100 and 101.

MULF 1, 102   multiply the contents of FPP register 1 by the FP number in memory locations 102 and 103. The result is left in the 32 bit register 1.

ADDF 1, 104   add the FP number from memory locations 104 and 105 to FPP register 1.

LD0 200   load CPU register 0 from memory location 200

LD1 201   load CPU register 1 from memory location 201

ADD 0, 1   add contents of registers 0 and 1.

In the above program the first three instructions use the FPP while the other three use the normal processor. The ADDF instruction must wait until the MULF operation has finished, during which time the normal processor is unused. Thus the following modification of the program reduces the execution time by allowing the three normal instructions to execute while the FPP is executing the multiplication.

LDF 1, 100
MULF 1, 102
LD0 200
LD1 201
ADD 0,1
ADDF 1, 104

8·3·5 Other Mathematical Functions

Subroutines are available for calculating other mathematical functions such as exponential, sine, cosine, tangent, etc. These routines repeatedly use the multiplication/division operations so that their efficiency is directly related to the arithmetic processing system employed.

These are rare examples of machines used in dedicated environments where, say, calculation of the trigonometric functions dominates the processing. This is an example where specially tailored microprograms can introduce these functions as part of the primary instruction set.

8·4 Memory Allocation and Protection

A memory management unit is an option used on bigger systems working in a multiprogramming environment. It forms a high level interface between the computer memory system and the operating system. Such a unit was explained in some detail in Section 7.8.5.

Other features of the main random access memory system are also to be considered.

8·4·1 Memory Protection

The memory management unit can provide memory protection through the operating system. Effectively the memory is treated as a number of blocks, the required number of blocks being allocated to any current program. A status register can be associated with each block which can be set to make that block read/write or read-only. This can be extended to make a block say read-only by the applications program but read/write by the operating system. Since the status register can be cleared or set up by the operating system, the memory protection is 'dynamic' and can be altered to suit the current situation.

The above technique is a software protection method, linking to the actual memory through the specialised hardware of the memory management unit. On some systems the memory itself includes an extra bit on each word which when set would inhibit any attempt to write into that word, making it effectively read-only. Such a technique is far less versatile than the dynamic allocation method.

8·4·2 Error Detection and Correction

Memory protection techniques described above imply protection of one program from corruption by another. Another form of protection required is to check for random errors caused by any reason such as transmission errors or electrical noise. The simplest technique is to include an extra bit with each word to give parity checking. Modern memory systems are proving of a high enough level of reliability to make this technique rare.

Error correction can be included but this involves more than the one redundant bit for each word. One 16 bit machine uses a 5 bit error correction code, increasing each word of memory to 21 bits. This expense is only justified in special high integrity applications, particularly in dedicated data communication systems.

8·4·3 Interleaved Memory

A technique introduced to increase memory speeds is available on some minicomputers known as interleaving or overlapping. Effectively the memory bank is split into two (or more) independent blocks, but so arranged that consecutive addresses are located in alternate blocks. In this way a second memory cycle to another block can be commenced as soon as memory access has been made in one block. This is particularly powerful with magnetic core memories, since the second block can be accessed while the re-write cycle is executing in the first block. Block data transfer rates can be virtually doubled by this technique.

8·4·4 Mixed Memory

With synchronous memory transfer the memory bank must be constructed with a similar type of speed of memory. With asynchronous memory transfer different types of memory can be mixed, e.g. 4 K of

600 nanosecond semiconductor, 4 K of 1 microsecond core and 8 K of 1·5 microsecond core. Programs would then be written to make use of the semiconductor store for the most frequently used access.

A powerful technique used is to add a small 'cache' memory to the main memory. The cache acts as a store for short blocks of data. When a memory location is referenced, the data is taken from the memory as usual. At the same time, concurrent with the processor operation, the next block of data from the locations immediately following the location just referenced are copied into the cache memory. The next memory access checks the cache memory to see if it currently contains the desired data, resulting in a 200 nanosecond transfer if it does or a normal speed transfer if it does not. The cache memory will probably store 4 to 8 blocks each of 4 to 8 words, with of course the addresses of the main memory locations which are currently duplicated. With the basically sequential nature of programs and data arrays, a high percentage of transfers will take place via the cache memory. Future machines will probably include the cache memory on an LSI CPU chip.

8·5 Multi-Processor and Multi-Computer Systems

The concept of one computer being used concurrently by more than one task is commonplace. The individual tasks may be different parts of one problem or they may be totally independent programs. The sharing and allocation of the one set of resources is known as multi-programming or multi-tasking and is run under control of a special purpose executive or operating system. Thus a dedicated software package is being employed to make the one hardware system appear to each user as though he had an individual (virtual) machine.

With more sophisticated software interfacing multiple users to the computer system becoming available, the total hardware power can be increased by improving the data processing. This can be achieved by faster hardware, but the main limitation lies in the sequential nature of the processing. Thus the concept of 'parallel-processing' becomes attractive. With a parallel-processing system multiple processors are employed, executing differing tasks concurrently, as allocated by the software system. This concept has a strong hold on modern computers at a low level, in the addition of special purpose, dedicated processors to the basic machine, e.g. intelligent DMA controllers, floating point processors, memory management units and I/O processors. In these examples special purpose processors, of differing power, are added to the one general purpose processor, but this can be extended to the true multi-processor concept of a number of general purpose processors, each with access to the same memory bank and peripherals, running under the one common operating system. In practice one of the processors will probably act in a supervisory role, allocating tasks to the other processors.

For a multi-processor system a common memory unit is required. This is normally configured as 2 to 4 blocks, each with its own data port. Thus different processors can be accessing different blocks of memory simultaneously, hesitating only when simultaneous access of the same block is required. However a special piece of hardware is required to create the multi-port memory access, sometimes called a memory/processor multiplexor, as shown in figure 8.3.

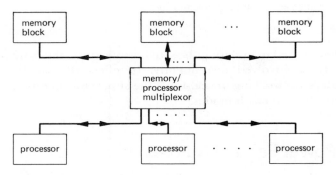

Fig. 8·3 A multi-processor computer configuration

An alternative configuration to the true multi-processor system is a network of communicating computers. Each computer is a separate entity, with its own memory and program, communicating with each other through I/O channels under program control. An obvious example is a minicomputer acting as a front-end processor to another computer. This concept is spreading in the use of intelligent terminals acting as satellite computers, probably geographically widely spaced, connected back to a central machine. In such a system two satellite computers can communicate with each other only indirectly, via the central computer. An alternative network may employ a hierarchical structure. As an example, in the system of figure 8.4, a data processing machine in a company's headquarters makes decisions as to what product is required at one of the outlying factories. This information is absorbed by a supervisory computer on site which sends out commands to various parts of the plant where local computers actually control the process. Data logging information is passed back to the supervisory machine for processing, any important results being fed back to the headquarters machine. Note that the satellite computers may be continually employed controlling the process; the supervisory machine

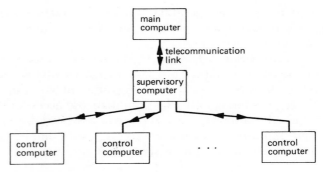

Fig. 8·4 A hierarchical multi-computer structure

will be dedicated to updating the satellite machines; the main machine will only be involved infrequently. In effect the satellite control computers are working in real-time, the supervisor in on-line and the main machine in batch modes.

8·6 Power Fail and Autorestart

When mains power supplies fail for any reason, processing must be suspended. It is most desirable that, when supplies are resumed, processing can continue from where it was suspended. The problem lies in the volatile nature of electronic storage devices, so that the contents of the CPU registers will be corrupted when power is re-instated. With magnetic core memory, the stored contents will not be effected by power fail, so that a few locations can be reserved to save the contents of the CPU registers. An optional hardware unit is required which continuously monitors the power supply. When a failure in the supply is detected, this power-fail unit generates an interrupt at the highest possible priority. The d.c. voltages will be held up by the smoothing capacitors for a few milliseconds before they fall low enough to corrupt the processor, which is long enough to execute a small program which stacks the contents of all the active CPU registers into memory. The PC contents will have been automatically saved by the interrupt. When power is returned, a new interrupt will be generated as soon as the d.c. supplies have stabilised, assuming that the computer is so designed as to start in a Wait state, which causes a routine to reload the registers from memory. Completion of this routine terminates the interrupt that was started by the power-fail, so that the original PC contents are restored and processing continues from where it left off.

With a volatile memory, e.g. LSI semi-conductor store, the problem is compounded. Back-up battery supplies are often used, switched on by the power-fail detector, which will stop corruption of the data for hours, particularly as with processing halted, it is not being accessed. Cassette tape recorders have been built into systems, so that with the memory on battery supply, a dump can be made. Power-up automatically causes a re-load before processing re-commences.

8·7 Real-Time Clocks

For any real-time system an internal clock is required. This option is simply a digital counter which causes an interrupt to be generated. The action taken in response to the interrupt is entirely the responsibility of the service routine, i.e. the clock only provides the signal to initiate a routine. The clock can generate a continuous train of regularly spaced interrupts or a single one. It can be turned on or off by program control.

The rate at which interrupts are generated can be varied, although the simplest devices generate interrupts tied to the 50 or 60 Hz mains supply. A truly versatile clock should be fully program controllable. A choice of basic oscillator frequency can be selected, commonly 1 MHz, 100 kHz, 10 kHz, 1 kHz or 50 Hz, often crystal controlled for accuracy. A register is provided which can be loaded with a number at run time; this number is then 'counted-down' by the oscillator pulses, generating the interrupt when it reaches zero. An extremely wide range of timing interval can thus be achieved by selection of the oscillator frequency and the number loaded into the counter register.

One specialised form of clock available is an optional unit called a *Watch-dog timer*. This timer can be set by program control to generate an interrupt after a specified time interval. While an application program is executing it must generate an instruction to reset the timer before the interrupt occurs. Thus if there is a CPU failure, the timer will not be accessed by the program and the resulting interrupt will signal the fault condition. These devices are only of use in dedicated real-time applications.

Chapter 9

Selecting a Computer System

9·1 Specifications

It is essential to specify the task which the computer is required to perform. The whole system requirement, not just the processor, can then be formulated from this specification and costed. There are far too many cost underestimates created by inadequate specifications.

It is equally important to allocate responsibility for the system. This can range from the user buying the hardware direct from the manufacturer and installing and programming the system himself, through to employing a systems house to undertake the complete job. Which is preferable is clearly dependent upon the size and skill of the staff employed by the user. If the general engineering expertise is available, but with no specialised knowledge of computer systems, a consultant firm may well bridge the gap.

In preparing a specification, the user must keep his feet on the ground. It is all too tempting to ask for every conceivable function which can be thought up. Many of the earlier failures of computer

The examples in this chapter lean towards instrument and control systems. The warnings apply equally to commercial or any other systems!

systems stemmed from too high a degree of sophistication – running before walking! Recent installations are far more state-of-the-art and are correspondingly more successful. Nevertheless it is as well to contemplate further developments, so that expandability may be a feature of the specification.

At all costs communication between the user and supplier must be good and fluent, a more difficult problem than may be anticipated due to the different backgrounds of the people involved and to security problems.

Lack of sufficient effort in the making of specifications and allocation of responsibility will involve serious problems, e.g. increase in cost due to underestimation of the less tangible items such as staff, programming, maintenance, etc. It could well lead to a choice of supplier with inadequate experience and the installation of inflexible or, at worst, inadequate equipment.

9·2 Choice of Supplier

If the project is purchased as a complete hardware/software package, a *turnkey* system, then the user has less interest in the criteria by which the system was selected. It is nevertheless advisable for the user to have some idea of the scale of his project, at least down to the type of computer, e.g. a mini or a maxi, and the principal peripherals.

The following factors should influence the choice of supplier:
(a) the ability to provide specialised hardware.
(b) the experience and ability to provide engineering systems support.
(c) the ability to write software.
(d) quality of documentation.
(e) the quantity and quality of any subcontracts.
(f) delivery times for the complete system.
(g) the views of other users.
(h) conditions of sale, warranty and maintenance agreements.
(i) training facilities and customer support.
(j) short and long term prospects of the supplier.
(k) cost effectiveness.

9·3 An Example of Computerising an Existing Technique in Instrumentation and Control

Instrumentation and control systems tend to grow-up. That is to say a rudimentary system is installed, which is successful in achieving its immediate aim, tends to highlight further requirements. At its simpler levels the problem can be resolved by conventional (digital voltmeter based) data loggers and printers and a number of single loop, possibly 3-term, controllers. As the size and complexity of the problem increases, more demands are made of complexity, speed and, probably most important, versatility. Often special purpose electronic logic systems are required to detect alarm levels and to actuate new sequences of events. It is at this stage, because of the versatility offered by the programmable nature, that the use of a digital computer as a 'nerve-centre' becomes attractive.

Data logging and display is a typical example of current interest, which exemplifies the situation.

The problems of transducers are assumed similar in all loggers. The conventional logger scans the transducers and passes each signal through a conditioning circuit (linearisation and scaling) and then prints the value, in a fixed format, on a printer. The value must actually be printed before the next reading can be taken (from the same or another channel). The analogue transducer signal is converted to a digital number to increase accuracy and to facilitate printing. The conversion is performed by a digital voltmeter, the BCD code of which is directly compatible with the printer. Great care is taken with the scanner to achieve high noise rejection and is commonly constrained to a maximum of 100 channels per second. In practice however this rate cannot be used since the printer speed (10 characters per second, say 5 characters per reading = 2 channels per second) is slower. If all channels are similar, using the same scan rate, linearisation and scaling, then the system is simple. Complexity starts to increase when differing transducers are connected and it is desirable to scan channels in a random order, and indeed at various rates. A high number of differing linearisation laws and scale factors can occur and it becomes obviously desirable to print out not only the measured variables converted to engineering units, but functions of the variables, i.e. *speed* × *torque* × *scale factor* to give *power*.

Thus a computer can be used to improve the logger on a number of counts:

(a) as a buffer between reading and printing, so that the maximum data rate as set by the scanner can be used. (The use of high speed, transient, sampling is possible, but is a more specialised problem.)
(b) as a calculator for scaling, linearising and computing functions.
(c) as a formatter to control the output; visual display units offer an alternative to printers.
(d) as a controller to select input channels, gains, rates, etc.
(e) to perform more sophisticated functions such as automatic calibration.

(f) to test readings to flag alarm conditions. Corrective actions can often be initiated by the computer.

(g) to enable interative control of an experiment by an operator via a console.

(h) to 'multiplex' a number of differing experiments.

This example also shows some of the problems that can be created. In fact a computer can be 'interfaced' to a conventional datalogger, but this has disadvantages. First the conventional DVM uses BCD code while the computer uses two's complement binary. The BCD to binary conversion can be done by special hardware or by software, both in their differing ways being expensive. In truth the DVM is not the ideal analogue-to-digital convertor for the computer controlled data logger.

It must also be realised that the increase in cost of the computer controlled logger over the conventional logger is due only in part to the cost of the computer. The scanner must be more sophisticated, with channel selection, gain, etc., set by commands from the computer. This also means more interfacing problems, involving extra hardware. Finally the software supplied will only be very basic and extra software costs will be involved if full advantage is to be taken of the facility offered.

The computer required for this task is simple and will require few peripherals other than the normal teletype. As usual however this can grow, so that one computer may control a number of scanners, printers and consoles, using disc and tape back-up for data storage. It is well to bear this in mind when installing the simpler computer system since a computer which can be expanded may well be used in future, larger systems, leading to machine compatibility.

9·4 System Requirements

From the specification the requirements of a particular system can be established. They should embrace the following:

The System
The number and type of peripherals
The type and size of computer
Backing storage
Environmental specification
Site facilities
Maintenance and specification of acceptance tests
Staffing requirements and training
Documentation
Delivery

Engineering support
Expandability
Price

The computer (hardware)
Processor performance
Memory size, type and speed
Input/output specification, i.e. number of channels and interrupt structure
Interfaces

Software
Utility packages
Executives
High level languages
Applications packages
Software support

9·5 Summary of Selection Criteria

It has been intimated that a computer should not be chosen for the processor alone, but for the system as a whole. It is impractical to even attempt to pick the best processor, the best disc, the best ADC, etc., since no one will take responsibility for the system as a whole and there will be no benefits to be gained from the development of standard software by the computer manufacturer. It is nevertheless usually necessary to employ more than one supplier, but this should be kept to a minimum.

The following points are offered as guidelines.

(i) *Cost.* Hardware costs are easiest to establish. Once the requirements have been determined, competing quotations can be requested from the suppliers. Care must be taken to look out for hidden costs in interfaces and signal processing. Use of price lists is not very helpful since it is never clear what discounts one does and does not qualify for. The cost of racking, special consoles, cabling etc. must also be estimated. Additional costs are often invoked in the more intangible replacement of existing instrumentation and control equipment.

Software costs are far more difficult to establish and specialist advice is most desirable. The amount of software supplied by the computer manufacturer is often not reflected in the hardware price, but it can have a marked effect on the final software cost. Applications packages may well prove most economic but are seldom satisfactory due to the diverse nature of everyone's problems. A rough estimate of £3000 for each 4 K words of store used is allocatable to software.

Running costs should also be considered, which are attributable to maintenance contracts, space, salaries, etc.

The following figures are quoted for an approximate breakdown of the cost of a system:

processor and memory   15%
peripherals, interfaces etc.   35%
software and documentation   25%
installation and maintenance   25%

(ii) *Performance.* The performance specification of the processor has been covered in some detail in previous sections. The obvious features to be considered are word length; speed; addressing features and the instruction set; input/output structure and the interrupt and interrupt-priority system; direct memory access; expandability.

(iii) *Software.* The problem of costing specific software has already been mentioned. This is governed to a large extent by the quality of the software provided as standard. This is in turn related to the hardware configuration since the more sophisticated executives and compilers require areas of core and back-up store.

If a satisfactory applications package can be adapted this will be the most economic, since the writing costs will be averaged over a number of users. More often however specific programs will have to be written for the particular project. This will be greatly eased if high level languages are available. Programs compiled from a high level language will be inefficient in terms of core and speed of execution compared to assembly language programming. This in effect increases hardware costs, but these will be more than offset by reduction in software writing costs. For larger systems an executive is essential, otherwise programs will have to be written to organise disc to memory swapping, multi-programming, etc. The executive must handle the interrupt system in an efficient manner. Special purpose executives are now becoming available to allow dedicated high level language programming for such tasks as process control; e.g. RTL/2, CORAL; with the executive handling special macros connected with real time, input/output devices and interrupts. It is in this field that major improvements are required in the next few years and standardisation would be a great help.

A computer with inadequate software support can be very expensive to program, not to mention very difficult!

(iv) *Systems Engineering.* It must always be remembered that the computer is only a component in a system. The engineering support required in most installations is not forthcoming from many computer suppliers. This point was stressed earlier when discussing responsibility.

Other, more direct, engineering problems should also be considered. Reliability is one of the more pertinent and most difficult to assess. Previous experience of any associate is often very enlightening. There are of course ways in which reliability can be increased if written into the specification (and costed!), by redundancy techniques. Ability to exert manual control in the event of computer failure is also helpful, and may be essential.

Compatibility with other machines in the same plant has obvious advantages with personnel training, maintenance and spares stocking. It may also help with software. Expandability is a common feature on modern machines and represents an intangible advantage.

(v) *Future Prospects of the Supplier.* The minicomputer market is currently rather cut-throat, with obvious price advantages to the user. This advantage will most certainly disappear if the supplier drops out of the market during or, for that matter, after the project. Care should be exercised in assessing the validity of claims for hardware or software to be produced 'in the near future'.

(vi) *General Services.* Installation, including siting, power, cabling, consoles, mimic displays, etc. involve specialist knowledge and close co-operation between user and supplier. Definition of acceptance tests must be considered, both before delivery to site (simulation) and in situ. The suppliers ability in this field will be limited by his experience. The standard of the documentation offered by the supplier should be assessed by insisting on examples of previous work or some very firm assurances. Staff training facilities offered must also be considered.

(vii) *Maintenance.* The supplier should offer a 12 month warranty to cover repairs, including parts and labour, which are his responsibility. This will not cover the cost of any software modifications which may prove necessary due to any weakness in the original specification.

Routine maintenance is another problem. The supplier should be prepared to offer a contract to cover all contingencies. The price of such a contract should be negotiated corresponding to the depth of service, including the time factor in responding to a request for help. The degree of supplier oriented servicing will depend upon the quality, quantity and experience of the users own maintenance.

9·6 Epilogue

It is far too easy to assess the desirability of a stand alone processor and to give less consideration to a complete system. This is most unwise since the cost of the processor may be only a small percentage of the total cost. Advantage of superior hardware can be easily lost in inadequate system software and lack of engineering support.

Care must be taken not to underestimate costs in general and software in particular.

Appendix 1

Number Systems and Arithmetic

Radix Number Systems

If $2^n = 10^x$ $x = n(0 \cdot 301)$

n	2^n	n	2^n	n	2^n
0	1	6	64	12	4096
1	2	7	128	13	8192
2	4	8	256	14	16384
3	8	9	512	15	32768
4	16	10	1024	16	65536
5	32	11	2048		

Any number can be expressed in any base or radix system. By convention the number is represented by a string of digits, the most significant to the left.

The common number system uses the base 10 and is called *Decimal*. Other commonly encountered bases are 2 (*Binary*), 8 (*Octal*) and 16 (*Hexadecimal*).

In general any number in any base can be related to a decimal number by the following rule:

$$(XYZ)_r = (X \cdot r^2 + Y \cdot r + Z)_{10}$$

i.e. the nth digit from the right represents the number of times r^{n-1} is included in the sum. The maximum size of number in any radix system is $r - 1$. This raises a problem in a hexadecimal system since the maximum digit size is fifteen, necessitating two digits if a normal numeric system is to be retained. This is overcome by using letters to extend the numbers, i.e. $A \equiv 10$, $B \equiv 11$, ..., $F \equiv 15$.
Thus

$$101101_2 = 1 \times 2^5 + 0 \times 2^4 + 1 \times 2^3 + 1 \times 2^2 + 0 \times 2 + 1$$

$$= 32 + 8 + 4 + 1 = 45_{10}$$

$$673_8 = 6 \times 8^2 + 7 \times 8 + 3$$

$$= 443_{10}$$

and

$$BCD_{16} = 11 \times 16^2 + 12 \times 16 + 13$$

$$= 3021_{10}$$

Octal and hexadecimal numbers are of importance in computers since they can be used as quick notations for binary numbers. This is because three binary digits can represent the numbers 0 to 7, i.e. the octal range, while four binary digits can represent the numbers 0 to 15, i.e. the hexadecimal range. Thus a binary number can be converted to octal by grouping the bits in threes from the right and converting each individual group. Similarly the conversion to hexadecimal is achieved by splitting into 4 bits groups, i.e.

$$1 \quad 001 \quad 111 \quad 011 \quad 000 \quad 011_2 = 117303_8$$

or

$$1001 \quad 1110 \quad 1100 \quad 0011_2 = 9EC3_{16}$$

Binary numbers are commonly organised as a fixed number of digits. Each binary digit is referred to as a *bit*. An n bit word can have 2^n possible combinations, representing numbers in the range 0 to $2^n - 1$. An 8 bit combination is termed a *byte* and 4 bits a *nibble*. Note that a byte could be directly expressed as a two digit hexadecimal number.

While the relationship between binary and decimal is not so simple as between binary and octal or hexadecimal, it must be given special consideration because of its common everyday use. One system that is used is to code each decimal digit as an individual group of 4 bits, although only ten of the sixteen possible combinations will be used. This is referred to as *binary-coded-decimal*, BCD.

Thus

$$5092_{10} = 0101 \quad 0000 \quad 1001 \quad 0010_{BCD}$$

This number can be expressed as a pure binary number by repeated division by 2, e.g.

$$
\begin{aligned}
5092 \div 2 &= 2546 \text{ remainder } 0 \text{ (LSB)} \\
&\ 1273 \text{ remainder } 0 \\
&\ \ 636 \text{ remainder } 1 \\
&\ \ 318 \text{ remainder } 0 \\
&\ \ 159 \text{ remainder } 0 \\
&\ \ \ 79 \text{ remainder } 1 \\
&\ \ \ 39 \text{ remainder } 1 \\
&\ \ \ 19 \text{ remainder } 1 \\
&\ \ \ \ 9 \text{ remainder } 1 \\
&\ \ \ \ 4 \text{ remainder } 1 \\
&\ \ \ \ 2 \text{ remainder } 0 \\
&\ \ \ \ 1 \text{ remainder } 0 \\
&\ \ \ \ 0 \text{ remainder } 1 \text{ (MSB)}
\end{aligned}
$$

$\therefore \quad 5092_{10} = 1001111100100_2$

Note that the pure binary number requires only 13 bits compared to 16 for the BCD number. With a 16 bit word the maximum number using BCD is 9999_{10} while using binary it is 65535_{10}.

Consider a normal 4 bit binary number. Since the left hand bit determines whether (1) or not (0) an 8 is needed, the next bit a 4, the next a 2 and the right hand bit a 1, this is often termed an 8421 code. This weighting of the significance of each bit position is essential in pure binary but not in BCD since all possible combinations are not used. Thus other weightings have been suggested, typically the 2421 code. In such a system two binary numbers may represent the same decimal number, e.g. 1101 and 0111. Another code that is used in mechanical systems, e.g. shaft encoders which generate a binary number representing an angular position, is the *Gray* or *Cyclic code*. In this code the individual bits are not uniquely weighted since the binary representation is arranged so that if the number is incremented or decremented only one bit changes, thus eliminating possible ambiguities when the shaft position is lying across two segments.

A 3 bit Gray code is shown in figure A1.1.

Signed Numbers

Signed numbers can be represented in a binary number by using the MSB to indicate the sign. Thus a 16 bit number can represent unsigned

0	000
1	001
2	011
3	010
4	110
5	111
6	101
7	100

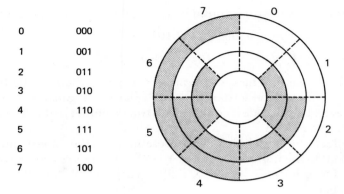

Fig. A1·1 Gray or Cyclic code

numbers in the range 0 to 65 535 or signed numbers in the range $-32\,768$ to 32 767. Three conventions are commonly encountered:

(i) *Sign and magnitude.* The MSB is set to 0 for positive and 1 for negative numbers; the remaining bits are used to represent the magnitude of the number as a normal unsigned integer number.

(ii) *Two's complement.* The true complement of a number is found by subtracting the number from the largest number representable, e.g. in a three digit decimal system the true complement (nine's complement) of 362 is $999 - 362 = 637$. In a binary system, subtracting the number from 'all the ones' simply results in replacing all ones by zeros and all zeros by ones, giving the one's complement. The 'radix complement' is given by simply adding 1 to the true complement, e.g. ten's complement = nine's complement + 1, and two's complement = one's complement + 1.

The ten's and two's complements can be used to represent negative numbers. As an example consider the odometer of a car. Starting from 000, if the car is driven forwards two miles it reads 002, but if the car is driven backwards it reads 998. Now 998 is the ten's complement of 2 $(999 - 002 + 1)$. In effect the three digit odometer is interpreting 000 to 499 as positive numbers and 999 to 500 as negative. As an example of a binary system consider a 5 bit number:

00000 (0_{10}) to 01111 (15_{10}) are the positive numbers.

-1 is given by the two's complement of 00001, i.e. $11110 + 1 = 11111$.

The largest negative number is -16_{10}, i.e. complement $(10000) + 1 = 01111 + 1 = 10000$. Note then, like the sign and magnitude convention, positive numbers have 0 in the MSB and negative numbers 1. Thus the number 10110 is a negative number; the

309

magnitude (it is not 6!) is found by taking the two's complement, i.e.

$$01001 + 1 = 01010 \equiv 10_{10}$$

$$\therefore 10110 \equiv -10_{10}$$

(iii) *Excess codes.* These codes are created by offsetting the binary number so that all the zeros represent the largest negative number. In practice the Excess code is equivalent to two's complement with the MSB only complemented.

In effect the number Y is represented by the binary number equivalent to the unsigned number $Y + 2^{n-1}$. For this reason the code is referred to as Excess X, where $X = 2^{n-1}$ in octal, i.e. Excess 200 for an 8 bit number.

The three codes defined above are compared for a 3 bit number in the table of figure A1.2.

Decimal	Sign and Magnitude	Two's Complement	Excess 4 Code
3	011	011	111
2	010	010	110
1	001	001	101
0	000	000	100
−1	101	111	011
−2	110	11C	010
−3	111	101	001
−4		100	000

Fig. A1·2

Two's complement is the method used in digital computers since addition and subtraction can be performed without further consideration of the sign of the numbers. With sign and magnitude representation the sign bits must be logically tested to determine what action to take with the magnitude, e.g. *subtract* (−2) from 3 requires the operation *add* 2 and 3.

Binary Fractions

With the integer number systems so far described, the smallest increment is one. The general number representation can be extended to include fractions* by introducing a 'radix-point', i.e. decimal or binary point. Thus

$$(XYZ \cdot PQR)_r = (X \cdot r^2 + Y \cdot r + Z + P \cdot r^{-1} + Q \cdot r^{-2} + R \cdot r^{-3})_{10}$$

$$\text{e.g. } 1011 \cdot 1001_2 = 8 + 2 + 1 + \tfrac{1}{2} + \tfrac{1}{16} = 11\tfrac{9}{16}$$

With a coded number, each digit is still treated separately, e.g.

$$1000\ 0110 \cdot 0011_{BCD} = 86 \cdot 3$$

Negative fractions can still be represented in the usual ways; the radix point however, must be situated so that the sign bit is always to its left. In calculating two's complement numbers the right-most bit must be incremented, independent of the position of the radix point.

The magnitude of a number is limited by the number of bits allocated to the integer part; limiting the number of bits in the fraction part restricts the accuracy. Thus truncation of an integer can cause errors while truncation of a fraction rounds-off the number, reducing accuracy.

Floating Point Representation

Using integer notation the range of number which can be represented is limited by the word length. An alternative method is to represent the magnitude of the number by a fraction with a separate counter to locate the radix point.

The following number equalities illustrate this point:

$$106 \cdot 372_{10} = 0 \cdot 106372 \cdot 10^3$$
$$-0 \cdot 00032_{10} = -0 \cdot 32 \cdot 10^{-3}$$
$$110 \cdot 1010_2 = 0 \cdot 1101010 \cdot 2^3$$

In general the number is represented by

$$\pm m \cdot r^e$$

where m is called the mantissa and e the exponent, r being the base. If the mantissa is adjusted so that the digit immediately following the radix point is the most significant non-zero digit, as in the above examples, the number is said to be 'normalised'.

Floating point numbers can be stored inside a computer by saving m and e only, r being implied. A typical representation is shown in figure A1.3. Since special software or hardware are required to manipulate floating point numbers, there is no special advantage to be gained in two's complement representation. In practice the mantissa is stored as

---

* Strictly speaking the fraction is that part of the number to the right of the radix point.

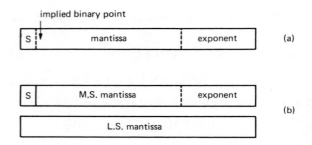

Fig. A1·3 Floating point number format (a) single precision (b) double precision

sign and magnitude. If numbers are always normalised before storing, then the MSB of the mantissa is always one and need not be stored, being assumed to exist in all calculations. The exponent is commonly stored in *excess* form. With a double precision word, the whole of the second word is used to extend the mantissa, thus more than doubling the number of significant figures without increasing the range of numbers.

Single precision in a typical high level language, e.g. FORTRAN, is normally 32 bits, 1 bit for the sign, 23 for the mantissa and 8 for the exponent. If the mantissa is normalised the MSB of the mantissa is always one and need not be stored, effectively increasing the mantissa to 24 bits. Since $2^{24} = 16\ 777\ 216_{10}$ approximately seven decimal places of accuracy are represented. The range of exponent is -128 to 127 so that the largest (normalised) number is $0.111\ldots1_2 \times 2^{127} = .17 \cdot 10^{38}$ and the smallest is $0.1_2 \times 2^{-128} = 1.47 \cdot 10^{-38}$

With double precision the mantissa is increased to 56 bits, giving approximately seventeen decimal places of accuracy.

With a 16 bit minicomputer two words must be used for single precision floating point, formatted as in figure A1.3(b) and four words are used for double precision, the exponent and sign being stored as part of the first word, the other three words extending the mantissa.

Binary Arithmetic

Unsigned Numbers

Addition

The normal rules of addition apply, except that a carry is generated when the result exceeds 1. Figure A1.4 shows the possible combinations of adding two 1 bit numbers A and B.

A	B	A + B	Carry
0	0	0	0
1	0	1	0
0	1	1	0
1	1	0	1

Fig. A1·4

Example:

Augend	101010		42
Addend	+11011	≡	27
Sum	1000101		69

Subtraction

When subtracting binary numbers the rules of figure A1.5 can be applied, borrowing when necessary from the next more significant bit.

A	B	A − B	Borrow
0	0	0	0
1	0	1	0
0	1	1	1
1	1	0	0

Fig. A1·5

Example:

Minuend	101010		42
Subtrahend	−11011	≡	27
Difference	001111		15

If the subtrahend is larger than the minuend a negative answer results. This will be discussed under the heading of signed numbers.

Multiplication

The rules for multiplication are given in the table of figure A1.6. Multiplication of unsigned numbers is discussed in some detail in Section 3.5.5.

A	B	A × B
0	0	0
1	0	0
0	1	0
1	1	1

Fig. A1·6

Example:

$$
\begin{array}{llr}
\text{Multiplicand} & 101010 & 42 \\
\text{Multiplier} & \times\,11011 \;\equiv & 27 \\ \hline
& 101010 & \\
& 101010 & \\
& 000000 & \\
& 101010 & \\
& 101010 & \\ \hline
\text{Product} & \overline{10001101110} \equiv 1134 &
\end{array}
$$

The five intermediate numbers in the above example are termed 'partial products'.

Division

Division can be performed by the conventional 'long division' techniques as shown in the following example. 42 is the 'dividend', 27 the 'divisor' and the answer the 'quotient'.

Example:

$$
\begin{array}{r}
1\cdot10001 \qquad \equiv 1 + \tfrac{1}{2} + \tfrac{1}{32} = 1\cdot531 \\
11011\,)\,\overline{101010} \\
11011 \\ \hline
11110 \\
11011 \\ \hline
110000 \\
11011 \\ \hline
101010 \\
\vdots
\end{array}
$$

Note that the error introduced in the truncated answer given above is quite large ($42 \div 27 = 1\cdot5556$); appreciably more binary places must be retained to give the equivalent decimal accuracy.

Signed Numbers

Since the MSB is used to represent the sign of the number it is most important to treat numbers as a fixed number of bits. In the following examples 5 bit numbers will be used.

Sign and Magnitude

The actual operation performed must be determined by a logical test of the sign bits involved and the operation demanded, e.g. A–B can involve the following, where |A| means the magnitude of A, etc.:

(a) A and B positive, |A| > |B|, *subtract* |B| from |A|
(b) A and B positive, |A| < |B|, *subtract* |A| from |B| and set sign bit of answer to negative.
(c) A positive, B negative, *add* |A| and |B|
(d) A negative, B negative, *subtract* |A| from |B|
(e) A negative, B positive, add |A| and |B| and set sign bit of answer to negative.

For multiplication (or division) the moduli can be multiplied (divided) and the sign bit set to positive if the sign of A and B are the same, negative otherwise.

Two's Complement

The major importance of two's complement arithmetic in digital computers is that the addition and subtraction of numbers can be performed as though they were unsigned numbers, without recourse to the logical sign bit tests required by sign and magnitude representation.

Examples:

$$
\begin{array}{cc}
00011 & 3 \\
-11110 \equiv -(-2) \\
\hline
00101 & 5
\end{array}
\qquad
\begin{array}{cc}
11011 & -5 \\
+11001 \equiv +(-7) \\
\hline
10100 & -12
\end{array}
$$

In both these examples, provided overflow does not occur, the borrow and carry generated are simply ignored.

In practice the subtraction is performed by adding the complement of the subtrahend and adding one to the result as shown in Section 2.5, irrespective of whether the numbers are positive or negative.

Multiplication and division of two's complement numbers is however not the same as that of unsigned numbers. A number of techniques are used.

(a) By converting negative numbers to sign and magnitude, multiply the magnitudes and determine the sign of the answer, complementing and adding one if the sign is negative to put the result back into two's complement form.

(b) By treating the numbers as though they were unsigned and then adding a correction factor if either or both the numbers are negative.

(c) By using specially developed algorithms which are modifications of the basic 'shift and add' technique, e.g. Booth's algorithm.

Excess Code

Addition and subtraction can be performed as per unsigned numbers but the MSB must be complemented to correct the result.

Floating Point

Addition and Subtraction

The smaller number is adjusted by shifting the mantissa right, filling in with leading zeros* and incrementing the exponent by one for each shift. This proceeds until the exponents are equal, when the mantissas can be directly added (subtracted) as sign and magnitude numbers. The resultant mantissa may exceed one, in which case it must be shifted right one place and the exponent incremented.

$$0\cdot11011 : 101 = +0\cdot84375 \cdot 2^1 = 1\cdot6875$$

$$+ 0\cdot10001 : 010 = + 0\cdot53125 \cdot 2^{-2} = 0\cdot1328$$

becomes

$$\begin{array}{l} 0\cdot11011 : 101 \\ +0\cdot00010 : 101 \\ \hline 0\cdot11101 : 101 = +0\cdot90625 \cdot 2^1 = 1.8125 \end{array}$$

Note that in shifting the smaller number, significant bits are lost, resulting in an error in the answer.

Multiplication and Division

If $A = m_1 r^{e_1}$ and $B = m_2 r^{e_2}$

then

$$A \cdot B = (m_1 \times m_2) r^{(e_1 + e_2)}$$

and

$$A/B = (m_1/m_2) r^{(e_1 - e_2)}$$

* if the MSB is implied rather than stored, the first shift right must fill in with a one.

Thus to multiply two floating point numbers the mantissas must be multiplied as sign and magnitude numbers and the exponents added (if Excess code is used, the MSB needs complementing). The mantissa may result in a zero in the left hand bit so that it must be shifted left and the exponent decremented.

Floating Point Decimal Arithmetic

In some applications in the data processing field, the small errors introduced by the finite length of the mantissa can be most annoying, e.g. a sum of £10·50 can be represented in normal floating point as, say, £10·499999. The answer is of course within a high degree of accuracy and special algorithms can be applied to round-off the answer to the desired number of figures. This however is difficult, since it is the equivalent decimal number that must be rounded, not the actual binary number stored. Thus BCD arithmetic is sometimes employed. Since each decimal character is individually coded, special arithmetic algorithms are required, e.g. a four digit BCD number can be stored in one 16 bit word; adding two such numbers however cannot be achieved with the normal ADD instruction, e.g.

$$
\begin{array}{cccccl}
0110 & 0010 & 0111 & 1001 & \equiv & 6279 \\
+0000 & 0001 & 0100 & 0110 & \equiv & +0146 \\
\hline
0110 & 0011 & 1011 & 1111 & \neq & 6425
\end{array}
$$

To arrive at the correct answer, the LS 4 bits of each number must be added. If the result is 9 or less then it stands; if it lies between 10 and 18, add 6 which generates a carry into the 5th bit and leaves 0 to 8 in the current 4 bits; for numbers between 10 and 15 the carry is generated when the 6 is added, whilst for 16, 17 and 18 the initial sum generates the carry. The next group of 4 bits are now added, along with any carry, until the sum is complete.

This technique is extended to a form of floating point number by implying the position of the decimal point to be between any of the 4 bit groups; thus an additional 4 bits in each BCD number can be used to count the decimal point position. The same rules of addition, multiplication, etc. as previously explained apply, treating the decimal point position counter as an exponent.

This form of number representation and arithmetic is commonly used in calculators and business machines.

Overflow and Carry

The carry bit effectively provides a 1 bit extension of a number being manipulated. Overflow is an indication that the result of an operation has exceeded the maximum number allowed. As an example consider the sum of two 5 bit unsigned numbers (range 0 to 31),

$$
\begin{array}{r}
10111 \equiv 23 \\
+10001 \equiv 17 \\
\hline
101000 \equiv 8 \text{ carry } 1
\end{array}
$$

In this case the overflow is directly indicated by the state of the carry bit. However with signed numbers the carry bit is not directly related to an overflow, i.e. the carry generated by the addition of the two's complement numbers -5 and -7, used in a previous example. The state of the carry bit after a subtraction depends upon the hardware involved; with the technique used in Chapter 2 the number to be subtracted is complemented and added to the other number.

When manipulating two 16 bit two's complement numbers any overflow from the fifteenth bit must effectively be detected. The overflow flag should be set to 1 under the following conditions:

(a) when *adding* two numbers of like sign, and the result is of opposite sign. Addition of two numbers of unlike sign cannot generate overflow.

(b) when *subtracting* two numbers of opposite sign and the difference is of opposite sign to the minuend, i.e. for $D = A - B$, if D and A differ in sign. Subtraction of numbers of like sign cannot generate overflow.

Appendix 2

Logic Systems

Introduction

In this appendix the basic components of binary logic systems are listed. The behaviour of the various gates and flip-flops are explained by truth tables.

Systems constructed from logic components can be broken into two classes, (i) *combinational* and (ii) *sequential.* The outputs of a combinational system depend only upon the current inputs; for a sequential logic system both the inputs and the current state of the system determine the output. A combinational system contains no memory elements, i.e. gates only, whereas a sequential system contains both combinational elements and memory elements, e.g. flip-flops.

A simple introduction to the arithmetic of logical systems is given, e.g. Boolean Algebra and DeMorgan's theorems. A few simple examples are included to indicate how the more complex logic circuits of the computer can be built up.

Logic units are described in terms of their logical behaviour, e.g. each variable can be in one of two states, 0 or 1. The actual physical gates are electronic circuits fabricated on 'chips', possibly more than one gate per chip. Different electronic techniques are employed, with

319

various characteristics which make one type more suitable for a particular application than another. These are summarised in Appendix 3.

Positive and Negative Logic

A positive logic system is one in which logical 1 is represented by a more positive voltage than logical 0, e.g. $1 \equiv +3\cdot5$ volts, $0 \equiv 0$ volts or $1 \equiv 0$ volts, $0 \equiv -10$ volts. Positive logic will generally be assumed, but it should be noted that, particularly in the I/O system, most computers employ some negative logic.

Assuming that TTL levels are used, i.e. $+3\cdot5$ and 0 volts, then it can be shown that a simple duality exists such that a positive logic AND gate can be used as a negative logic OR gate. Similarly the positive logic OR, NAND and NOR gates can be used as negative logic AND, NOR and NAND gates respectively.

Obviously gates can only be used with their designed voltage levels so that to use mixed types of logic, voltage level-changers are needed to interconnect units.

AND (multiplication)

$1 . 1 = 1$
$1 . 0 = 0$
$0 . 0 = 0$
$A . 1 = A$
$A . 0 = 0$
$A . A = A$ – idempotence law –
$A . \bar{A} = 0$ – complementarity –
$A . B = B . A$ – commutativity –
$A . (B . C) = (A . B) . C$ – associativity –
$\bar{\bar{A}} = A$ – involution

OR (addition)

$1 + 1 = 1*$
$1 + 0 = 1$
$0 + 0 = 0$
$A + 0 = A$
$A + 1 = 1$
$A + A = A$
$A + \bar{A} = 1$
$A + B = B + A$
$(A + B) + C$
$\quad = A + (B + C)$

$$\left.\begin{array}{l} A + AB = A \\ A(A + B) = A \\ A + \bar{A}B = A + B \end{array}\right\} \quad \text{absorption law}$$

$$\left.\begin{array}{l} \overline{A + B} = \bar{A} . \bar{B} \\ \overline{A . B} = \bar{A} + \bar{B} \end{array}\right\} \quad \text{De Morgan's laws}$$

Basic Logic Gates

The basic logic gates are summarised in figure A2.1. The Boolean expressions and the truth tables are also shown in the figure.

---

* Only in this term does Boolean and Binary arithmetic differ. Hence the exclusive −OR is defined such that $1 \oplus 1 = 0$ An example is given later in the design of a half-adder.

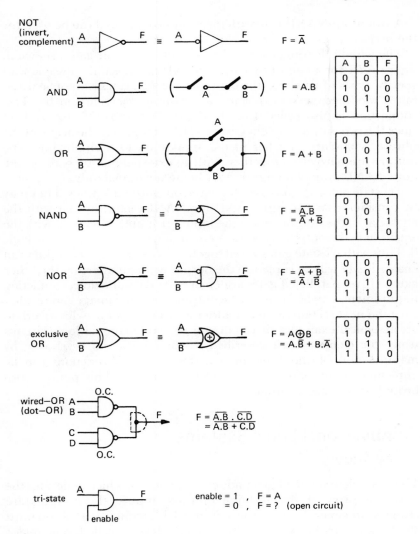

Fig. A2·1 Basic logic gates

The 'dee' type symbol is used to represent the AND function and the 'shield' the OR function. The small circle on a signal line means that the variable is inverted.

Each gate is shown with two inputs, except the invertor. In practice multiple input gates can be obtained; thus for a NOR gate with three inputs, A, B and C,

$$F = \overline{A + B + C} = \overline{A} \cdot \overline{B} \cdot \overline{C}$$

321

A two input NAND gate with the inputs commoned can be used for the NOT function.

The wired-OR connection of the outputs of similar gates, shown in figure A2.1 for a pair of two input NAND gates, is only possible with specific types of gate, e.g. the conventional TTL gates cannot be wired but a modified version, termed an *open-collector* gate can be. This connection is also called Dot-OR-ing or Dot-AND/OR-ing. Indeed since the two outputs are effectively AND-ed together the origin of the phrase is obscure and lies in the application to multiplexing. The outputs are hardwired together, with an external pull-up resistor, the dotted AND symbol on figure A2.1 being notational only.

Tri-state gates are also used for wired output connections. They may be considered as two input AND (or NAND) gates in that with the enable at 1, the output equals the input (or input). However, with the enable at 0, the output becomes open-circuit, i.e. it 'floats', and *not* logic 0. Thus with tri-state gates wired together at the output, the input to an enabled gate will be copied to the output, without affecting the other gates. If two paralleled gates are enabled at the same time, conflicting requirements can be made on the output line and damage can result.

In the next sections a binary adder and a decoder are described, to act as typical examples of the design of combinational logic circuits using the elements just described. In practice it can be shown, by manipulation of the Boolean equations, that all functions can be implemented by networks of NAND gates only. This point is also brought out in the examples.

Combinational Logic Systems
Binary Adders

The basic element of a binary adder is a logic unit which generates the sum and carry of the addition of three inputs; three inputs are required in general since a carry from a less significant addition must also be added to the two input digits. Such a device is called a *Full Adder*, figure A2.2(b). 'n' such units can then be connected into a parallel word-orientated adder as shown in figure A2.2(c). The simpler one-bit adder with just two inputs, figure A2.2(a) is called a *Half Adder*.

With the simple parallel adder of figure A2.2(c) the carry bits will be propagated from the LSB upwards and the more significant sum bits may change transiently, until the less significant full adders have completed. This is termed 'ripple-through' and the n bit sum is not complete until n times the time taken for the individual carry bits to set. More complex circuits are used in practice with 'carry-look-ahead' to speed up the operation.

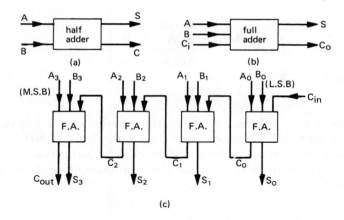

Fig. A2·2 (a) Half adder (b) Full adder (c) A 4 bit parallel adder

Half Adder

The truth table required for figure A2.2(a) is:

A	B	S	C
0	0	0	0
1	0	1	0
0	1	1	0
1	1	0	1

The defining Boolean expression for any function can be written down from the truth table directly, viz. for any 1 in the function column the corresponding input conditions must be AND-ed; this must then be OR-ed with the conditions for any other combinations which result in the functions being 1. Thus for the above truth table

$$S = A \cdot \bar{B} + \bar{A} \cdot B = A \oplus B$$

and

$$C = A \cdot B$$

The exclusive-OR function required for the sum can be directly implemented as shown in figure A2.3(a). However, using the rules given previously,

$$F = A \cdot \bar{B} + \bar{A} \cdot B = \overline{\overline{(A \cdot \bar{B})} \cdot \overline{(\bar{A} \cdot B)}}$$

323

Now

$$\overline{A . \bar{B}} = \overline{A . \bar{A} + A . \bar{B}}$$
$$= \overline{A . (\bar{A} + \bar{B})} = \overline{A . \overline{A . B}}$$

Similarly

$$\overline{\bar{A} . B} = \overline{B . \overline{A . B}}$$

Thus as shown in figure A2.3(b) the function can be implemented entirely with NAND gates. Note that only four NAND gates are required compared to a total of five gates, of various sorts, for the direct implementation. Further the complement of C is directly available.

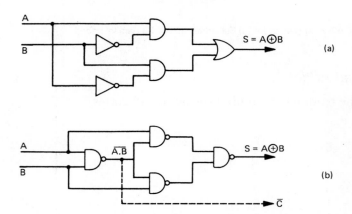

Fig. A2·3 The Exclusive-OR function (a) direct implementation (b) NAND gate implementation

Full Adder

The truth table for the full adder is:

A	B	C_i	S	C_o
0	0	0	0	0
1	0	0	1	0
0	1	0	1	0
1	1	0	0	1
0	0	1	1	0
1	0	1	0	1
0	1	1	0	1
1	1	1	1	1

324

Hence

$$S = A \cdot \bar{B} \cdot \bar{C_i} + \bar{A} \cdot B \cdot \bar{C_i} + \bar{A} \cdot \bar{B} \cdot C_i + A \cdot B \cdot C_i$$

and

$$C_0 = A \cdot B \cdot \bar{C_i} + A \cdot \bar{B} \cdot C_i + \bar{A} \cdot B \cdot C_i + A \cdot B \cdot C_i$$

These equations can be simply implemented by two half adders and a NAND gate, as shown in figure A2.4.

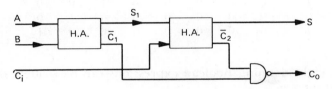

Fig. A2·4 Full adder

The above equations, derived directly from the truth table, are correct but may contain redundant information. The individual product terms, each involving some combination of all variables, in these expressions are called *minterms*. If the expression can be simplified then the resulting product terms are called *implicants*, i.e. the implicants are the product terms of a minimal realisation. To determine the minimal realisation of expressions such as those above is not trivial. Boolean algebraic simplification can be used but graphical methods, such as Karnaugh maps, are used for the more complex functions.

As an example of Boolean simplification consider C_0. The minterm ABC_i can be OR-ed in the equation another two times and grouped as follows

$$C_0 = A \cdot B \cdot \bar{C_i} + A \cdot B \cdot C_i + A \cdot \bar{B} \cdot C_i + A \cdot B \cdot C_i + \bar{A} \cdot B \cdot C_i + A \cdot B \cdot C_i$$

$$= A \cdot B \cdot (\bar{C_i} + C_i) + A \cdot C_i \cdot (\bar{B} + B) + B \cdot C_i \cdot (\bar{A} + A)$$

$$= A \cdot B + A \cdot C_i + B \cdot C_i$$

$$= \overline{\overline{A \cdot B} \cdot \overline{A \cdot C_i} \cdot \overline{B \cdot C_i}}$$

Decoders

A *decoder* is a device which activates one specific output line, selected by a binary number on the input lines. Thus a 3 input line decoder can select one of 8 output lines, a 4 input one of 16 outputs, etc.

The truth table for a one of 8 decoder is:

A_2	A_1	A_0	F_0	F_1	F_2	F_3	F_4	F_5	F_6	F_7
0	0	0	1	0	0	0	0	0	0	0
0	0	1	0	1	0	0	0	0	0	0
0	1	0	0	0	1	0	0	0	0	0
0	1	1	0	0	0	1	0	0	0	0
1	0	0	0	0	0	0	1	0	0	0
1	0	1	0	0	0	0	0	1	0	0
1	1	0	0	0	0	0	0	0	1	0
1	1	1	0	0	0	0	0	0	0	1

Thus eight defining Boolean expressions can be written, one for each output, e.g.

$$F_2 = \bar{A}_0 . A_1 . \bar{A}_2$$

and

$$F_7 = A_0 . A_1 . A_2$$

This can be directly implemented with three invertors and eight 3 input AND gates as shown in figure A2.5. The AND gates in practice may well be NAND gates followed by invertors.

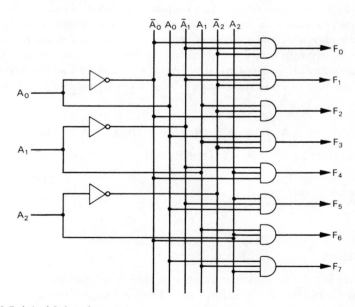

Fig. A2·5 A 1-of-8 decoder

Sequential Logic System

Sequential logic systems must contain memory elements to save the logic level of a current state, which may be used to affect some future state. The analysis of sequential circuits is beyond the scope of this book, but some knowledge of the basic memory elements is required. Such devices are collectively called *bistables, latches,* or *flip-flops.* As with gates they can be constructed in positive or negative logic and in a variety of technologies, i.e. bipolar or MOS, so that they can be made compatible with each range of gates.

There are a number of variants on the basic flip-flop, largely determined by specialised input gating, which are outlined below.

The R-S Flip-Flop

The phrase R-S stands for *reset-set,* where *reset* means to establish the logical output variable at level 0 and *set* at level 1. Alternatively the term *clear* is used rather than reset, but here clear-preset will be used as a rather special R-S function, as will be explained later. The basic R-S flip-flop is the basis of all other flip-flops.

Two implementations of the R-S flip-flop are shown in figure A2.6, one using NOR gates and the other NAND gates. They are similar except for the case of $R = S = 1$, a state which is to be avoided.

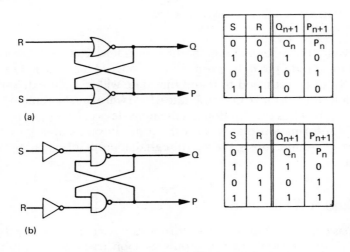

(a)

S	R	Q_{n+1}	P_{n+1}
0	0	Q_n	P_n
1	0	1	0
0	1	0	1
1	1	0	0

(b)

S	R	Q_{n+1}	P_{n+1}
0	0	Q_n	P_n
1	0	1	0
0	1	0	1
1	1	1	1

Fig. A2·6 R-S flip-flop (a) using NOR gates (b) using NAND gates

327

Consider the NOR gate system. The Boolean equations defining each output are

$$Q = \overline{R + P} \quad \text{and} \quad P = \overline{S + Q}$$

Thus for $R = 1, S = 0$

$$Q = \overline{1 + P} = 0 \quad \text{and} \quad P = \overline{0 + Q} = \overline{Q} = 1$$

For

$$R = 0, S = 1 \qquad Q = \overline{0 + P} \quad \text{and} \quad P = \overline{1 + Q} = 0$$

thus

$$Q = 1$$

For

$$R = 0, S = 0 \qquad Q = \overline{P} \quad \text{and} \quad P = \overline{Q}$$

Thus for $S = R = 0$, the flip-flop is in a 'do-nothing' state which maintains the logical levels of P and Q which have been determined by some previous value, e.g. at power-on either state may occur at random. Note however that, except for $R = S = 1$, $P = \overline{Q}$. Thus the two outputs from a flip-flop are the true output, Q, and its complement, $\overline{Q}$, as shown diagramatically in figure A2.7.

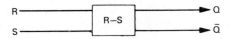

Fig. A2·7 Schematic diagram for the R-S flip-flop

Consider the quiescent state of the inputs R and S to be 0, then Q can be set to 1 (and $\overline{Q}$ to 0) by raising S to 1; once Q has reached its stable state, S can be returned to 0 and that state will be retained. Similarly raising R to 1 will make $Q = 0$, a state which will again be retained when R returns 0. Thus the flip-flop is a memory device, its output retaining the last information that was on the input lines, assuming that both were not simultaneously 1, even though that input information may be transient.

Clocked R-S Flip-Flops

The basic R-S flip-flop is an asynchronous device in the sense that the outputs will respond to the inputs as soon as they are applied. A synchronous version can be derived by additional input gating, as

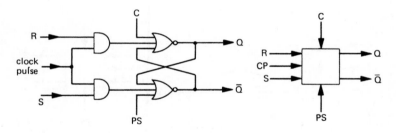

Fig. A2·8 Clocked R-S flip-flop

shown in figure A2.8. In this case either R and the clock-pulse, or S and the clock pulse must both be 1 to reset or set Q. Thus information contained on either R or S is only memorised by the flip-flop when the clock pulse occurs. The clock pulse must stay at 1 long enough for any transitions to take place, but preferably no longer. S and R must not change while the pulse is high and S = R = 1 must be avoided. The initial state of the flip-flop can be pre-established by retaining asynchronous entry points after the input gating, labelled PS and C, e.g. preset and clear. Normally PS and C will stay at logical 0.

It has been stressed previously that the R = S = 1 state must be avoided. With a clocked input however the quiescent state R = S = 0 need not be maintained (cp = 0 has the same effect) so that an unambiguous input system can be used, as shown in figure A2.9. This is termed D-type input; the cp will set Q to 1 if R/S = 1 and reset Q to 0 for R/S = 0.

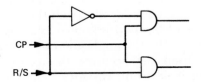

Fig. A2·9 Modification of input gating of figure A2·8 to give D-type input

J-K Flip-Flops

Figure A2.10 shows a modification to the clocked R-S flip-flop employing feedback from the output to the input.

It can be easily verified that for the input conditions J = K = 0; J = 0, K = 1 and J = 1, K = 0, the performance is unaffected and J ≡ S and K ≡ R.

329

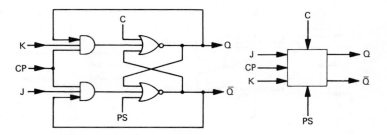

Fig. A2·10 A J-K flip-flop

The difference occurs when J = K = 1. Assume for the moment that CP is also held at 1. Then while this condition exists, Q is directly connected to R and $\bar{Q}$ to S. Thus if Q = 1 and $\bar{Q}$ = 0, the flip-flop will be reset, changing Q to 0 and $\bar{Q}$ to 1. Now however the input to S is 1 so that Q changes back to 1 and $\bar{Q}$ to 0. In fact an unstable state has been reached and Q and $\bar{Q}$ will continue to oscillate. If now however the clock pulse is timed so that it stays at logic 1 long enough to initiate the transition in output state, but then falls to 0 before the transition is complete, the input gates will be inhibited and the second and subsequent transitions will not be allowed. Thus the net effect of J = K = 1, combined with an accurately timed pulse duration results in the flip-flop simply changing state, i.e. the output is complemented.

Toggling or Edge-Triggered Flip-Flops

If a flip-flop is to be used exclusively for complementing, individual J, K and CP inputs are not required; effectively they can be paralleled into one input. This type of flip-flop is known as a 'toggle', the output of which is complemented by the application of a pulse at the input, T. The dependence upon the accurate timing of the input can be eliminated by internal electronic circuitry.

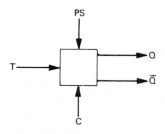

Fig. A2·11 Schematic diagram for a toggle flip-flop

330

The CP is differentiated, generating a positive pulse as the CP rises and a negative pulse as it falls back to zero. The output of the differentiator is then rectified, resulting in a controlled width pulse being fed to the flip-flop, synchronised to the leading-edge of the CP, independent of its duration. If an invertor is included before the rectifier then the positive pulse fed to the flip-flop is generated by the trailing-edge of the CP, independent of the rising-edge. Trailing-edge triggered toggles are usually indicated on block diagrams by an invertor 'dot' on the toggle input, as in figure A2.13.

Master-Slave Flip-Flops

Master-slave flip-flops employ two cascaded clocked flip-flop elements. The outputs of the first (master) flip-flop are coupled into the inputs of the second (slave) flip-flop. A common CP is used, except that it is inverted before being fed to the slave.

While the CP is at zero, the slave is enabled, due to the CP inversion, and the output from the master is copied into the slave, e.g. if $Q_1 = 1$, Q is set to 1.

When the CP is raised to 1, input information is transmitted to the master flip-flop, setting or resetting Q_1 and $\bar{Q}_1$ as required. However, the slave is now inhibited so that Q and $\bar{Q}$ do not yet change. Thus while the clock pulse is high the master-slave flip-flop stores both the new and the old information, in the master and slave respectively. When the CP falls back to zero the new data is copied to the slave and the old data lost.

The use of this type of flip-flop in a shift register will be shown later. One immediate use however is that the output Q can be fed back to the input R and $\bar{Q}$ to the input S to create a toggling flip-flop, the buffer created by the master stopping the oscillation encountered with a normal clocked flip-flop. Thus a flip-flop as shown in figure A2.12 can be used as a trailing-edge toggle simply by externally wiring Q to R and $\bar{Q}$ to S and using the CP as T.

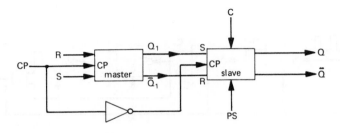

Fig. A2·12 A master-slave flip-flop

Minicomputers and Microprocessors

Note that a register used in a computer as an accumulator must be constructed of master-slave flip-flops. The output from the adder can be copied into the master while the slave still supplies the original data to the inputs of the adder; when the CP falls back to 0 the new data is copied to the slave which will alter the input to the adder and hence its output, but this is ignored by the master since it is now inhibited.

Binary Counters

Figure A2.13 shows a 4 bit binary up-counter. Trailing-edge triggered toggles are employed. A pulse is initially applied to the clear line to clear each flip-flop to 0. The train of pulses to be counted is applied to the first flip-flop. Q_0 switches from 0 to 1 when the first input pulse falls back to 0. The input T_1 is now high, but does not trigger Q_1. The second pulse rising to 1 does nothing but when it falls back to 0, T_0 is again triggered, changing Q_0 from 1 to 0. This in turn causes T_1 to fall to 0 and complements Q_1 from 0 to 1, etc.

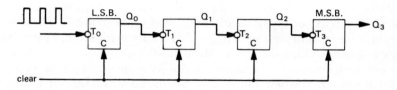

Fig. A2·13 A binary up-counter

A BCD counter can be made by noting that $10_{10} = 1010_2$. Thus when Q_1 and Q_3 are both 1 a carry should be generated to the next 4 bit counter representing the next most significant decimal digit and the first 4 bits must be cleared. This is shown in principle in figure A2.14.

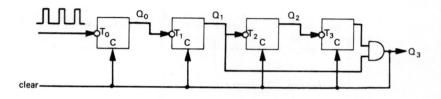

Fig. A2·14 One digit of a BCD counter

332

Shift Registers

A shift register is used to store a serial string of binary digits, synchronously. Referring to figure A2.15, each bit of input data is sequentially applied to the R/S line and is transferred into the shift register by a clock pulse. Thus the rate at which the input data is presented must be related to the clock pulse rate. The shift register must have as many 'cells' as there are bits to be stored.

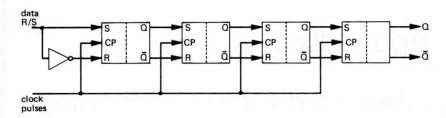

Fig. A2·15 A 4 bit shift register

Master-slave flip-flops must be used so that the contents of one cell are shifted into the master of the next while the slave of that cell provides the correct data to the next master. When the clock pulse falls back to 0, the masters copy to the slaves but communication between cells is inhibited. The system shown will only shift-right. By appropriately reconnecting the outputs to inputs to the left a shift-left can be achieved. In practice appropriate gating can be incorporated to shift either right or left, determined by whether a control signal, SC, is 1 or 0, e.g.

$$S_n = Q_{n+1} . \overline{SC} + Q_{n-1} . SC$$

where S_n is the input to the nth flip-flop, Q_{n-1} is the output from the left-adjacent flip-flop and Q_{n+1} the output from the right-adjacent flip-flop.

The data can be 'read' out of a shift register serially from the output $\overline{Q}$ line by applying the appropriate number of clock pulses. Alternatively the individual flip-flop outputs can be accessed in parallel.

Appendix 3

Integrated Circuit Technology

Integrated circuits are simply electronic circuits constructed on one piece of semiconductor material as distinct from external connections between discrete components.

Circuits such as a gate or possibly four separate gates on the one component are classed as *medium scale integration* (MSI) while the circuits with larger numbers of components, e.g. 1024 bit memory, are classed as *large scale integration* (LSI). The earlier LSI circuits were repetitive, simple sub-circuits, like memories, but more complex CPU structures are now being fabricated.

Two fundamental technologies are used, based on the *Bipolar transistor* or the *field effect transistor* (FET). The FET circuits are loosely classed as *metal oxide silicon* (MOS) systems. Currently Bipolar circuits are faster but more restricted in scale so that most LSI devices use MOS in one form or another. All transistors can be made p-type or n-type (p-channel or n-channel in MOS). Thus variants such as PMOS and NMOS appear. A significant development is an integrated MOS circuit which includes some PMOS and some NMOS transistors connected back-to-back. This is called *complementary* MOS (CMOS) and is much faster since transistors can be kept out of saturation. Another innovation is to use an insulating substrate, sapphire, termed *silicon-on-sapphire* (SOS).

The following table summarises some of the characteristics of MSI and LSI circuits. The wide range of figures for the MOS device is related to the wide scale of integration, e.g. a 1 K bit memory is approximately twice as fast as a 2 K bit memory chip.

Type	Stage Delay (nano sec)	Power Dissipation (mW/gate)	Chip Density (mil²/ gate)	Noise Immunity (volts)	Power Supply Voltage (volts)
MSI (all Bipolar)					
RTL	20	12		0·2	+3·6
DTL	16	14		0·4	+5
TTL (low power)	25	1–2	50–120	0·4	+5
TTL (medium speed)	8	5–10	50–120	0·4	+5
TTL (high speed, Schottky clamped)	2	18–23	50–120	0·3	+5
ECL	0·3–1	30–250		0·2	−5·2
LSI Bipolar (TTL compatible)	5–50	0·5–30	5–10	0·4	+5
PMOS	100–1000	0·05–0·7	2–15	1–2	+5, −9
NMQS	50–300	0·05–0·7	2–15	0·4–1	+12, +5, −5
CMOS	10–100	0·1–2	5–35	3·5–4	+5 to +15
SOS	1–100	0·1–1	2–25	0·4–4	+5, +12

The output from any logic circuit has two states, the 0 and the 1 states. Electrically the equivalent circuit of the output is an emf in series with a resistor, as shown in figure A3.1. The effective emf *and*

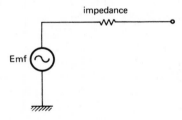

Fig. A3·1 Equivalent circuit for the output of a logic element

impedance will change from one state to another, factors which are taken into account in interconnecting circuits. The following table summarises typical values for the common types of circuit.

335

Minicomputers and Microprocessors

Logic Type	Impedance (ohms)		Emf (volts)	
	Logic 0	Logic 1	Logic 0	Logic 1
RTL	25	650	0·2	1·1
DTL	25	2000	0·2	5
TTL	12	140	0·2	3·5
ECL	15	15	−1·58	−0·75
CMOS	1500	1500	0	10

Appendix 4

Random Access Memory

Introduction

Memory systems as employed in digital computers can be split into two categories, *random access* and *sequential access*. Random access is required for fast, main memory and sequential access, being cheaper, is used for bulk or back-up storage. Bulk storage devices, e.g. magnetic tape or disc, are discussed in detail in Section 6.6. Brief descriptions of random access memory are included in Section 2.3 and this is explained in greater detail here.

Random access memory systems are word orientated, that is each unit of data stored at a unique location comprises a multiple number of binary digits, commonly 8 bit bytes or 16 bit words. Each memory location must thus have the number of bits of storage. Each location will be uniquely identified by an address. Comment is made at the end of this appendix on 'content addressable memory', but normal memory is accessed solely by address; it is the responsibility of the computer system to ensure that the required data is stored in that address.

To be of use in the conventional digital computer architecture the memory bank must be capable of communicating with any word, but only one at a time. This word of data will pass along a common data bus,

337

the specific location being identified by an address word, independent of the data word, as indicated in figure A4.1

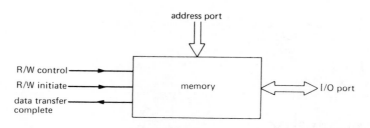

Fig. A4·1 A general random access memory system

Classification of Random Access Memories

(i) *Read–write memory.* This is the common type of memory where a word of data can be written into a location, overwriting any previously stored data or can be read out from a selected location. The read action may be destructive or non-destructive. For most applications non-destructive-read-out (NDRO) is required and devices which are fundamentally destructive-read-out, e.g. magnetic core, must be modified to create an effective NDRO. Since this is the common memory type it is referred to simply as RAM, rather than the strictly accurate read–write-RAM.

(ii) *Read-only memory.* A random access memory can be made with data loaded into it during its fabrication. The data stored in any location can be read but it cannot be altered. This type of memory is called ROM, although random-access-ROM is strictly accurate.

In a computer system, normal RAM can be made non-writable or writable but non-readable if needed, by logical control of the external circuitry.

(iii) *Programmable read-only memory.* A type of ROM is available which is fabricated without a preset data load. These are termed PROMs and a data pattern can be loaded into them once only by using a special programming device, but not by the computer, e.g. techniques such as burning out internal diodes by high voltage application to create logical 1's are used. A true ROM is expensive in small quantities, whereas a PROM is relatively cheap. In larger quantities the price advantage reverses.

A form of PROM is available, which must also be specially programmed, but which does not experience irrevocable 'damage'. These devices can be cleared back to all zero by exposure to ultra violet light, to which end a quartz window is built into the memory chip. Once cleared they can be reprogrammed and as far as the computer is concerned are ROMS. These devices should be called *erasable* PROM (EPROM), *reprogrammable* ROMS (RPROM) or *electrically alterable* ROMS (EAROM), but the term PROM is used rather indiscriminately. These devices are also known as 'read-mostly' or 'fast read-slow write' memories.

Types of Memory

A number of different technologies have been applied to random access memory construction over the years. Magnetic cores have been far and away the most successful, but this is now being challenged by integrated circuit semiconductor techniques; these two techniques will be explained in the following. It should be noted however that plated-wire memories, networks of thin wire, plated with a magnetic material, have been used in larger machines. These memories were much faster than cores, but have proved more expensive to manufacture. Attempts to produce thin-film magnetic memories were disastrous.

It is possible to make magnetic core ROM, but this is uncommon nowadays. Thus in practice only RAM magnetic core memories are encountered while semiconductors are used for RAM, ROM and PROM.

Magnetic Core RAM Systems

Ferrite Cores

Each bit of the memory requires an individual core, and annular ring of ferrite. Cores range from 2000 to 500 μm outside diameter, 1300 to 400 μm inside diameter and 640 to 130 μm thick. It is desirable to use smaller cores, since they will switch at faster rates, e.g. 2000 μm cores result in 6 μsec cycle time while 500 μm cores can be used down to 0·5 μsec.

The type of ferrite used is critical and must display the 'square-shouldered' B-H loop of figure A4.2. The core can be magnetised so that it will retain a high degree of permanent magnetism. When polarised in one direction it will be used to represent logical 1 and the reverse polarity logical 0. In this way the logical data stored is 'permanent' and does not require any external power supplies. The polarity can be controlled by passing a current through a wire which is threaded through the core, as shown in figure A4.3. The choice of which polarity represents logical 0 and which 1 is arbitrary.

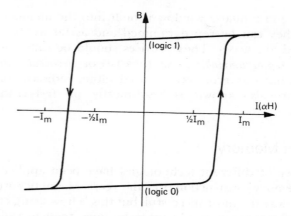

Fig. A4·2 B-H loop for ferrite core

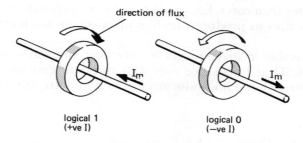

direction of flux

logical 1
(+ve I)

logical 0
(−ve I)

Fig. A4·3 Magnetic cores

Refer now to figure A4.2. Assume the core to be storing logical 0, with I = 0. If I is increased to $+\frac{1}{2}I_m$ and then reduced to 0, the knee in the B-H curve will not have been passed and the magnetisation will stay in the logical 0 state. However if I is increased to I_m, the magnetisation will be reversed to the logical 1 state, which it will retain when I returns to 0. Thus the core will not be switched by any current of $\frac{1}{2}I_m$ but will be driven to 1 by $+I_m$ or 0 by $-I_m$, irrespective of the initial state. Thus data can be written into the memory core.

To read the stored data it is necessary to determine the polarity of the magnetism, which cannot be directly achieved; in fact a destructive read-out process must be used. A second wire is passed through the core, termed a 'sense wire'. A current $-I_m$ is passed through the drive wire, the same wire used for writing, which results in a logical 0 state being forced. If the initial data stored was 0 then no flux change will take place and there will be no output voltage induced in the sense

340

winding. If however a 1 was stored initially then the flux will have been reversed, which will induce a voltage into the sense wire. Thus the data stored prior to the application of the $-I_m$ current can be detected by the presence (1) or absence (0) of a pulse on the sense wire.

The final state of the core after reading is always 0, so that to create a non-destructive read-out, a second operation must be initiated to re-write the data just read back into the core. Thus the complete memory cycle comprises two cycles, a read cycle, followed by a write cycle. This will be shown in more detail later.

A 2-D Core Store

An N word store of n bit words is shown in figure A4.4. Since only one drive line at a time can be activated, the one sense wire can be passed through the corresponding bit in every word, resulting in N drive wires and n sense wires. The n inhibit wires will also be needed for writing.

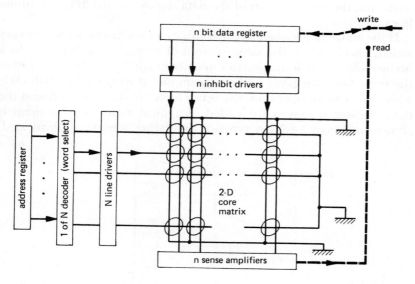

Fig. A4·4 A 2-D magnetic core system

The 1 of N decoder accepts the address from the address register and enables one unique drive line, which passes through every bit of the selected word. For an n bit address register $N \leqslant 2^n$.

(a) *Write Operation*

A current $-I_m$ is passed through the drive line selected by the address register contents, which clears each bit of the selected word to 0. A current $+I_m$ is then passed through the same wire. At the same time however the data to be written, which is stored in the data register, is used to direct currents down the inhibit wires. The current in the inhibit wire is zero if the corresponding bit in the MBR is 1 and $-\frac{1}{2}I_m$ if it is 0. Thus on the row of cores selected the net current will be either $(I_m + 0)$ for logical 1 or $(I_m - \frac{1}{2}I_m = \frac{1}{2}I_m)$ for logical 0, as required. Since the inhibit wires pass through every core all other cores may be subjected to magnetising currents, but none except the drive selected row will exceed $\frac{1}{2}I_m$ so that they will be unaffected.

(b) *Read Operation.*

A current $-I_m$ is passed through the selected drive line, clearing each bit to 0. An emf will be induced in the sense wire if the previous state of that bit were 1 and no emf for logic 0. The sense amplifiers, one per bit, drive the data register. Each sense wire passes through the appropriate bit of every word, but only the selected one will change state.

Since the selected word has been cleared, it must be re-established to give NDRO. Thus a second cycle is initiated exactly as for the write sequence, the new contents of the data register controlling the inhibit lines.

If the above two sequences are compared they can be seen to be very similar. Both follow the same pattern of a 'read cycle' followed by a 'write cycle', the pair making one 'memory cycle'* For a read operation the sense lines are gated to the data register during the first half cycle while for a write operation the sense lines are disconnected and the data register is externally loaded. A typical gating arrangement is shown in figure A4.5. In practice the gating is more sophisticated,

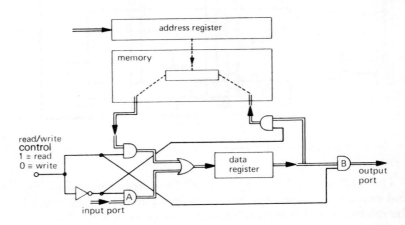

Fig. A4·5 Gating to control the read or write operation

*Beware the confusion between the read and write operations and cycles.

incorporating accurately timed strobe pulses, to clean-up the sense wire signals.

A 3-D Core Store

The word select system forms one dimension of the 2-D store. This is split into a two dimensional co-ordinate system in the 3-D system, the n bits of the word forming the third dimension. Consider first a 1 bit word system as shown in figure A4.6.

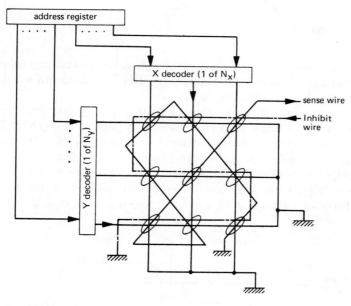

Fig. A4·6 A 3-D coincident current 1 bit word system

The address is split into two parts, each individually decoded to select one X and one Y line. A current $\frac{1}{2}I_m$ is passed along each selected line. Thus cores not on the selected lines see no current; cores on the selected lines see $\frac{1}{2}I_m$ and therefore do not switch except for the core at the intersection which sees $\frac{1}{2}I_m + \frac{1}{2}I_m$ and will switch. Since only the selected core can be affected, one sense wire and one inhibit wire can be threaded through all cores. The threading pattern is carefully arranged to minimise cross coupling.

The matrix need not be symmetric, but a sensible maximum configuration is to make $N_x = N_y = \sqrt{N}$ where, as in the 2-D system, $N = 2^n$, i.e. N_x and $N_y \leqslant 2^{n/2}$.

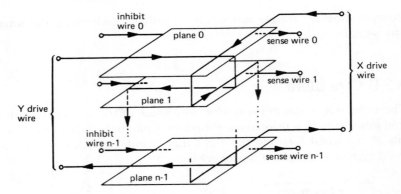

Fig. A4·7 A 3-D n bit system

For an *n* bit word system, n planes must be stacked together, each with individual sense and inhibit wires, but with common word select wires, as indicated in figure A4.7.

The read and write cycles are exactly the same as described for a 2-D system. When writing a 0 a current $-\frac{1}{2}I_m$ is passed through the inhibit wire. Cores on the non-selected wires then see only the $-\frac{1}{2}I_m$ from the inhibit wire; cores on the selected lines see $\frac{1}{2}I_m - \frac{1}{2}I_m$ except for the coincident core which sees $\frac{1}{2}I_m + \frac{1}{2}I_m - \frac{1}{2}I_m$. No core therefore sees a current bigger than $\frac{1}{2}I_m$ and no switching occurs. Typical current waveforms are shown in figure A4.8, together with typical sense wire

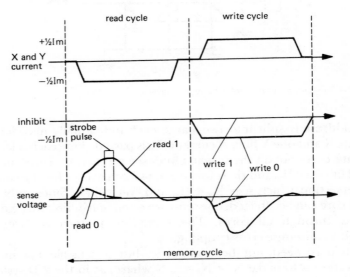

Fig. A4·8 Typical current and voltage waveforms

344

voltages. The unwanted negative voltages can be eliminated by rectification. The output when reading 0 is small, but non-zero (the $\frac{1}{2}I_m$ currents in all the cores linked by the sense wire will induce small emfs since the B-H curve can never be exactly 'square'). Thus by gating the sense wire voltage with a narrow strobe pulse, as indicated, the signal can be cleaned-up.

Comparison of 2-D and 3-D Systems

During the read cycle, with a 3-D system $\frac{1}{2}I_m$ currents are passed through $N_x + N_y$ cores, which produce individually negligible flux changes, except for the selected core. However, the resultant sum of all these small emfs can result in an undesirable noise emf, as shown in figure A4.8. With a 2-D system only the selected word sees any current and the noise problem is avoided.

With a 2-D system the requirements are:

N line drivers and decoders

n inhibit drivers

n sense amplifiers

With a 3-D system the requirements are

$2\sqrt{N}$ line drivers

n inhibit drivers

n sense amplifiers

Thus the 3-D system is cheaper. However since four wires must be threaded through each core for the 3-D system, compared to three for the 2-D, some of the cost advantage may be lost in production difficulty, particularly with smaller, faster cores.

It is possible, for both systems, to combine the sense and inhibit wires, using external logic to isolate the current function, e.g. as a sense wire during the read cycle, and an inhibit wire during the write cycle.

A 2½-D Core Store

The $2\frac{1}{2}$-D system is a compromise between 2-D and 3-D. The system is similar to figure A4.7, except that in place of the common X drive to each plane, n individual X drives are used. The inhibit wire is now not needed, since the individual X drives can be gated to pass the $\frac{1}{2}I_m$ current for writing logical 1 but to inhibit it for writing logical 0.

Semiconductor RAM Memories

The memories are fabricated on LSI chips as a multicell structure. Each cell can store 1 bit of data. Data can either be read-out (nondestructively) or written-in, with no requirements for the read-write cycles necessary with magnetic core. This is the major reason for the fact that *semiconductor* (SC) memories are generally faster than core, rather than any fundamental physical features. The time taken to read or write data from or into a cell is called the 'access time', but the full memory cycle must include a further time allowance for decoding the memory address and activating the cell control gates.

Semiconductor RAM memories are volatile, that is if the power is switched off the data is irretrievably corrupted.

The cells are arranged in a matrix pattern similar to a 1 bit, 3-D store. Grouping into n bit words is arranged by external logic circuitry. The same principle of X and Y decoding can be used, and the decoders are usually fabricated on the chip along with the memory cells. A typical cell read/write select logic is shown in figure A4.9. The data-in, write-enable and read-enable lines are common to every cell. The data-out is also a common line so that each of the output AND gates are wire-OR-ed together, probably using tri-state techniques.

The storage element in the cell may be one of two types, static or dynamic.

(i) *Static.* The storage element is a conventional flip-flop, as described in Appendix 2. It may be fabricated in Bipolar technology, with two transistors per cell or in MOS, probably using four FETs per cell. The comments made in Appendix 3 relating speed, size, cost, etc. apply. Thus commercially available SC memories use Bipolar techniques for smaller, faster (scratch pad) applications and MOS for main memories.

(ii) *Dynamic.* The storage element is a capacitor, charged to one voltage for logical 1 and to another for logical 0. These devices are always fabricated in MOS. The charge on the capacitors will decay in fractions of a second, so that they must be continually refreshed. A read-write operation must be performed sequentially on every cell a

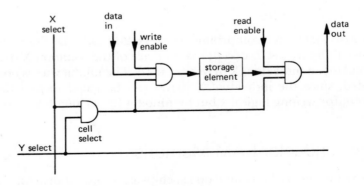

Fig. A4·9 One cell of a semiconductor memory matrix

minimum number of times per second to avoid information loss. The refresh is executed by dedicated circuitry, sometimes integral with the chip, 'interrupted' by read or write operation requests. Dynamic stores are low on power consumption, since there is no steady drain.

Content Addressable Memories

Content addressable memories (CAM) or *Associative memories* are more complex systems, involving more logic with each memory cell. They have three modes of operation, Read, Write and Search (or Match), the first two being similar to normal RAM memory systems.

In the Search mode however the contents of each word of memory are compared with a given data word. If a match is detected then a flag bit, one of which is associated with each word, is set. Multiple matches may well be detected in the one operation.

The technique is made far more powerful by allowing matching of only part of a word to set the indicator flag. This is achieved by using a separate Mask register; only the bits in the Search register which correspond to ones in the Mask register will be compared with the memory contents. Thus in the example of figure A4.10 all memory

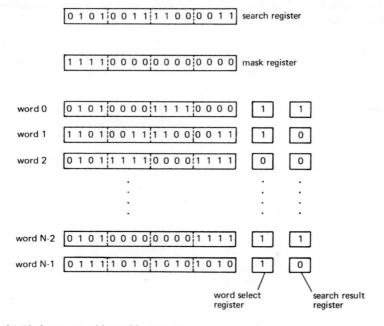

Fig. A4·10 A content addressable memory

locations which have 0101 in the left hand 4 bits will have the associated Search Result flag set, irrespective of the contents of the remaining 12 bits as dictated by the Mask Register contents.

A further refinement is to attach a second flag to each stored word which can be cleared to exclude that specific word from the search. This is called the Word Select flag. The Word Select and Search Result flags can be considered as separate registers. Note that the Search and Mask registers are n bit registers but the other two are N bits long.

CAMs have not yet found application in computer systems, partly because of cost but largely because they involve whole new concepts which the standard computer architecture does not efficiently cope with. Far longer words are required into which whole records can be stored. Thus for a register of racing horses; the horse's name, the trainer's name and the owner's name can be stored in each word. By setting an owner's name in the search register, with the appropriate bits in the mask, then all the horses that are recorded as owned by that person will set the appropriate bit in the search result register. A subsequent program can then print out the names of all horses owned by the particular person by interrogating the contents of all locations with the search result bit set. The same data bank can then be used to find the names of all the horses trained by Joe Bloggs by repeating the process with new data in the search and mask registers. In practice each horse, owner and trainer would be identified by a code number to simplify the stored record.

Bibliography

The following textbooks are recommended as directly related reading.

1. Barna, A and Porat, D. I. *Intergrated Circuits in Digital Electronics* (Wiley, 1973).
2. Bartee, T. C. *Digital Computer Fundamentals* (McGraw-Hill, 1972).
3. Flores, I. *Computer Organization* (Prentice-Hall, 1970).
4. Foster, C. C. *Computer Architecture* (Van Nostrand, 1971).
5. Korn, G. A. *Minicomputers for Engineers and Scientists* (McGraw-Hill, 1973).
6. Lewin, D. *Theory and Design of Digital Computers* (Nelson, 1972).
7. Peatman, J. B. *The Design of Digital Systems* (McGraw-Hill, 1972).
8. Weitzman, C. *Minicomputer Systems: Structure, Implementation and Application* (Prentice-Hall, 1974).
9. Woollons, D. J. *Introduction to Digital Computer Design* (McGraw-Hill, 1973).
10. *The Value of Power*, published by General Automation Inc., 1973.
11. *The Value of Micropower*, published by General Automation Inc., 1974.

The following books will also be of interest to readers of this book.

Digital Techniques

12. Baron, R. C. and Piccirilli, A. T. *Digital Logic and Computer Operations* (McGraw-Hill, 1967).
13. Lewin, D. *Logical Design of Switching Circuits* (Nelson, 1972).
14. Morris, R. L. and Miller, J. R. (Eds.) *Designing with TTL Integrated Circuits* (McGraw-Hill (Texas Instruments), 1971).
15. Phister, M. *Logical Design of Digital Computers* (Wiley, 1958).
16. Richards, R. K. *Arithmetic Operations in Digital Computers* (Van Nostrand, 1955).
17. Wickes, W. E. *Logic Design with Integrated Circuits* (Wiley, 1968).

349

Computer Design, Systems and Components

18. Black, W. W. *An Introduction to On-line Computers* (Gordon and Breach Science Publishers, 1971).
19. Davis, G. B. *Introduction to Electronic Computers* (McGraw-Hill, 1971).
20. Flores, I. *Computer Design* (Prentice-Hall, 1967).
21. Fry, T. F. *Computer Appreciation* (Newnes–Butterworth, 1970).
22. Gschwind, H. W. *Design of Digital Computers* (Springer-Verlag, 1967).
23. Heath, F. G. *Digital Computer Design* (Oliver and Boyd, 1969).
24. Hodges, D. A. (Ed.) *Semiconductor Memories* (I.E.E.E. Press, 1972).
25. Renwick, W. and Cole, A. J. *Digital Storage Systems* (Chapman and Hall, 1971).
26. Sobel, H. S. *Introduction to Digital Computer Design* (Addison-Wesley, 1971).

Software

27. Barron, D. W. *Assemblers and Loaders* (Macdonald–Elsevier, 1972).
28. Barron, D. W. *Computer Operating Systems* (Chapman and Hall, 1971).
29. Gries, D. *Compiler Construction for Digital Computers* (Wiley, 1971).
30. Higman, B. *A Comparative Study of Programming Language* (Macdonald–Elsevier, 1969).
31. Hopgood, F. R. A. *Compiling Techniques* (Macdonald-Elsevier, 1969).
32. Lister, A. M. *Fundamentals of Operating Systems* (Macmillan, 1975).
33. Wegner, P. *Programming Languages, Information Structures and Machine Organization* (McGraw-Hill, 1968).
34. *Computer Software for Process Control* (BISRA, 1969).

Software/Hardware Systems

35. Bell, C. G. and Newell, A. *Computer Structures: Readings and Examples* (McGraw-Hill, 1970).
36. Organick, E. I. *Computer System Organisation* (Academic Press, 1973).
37. Watson, R. W. *Timesharing System Design Concepts* (McGraw-Hill, 1970).
38. Wilkes, M. V. *Time-sharing Computer Systems* (Macdonald–Elsevier, 1968).

Applications

39. Coury, F. F. (Ed.) *A Practical Guide to Minicomputer Applications* (I.E.E.E. Press, 1972).
40. Hebditch, D. *Data Communication: an Introductory Guide* (Paul Elek, 1975).
41. Mace, P. W. *Visible Record Computers* (Business Books Ltd., 1974).
42. Martin, J. *Introduction to Teleprocessing* (Prentice-Hall, 1972).
43. Martin, J. *Telecommunications and the Computer* (Prentice-Hall, 1969).
44. Sanders, D. H. *Computers and Management: in a Changing Society* (McGraw-Hill, 1974).
45. Schoeffler, J. P. and Temple, R. H. (Ed.) *Minicomputers: Hardware, Software and Applications* (I.E.E.E. Press, 1972).
46. Smith, C. L. *Digital Computer Process Control* (Intext Educational, 1972).
47. Soucek, B. *Minicomputers in Data Processing and Simulation* (Wiley, 1972).

Index

351

Index